CINEMAS

OF

BISEXUAL TRANSGRESSION

A CAMERA OBSCURA BOOK

CINEMAS OF

Duke University Press   *Durham and London*   2026

BISEXUAL TRANSGRESSION

JACOB ENGELBERG

Project Editor: Liz Smith
Designed by Courtney Leigh Richardson
Typeset in Portrait and Retail by Westchester Publishing Services

Library of Congress Cataloging-in-Publication Data
Names: Engelberg, Jacob, [date] author.
Title: Cinemas of bisexual transgression / Jacob Engelberg.
Other titles: Camera obscura book (Duke University Press)
Description: Durham : Duke University Press, 2026. | Series:
A camera obscura book | Includes bibliographical references and index.
Identifiers: LCCN 2025020374 (print)
LCCN 2025020375 (ebook)
ISBN 9781478032984 (paperback)
ISBN 9781478029526 (hardcover)
ISBN 9781478061731 (ebook)
Subjects: LCSH: Bisexuality in motion pictures. | Bisexuality. |
Lesbianism in motion pictures. | Sex in motion pictures. |
Motion pictures—Social aspects.
Classification: LCC PN1995.9.B57 E54 2026 (print) |
LCC PN1995.9.B57 (ebook)
LC record available at https://lccn.loc.gov/2025020374
LC ebook record available at https://lccn.loc.gov/2025020375

Cover art: Film still from *Basic Instinct* (Paul Verhoeven, 1992).

For my teachers

The pleasures I tried to deny myself only assailed my mind all the more ardently.
—Madame de Saint-Ange, in Donatien-Alphonse-François de Sade,
La Philosophie dans le boudoir

It is important to resist that theoretical gesture of pathos in which exclusions are simply affirmed as sad necessities of signification. The task is to refigure this necessary "outside" as a future horizon. . . . But of equal importance is the preservation of the outside, the site where discourse meets its limits, where the opacity of what is not included in a given regime of truth acts as a disruptive site of linguistic impropriety and unrepresentability, illuminating the violent and contingent boundaries of that normative regime precisely through the inability of that regime to represent that which might pose a fundamental threat to its continuity.
—Judith Butler, *Bodies That Matter*

It is precisely bisexuality's ontological, epistemological and representational *polysemy* that generates its subversive potential to lay bare the mutability, contingency and inherent transgressiveness of desire.
—Maria San Filippo, *The B Word*

Non-decidability defines a *praxis*.
—Roland Barthes, *S/Z*

Contents

Preface

This Capacity

Bisexuality is an imperfect term. It seems, at once, too particular and too general. It might evoke the idea of the bisexual as an ahistorical subject or bisexuality as a category of social-scientific taxonomy, notions that queer studies and queer politics have sought to trouble. Or perhaps it recalls various ideas of the not-now or the not-here. Bisexuality has been cast invariably, as Steven Angelides outlines, as "an artifact of our evolutionary prehistory, a state outside or prior to culture or civilization, a myth, a catachresis, and a (utopian) sexual impossibility."[1] The term can feel awkwardly imprecise. To use it is to invite challenges as to its definitional coherence, aspersions as to its critical necessity, suspicions as to its very possibility. Whereas *queer* has, across the past four decades, enjoyed and enjoined critical attention across disciplines and, outside of the academy, has proliferated across discourses of sexuality and politics, *bisexual* stands awkwardly, its ungainly sibling, purportedly out of touch and out of time. Nevertheless, it is the word I will use. Insofar as the use of words is conceptualized by Sara Ahmed as how words are "put to work or called upon to do certain kinds of work," I contend it is the work *bisexuality* can do—with its abundance of discursive, genealogical, and critical affordances—that renders it indispensable for a radical recalibration of the terms of queer film studies as we know it.[2]

Bisexuality's conceptual utility lies in its ability to describe a desirous sexual capacity beyond the dominant and dominating heterosexual-homosexual binary through which human sexuality has been organized in the West since the nineteenth century. Across this history, Angelides observes how bisexuality has tended to function as the "internally repudiated other" within the "logical or axiomatic structure of the hetero/homosexual dualism" in Western epistemologies of sexuality.[3] Despite the dominance of heterosexuality and homosexuality—the binary of *mono*sexuality—in these epistemologies, the capacity for forms of desiring beyond these strictures has always haunted the heterosexual-homosexual binary's coherence.

This capacity for desire beyond monosexuality has not always been articulated under the sign *bisexual*. Diederik F. Janssen's extensive research into late nineteenth-century medical discourses reveals a plethora of terms through which it was described.[4] Karl Heinrich Ulrichs calls it "uranodionism."[5] For Eugène Gley, it is a "double direction of the sexual instinct" that describes this capacity's intermittent appearance.[6] For Benjamin Tarnowsky, this intermittence of desires is characterized as "periodic pederasty."[7] Richard von Krafft-Ebing and Albert Moll articulate this capacity as "psychical" or "psychosexual hermaphroditism," whereas Albert Eulenburg recognizes this capacity as a "light form or precursor" to sexual inversion.[8] For Marc-André Raffalovich and Georges Saint-Paul, these capacities are to be found in a sexual type they call "indifferents."[9] Through these examples, Janssen pinpoints how, at this formative time in the development of sexual science, terminology describing this particular capacity proliferated. Around the turn of the twentieth century, Sigmund Freud began to take an interest in this capacity, something that he describes in different ways, and with different emphases, throughout his career: the infant's "polymorphously perverse disposition," the "amphigenic" and "contingent" inversions of certain adults, the physiological and psychical "bisexuality of all human beings."[10] In their later sexological tabulations, this capacity was to be found between the 2 and the 5 of Alfred Kinsey's Heterosexual-Homosexual Rating Scale and Fritz Klein's Sexual Orientation Grid.[11] This capacity has been afforded different names in twentieth-century psychological discourses around sexuality, from *bisexuality*, to *ambisexuality*, to *omnisexuality*.[12] This is the capacity described by the contributors to *Semiotext(e)*'s 1981 special issue named "Polysexuality."[13] In social and activist discourses, this capacity has been articulated under a plethora of signs, including *bisexuality, bi+,* the *bisexual umbrella, pansexuality, sexual fluidity, heteroflexibility* and *homoflexibility, queerness, nonmonosexuality,* and, most recently, *plurisexuality* and the *multiattraction spectrum*. Beyond the English language, of course, further terms proliferate. Under whichever sign they travel, these terms attest to something troubling for dualistic epistemologies of sexuality: desire's capacity to exceed heterosexual-homosexual divisions.

The preeminence of the term *bisexuality* in naming this phenomenon in Western discourses provides us with a useful discursive genealogy. The term *bisexuality* has populated psychomedical discourses from the late nineteenth century to the present day; *bisexuality* emerged in the twentieth century as a popular term for individuals articulating their own desires, later appearing in the acronym that became popularized transnationally, LGBT, and its variations; from the 1970s onward, it was the term under which political organizing took place as bisexual politics; and in the 1990s, bisexual theory emerged as a critical practice vis-à-vis the paltry attention bisexuality was afforded in gay and lesbian studies and queer theory alike. The term *bisexuality* affords us a critical history to think through the cultural, social, and political import of desires toward people of more than one gender.

Yet, a recurrent problem *bisexuality* has posed as a term for those seeking to articulate sexuality beyond dominant frameworks is the twoness that seems to be implied in its *bi-* prefix, suggesting desire toward people of *two* different genders. This conception of *bisexuality* has, indeed, been articulated throughout the term's history in a way that is complicit with the dominant epistemology of an oppositional and discrete sex binary, which gained preeminence in Western medicine between the eighteenth and nineteenth centuries, and the concept of the gender binary, which was popularized in the mid-twentieth century, first emerging in sexology before being reappropriated for feminist politics and theory.[14] A shift that occurred between the 1980s and 1990s, however, saw bisexual activists and theorists rearticulate their understandings of *bisexuality* away from these binaries in ways that chimed with transgender politics' problematization of discrete categories of sexual taxonomy.[15] These examples of articulations of *bisexuality* away from the gender binary should not suggest that bisexuals have never deployed binary definitions, nor should it elide the popularity of these definitions throughout the twentieth century. What they do suggest, however, is how certain bisexual thinkers have worked to conceptualize *bisexuality* in ways that exploit its potential to challenge not only the hetero/homo sexuality binary but also that of man/woman. I am sure some might suggest that terms like *pansexuality, plurisexuality,* or *omnisexuality*—with their Greek (*pan-*, all, every) and Latin (*plūri-*, many; *omni-*, every) prefixes denoting multitude as opposed to twoness—would be better suited for speaking nonsingular sexual desire beyond binary gender. However, my decision to use *bisexuality* is predicated on the conceptual, political, and theoretical work that has operated under this sign, especially insofar as this work has perverted the normative meaning of the *bi-* prefix to pluralistic ends. And even in discourses around *bisexuality* in which a bothness seems to be in operation, I draw attention to how, often, this bothness works dialectically to precipitate a binary's destabilization and the emergence of polyvalent possibilities beyond its confines.

Although problems are likely to arise with any choice of terminology around gender and sexuality, I want to clarify how and why I will be using

certain terms in this book. My use of the term *bisexuality* will be capacious, referring to the capacity for desiring beyond a single gendered object. Both the adjective *capacious* and the noun *capacity* take as their roots the Latin *capāx* and
capāci, which, fittingly, describe the ability "to take in." In this sense, we might
think of bisexual capacity as a kind of open receptivity to desirous possibility.
When naming phenomena as "bisexual," I am not making an ontological claim
of the correctness or incontrovertibility of bisexual categorization. Rather, I
do so to draw attention to such phenomena's attestation of desirous possibilities beyond unidirectional gendered object choice. I will privilege the term
gender over *sex*, as I recognize the organization of material bodies into discrete
sexes on the basis of an assumed or ideal reproductive function to be a fundamentally social phenomenon, with *gender* foregrounding this particular valence.[16] Correspondingly, my use of the terms *male* and *female* do not adhere
singularly to the notion of sex; instead, I use them as adjectival forms correspondent to *man* and *woman*, respectively. In accounting for desirous forms of
relationality between gendered subjects, I will eschew the terms *heterosexual*
and *homosexual* to avoid the assumption that certain relational forms necessarily indicate a single (mono)sexuality. My imperfect remedies are the terms *intragender* and *extragender*, which delineate desirous relations between people of
a shared gender and between people of different genders, respectively. Admittedly, this formulation articulates a binary not dissimilar to the hetero-homo
binary, yet its usefulness lies in its nonexclusivity, its resistance to inferring
direct correspondences between forms of desirous relation and specific formations of sexuality, and its foregrounding of the operations of similarity and
difference herein. I will also use the term *queer* throughout this book; when it
is not paired with *theory*, *studies*, or *politics*, which refer to those respective traditions, I take *queer* as an adjective describing that which falls outside heterosexuality or cisgenderness. The process of identifying genders on screen in the
first place is to operate within the terms of a cissexist economy of signification.
In other words, our ability to read a figure as man, woman, or even an ambiguous gender is to apply a cisnormative yardstick regarding how certain genders
appear conventionally. The visual is, in Amy Villarejo's words, "the terrain . . .
that gender binarism is most strictly enforced."[17] I contend, however, that we
cannot speak of sexuality's signification on screen without attention to, and
critical use of, the cissexist economy of signification through which sexuality
tends to be read. It is with critical knowledge of the conventions of this visual
system of gender signification that we can come to understand how they are
transgressed and through which bisexuality's potential to trouble sexual dual-
isms comes into view.

If you are still unconvinced of the utility of *bisexuality* as the term through which to do this work, let me stress that engagement with the potential to desire beyond strict and exclusive heterosexual-homosexual organization is what grounds it. This is a potential that we can explore—and, indeed, that has been explored—under various appellations. While I hope to demonstrate the affordances of *bisexuality*'s particular use, I posit that any discomfort with the term should not preclude engagement with its conceptual deployment. The work herein involves attention to those excessive forms of desiring that involve mutability rather than stasis, nonlinearity rather than unidirectionality, polysemy rather than univocal signification. Certain deployments of film form, I will suggest, are particularly suited to conveying these desirous possibilities in the formation of cinemas wherein monosexual interpretation cannot hold, wherein the rules of monosexual taxonomy are transgressed. While I will call these extensive desirous capacities "bisexuality," I endeavor to preserve the term's instability. Thus, any lingering discomfort with it need not be suppressed but, instead, can be stayed with as a generative force of disorientation. Such a disposition may prove useful as we work to unmoor the security and reliability of structures of sexual organization and proceed without their guarantee.

Introduction

Bisexuality, Transgression, Cinema

Salò, or The Seventeen Genderless Asses

DUKE.	Lights out!
. . .	
BISHOP.	Before we begin, I have a proposal.
DUKE.	Tell us, tell us!
BISHOP.	We have not yet decided what prize to give to him or to her whose behind is judged to be the best. Here is my proposal: he or she whose behind is judged to be the best will be killed immediately.
DUKE.	Agreed. This way—without knowing to whom they belong—we are sure to be impartial.
. . .	
MAGISTRATE.	Knowing that an ass belongs to a boy rather than a girl could influence our decision. Instead, we must be absolutely free to choose.

—*Salò, or The 120 Days of Sodom* (Pier Paolo Pasolini)

Salò, or The 120 Days of Sodom (Pier Paolo Pasolini, 1975) transposes Donatien-Alphonse-François de Sade's *The 120 Days of Sodom* into the Republic of Salò, a short-lived German puppet state that operated in Italy during the final two years of the Second World War. This historical setting is the backdrop against which a group of fascist libertines, in collaboration with others, kidnap a group of teenagers and imprison them in a remote palace. In an expansive room, a competition is facilitated to determine whom among their captives

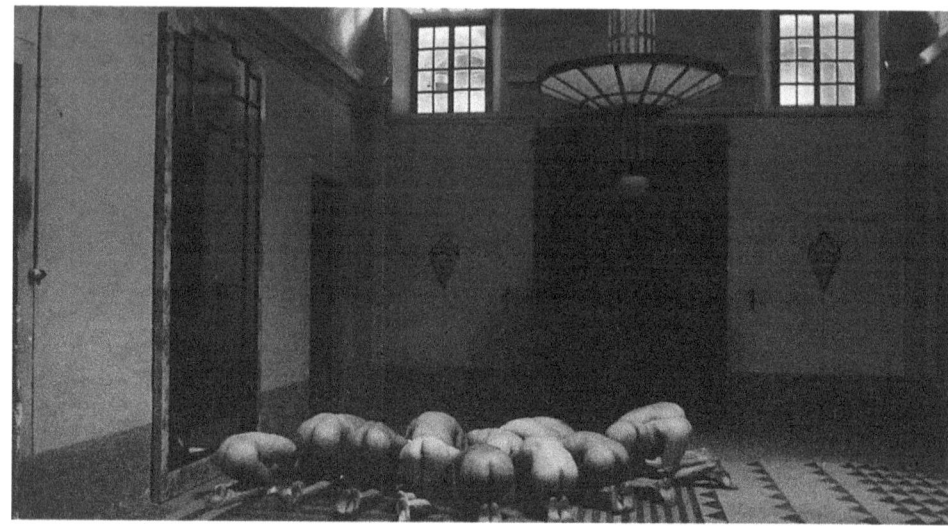

FIGURE I.1 A tableau of genderless asses. *Salò, or The 120 Days of Sodom* [*Salò o le 120 giornate di Sodoma*] (Pier Paolo Pasolini, 1975). Digital screen capture.

has the best ass. The adolescents are naked and bent prone, their heads covered with sacks and their rears pointed upward. As the libertines evaluate the asses on display, the Magistrate (Umberto Paolo Quintavalle) remarks how this formal presentation—lights off, heads covered—ensures impartiality regarding the genders of their surveyed objects.

The ass has no gender. In the various systems of social organization that have operated throughout history as a means of determining gender, the ass has never been a trustworthy physiological signifier. If, as psychoanalyst Lou Andreas-Salomé argues, ego formation involves the repudiation of the anus in favor of genital sexuality, then this display of bodies—centering the ass— might remind us of that which precedes ego formation, the anality shared by all rather than the site of genitality upon which sex division is violently articulated.[1] In *Salò*'s tableau of seventeen genderless asses, we glimpse the possibilities of desire undetermined by gender, a bisexual erotics.[2] Single-gendered object choice became the ascendent form of sexual subjectivity in the West from the late nineteenth century onward—the heterosexual configuration aligned to normality and the homosexual configuration aligned to pathology. This Manichean system of social organization posits, at once, a dualism of gender or sex, determined fundamentally by the appearance of the genitals, and a dualism of sexual desire. *Salò*'s brief configuration of bodies illuminates, through the genitals' concealment and the ass's exposure, the possibility of desire beyond the regime of sexual difference.[3]

Whereas this tableau figures the possibility of desiring beyond single-gendered object choice through elision of the symbolically dense genitals, elsewhere, *Salò* speaks to this same possibility through the serialized exposure of frontally naked bodies. Throughout the film, the unclothed bodies of captives are rendered objects of monstration. Viewing the genitals of Franco (played by Franco Merli) and Sergio (Sergio Fascetti) in close-up, or the frontal display of Renata's (Renata Moar) naked body, we are confronted not with an image of genderlessness but with a fleshy, genital array of differently gendered bodies. Although the genderless asses conceal those primary and secondary sex characteristics made meaningful in a cissexist signifying economy, and the latter examples provide serial representations of these body parts, both eschew the demand that desire be oriented toward objects of a single intelligible gender. In the camera's scopophilic refusal to taper its gaze—either to intelligibly gendered objects or to objects of a single discernible gender—*Salò*'s spectator is invited to participate in a bisexual form of primary identification.[4]

Yet, these cinematic images cannot be divorced from the diegetic context from which they emanate: that of violence, coercion, cruelty, humiliation, fascism. Presenting, at once, the paradoxical fascist preoccupation with the notion of freedom ("we should be absolutely free to choose") and fascism's envisaging of social homogeneity—figured in the uniformity of the asses on display—*Salò*'s images of free sexual choice unencumbered by sexual difference are inseparable from the force of domination.[5] Although it may trouble us that this image of bisexual erotics is rendered through violent subjugation, this is a trouble with which it is worth staying. Franco is the captive who is determined to have the best ass, and he is wrestled to his feet, a gun pressed to his temple, as he anticipates his prize: death. The trigger is pulled but the gun is unloaded. To Franco's dazed bemusement, the Bishop announces that the promise of the release of death as his prize was, in fact, a ruse: "You fool! How could you think we would kill you? We would want to kill you a thousand times over, to the limits of eternity, if eternity had limits." Franco and his fellow captives' cycle of torture continues.

A film whose enduring power pivots around the implication of the pernicious in the pleasurable, *Salò*'s rendering of bisexual erotics through the transgression of various moral standards instantiates a tendency in various cinemas' figurations of bisexual possibility. This relation—between the cinematic figuration of bisexual possibility and transgression—is the phenomenon this book traces. To begin with the example of *Salò* is to posit that an analysis of this relation need not be limited to those transgressions we deem aspirational, reclaimable, or positive. But equally, this analysis need not be circumscribed by an approach that repudiates these images as circulating phobic, deleterious, or negative ideas about bisexuality. Instead, my analysis proceeds via an interrogation of the compelling relation between the cinematic figuration of bisexual possibility and the breaking of various standards: social and political rules, ethical and moral norms, conventions of film form.

This book traces cinematic figurations of bisexual transgression that, like *Salò*, offer glimpses of bisexual possibility through their transgression of various rules. Although monosexuality—the structure of sexuality involving desire toward people of only one gender—may be culturally ascendent and naturalized on film through formal conventions in sexual signification, bisexual possibility can be found in what Maria San Filippo identifies as those "bisexual spaces . . . that represent and appeal to interstitial, fluid spectatorial identifications, and thus have the potential to subvert, or 'unthink,' monosexuality," as well as those "sites (textual and extratextual locations) and sights (ways of seeing) that resist monosexuality and that attribute desire to physical, emotional, and material determinants beyond gendered object choice."[6] That bisexuality is figured persistently on film through a relation to transgression is far from incidental. Bisexuality being figured as a possibility is itself a transgression of the rule that humans are necessarily heterosexual or homosexual, and, as we will see, the transgression of bisexuality is made meaningful on film—persistently—through other forms of transgression. This analysis invites a turn to those transgressive cinemas, transgressive films, and moments of transgressive figuration in which bisexual possibility comes into view amid the troubling thrills that rush as a border is crossed. In *Salò*, a film indebted to Sade's original tale set in the milieu of French libertinism, we can certainly find evidence of such processes at play, but these pleasures are also described evocatively in another Sade work: *Philosophy in the Bedroom* (1795).[7] At the beginning of this dramatic dialogue, Madame de Saint-Ange reflects on her efforts to quell her sexual appetite by restricting her lovers to women. Alas, she finds that her abstinence from male lovers only meant that these pleasures "assailed [her] mind all the more ardently."[8] This relation between prohibition and pleasure, and the entanglements of this dynamic with bisexual possibility, is one we shall trace across a number of cinematic contexts. While monosexuality may rule cultural understandings of sexual subjectivity, as it rules conventions in cinema's signification of sexuality, bisexuality emerges as a disruptively compelling transgressor, inviting us to look scopophilically upon the genderless ass and asking us, "Well, wouldn't you?"

Bisexual transgression is a prevalent and persistent phenomenon discernible across disparate cinematic contexts. Attention to this phenomenon is instructive not only insofar as it foregrounds a bisexual focus in a critical landscape in which bisexuality is rarely prioritized but also to the extent that it recalibrates the terms upon which inquiries into gender, sexuality, and transgression on-screen are predicated. Centering bisexual transgression enables a dynamic approach to questions of cinematic sexuality, directing us toward the fecund ground between and beyond polarities of gender and sexuality and in contravention of rules of sexual, social, and aesthetic organization. The geographic scope of the corpus I consider encompasses Europe, North America, and Australasia: areas traditionally associated with ideas of the West. This focus reflects my attention to Western genealogies of sexual epistemology; although I attend to various national and cultural differences herein, these contexts share a historical relation to certain discourses of gender and sexuality that affect the figurations of bisexuality they produce. Nevertheless, in my afterword, I outline some of the figures of bisexual transgression populating cinemas beyond the West. These constitute suggestions for the future direction of investigations into bisexual transgression that should attend to these films' respective contexts of sexual epistemology while reflecting on the operations of globalization herein. This book thus maps how cinemas have grappled with bisexuality in a context of sexual epistemology in which bisexuality's very existence has been deemed questionable. Importantly, this is a context in which Western conceptions of gendered and sexual binarism—which, in turn, have functioned as conceptual teloi in notions of Western civilizational development and white supremacy—find themselves disturbed. To analyze cinematic sexuality with these considerations in tow affords us a vantage point from which to consider cinema's potential to unmoor interlocking structures of sexual-social organization.

This introduction begins with a critical history of bisexuality across scientific, social, political, and theoretical discourses to establish the term's genealogy and critical utility. I then consider bisexuality's marginal position within queer studies, in which it has often been dismissed as irrelevant, unfruitful, or even anathema to queer inquiry. Next, I outline some of bisexual theory's interventions in queer studies, particularly as they relate to sexual epistemology, before assessing the utility of the contested terms *monosexuality* and *monosexism*. I then trace various uses of *bisexuality* in theoretical approaches to film and media, first, in aesthetic and film theories deploying it as a critical term and, second, in expressly bisexual film and media critiques characterized by two different approaches: axiological and critical. In conversation with the latter, I propose thinking of bisexuality's intelligibility on film as a hermeneutic problem requiring a critical bisexual hermeneutics. I also stress the conceptual utility of figures and figurations in accounting for cinematic bisexuality, as opposed to notions of bisexual subjectivity. Next, I assess various theories of transgression and their relation to bisexuality, defending the notion of bisexual transgression against its disparagement in some strands of bisexual theory. I outline how various figures of bisexual transgression have been deployed in critical bisexual writing and assert the potential these hold for illuminating cinematic spaces where bisexual possibility is figured as transgressively knowable.

Discursive Bisexualities

"Bisexuals"/polymorphous perverts . . . were an endangered species after 1870, for they were (and are), in fact, thoroughly *endangering*, undermining the binarisms through which life was (and is) rendered comprehensible.
—Donald E. Hall, "Graphic Sexuality and the Erasure of a Polymorphous Perversity"

The bisexual group is found to introduce uncertainty and doubt.
—Henry Havelock Ellis, *Studies in the Psychology of Sex*

Bisexuality's potential to disturb binary models of human sexuality is a quality inherent throughout much of its discursive history. The roots of the term lie in late eighteenth-century botany, where it described flowers possessing both carpels and stamens, signaling a coincidence of reproductive functions deemed female and male, respectively.[9] During the nineteenth century, the term was increasingly applied to animals exhibiting sexual characteristics deemed both male and female, also called "hermaphroditism."[10] In Charles Darwin's widely read 1871 monograph *The Descent of Man*, he elucidates his theory of sexual selection, proposing that hermaphroditism is a feature of lesser-evolved organisms and that, as species evolve, they atrophy and become sexually dimorphic: either male or female.[11] Naturalist Ernst Haeckel transposes these ideas regarding the evolution of species onto the development of individual organisms in his claim, in 1874, that "phylogenesis [the evolution of species] is the mechanical cause of ontogenesis [an individual organism's development]," what is commonly known as recapitulation theory.[12] While these debates in the natural sciences may seem far removed from articulations of bisexuality in the twentieth and twenty-first centuries, we must remember that the genesis of bisexuality's discursive history occurred within an epistemological framework in which distinctions between sex, gender, and sexuality did not operate as they tend to today. In the late nineteenth century, assumptions of contingency between human physiology and the constitution of humans' sexual desires were commonplace in the medical sciences. The lesser-evolved physiological bisexuality that natural scientists purported to observe in certain species would thus come to effect conceptions of a psychical bisexuality.[13]

For Sigmund Freud, the term *bisexuality* had shifting resonances throughout his career, but all involved a compresence of phenomena commonly understood to be exclusively male or female: fluctuations in individuals' perceptions of their gender, their multiply gendered object choices, or the sexual complexity of all our physiologies.[14] Freud's thinking on bisexuality was influenced integrally by Wilhelm Fliess, who argues that "all living things bear a bisexual [*zweigeschlechtigen*] character."[15] Freud is convinced of the argument, in the biological sciences, that "an originally bisexual physical disposition has, in the course of evolution, become modified into a unisexual one."[16] He is wary, however, of purporting a straightforward correspondence between physiological and psychical bisexuality, which he deems "independent of each other."[17] Instead, Freud proposes that sexual object choice tends to develop— both phylogenetically and ontogenetically—from a range of sexual objects into a single one:

> The object choice of the pubertal period is obliged to dispense with the objects of childhood and to start afresh as a "sensual current." Should these two currents fail to converge, the result is often that one of the ideals of sexual life, the focusing of all desires upon a single object, will be unattainable. . . . A disposition to perversions is an original and universal disposition of the human sexual instinct. . . . The sexual drive of adults arises from a combination of a number of impulses of childhood into a unity, an impulsion with a single aim.[18]

Freud's specification of the singular sexual impulse of adulthood marks the outcome of his famous Oedipus complex theory, yet the means through which this outcome is attained are theorized differently for boys and for girls.[19] First, the boy must retain the mother as the original object, while the girl is obliged to abandon the mother as the original object. Second, the boy's narcissistic identification with his penis is retained, while the girl's narcissistic identification with the clitoris must be abandoned.[20] These differences between the genders' Oedipus complexes mean, for Freud, that "there can be no doubt that the bisexuality, which is present . . . in the innate disposition of human beings, comes to the fore much more clearly in women than in men."[21] I suggest we understand this point from Freud as an attestation not of a natural bisexuality more prevalent in women but instead of bisexual potential's greater social perceptibility among women, chiming with the gendered dynamics of bisexual intelligibility I trace later. These differences aside, the overriding lesson from Freud is that no human is ever entirely free of this bisexual predisposition. Although it may be repressed by most, its endurance in the unconscious was paramount.[22]

The universalizing claims around bisexuality in Freud can certainly be problematized along the lines Judith Butler does when they write that "to presume the primacy of bisexuality . . . is still not to account for the construction of these various 'primacies.'"[23] The ideas of Freud and other psychoanalysts have also been critiqued routinely by thinkers in both bisexual activism and theory. The most common protests are as follows: His ideas seem to preclude the possibility of a mature adult bisexuality; they might be said to relegate bisexuality to a past, forever inaccessible in the present; they deploy bisexuality only insofar as it can be a fulcrum upon which heterosexuality and homosexuality are predicated; and they promote racist-colonialist understandings of bisexuality as the domain of the uncivilized and monosexuality as the domain of the civilized. My response to these critiques, however, stresses the utility of understanding Freud and his contemporaries not as observers of a naturalized or biologized truth of human sexuality. Instead, we should understand them, first, as analysts of social and cultural processes at play in the contexts in which they wrote and, second, as theorists of the drives that animate the psyches of individuals navigating these contexts. Freud himself is consistent in his description of heterosexuality's attainment as an "ideal," and it is in this sense that his theories' utility is not ontological but diagnostic. With bisexuality, what remains useful in Freud and his contemporaries is their attestation of the psychic endurance and prevalence of bisexual possibility in societies in which a mature monosexuality is either naturalized, in the case of heterosexuality, or pathologized, in the case of homosexuality. Freud observes cultural processes at play in which this curtailment of desire functions as a cultural demand, out of which one or other monosexuality is naturalized.[24] In cultures stipulating a binary model of sexual organization, the persistence of bisexuality continued to operate, as Henry Havelock Ellis observes, as a sign of "uncertainty," which, in the words of Donald E. Hall, was "thoroughly endangering" to the self-aggrandizing neatness of binary taxonomy.[25]

It is during the twentieth century that bisexuality came to be taken up as an identity category through which individuals understood their own sexualities. Similarly to the discursive history of homosexuality, bisexuality was repurposed from scientific discourses to be redeployed socially. The

1970s saw the first expressly politicized formations of bisexuality take shape in the United States, with the 1972 formation of the National Bisexual Liberation Group in New York and the Ithaca-based Quaker group the Committee of Friends on Bisexuality.[26] This decade also saw the first use of the term *bisexual chic*, referring to the perceived popularity of bisexuality within various countercultures. A *Newsweek* article from 1974 declares, "There is a new vibration to spring this year. . . . Bisexuality is in bloom."[27] Discussing the purportedly increased popularity of bisexuality with *Playboy*, controversial sexologist John Money remarks, "I wouldn't be surprised if the Seventies earned the sobriquet of the bisexual decade."[28] The 1980s saw a growth in bisexual political movements both within and beyond the United States, emerging in England, Scotland, West Germany, and the Netherlands. In the same decade, male bisexuality in particular received greater attention in the wake of the AIDS crisis, with fears around the transmission of HIV into the heterosexual family unit effecting bisexual men's stigmatization. Between the 1970s and the 1990s, there was also fervent discussion around bisexual women within lesbian communities, in which they occupied a contested position. By the 1990s, bisexual activist communities had expanded further, bringing with them magazines, activist edited collections, and, in the academy, bisexual theory. Seemingly forgetting their 1974 announcement, a 1995 cover of *Newsweek* proclaims, "Bisexuality: Not Gay. Not Straight. A New Sexual Identity Emerges."[29] This is, admittedly, only a cursory tour of a thirty-year period that does not do justice to the various tensions, contradictions, and complexities around bisexuality herein. While I explore these shifting dynamics in greater detail in my case studies, for now I seek only to underscore the intense proliferation of cultural and political attention toward bisexuality across these decades. This book's predominant attention to films made between 1970 and 2000 is thus rooted in the contextual richness that bisexuality's increased discursive circulation affords a historically informed film analysis.

Gendered Bisexualities, or Delineations of Nonexistence

A regular observation across much bisexual writing involves the markedly gendered differences in common understandings of bisexuality that also seek to establish its nonexistence. The adage goes that, among women, bisexuality is unremarkable, a capacity of all women whose desires toward other women, as long as they are concurrent with desires toward men, can be rewritten as heterosexuality. Insofar as female bisexuality can be demarcated as nonthreatening—an erotic spectacle, a frivolous experiment, a permissible peccadillo—female bisexuality's queerness is often depoliticized and subsumed into hypersexual forms of female heterosexuality. Part of the alignment between female bisexuality and dominant notions of (heterosexual) womanhood is rooted in what Shiri Eisner terms bisexuality's association "with multiplicity rather than singularity or 'oneness.'"[30] As theorized most famously by Luce Irigaray, the woman's sexuality is considered "at least double, goes even further: it is *plural*."[31] It is through this association that female bisexuality can be discursively transformed into something befitting dominant heteropatriarchal understandings of gender and sexuality. As Eisner notes, this cultural process works to "neutralize the 'sting'" carried by female bisexuality so that it is made into a nonthreatening erotic spectacle and "converted and rewritten into . . . something that's both palatable and convenient to patriarchy."[32] We should note, however, that just because this resignification of female bisexuality takes place, its effects are not necessarily normalizing. Beyond the social alienation produced by the demarcation of bisexual women as heterosexual, research in the social sciences has made troubling links between the treatment of bisexual women as hypersexual heterosexuals and the disproportionate rates of sexual violence they have been shown to face across a variety of cultural contexts.[33] Moreover, the resignification of female bisexuality as a form of heterosexuality is, importantly, not simply a framework through which female bisexuality simply becomes female heterosexuality. Instead, there is a specific process at play here whereby female bisexuality is taken to be the ne plus ultra of depoliticized womanhood, acquiescent to patriarchy and its demands of female sexual spectacle.

The corollary perception of bisexual men, however, involves bisexuality being rewritten as homosexuality; here, sexual desire toward other men produces a totalizing effect in the opposite direction. In the man assumed to be heterosexual, a single deviation into intragender desire holds the potential to undo his heterosexuality irreversibly.[34] From the second half of the twentieth century onward, some of the most prominent figures in psychoanalysis and psychology would reify understandings of male bisexuality as male homosexuality. Psychoanalyst Edmund Bergler writes in 1957 that male bisexuality "is an out-and-out fraud, involuntarily maintained by some naïve homosexuals, and voluntarily perpetrated by some who are not so naïve. The theory claims that a man can be—alternately or concomitantly—homo and heterosexual. The statement is as rational as one declaring that a man can at the same time have cancer and perfect health."[35] For Bergler, bisexual men are, whether intentionally or not, homosexual charlatans whose purported desires are irrational in his medical framework. Czechoslovakian sexologist Kurt Freund comes to similar conclusions through his experiments measuring penile tumescence in relation to pornographic stimuli as an index of sexual arousal. With these experiments in 1974, Freund determines that there is no evidence for what he terms "bisexuality proper" among men.[36] Freund's conclusions were influential for American psychologist J. Michael Bailey, who led similar experiments to Freund's in the 2000s that purported to prove the nonexistence of what he calls "physiological" male bisexuality.[37] As Bailey summarizes: "Freund . . . was never able to find a subset of men who appeared bisexual in the lab. Although their data are less scientific, gay men share Freund's skepticism. They have a saying: 'You're either gay, straight, or lying.'"[38]

Attention to the gendered forms taken by common understandings of bisexuality is thus central to any bisexual cultural analysis. Importantly, these common understandings carry with them an assumed cisgenderness. Rooted as they are in patriarchal and heterosexist frameworks, so too do they carry an inherent cissexism that treats expressions of transness as deviant maleness or femaleness, determined by sex assigned at birth. These common gendered understandings of male and female bisexuality, therefore, cannot but reproduce a gender binary in which trans and nonbinary gender are deemed nonexistent. Yet, as we have seen, cultural attitudes toward female and male bisexuality involve their being rewritten as heterosexuality and homosexuality, respectively, thus consolidating notions of bisexuality's general nonexistence. Similar discursive moves are observable in recent antitransgender thinking, whereby transness is treated as nonexistent by recasting it as a confused homosexuality, as male paraphilia, or as symptomatic of mental illness or neurodevelopmental disorder.[39] What these characterizations share with those professing bisexuality's nonexistence is their function as epistemological frameworks that resignify phenomena attesting to a binary's insufficiency or nonexclusivity to befit dominant conceptions of gender, sex, sexuality, and medicine. A compelling parallel thus emerges through which sexualities that contest neat binary organization and genders that contest neat binary organization must be rendered nonexistent in order that these binaries maintain their purported ontology.

The question thus emerges as to how to discuss the cultural implications of phenomena that are culturally assumed to not exist. One analytic offering a potential egress here is Georg Wilhelm Friedrich Hegel's conceptualization of the dialectic of being and nothing: that *that which is* is inseparable from *that which is not*.[40] For Hegel, the dissolution of this opposition between being and nothing involves a movement toward *becoming*.[41] With this analytic in place, we should pause before countering assertions of bisexuality's nonexistence simply with exclamations of "Bisexuality exists!" Instead, we can understand the assertion of "monosexuality *is*, bisexuality *is not*" as an unstable mantra haunted by its negations. The critical task thus involves posing challenges to the exclusivity and taxonomical stability of sexual formations, eschewing the zero-sum games of being and nothing, and giving way to a space of potentiality where sexuality is understood as always able to be otherwise, always becoming.[42] One of the central ways in which such potentialities have been explored, albeit without recourse to Hegel, is bisexual theory. A series of interventions into queer studies as it was emerging in the 1990s, bisexual theory posed epistemological trouble in its exploitation of values with which bisexuality has tended to be cast, bringing uncertainty, unintelligibility, and the contestation of binary thinking to the critical fore.

Queer Theory and Its Bisexual Interventions

Bisexuality is not merely a problem of an unrecognized or vilified sexual preference that can be solved, or alleviated, through visibility and legitimation as a third sexual option. . . . I propose, therefore that we assume bisexuality . . . as an epistemological as well as ethical vantage point from which we can examine and deconstruct the bipolar framework of gender and sexuality.
—Elisabeth D. Däumer, "Queer Ethics"

Although the genesis of queer theory was characterized by a call to depart from the "ideological liabilities" of the terms *lesbian* and *gay*, and to embrace how "the constituent elements of anyone's gender, of anyone's sexuality aren't made (or *can't be* made) to signify monolithically," the role of bisexuality herein has often been dismissed.[43] Around two decades after its genesis, David M. Halperin observes that while "'queer theory' was once the name for the field of study that capitalized on the crisis of sexual definition, on this breakdown in our conceptual categories . . . *queer* has lost its sense of unassimilable and irredeemable sexual deviance, and subsided into a mere synonym of *gay*."[44] Notwithstanding discussions of Freud's theories of bisexuality, allusions to bisexuality in queer studies tend only to be found in parentheses and endnotes, if not prescinded from altogether. When it has been addressed, queer theorists have often been skeptical of bisexuality's critical utility. For Lee Edelman, the "hetero/homo binarism . . . [is] more effectively reinforced than disrupted by the 'third term' of bisexuality. . . . The category of 'bisexuality' can appear to position itself between reified polar opposites of 'heterosexual' and 'homosexual.'"[45] In an online discussion, Eve Kosofsky Sedgwick warns against how "the political concept of 'bisexuality' seems to offer a *consolidation and completion* of an understanding of sexuality as something that can be described adequately, for everybody, in terms of gender-of-object-choice. . . . As though . . . you have now covered the entire ground and collected the whole set."[46] Edelman's and Sedgwick's conceptual reticence toward bisexuality is rooted in their perceptions of its consolidating effect over dominant understandings of sexuality.

Steven Angelides critiques these positions, however, as enacting the limitations they purport to observe. He writes that these arguments are structured by "a curious *dis/avowal* of bisexuality, where only some of its possible meanings have been authorised."[47] Although Angelides acknowledges that bisexuality can be deployed in a consolidatory fashion, he stresses that this is just one of its potential deployments. Bisexuality, for Angelides, is most threatening to hegemonic conceptions of sexuality when engaged in the present tense: "It is *not* bisexuality *per se* that reinforces our binary categories of sexuality. Rather, it is the temporal framing of bisexuality—*the persistent epistemological refusal to recognize bisexuality in the present tense*—that has functioned to reinforce the hetero/homosexual binarism."[48] To recognize bisexuality's presentness is to facilitate its use as that which troubles the heterosexual-homosexual binary's very epistemological grounding: the nowness of bisexual possibility.

Bisexual theory's foundational contention lies in the epistemological utility of a bisexual focus in queer approaches to gender and sexuality. The concerns that came to characterize bisexual theory are expressed earliest by Elisabeth D. Däumer in her 1992 article that proposes "we assume bisexuality . . . as an epistemological as well as ethical vantage point from which we can examine and deconstruct the bipolar framework of gender and sexuality."[49] Däumer's articulation of such a vantage point is as suspicious as Edelman's and Sedgwick's toward consolidatory approaches to bisexuality. She insists that "bisexuality is not merely a problem of an unrecognized or vilified sexual preference that can be solved, or alleviated, through visibility and legitimation as a third sexual option. . . . The effort to disambiguate bisexuality and elevate it into a sign of integration might counteract the subversive potential of bisexuality as a moral and epistemological force."[50] Instead, Däumer proposes that bisexuality's critical position *"between* identities" is a useful vantage point from which difference can be explored without recourse to oppositional binaries.[51]

It is in the aftermath of Däumer's call that scholars consider in greatest detail what a bisexual epistemological position might look like. For Clare Hemmings, what is most epistemologically useful in bisexuality is its "insistent partiality," which "makes visible the process by which we all become sexual and gendered subjects."[52] A bisexual epistemology brings into view those qualities of dominant sexuality—"separation, self-reflection, stasis"—that exert a constricting force over all forms of sexuality.[53] The conception of bisexual epistemology I find most compelling comes from Maria Pramaggiore, who reappropriates the cliché that bisexuals are "on the fence" to theorize a bisexual "epistemology of the fence." Pramaggiore elucidates:

> The fence, in its nominal form, identifies a place of in-betweenness and indecision. Often precariously perched atop a structure that divides and demarcates, bisexual epistemologies have the capacity to reframe regimes and regions of desire by deframing and/or reframing in porous, nonexclusive ways. Fence-sitting . . . is a practice that refuses the restrictive formulas that define gender according to binary categories, that associate one gender or one sexuality with a singularly gendered object choice, and that equate sexual practices with sexual identity. Bisexual epistemologies—ways of apprehending, organizing, and intervening in the world that refuse one-to-one correspondences between sex acts and identity, between erotic objects and sexualities, between identification and desire—acknowledge fluid desires and their continual construction and deconstruction of the desiring subject.[54]

In Pramaggiore's evocative conception, bisexual epistemologies are characterized by a nonexclusive approach to knowledge formation, which underscores, in relation to sexuality, the various ways in which experiences and expressions of sexuality do not correspond conventionally. Central here is desire's capacity to transform: an affirmation of desire's contingency and mutability.

Attention to desire's potential to be nonsingular in its directionalities, and wont to change, involves a reckoning with that which dominant notions of heterosexuality and homosexuality must negate in their efforts toward stable meaning. Hemmings outlines how both heterosexuality and homosexuality maintain their epistemological coherence through a repudiative relation between the terms.[55] Here, the positive demarcation of the gender of one's object choice is made meaningful through the negative demarcation of another possible gendered object; the latter is the subtrahend in whose deduction the positive gendered object choice is affirmed. In thinking through how to handle conceptual oppositions, we might return once more to Hegel in his perspicuity that "it is explicitly what contains . . . oppositions at which the understanding stops short . . . and contains them as something sublated within itself."[56] Among queer theory's founding texts, we find critical analysis of heterosexuality's negation of homosexuality—from Judith Butler's discussion of heterosexuality and melancholia to Eve Kosofsky Sedgwick's analysis of heterosexuality's "simultaneous subsumption and exclusion" of homosexuality in the hetero-homo dyad.[57] These analyses, however, stop short of recognizing bisexuality's conceptual utility in working through the oppositions they wish to deconstruct. To limit our discussion of the heterosexual-homosexual opposition to the ways in which the former negates and internalizes the latter, or vice versa—or even to their compelling overlaps—is, still, to bottleneck our understanding. Such an approach maintains the sublations that form the opposition, even while professing to unconceal them. To think about sexual epistemology only through the given oppositional terms is to secure their sublations. Instead, I suggest we should take the route Hegel describes as the speculative moment, which "grasps the unity of the determinations in their opposition, the *affirmative* that is contained in their dissolution and their passing over into something else."[58] The dissolution of the heterosexual-homosexual opposition can thus work to affirm something else, a bisexual possibility that expands and complicates the epistemic landscape's cartography. To enact such a speculative moment, however, we must take a critical stance toward what has become a contested term in sexuality studies: *monosexuality*.

The Problem of Monosexuality

Theoretical formulations of bisexual inquiry have worked to shift a queer intellectual focus onto how dominant formulations of heterosexuality and homosexuality often share certain investments: teleological narratives of sexual becoming, a belief in sexuality's naturalness, a conception of sexuality as an unchanging expression of an inner truth, and a structure of mutual oppositionality wherein each sexuality renders the other meaningful through the repudiation of its opposite. Although all bisexual theory is attentive to the vantage point bisexuality provides in critiquing these dominant ideas, there is disagreement as to the utility of grouping together heterosexuality and homosexuality under the term *monosexuality*. *Monosexuality* describes desires toward people of only one gender (heterosexuality and homosexuality), and *monosexism* describes "a social structure operating through a presumption that everyone is, or should be, monosexual."[59] While many bisexual activists and bisexual theorists deploy these terms, a number of British bisexual theorists argue against their use. The strongest critiques to this effect come from Hemmings, who writes that "to term all non-bisexuals *monosexuals* erases the differences between lesbians/gay men and heterosexuals, equating the power dynamics that exist between bisexuals and lesbians/gay men with those between homosexuals and heterosexuals. Such a gesture refuses to acknowledge the social hierarchies of sex, gender, and sexuality that have historically influenced and continue to influence, subject and community formation."[60] Hemmings contends that the use of *monosexual* as a descriptor erases the operations of structures of homophobia and sexism. It is unclear, however, why Hemmings believes that the former necessitates the latter. Hemmings claims that "in this rubric bisexuals are uniquely oppressed by monosexism. . . . By setting up this division, the differences between lesbians and gay men and heterosexuals in terms of power are elided."[61] However, the acknowledgment of a social rule stipulating the normality, maturity, or legitimacy of attraction toward only one gender, while casting attractions toward more than one gender as non-normative, immature, or illegitimate, need not suggest that this rule operates independently of others. There seems to be a reluctance on Hemmings's part to recognize that systems of sexual oppression can operate in more than one way.[62] While Hemmings suggests that the term *monosexuality* "erases the differences between a lesbian feminist position and a heterosexual male position in relation to structures of power," her example already shows that strict divisions of sexuality cannot be thought of independently: the woman figure she cites is homosexual, the male figure she cites is heterosexual, yet she still deploys these sexuality terms while noting gendered differences herein.[63] Hemmings's resistance to the term *monosexuality* is thus rooted in what I contend is an error whereby attention to the social stipulation that people should only desire people of a single gender is misconstrued as a denial that other social stipulations exist.

Another issue with Hemmings's critique is its elision of an important locus of critical attention: the mutual investments and workings of heterosexuality and homosexuality. These investments are parsed in detail in legal scholar Kenji Yoshino's article "The Epistemic Contract of Bisexual Erasure." With attention to sexual epistemology, Yoshino illuminates the multiple sites of mutual interest between liberal gay rights movements and heterosexist norms that rely upon the erasure of bisexuality for their mutual coherence.[64] Yoshino does not seek to elide power differentials between heterosexual and homosexual people but, instead, identifies those points of shared investment between a liberal gay politics defining queer sexuality as heterosexuality's equal opposite—natural, immutable, secure—whose coherence is dependent on bisexuality's elision. Instructive critical interventions like Yoshino's are impossible without attention to monosexism.

Hemmings also critiques the term *monosexuality* because she sees it as "attempting to mark out bisexuals as somehow 'beyond' sex and gender . . . creating a boundary around bisexuality (that only the most enlightened and gender-free may cross?)."[65] In this usage, Hemmings argues, monosexuals are considered "politically duped into believing in a two sex, two-gender system."[66] Hemmings's contention is that the identification of monosexuality creates a hierarchy of sexual radicalism in which bisexuality's ability to operate within a sex or gender binary is elided. While I agree that bisexuality does not per se contest a binary system of gender, Hemmings seems uncurious to entertain how it might hold the potential to do so. It seems uncontroversial, to me, to suggest that bisexuality can describe desire beyond gender. It is the beyondness of our desires that characterizes their nonsingularity: We desire beyond single-gendered objects, our sexualities are constituted beyond the present in a way that embraces our pasts and potential futures. To attest to this beyondness is not to assert bisexuality as being beyond the reaches of discourse or beyond social exigencies but, instead, to mobilize bisexuality's ontological capacity for desiring beyond single-gendered object choice toward a destabilization of sexual norms that cement rigid gender and sexuality binaries. This is not a trouble we should avoid lest some be considered unenlightened or unradical. On the contrary, it is new forms of knowledge and radical challenges to extant systems of gender and sexuality to which our critical thinking must be drawn.

Monosexism thus describes one facet in a web of sexual organization that, rather than isolating a particular form of sexual oppression without attention to others, in fact, complexifies and particularizes our understanding of varying dynamics at play here. While Hemmings is "deeply concerned by the discursive and political effects that the creation of the monosexual/bisexual binary has," this concern is misattributed.[67] The monosexual/bisexual binary is already at play socially: It operates in state systems of border control deeming the legitimacy of those seeking asylum on the basis of their sexualities, it affects the interpersonal relations of bisexual people in the world, and, as social scientists have observed across decades, it marks disparities in health, exposure to violence, and material conditions of bisexual people in varied cultural contexts.[68] The issue lies, therefore, not in naming monosexism but in monosexism itself.[69]

Bisexuality's Uses in Aesthetic Analysis

BISEXUAL AESTHETICS, BISEXUAL SPECTATORSHIP

Prior to the emergence of bisexual theory, and its fitful articulations in film and media studies, bisexuality's deployment for critical approaches to aesthetics appeared most pronouncedly in two loci: the cultural-aesthetic theory of Sergei Eisenstein and feminist theories of film spectatorship.[70] Strange bedfellows they may be, yet their scholarship shares an investment in bisexuality as a means of accounting for the relations between gender, sexuality, and aesthetics. Bisexuality is a topic that fascinated Eisenstein, first, in relation to the theories of Otto Weininger and, later, in relation to the work of Magnus Hirschfeld, whose Institute for Sex Research he visited in the early 1930s.[71] Eisenstein proposes that "the dialectical principle in sex is bisexuality."[72] His understanding of bisexuality encompasses notions of sex (intersexuality or hermaphroditism), gender (the coincidence of masculinity and femininity), and sexual desire (bisexuality in its current sense).[73] Theorizing the application of the dialectical method to questions of sex, Eisenstein posits these bisexual dynamics as undergirding the terrain of inquiry.

Bisexuality, Eisenstein argues, must be "rethought of as a social process eliminating contradictions, establishing legal equality and equal participation in labor and achievements—no longer by the mystical feminine and masculine 'elements,' and much less by biological 'categories.'"[74] Remarkably, Eisenstein proposes what is effectively a proto-queer thesis, arguing for social change through a denaturalization of sexual taxonomies. For Eisenstein, the function of bisexuality in these denaturalization efforts involves its reminder of the simultaneous presence of that which is deemed masculine and feminine, male and female, and even heterosexual and homosexual in us all. These arguments anticipate the later work of sexual revolutionaries like Shulamith Firestone and Mario Mieli, whose imaginings of a postrevolutionary future involve the nonexclusivity of the dyads Eisenstein traces.[75] Eisenstein stresses that "these ideas about bisexuality here bear no relation to any narrow sexual problem. We are interested in the issue of the 'lifting' of this biological field of application of the conceptual opposites."[76] The utility of bisexuality for Eisenstein thus lies not in reproducing overdetermined biological accounts of bisexuality but in engaging bisexuality dialectically as a means of parsing that which society has dichotomized.[77]

Especially pertinent for my investigation is how Eisenstein conceptualizes such bisexual possibilities as discernible in certain aesthetic works. He discusses a scene from Jacques Deval's 1935 play L'Âge de Juliette in which a young couple, Serge and Mietta, exit their hotel room to an offstage bathroom while mechanics fix a radio; upon their return, the couple is wearing each other's bathrobes. Eisenstein concludes that this sequence not only conveys Serge and Mietta's having been intimate with one another, it also evokes "the restoration of this initial, primary, unitary bisexual element."[78] For Eisenstein, this example attests to a bisexual potential he deems a "precondition in all creative dialectics": the presence of that which reminds us of the possibilities beyond strict male/female, masculine/feminine, heterosexual/homosexual divisions.[79] In his application of a bisexual dialectical method to Deval's play, Eisenstein demonstrates a potential aesthetic works hold for us to glimpse possibilities beyond dominant sexual taxonomies, a potential to which trans and bisexual interventions in film and media studies would also later attest.[80]

Bisexuality's utility as a descriptor of gender and sexuality's mutability is also key for feminist theoretical engagements with questions of film spectatorship. An early example of this critical trend can be found in Laura Mulvey's articulation of a female spectator's identification with male characters as a "transsex identification . . . shift[ing] restlessly in its borrowed transvestite clothes."[81] While not naming this identification across gender lines as "bisexual," Mulvey's theorization suggests the potential to understand cinematic spectatorship as a protean process that can take place across categories of gender. Yet further, in her description of a female spectator identifying herself with a male protagonist, Mulvey is articulating not only a gender transgression (which trans media theorists have since developed beyond the clumsy transsexuality/transvestism metaphor) but a potential desirous transgression.[82] Here, Mulvey also attests to how a female spectator might vicariously desire a heterosexual male protagonist's female object of desire: the female spectator might desire a female object *as man*. Elizabeth Cowie's later article "Fantasia" speaks to this potential to identify and desire in unfixed ways. Cowie draws upon Jean Laplanche and Jean-Bertrand Pontalis's articulation of fantasy not as the object of desire but as its setting, its "mise-en-scène."[83] Cowie contends that "what is necessary for any public forms of fantasy . . . is not universal objects of desire, but a setting of desiring in which we can find our place(s). . . . While the terms of sexual difference are fixed, the places of characters and spectators in relation to those terms are not."[84] Within this framework, a spectator might experience multiple sites of identification and desire, caught amid various forms of sexual alignment within the fantasy space of cinema. Cowie later turns to bisexuality—as do other feminist film theorists, including Janet Bergstrom, Carol Clover, Miriam Hansen, Tania Modleski, Margaret Morse, Gaylyn Studlar, and Linda Williams—as a means of describing the sexual and gendered flexibility experienced in film spectatorship.[85] "This notion of bisexuality," writes Cowie, "emphasizes the complexity as well as the interdependency of the multiple positions constructed in film."[86] Feminist theoretical accounts of spectatorship seeking to map the numerous positions that constitute film viewing have sometimes found in bisexuality a model for doing so, useful in its potential to capture the inherent plasticity of our spectatorial identifications and desires.

Such potentialities might even be glimpsed in the earlier writing of André Bazin. Although Bazin is not generally understood as theorizing questions of gender or sexuality, in his account of eroticism and the cinema, he writes that "the cinema unreels in an imaginary space which demands participation and identification. The actor winning the woman gratifies me by proxy. His seductiveness, his good looks, his daring do not compete with my desires—they fulfill them."[87] Bazin's comments serve as a reminder that, in film spectatorship, identification and desire are never discrete processes; his gratification is rooted not only in the assumedly beautiful woman described but in his ability to identify with a seductive, good-looking (read: desirable) man. Bazin's reflections, in fact, speak to Jackie Stacey's later warning against "the rigid distinction of *either* desire *or* identification," and her call for theories that "address the construction of desires which involve a specific interplay of both processes."[88]

One site in which the dynamics undergirding Bazin's spectatorial account have been developed, and Stacey's call for thinking desire and identification together has been taken up, is expressly bisexual film studies scholarship. Pramaggiore's bisexual intervention in discussions of spectatorship highlights "the spectatorial difficulty of clearly distinguishing between wanting to 'be' a character . . . and wanting to 'have' a character."[89] In a similar vein, Maria San Filippo suggests that "we are welcomed *out* of the closet by the cinematic experience" and that "screen media offer a liberating space for the accommodation of subjectivities and desires beyond monosexuality."[90] In these bisexual theorizations, film spectatorship carries with it the potential to desire, albeit transiently, in ways that transgress the heterosexual/homosexual division. Film's recurrent invitations to desire and to identify in partial, protean, and impermanent ways proffer bisexual possibilities wherein various desires and identifications might be experienced vicariously.[91]

These theoretical contributions speak to the utility of bisexuality as a critical framework through which to explore cinema's potential to remind us of sexuality's extensive capacities, both conceptually, at the level of signification, and intersubjectively, at the level of the spectator's desires and identifications. Yet this critical impulse can and has been taken further afield in critical practices where bisexuality functions not only as a concept for critical deployment but also as the primary position from which film criticism emanates—as, in other words, a bisexual film criticism. These critical practices tend to consider the relation between bisexuality, cinema, and sexual politics, lingering longer on the question of bisexuality's textual representation or representability. Although bisexual theoretical approaches are those I find richest in exploring these questions, a significant history of bisexual film criticism developed through different approaches more aligned with bisexual activism. Both critical genealogies provide insights into the fraught position of bisexuality vis-à-vis cinema: its problems, its conflicts, but also its potential affordances.

BISEXUALITY AND MEDIA: THE AXIOLOGICAL APPROACH

As with other minority peoples, few images of Bisexuals appear in the popular media. It is unconscionable that when Bisexuals are portrayed, it is as sick depraved creatures.

—ACT UP New York, "NBC Protest"

An early milestone in expressly bisexual media critique occurred in 1988 in concert with a series of protests that responded to an episode of the American television series *Midnight Caller*. The late 1980s saw bisexual American groups' increased militantism, with calls for participation and attention in gay political campaigns becoming demands whose urgency was heightened by the AIDS epidemic.[92] This politics was in full force in the response to the episode, entitled "After It Happened," which depicts an HIV-positive bisexual man who purposely transmits the virus to others. Following the leaking of the episode's screenplay, the New York Area Bisexual Network and the Bisexual Support Group joined forces with AIDS activist group ACT UP New York to protest the series' portrayal of bisexuality.[93] In an activist landscape in which attentions were turning to the import of screen representation, bisexual politics was finding a place for itself.

These emergent bisexual media critiques are observably influenced by approaches in gay media critique circulating during the late 1970s and 1980s that considered negative portrayals of certain sexuality groups as either symptomatic of queerphobia or precipitative of queerphobic attitudes and even violence. New Line Cinema's 1974–1975 lecture series "Presentations" included a talk by Vito Russo that was later included in his book *The Celluloid Closet*; their catalog description calls the talk "an insight into the power of the media to perpetuate social stereotypes."[94] Five years later, New Line would showcase a similar lecture, this time, with a bisexual angle, delivered by Don Fass, the founder of the National Bisexual Liberation Group. The promotional text for the presentation promises a discussion of "the bisexual experience" alongside illustrative film clips.[95] Although precise information about the content of Fass's presentation is difficult to find, it is reasonable to suspect that it followed a similar approach to those of New Line's other speakers, which, alongside Russo's focus on homosexuality, featured Molly Haskell on "the treatment of women in the movies" and James Murray on "blacks in films."[96] These

FIGURE I.2 An ACT
UP New York pam-
phlet for a protest
of *Midnight Caller* at
NBC. Document scan.

NBC POLICY ON AIDS:
TO FRIGHTEN OR ENLIGHTEN?

An upcoming episode of NBC's "Midnight Caller" portrays a bisexual man infected with HIV (the "AIDS virus") who knowingly spreads the disease to male and female partners. A woman he has infected then hunts him down and tries to kill him.

This episode does more than merely sensationalize the plight of the estimated 1.5 million people currently living with HIV infection in this country. . .

IT ENDANGERS THEIR VERY LIVES!

The premise of a vindictive Person With AIDS (PWA) purposefully infecting others plays into the public's darkest, ill-founded fears about AIDS transmission and further pumps up an already highly-charged atmosphere of national AIDS hysteria.

This dangerous scenario, with its "Innocent Victim" becoming infected by the "Guilty/Evil HIV Carrier" then goes on to promote violence and vigilantism as a valid response to the AIDS Crisis!

WHAT IS NBC TELLING THE PUBLIC?

A recent Roper study states that the American Public uses Television as their major source for AIDS Information and Education. But instead of educating the Public about AIDS or helping to bring a more compassionate response to people who are living with AIDS or HIV Infection, NBC is cynically choosing Ratings Points over Broadcasting Ethics.

What is at issue here is not censorship, it is ethics.

We demand that NBC apply the same standards to people infected with HIV as they do to other racially or sexually sensitive subjects.

We demand that NBC stop playing ratings games with people's lives!

We demand that NBC recognize its responsibility to the American Public and cancel this episode of "Midnight Caller" immediately!

We are ACT UP, the AIDS Coalition to Unleash Power, a diverse, non-partisan group of individuals united in anger and committed to direct action to end the AIDS crisis. For more information, please call 212-533-8888.

presentations' use of film as a means through which to explore issues of social justice regularly took the form of identifying stereotypes and censuring cinema's role in perpetuating prejudice. This tenor of argument can be found in the 1985 revised edition of Russo's *The Celluloid Closet*, where he writes: "Open violence against gay people in America has reached epidemic proportions, fueled by films that encourage young people to believe that such behavior is acceptable."[97]

The arguments proffered by Russo, his contemporaries in the Gay and Lesbian Alliance Against Defamation (GLAAD), and ACT UP New York are characterized by an approach that would come to be known as "media effects theory." The definitive premise of media effects theory involves the idea that media can have direct, measurable influences on the attitudes and actions of its viewers.[98] The problem with this premise is not that media cannot affect its audience's perceptions of the world. Instead, it is the characterization of the media text as producing linear, unidirectional, and univocal messages, devoid of textuality, stripped of social context, and impervious to the interpretive faculties of those who receive them. That representations can affect the social perception of social groups—a phenomenon explored more delicately by scholars like Stuart Hall and Richard Dyer—does not mean that all social groups are equally intelligible, nor does it mean that processes of comprehension are directly predictable.[99] This phenomenon also cannot be taken to mean that the truth about a group is definitively representable, nor does it mean that images certain people deem to be negative necessarily invoke negative social outcomes (yet, in media effects approaches, the first contention often dovetails with the latter). In these approaches, sprawling and pervasive issues like social queerphobia become conveniently crystallized in a repudiable bad object.

Much bisexual writing has engaged the language of negative representation, stereotypes, or tropes—and the presumptions of media effects—to discuss cinema, from the scholarly and para-academic writing of Wayne M. Bryant, Justin Vicari, and Jonathan David White, to listicles in online publications with titles like "11 Bisexual Tropes I'm Honestly Tired of Seeing in TV and Movies" and "9 Bisexual TV and Film Characters Who Deserved Better than Tired Tropes," to an entry on the wiki TV Tropes that lists media objects containing the purported trope of "the Depraved Bisexual."[100] Admittedly, there is some utility to this work: the identification of stereotypes and tropes works to map the textual terrain with an eye for repetition, drawing our attention to where notable recurrences take place and the persistent meanings with which bisexuality is often invoked. The efforts of a researcher like Bryant in his encyclopedic *Bisexual Characters in Film: From Anaïs to Zee* (1997) endures as a valuable resource in the sheer breadth of films it identifies as potentially open to bisexual inquiry. Where these pieces of writing lack rigor, however, is in their mode of reading, tending to proceed by identifying in certain media texts a character they read as bisexual and whose representation, they argue, is either beneficial or deleterious for perceptions of bisexual people.[101] The examples they cite in the negative range from *The Berlin Affair*'s (Liliana Cavani, 1985) seductive art student Mitsuko (Mio Takaki) and *Blue Velvet*'s (David Lynch, 1986) paraphiliac gangster Frank (Dennis Hopper) to the unnamed gay-man-turned-woman-desiring-misogynist (Rocco Siffredi) of Catherine Breillat's allegorical art film *Anatomy of Hell* (2004). While I am sensitive to the frustrations that undergird the readings of these films, they make a critical error. The regular suggestion one finds is that representations of bisexuals behaving badly are untruthful.

This assertion speaks, first, to the presupposition that media can represent the truth about a social group.[102] Here we would be wise to remember Gayatri

Chakravorty Spivak's careful articulation of the difference between representation qua *Vertretung*, "representation in the political context," and representation qua *Darstellung*—"the philosophical concept of representation as staging, or, indeed, signification."[103] In Spivak's exposition, we are warned that confusing these two senses of *representation* nullifies political work into a shallow reading practice whereby representational visibility is embraced uncritically as a metric of social transformation. Spivak's ideas are developed in the film studies scholarship of Kara Keeling and echoed in that of Rey Chow, both of whom criticize the tendency to understand aesthetic representations as, in Keeling's words, "political proxies."[104] What is ineffectual, therefore, in approaches to film that seek truth, coherence, or proxies of the political is a fundamental misapprehension of the aesthetic that risks reproducing dominant discourses that conflate narrow notions of what cultural groups are said to look like with what these groups are or might be.

Second, these critics' characterizations of such a truth about bisexuality regularly involve loosely defined notions of goodness, which can, under no circumstances, conform to stereotypes about bisexual people. Shiri Eisner reminds us that "this outright denial of [bisexual] stereotypes creates a mirror image of the bisexual imagined therein. . . . This bisexual is reassuring, harmless, stable and safe . . . unthreatening and docile . . . a harmless and benign sexual citizen . . . answering each and every call for normativity with enthusiastic consent."[105] The critical weakness in an antistereotype bisexual approach to media lies in its acquiescence to normative notions of recognizability and virtue, notions that should be interrogated rather than reasserted. These approaches to reading media images are axiological: They are guided by a normative value system through which truthfulness, virtue, and positivity are determined. What hamstrings them is thus an assumption that bisexuality is definitively recognizable in media (and that media viewers will necessarily perceive bisexual people in the same ways a media text represents them), alongside bromides involving a broadly defined aspiration toward supposedly positive representation that, more often than not, reveal themselves as calls for either normativity or respectability.[106]

More critical approaches to representation, however, are mindful of the contingency of mediated meaning-making and skeptical toward the promise of good representation, the likes of which have recently been developed within trans media studies in ways that speak to important alliances between critical bisexual and transgender media analysis. When Jo Eadie intervenes in conversations around bisexual representation, he warns against reading bisexual filmic figures' embodiments of excess and transgression simply as evidence of

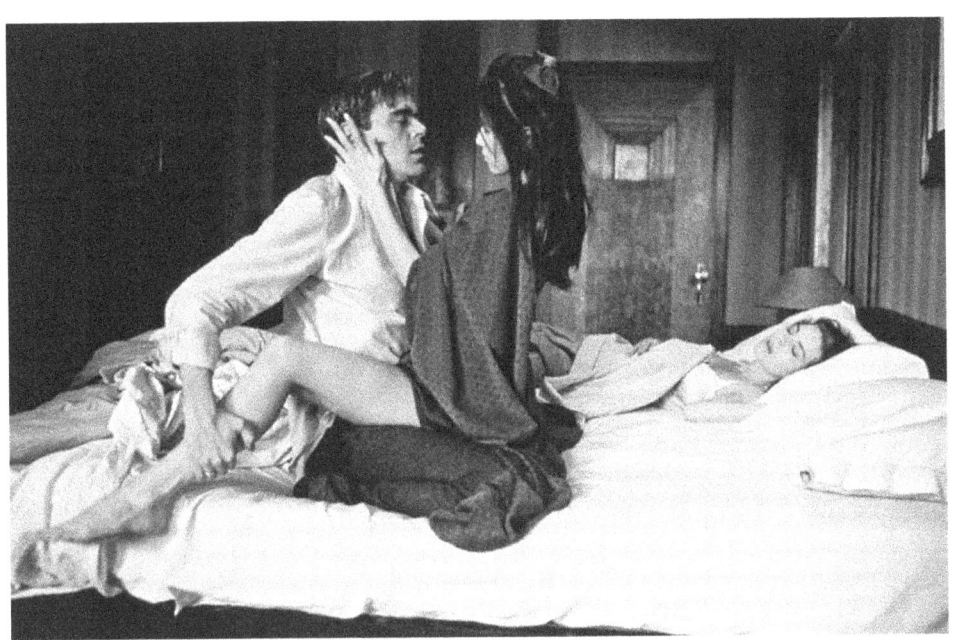

FIGURE I.3 Mitsuko (Mio Takaki) seduces Heinz (Kevin McNally) while Louise (Gudrun Landgrebe), her lover, sleeps. *The Berlin Affair* [*Interno Berlinese* / *Leidenschaften*] (Liliana Cavani, 1985). Promotional image.

bisexuality being "stereotyped." Instead, he suggests that "we may learn something here about the discursive regulation of bisexuality . . . how bisexuality is made socially meaningful."[107] Eadie's proposition moves us away from the ruse of thinking representation as both a signifier of truth and the originator of supposedly negative media effects to consider, instead, the discursive practices through which bisexuality is aligned with certain social meanings, often involving the transgression of a limit. Eadie's impulse is mirrored in the recent work in trans media studies led by Cáel M. Keegan, who describes the dismissal of what he terms "bad trans media objects" as enacting a politics that grants the "least disruptive" of these objects "a marginal amount of inclusion."[108] Keegan's critique of good trans media objects—representations of ethical, happy trans figures presented through codes of authenticity—involves them being the least challenging to extant systems of gender, the trans figure working to naturalize the cisness of other diegetic figures.[109] The bad trans media object, however, exploits the capacity in badness to indicate "the presence of something unclassifiable within the established categories used to delimit sex and gender."[110] This critical approach allows Keegan to revisit some of trans representation's most repudiated figures among popular trans media criticism—from *Tootsie*'s (Sydney Pollack, 1982) Michael/Dorothy (Dustin Hoffman) to *The Silence of the Lambs*' (Jonathan Demme, 1991) Buffalo Bill/Jame Gumb (Ted Levine)—to consider the ways these figures pose a disruption to dominant paradigms of gender and sex, a disruption that is not contained but, rather, poses challenges to cissexist forms of governmentality.[111]

I share with Eadie and Keegan an investment in looking to bad media objects not simply as evidence of prejudicial attitudes but as usefully disruptive representations in which social anxieties, systems of sexual signification, and models for queer forms of dissidence come into view. The alliances to be forged between critical bisexual and transgender approaches speak to some important sites of mutual solidarity in our work.[112] As Shiri Eisner reminds us, transgender and bisexual people (who are, empirically speaking, groups that overlap significantly, with significant proportions of each group identified as both) embody certain challenging forms of social being while also facing similar accusations from those dismissive of their political legitimacy.[113] Eisner details how both bisexuality and transness speak to our capacity for change, for sexual becoming, in contrast with notions of sexual immutability. Both also have a complex relation to notions of passing, the unreadability of their queerness sometimes voluntarily taken on and sometimes coercively enforced. Relatedly, both groups are regularly accused of desiring or having straight or straight-passing privilege and of acquiescing to a dominant gender binary. While taking pains not to treat this shared ground as a space of direct parallels or equivalences, Eisner's work outlines pertinent homologies between bisexuality and transness within dominant sexual epistemologies. Their analysis illuminates two particular anxieties that both bring to bear: first, the capacity for our sexual selves to change, to be different in the future to how they were in the past and, second, the ability for that which looks normative—cisgender, heterosexual, or of a binary gender—to reveal the insufficiency of dominant codes of sexual signification in the presence of an unintelligible queerness. When reconceptualized as such, we find clues to the particular affordances of moving images with regard to troublesome, transgressive, or disruptive figurations of transness and bisexuality. The durational nature of the form allows for change or becoming to take place; its visuality allows for questions around sexual epistemology's relation to perception to take shape. These questions around cinematic temporality, visuality, and sexual epistemology animate this book, with trans media theory recurring as an important accomplice in staging my bisexual intervention. What this mode of inquiry requires, however, are more critical approaches than axiology can afford.

CRITICAL BISEXUAL APPROACHES TO FILM AND MEDIA: HERMENEUTICS AND FIGURATION

Donald E. Hall's introduction to an edited collection on bisexuality and representation submits that "BISEXUALITY cannot be definitively represented."[114] The operative word in Hall's provocation is "definitively." Whereas heterosexuality and homosexuality have associated with them comprehensible, intelligible representational forms, bisexuality carries no such certitude. Consider bisexual activist Robyn Ochs's question:

> What kind of behavior would I—as a bisexual—have to engage in for other people to see me as bisexual? I could walk into the room with a man and a woman, one on each arm, engaging in public displays of affection with each in a way that makes it obvious that we're sexual partners. Or I could be known to have multiple partners, including at least one man and one woman. Or I could leave someone for someone else of a different sex than the partner I have left. (Interestingly, in this scenario, many people still might not read me as bisexual. Rather, they might interpret me as having finally "finished coming out" or decide that I have "gone straight").[115]

Ochs's reflections highlight how the dominance of a monosexist frame of interpretation works to preclude bisexuality as an interpretive possibility. Bisexual theorists have worked to parse precisely why and how bisexuality is rendered intelligible or unintelligible in a text and to develop bisexual frameworks of interpretation that embrace partiality, mutability, and interstitiality. In the major works of queer film theory, however, scant attention has been paid to issues around bisexuality, favoring, broadly speaking, an implicit focus on the figure of the homosexual (including particularized variations, such as the pansy or the butch), the gender transgressor, or on notions of gay, lesbian, or queer cinema. The most critical scholarly work on bisexuality and film has come from Maria Pramaggiore, Jo Eadie, Alexander Doty, Maria San Filippo, and B. C. Roberts. The work of these scholars is linked by a critical relation to notions of good representation and a questioning of the very terms upon which (bi)sexual representation is predicated. I call these approaches "critical" because of their interrogation and problematization of presuppositions regarding sexuality's representability on film. These thinkers do not assume that film form is a tabula rasa upon which any sexuality might be represented; instead, they attend to the epistemological and formal exigencies through which cinematic sexuality is constructed.

Pramaggiore reminds us that "even when texts are 'about' queers or queerness, textual elements can repress or express possibilities for bisexual desires, that is, nonsingular desires that may be detached from strict sex and/or gender oppositions."[116] Pramaggiore's invitation for us to consider the construction of such desires on film spells the critical impulse found throughout these scholars' work on bisexuality and film, wherein film's capacity for figuring desire in nonlinear, nonexclusive ways is anatomized. These scholars, whose work I engage with throughout the book, share some central foci: bisexuality's temporal dimensions and how these interact with narrative; bisexuality's relation to cinematic space and how mise-en-scène and editing affect relational structures between different characters; and the preponderance of cinematic bisexual figures in whom other issues or identities are metaphorized. Attention to these aspects of cinematic sexuality foregrounds the contingencies that determine bisexuality's very figurability.

To return to Hall's contention that bisexuality "cannot be definitively represented," we must remain cognizant of how bisexuality's representability is stymied by epistemological and significatory conventions befitting monosexual interpretations. San Filippo reminds us that, conceptually, bisexuality is produced through a "crisis of signification," that its very intelligibility is obscured "by modes of representation and reading confined within monosexual logic."[117] In order to address questions of bisexuality and cinema, therefore, we must attend first to the question of sexuality's very interpretation. One of the primary difficulties in approaching texts through a bisexual lens is the inevitable question as to what counts as bisexuality or who counts as bisexual. My approach to identifying moments of bisexual interest on film, however, is not definitive but capacious, stressing how particular hermeneutic approaches work to bring bisexual meaning into view. I am disabused of the notion that any text can be said to signify a certain sexuality in a totalizing, replicative fashion; semiotics' enduring reminder for scholars of representation stipulates the social contingency of signification and meaning.[118] That different readers and different approaches to reading effect the garnering of different meanings must be the starting point for questions of bisexual representation.

Let us consider Ang Lee's *Brokeback Mountain* (2005). For some viewers of the film, the tale of Jack (Jake Gyllenhaal) and Ennis (Heath Ledger) reflects the pains of the closet: Their heteronormative family lives constitute an inauthentic space where they must keep up the pretense of heterosexual masculinity, the mountains they wander as their love burgeons are spaces of authenticity, where a true gay self roams free. Such is the reading made by Gary Needham, for whom *Brokeback Mountain* narrates "the drama of homosexual desire and repression," yet, for a different viewer employing different interpretive frameworks, other meanings might be taken.[119] This latter viewer might look to the affection and desire shown between Jack and Lureen (Anne Hathaway), as well as Ennis and Alma (Michelle Williams), as authentic. This viewer might see the desires expressed by Jack and Ennis toward their wives, as well as toward each other, not necessarily as in opposition but as constitutive parts of these figures' desirous capacities. While one such desire is socially sanctioned and the other carries social sanctions, these social rules need not determine our reading the sincerity of the desires of those navigating them. Read differently, San Filippo determines that *Brokeback Mountain* "takes pains to establish that for neither man is sexuality predicated on gendered object-choice," effecting a "consistent refusal to toe the line of monosexuality."[120] I provide these interpretive examples not to suggest that San Filippo's is the correct reading and Needham's the incorrect reading but, instead, to show how the process of interpretation informs readings of textual sexuality. While the gay reading is no less justifiable than the bisexual reading, I want to stress how monosexual assumptions determine the dominant way in which sexuality is read textually. It is through the use of a critical bisexual frame of interpretation that different meanings come into view. To read with a critical bisexual eye is to contest the ascendency of a monosexist hermeneutic.[121]

In my identification of bisexual figures and bisexual meaning in film, I use a critical bisexual hermeneutic that is attentive to those moments when a monosexist expectation is dashed, those moments that defy monosexual interpretation, those moments in which bisexual possibilities make themselves known. In philosophical hermeneutics, these moments might be compared to Hans-Georg Gadamer's discussion of the phenomenon of *"Anstoß nehmen"*—of "being pulled up short," "being affronted," or "being irked"—"by the text."[122] This phenomenon takes place, Gadamer continues, when either the text "does not yield any meaning at all or its meaning is not compatible with what we had expected."[123] The appearance of bisexual possibility in film occurs through this phenomenon of *Anstoß nehmen*, in which the conventional process of monosexual interpretation is stopped.

In order for a critical bisexual hermeneutic to work, an interpreter must be open to the possibility of a multiplicity of interpretations, resonances, evocations, and meanings. It must reject the monosexist hermeneutic's logical roots in the rule of the "either/or." Poet and bisexual activist June Jordan contends

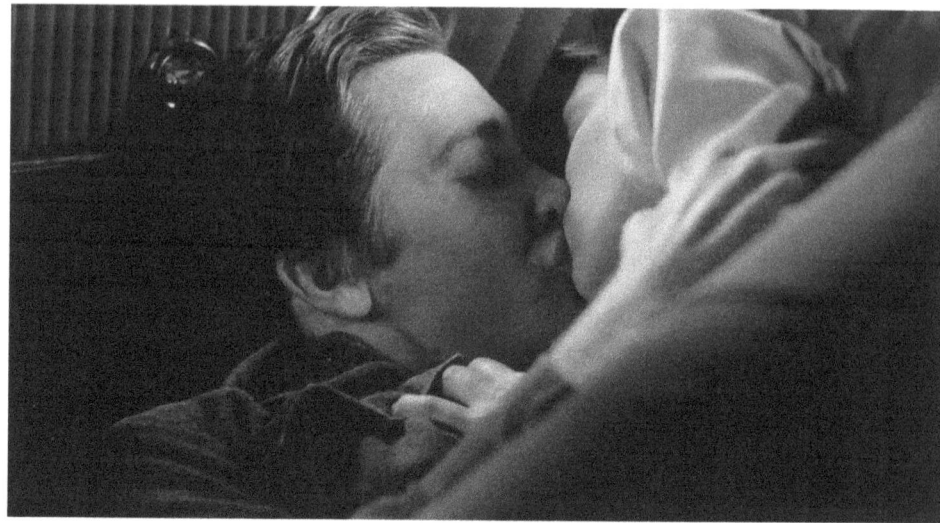

FIGURE I.4 A monosexist hermeneutic requires that we negate moments like this scene of desire between Jack (Jake Gyllenhaal) and Lureen (Anne Hathaway)—either by ignoring it or interpreting it as inauthentic—in the service of a gay reading. *Brokeback Mountain* (Ang Lee, 2005). Digital screen capture.

that bisexuality "invalidates either/or formulation, either/or analysis."[124] Jordan's words speak to the necessity of rejecting mutually oppositional binaries in the formulation of bisexual meaning. Such a hermeneutic position might be elucidated through what Roland Barthes calls "the role of an *and/or*," in relation to a text's having two possible means of interpretation (codes).[125] Barthes asks: "Is one more important than the other? . . . If we want to 'explicate' the sentence . . . must we *decide* on one code or the other?"[126] Barthes's answer is that to decide upon one or the other code is "impertinent," that to be attentive to the "and/or" at play here involves recognizing the text's "plurality," "non-decidability," its "polysemic chain."[127] A critical bisexual hermeneutic must work through what Barthes calls the "praxis" of "non-decidability."[128] Just as the bisexual refuses the choice between heterosexuality and homosexuality, so too must a critical bisexual hermeneutic refuse the tyranny of the "either/or." San Filippo underscores how "it is precisely bisexuality's ontological, epistemological and representational polysemy that generates its subversive potential to lay bare the mutability, contingency and inherent transgressiveness of desire."[129] Such is the value of a critical bisexual positioning that, in order to illuminate bisexually polysemous possibilities, must transgress the rules of monosexual monosemy.[130]

A final way in which my approach to bisexuality and cinema will be guided is by an insistence in looking to bisexual figures and figurations. The figure has constituted a critical term for poststructuralist philosophers, like Jean-François Lyotard, for its potential to disturb the strict division between the symbol and that to which it refers, to describe that which is irreducible to signification.[131] The use of the figure for film studies involves, for Belén Vidal, a means for us to attend to "the elements of visual form which resist the culturally regulated exercise of decoding into the 'flat' space of reading, in favor of the 'mobility' . . . of the visual."[132] The figure allows for a circumvention of erroneous assumptions of one-to-one alignments between the cinematic and the extratextual, allowing, instead, for an approach that embraces polysemy, nondecidability, and mutability. My attraction toward the figure in accounting for cinematic bisexuality is rooted in its inherent suspicion toward the cinematic image as a direct representation of a referent in the world.[133] The figure's personified articulation should not, however, be conflated with notions of subjectivity. Conceptions of the bisexual subject often presume a comprehensive form of bisexual subjectivity in the world, yet the figure carries no such assumptions. What we find more regularly in film, I suggest, is how the invocation of a bisexual possibility, in fact, troubles notions of sexual subjectivity as it troubles the assumption of sexuality's intelligibility.

Bisexuality's resistance to dominant notions of sexual subjectivity has been a central concern in much bisexual theory.[134] If we understand subjectivity in the Althusserian sense as the means through which ideology hails subjects, bisexuality's preclusion herein is rooted in dominant ideology's refusal to recognize bisexuality as a possibility.[135] The invocation of bisexual possibility thus disturbs these terms' binary logic and undermines notions of sexual subjectivity. To speak of cinema's bisexual figures is therefore different from assertions of cinematic bisexual subjects: these figures deride the farce of sexual subjectivity, allowing room to discuss that which wreaks trouble herein.

To this end, one of the most useful philosophical articulations of the figure for my project comes from Donna Haraway, who describes figures as "material-semiotic nodes . . . in which diverse bodies and meanings coshape one another."[136] For Haraway, such figures are imbued with intense affective resonances rooted in their connection to story: "Figures collect up hopes and fears and show possibilities and dangers. Both imaginary and material, figures root peoples in stories and link them to histories."[137] This book embraces the potentials of such an entity, the bisexual figure, in whom the troubled relations between sexuality's social, political, historical, epistemological, and aesthetic dimensions can be encompassed.[138] Although Haraway uses the terms *figure* and *figuration* synonymously, I use the former to stress a singular distillation of meanings around a particular filmic character and the latter to underscore the processual dynamics of meaning-making both within and beyond a particular cinematic figure.[139] Behind every figure—particular, compelling, singular—are processes of figuration.

Toward a Film Theory of Bisexual Transgression

The close, mutually constitutive relation between bisexuality and transgression on film is evident in the prevalence of filmic examples in which the limits of heterosexual-homosexual organization are contested in concert with other limits' contestation. In a similar vein to June Jordan and Maria San Filippo, bisexual theologian Ibrahim Abdurrahman Farajajé reminds us that "in cultures that prioritize either/or thinking . . . anything that occupies a liminal, an intersectional, an interstitial location is seen as a threat."[140] The relation Farajajé traces between interstitiality and threat brings to bear how the confounding of the either/or hermeneutic is structured as a transgression. Transgression involves a movement beyond an established limit, the violation of a standard, the contravention of a rule. In this sense, transgression is fundamentally defined by its relation to a structure of lawful containment, prohibition, or limited possibility. Transgression poses challenges to this structure's purported boundaries, but, simultaneously, transgression is limited by this relation insofar as it is dependent upon the rigidity of the structure to which it responds in order that it be enunciated. Jacques Lacan describes how "transgression in the direction of *jouissance* [the near-intolerable excess of enjoyment] only takes place if it is supported by the oppositional principle, by the forms of the Law."[141] Transgression is thus, crucially, dependent upon the Law, the rule, the limit, in its manifestation.

Against conceptions of transgression as involving the destruction of a rule or a limit, Michel Foucault adumbrates it as "a spiral which no simple infraction can exhaust."[142] With this helical metaphor, Foucault underscores the circular, relational dance between transgression and the rule. For Foucault, the operation of transgression is not the rule's obliteration but its illumination, described as "like a flash of lightning in the night which, from the beginning of time, gives a dense and black intensity to the night it denies, which lights up the night from the inside, from top to bottom, and yet owes to the dark the stark clarity of its manifestation, its harrowing and poised singularity."[143] Transgression's taking-place illuminates the constitution and operations of rules themselves: by contesting the rule, the rule and its workings come into view. In working toward a theory of bisexual transgression, we can thus understand this phenomenon as necessarily involving the exposure of monosexism's workings, the structuring principles of a monosexual norm. Foucault's ideas also help to clarify transgression's workings as interstitial, never simply oppositional, in ways that complement bisexuality's conceptual location beyond, between, or simultaneously within categories commonly understood to be incompatible. Bisexual transgression reveals an underacknowledged stratum of sexual organization while gesturing, simultaneously, to possibilities beyond its strictures.

Transgression's relation to the sexual or the erotic is, similarly, central to its use for considerations of bisexuality. Georges Bataille writes that "the history of eroticism is by no means that of sexual activity allowed within the limits defined by the rules: indeed eroticism only includes a domain marked off by *the violation of rules*."[144] Bataille's interrogations of eroticism's workings stress how erotic desire regularly involves the breaking of a rule, a norm, an expectation, that the thrill of the erotic cannot be separated from the thrill of sexuality's associations with the verboten or the taboo. In this sense, all forms of eroticism might be said to be inherently transgressive, yet what marks bisexuality's singularity here is the foundational erotic transgression by which it is constituted. Further, we can consider how the experience of erotic transgression has been conceptualized as a form of sexuality in which gendered object choice is deprioritized. Tim Dean, for example, states that "transgression involves an experience of sexuality in which the gender of the partner remains secondary, if not altogether irrelevant."[145] Where bisexuality is understood as the capacity for desire beyond a single-gendered object, this quality is discernible as a persistent feature of various forms of sexual transgression in which knowably gendered objects recede from the priorities of desire.

Discussions of bisexuality in relation to transgression have been met with some fervent critiques, again within British bisexual theoretical circles. For Hemmings, "presumptions of de facto bisexual transgression have [a] foreclosing . . . effect on the range of bisexual knowledges and ontological possibilities."[146] Later, she elaborates that "instead of celebrating dubious bisexual transgressions . . . I advocate an approach that insists that bisexuality's capacity to generate radical reconfigurations of [sexual] oppositions resides not outside but within social and cultural meaning."[147] Hemmings's critique of bisexual transgression is rooted in an understanding that attestations of bisexuality's transgression foreclose a multiplicity of possibilities regarding what bisexuality might be, that they present bisexuality in an uncritically celebratory fashion, and that they assume bisexuality to be outside spaces of society and culture. I contend, however, that Hemmings's remarks, at worst, misrepresent what transgression is or, at best, use transgression to name something altogether different from what I am naming.[148] With the conception of transgression I have outlined, the identification of bisexuality's alignment with and enactment of transgression does not necessarily spell its capacity to be celebrated, its political or social radicalism, or its operation outside of society and culture. Foucault reminds us that a discussion of transgression "must be detached from its questionable association to ethics if we want to understand it. . . . It must be liberated from the scandalous or subversive, that is, from anything aroused by negative association."[149] In speaking of bisexual transgression, we therefore need not treat it as something we can expect, in Jonathan Dollimore's words, "miraculously to change the social order."[150] Instead, as Dollimore continues, if transgression involves any subversion, it is that of "the dangerous knowledge it brings with it, or produces, or which is produced in and by its containment in the cultural sphere."[151] Foucault's warnings and Dollimore's corrective allow for an articulation of bisexual transgression that is not simply an empty call for scandalous negativity as politics but, instead, an analytic through which we can trace how transgressive renderings of bisexual possibility illuminate certain rules structuring our sexual episteme. This is a process that takes place not from the outside this episteme but from within.

Although instances of bisexual transgression on film might align themselves with scandal, subversion, or negativity, the allure of these associations is something to which we can attend critically. Our approach will be limited, however, if it concerns itself only with the ethics of figurations of bisexual transgression. To do so in the context of film analysis is to replicate a model of engagement I have critiqued in which film is assumed to tell us the truth about that which it represents, thus dovetailing into axiology. This book necessarily encompasses both instances of bisexual transgression that might be pleasurably scandalous alongside those that might be deemed ethically reprehensible. Bisexual transgression is just as discernible in figures of pleasurable seduction—such as the suave Konrad (Michael York) of *Something for Everyone* (Harold Prince, 1970) and the sultry Ariane (Bulle Ogier) of *Maîtresse* (Barbet Schroeder, 1976)—as in disturbed serial killer figures, like Otis (Tom Towles) of *Henry: Portrait of a Serial Killer* (John McNaughton, 1986) and Camille (Richard Courcet) of *I Can't Sleep* (Claire Denis, 1994). To discuss these examples as constitutive of a wider alignment between bisexuality and transgression on screen is not to posit their shared ethical dimensions, nor is it to posit that all representations of transgression operate in shared ways politically. Instead, these varying examples help us to trace the persistence of this alignment across remarkably disparate contexts where, in turn, they bring rules of sexual-social organization into clearer view.

That some of these examples might be pleasurable or productive of a subversive thrill and some might effect displeasure or forms of social consolidation suggests a diversity of representations to be analyzed, not eschewed. Further, to be attentive to transgression's workings is to acknowledge that textual representations of ethically dubious acts can often produce thrilling pleasures, from the stylish murders perpetrated by dapper film noir villains to the simulation of nonconsent in hardcore pornographic film. As Dean reminds us, a transgressive text's "risk does not need to be politically defensible in order to be experienced as exciting; indeed, the reverse may be true."[152] Images of bisexual transgression provide us not with a single relation between bisexuality and ethics but with a *singular* relation between bisexuality and transgression. My work involves neither celebrating nor disparaging these representations; it attests, instead, to the value in looking at their workings critically.

The Cinematic Figure of the Bisexual Transgressor

The bisexual transgressor is the figure around which this investigation pivots: the cinematic figurations to which they give form and, through which, they are given form. Outside of film studies, this figure has appeared throughout bisexual writing in various guises that provide productively interdisciplinary models through which to approach film. For psychologist Fritz Klein, "the bisexual resembles the spy in that he or she moves psychosexually freely among men and among women. The bisexual also resembles the traitor in that he or she is in a position to know the secrets of both camps, and to play one against the other. The bisexual, in short, is seen as a dangerous person, not to be trusted, because his or her party loyalty, so to speak, is nonexistent."[153] Klein's discussion of perceptions of bisexual people uses the figure of the spy or traitor in order to explore bisexuality's conception as being doubly aligned between spaces of heterosexuality and homosexuality. Similar associations can be traced in Hemmings's articulation of the "bisexual double agent," with her "often frightening and sinister knowledge of both the inside and the outside."[154] In the light of Klein's and Hemmings's figures, we might recall some of cinema's bisexual spies, from *The Last Emperor*'s (Bernardo Bertolucci, 1987) Eastern Jewel (Maggie Han) to *Atomic Blonde*'s (David Leitch, 2017) Lorraine (Charlize Theron). These cinematic characters' ability to inhere in disparate spaces are metaphorized in their ability to seduce across lines of gender. A similar figure proposed outside of film studies is legal scholar Naomi Mezey's "bisexual saboteur," whose "excess of the hetero/homo regime" renders the categories around them incoherent.[155] Here, we might think of a character like *The Doom*

Generation's (Gregg Araki, 1995) Xavier (Jonathon Schaech), whose intrusion into the lives of couple Amy (Rose McGowan) and Jordan (James Duval), and seduction of both, effects confusion regarding the characters' identities. Or perhaps we might look to *The Does* (Claude Chabrol, 1968), a film whose narrative is animated by an ambivalence regarding which of its two central female characters—Frédérique (Stéphane Audran) and Why (Jacqueline Sassard)—is manipulating the other. Both these figures' duplicities are figured through their bisexualities: Their relations to Paul (Jean-Louis Trintignant) and to one another are wracked by an uncertainty as to the sincerity of these attachments. *The Does*' very narrative intrigue is made meaningful through this difficulty in discerning the sincerity of Frédérique's and Why's bisexual relations. Again, a bisexual figure's transgressions effect epistemological confusion.

Yet, in transposing these evocative bisexual figures to film studies, we can delve deeper to consider how the anxieties, movements, and machinations of these figures come to be expressed in and through film form itself. The bisexual transgressor's battleground is sexual epistemology. In narrative cinema, this becomes the terrain of narrative comprehensibility, where sexual knowability circulates in a wider narrative economy determining that which is known, that which is unknown, and that which remains ambiguous. These epistemological issues are often rendered all the more precarious on film by the unreliability of the visual in ascertaining knowledge. Film's various forms of visuality carry with them anxieties around any form of mediation's capacity for dissimulation. From questions of the image's diegetic veracity to the more fundamental issues of what lies beyond the frame, or what lies out of focus, narrative film depends upon systems of knowing-through-seeing while, simultaneously, remaining haunted by the dissimulative potential of these very systems. The bisexual transgressor is also characterized by particular anxieties concerning questions of spatial alignment and temporal predictability, from questions of the camp to which they are aligned to curiosities around where they have been and where they might go. On film, these issues can be explored with attention to cinematic space's sexual significations, with figures' alignments to location and to mise-en-scène expressing and reflecting issues around sexual alignment. It is also a ripe medium for exploiting issues around sexual temporality. While classical approaches to cinematic temporality can, of course, naturalize linear modes of sexual becoming—from the heterosexual marriage plot to the linear coming-out journey—different approaches hold the potential for different renderings entirely, exploiting the endurance of the past and the unpredictability of the future in ways that challenge notions of sexual unidirectionality. A film theory of bisexual transgression requires attention to the inseparability of cinematic

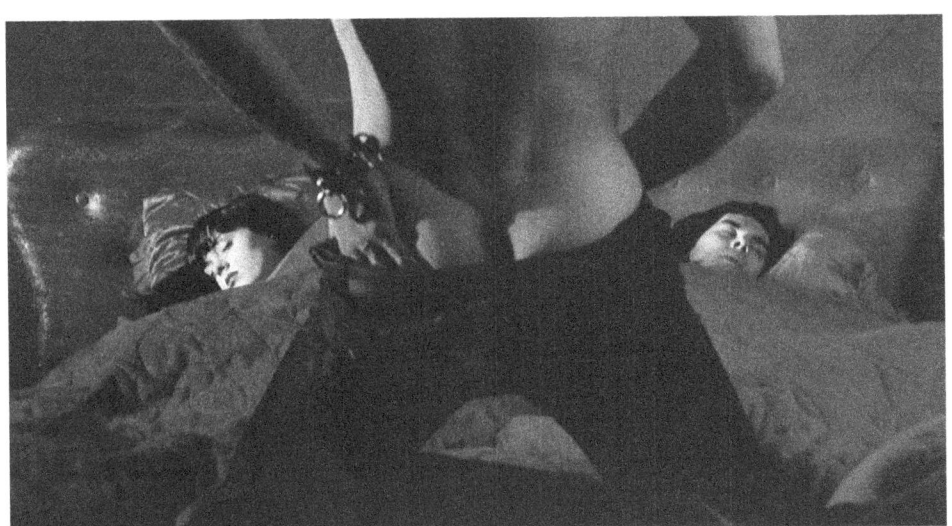

FIGURE 1.5 Xavier (Jonathan Schaech) masturbates as he watches Amy (Rose Mc-
Gowan) and Jordan (James Duval) sleep. *The Doom Generation* (Gregg Araki, 1995).
Digital screen capture.

sexuality from film form as the very matter through which monosexual conventions and their bisexual contraventions are rendered knowable.

A final observation when attending to these cinematic figures of bisexual
transgression involves these figures' illumination of the monosexual binary's incoherence in concert with a revelation of others binaries' incoherence. Maria
San Filippo terms this phenomenon "bi-textuality," a cinematic mode that
works to "formulate and convey ... a metaphor between bisexuality and an
analogous identity construct that also resists containment within a binary
taxonomy.... Bi-textuality ultimately works, therefore, to expose the fallacy
of ordering sexuality (or any identity construct) to simplistically and constric-
tively as binary systems do."[156] San Filippo outlines an array of filmic figures
who operate through this bi-textual mode: the "bisexual-bohemian," whose
wanderlust and hedonism precipitates her navigation of spaces of normativity
and otherness; the "dreamgirls" and "dreamboys" who defamiliarize "the social-
sexual subject's constructed self"; and the bisexual significations of the "rich
bitch" and her "dependent double," in whom bisexuality is fashioned as "the
primary weapon of the characters' dual (and dueling) economic and sexual
showdown."[157] These figures, which I engage in later analyses, demonstrate
how cinema's bisexual transgressors are regularly made meaningful through
parallel transgressions, recalling Jo Eadie's insistence that the bisexual cinematic

figure serves as "an indicator that a cultural tension is being broached, whose contours the bisexual enables the audience to negotiate, and whose dangers the bisexual always embodies."[158] A critical bisexual theoretical approach need not lament this work of metaphor in the hopes of a purist illusion of unspoiled sexual-cinematic representation. Instead, attention to these bi-textual alignments allows for a broader account of cinematic sexuality's imbrication in, and reliance upon, a variety of discourses and systems of signification in which networks of transgression are mapped.

Cinemas of Bisexual Transgression proceeds via four chapters that look at respective cinematic contexts in which figures of bisexual transgression have circulated, with each chapter foregrounding one film for close analysis. Chapter 1 considers female vampires of 1970s European and North American exploitation cinema, figures who have commonly been referred to as "lesbian vampires" but who, I will argue, are better accounted for by my term *les(bi)an vampires*. While much ink has been spilled on these films and the seductive vampires they center, I propose an original way of approaching them that is attentive to bisexual meaning. With a key focus on José Ramón Larraz's *Vampyres* (1974), I perform close readings of the les(bi)an vampire's inventive sex acts, which often exploit the ungendered-wound-as-object-choice; her relation to glamorous femininity, whose intersections with discourses around female bisexuality have not been prioritized; and her racial-national ambiguity, which serves as a persistent bi-textual point of parallelism that brings to the fore relations between bisexuality, national identity, and race. Chapter 2 moves to a radically different cinematic locus—lesbian narrative cinema—where anxieties around female bisexuality have circulated in some ways that are unique but in other ways that are consistent with broader tendencies around bisexual transgression on film. I begin by establishing cultural and political lesbian histories between the 1970s and 1990s, tracing where female bisexuality has been articulated through a particular credo that I term *bi-exclusionary lesbian ethics*. Centering Sheila McLaughlin's *She Must Be Seeing Things* (1987), I analyze how the mise-en-scène deploys cinematic indices of a woman's desire toward men in ways that precipitate her lesbian partner's paranoia. The film's expressive rendering of this paranoia involves stirring manipulations of visual coherence and notions of diegetic reality, which work, within a specifically lesbian-feminist context, to raise questions around the relation between perspective and sexual intelligibility. Here, I trace a hitherto untheorized tendency in lesbian narrative cinema's deployment of the figure of the bisexual transgressor to effect an intracommunal critique of bi-exclusionary lesbian ethics.

Whereas the first two chapters consider female articulations of bisexual transgression, chapter 3 considers the figurations of transgressive male bisexuality to be found in European art cinema, with a particular focus on films emerging in the wake of HIV/AIDS. I first consider the amenability of art cinema to renderings of bisexual possibility, with its germane investments in polysemy, ambiguity, and nonlinearity. These qualities also emerged in wider discourses around male bisexuality in the first decades of HIV/AIDS, with persistent references to the bisexual man's dangerous unknowability. With an extensive reading of Cyril Collard's *Savage Nights* (1992), I consider these alliances between art film aesthetics and bisexuality and the significance of the film's presentation of male bisexual seropositivity. Central to this analysis are notions of bisexual tourism, which animate the movements of the film's protagonist; expressions of bisexual relationalities through film form, which art cinema has deployed inventively against formal conventions that naturalize monosexual monogamy; and a bisexual ethics of ambiguity that characterizes *Savage Nights'* embrace of bisexual transgression as a form of relation amid social fragmentation.

In chapter 4, we arrive at what is perhaps the most renowned example of bisexual transgression in cinema: Paul Verhoeven's *Basic Instinct* (1992). I situate this hotly debated film in the context of the erotic thriller genre, in which I locate a transgressive bisexual erotics. I proceed with an assessment of Sharon Stone's star image, particularly insofar as it has been informed by the emergence of the postfeminist sensibility and notions of bisexual marketability. Rather than simply reading these phenomena as symptoms of bisexual female depoliticization, however, I consider their historical emergence in relation to political economy, with a focus on nineties financialization and its risky investment in normative forms of homosexuality. Through this history, I examine the erotic thriller's depictions of bisexual elites and embezzlers as symptomatic of anxieties around investment in pink economies. These anxieties among others, I argue, are crystallized in the figure of the bisexual murderer, whom I analyze in relation to the erotic thriller's narratives of ratiocination and how murderousness and queerness dovetail in these dramas of (in)visible evidence. Here I also trace pertinent parallels with transfeminine figures stalking the erotic thriller to anatomize the sexual, corporeal, and visual forms of unintelligibility that render these figures both dangerous and alluring while also pointing to fruitful nexuses between bisexual and transgender media theories. The afterword begins with a figure who perhaps serves as a limit case in cinemas of bisexual transgression: the rapist in the shadows of Gaspar Noé's *Irreversible*

(2002). With this figure, I return us to the foundations of my nonaxiological approach to transgressive bisexuality on film to consider what we are afforded when we depart from this interpretive mode. I also offer some reflections on future directions of research into cinemas of bisexual transgression, ending with a meditation on the capacity of these cinemas, and a bisexual theoretical approach to them, to radically recalibrate queer film studies.

Cinemas of Bisexual Transgression looks to figures of transgressive bisexual possibility as critical sites of interplay between sexuality, cinematic signification, and rules of social organization. Such a focus works to foreground both sexual-cinematic phenomena and approaches to sexual epistemology, which embrace partiality and proteanism—qualities with which bisexuality has been aligned historically. Correspondingly, this focus works to destabilize assumptions of wholeness and situatedness in relation to both sexual-cinematic signification and sexual epistemology in ways that expand a queer theoretical sensibility and reaffirm its foundational embrace of that which exceeds sexuality's dominant ideological categorizations. The critical approach I deploy toward images of bisexual transgression on film is attentive to bisexuality's functions on film, not as a means through which ideas of bisexual subjectivity might be consolidated but, instead, as sexual and significatory transgressions constituted by and begetting further transgressions. To read the bisexual transgressor closely in the contexts of aesthetics, epistemology, and historiography is to expand the plane of queer inquiries into film. This focus necessarily looks beyond cinema's ritualistic reassertions of heteronormativity, as it looks beyond oppositional, implicitly homosexual, cinematic figures of queer alterity. It looks, instead, toward the richly interstitial ground of bisexual transgression, where bisexuality operates along the lines first observed by Däumer as "a sign of transgression, ambiguity and mutability."[159] Attention to cinematic figurations of bisexual transgression exposes the precarities and anxieties of sexuality's binary organization as it illuminates cinema's potential to embrace sexuality's mutability, fragmentedness, and draw toward the forbidden.

CHAPTER 1

THE LES(BI)AN VAMPIRE'S CARNAL STAKES

Vampyres (1974)

In Harry Kümel's sumptuous vampire film *Daughters of Darkness* (1971), Countess Elizabeth (Delphine Seyrig) sits in the lobby of an art deco hotel in Ostend, Belgium, talking with a newlywed couple about the murder of a young woman. When a middle-aged man (Georges Jamin) enters, he begins to discuss the crime with the group. "Monsieur is a policeman," Elizabeth remarks, explaining that the man's interest in the matter is professional. But with this offhand comment, Elizabeth reveals too much; the man is, in fact, a *retired* policeman. Elizabeth's knowledge inadvertently discloses her preternaturally impossible age, incommensurate with her appearance. As Elizabeth takes out her compact to attend to her makeup, the retired policeman peers over her shoulder where he views her lack of reflection. The compact does not reflect her face, only her red nails fluttering in the air. Realizing she is being watched, Elizabeth snaps the compact shut, momentarily shaken at the second unintentional revelation: her nonreflection. Although the myth of the vampire's nonreflection is common across vampire films, we can consider this moment beyond its generic moorings. Maria San Filippo interprets cinema's bisexual vampires' nonreflection

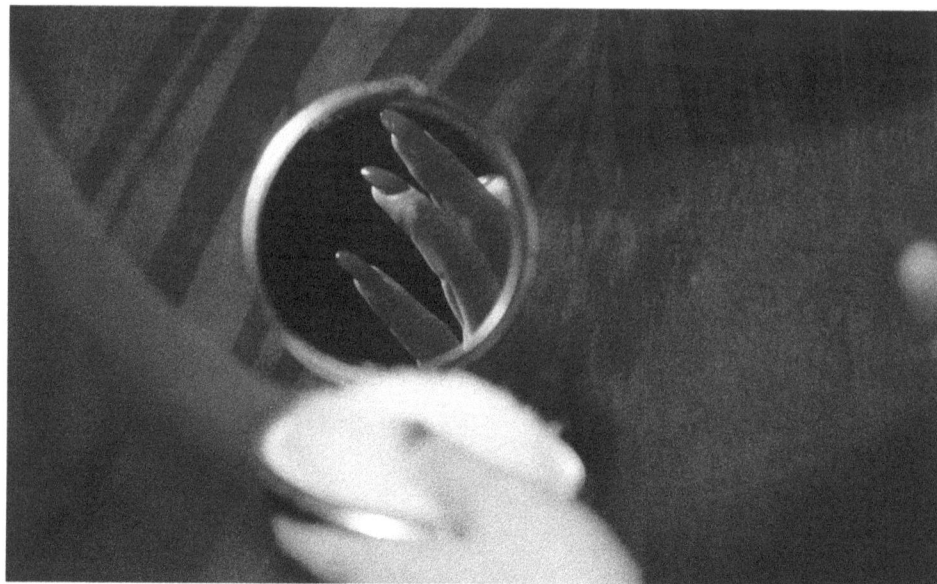

FIGURE 1.1 Countess Elizabeth's (Delphine Seyrig) partial nonreflection. *Daughters of Darkness* [*Les Lèvres rouges* / *Le Rouge aux lèvres*] (Harry Kümel, 1971). Digital screen capture.

through Jacques Lacan's theory of the mirror stage, suggesting "that she circumvents inscription within the Symbolic Order . . . as unnamable and (in)-visible as the bisexual."[1] If, for Lacan, the mirror stage establishes the subject's "I" function, bisexuality's preclusion from dominant forms of sexual subjectivity is figured here as reflective absence, a visualization of Clare Hemmings's provocation: "To say 'I am bisexual' is to say 'I am not "I."'"[2] Instead of a face, the mirror reflects signs of feminine adornment—Elizabeth's claret acrylics metonymizing her being simulation-of-woman. Yet, further, it is Elizabeth's efforts to conceal her vampirism—her timelessness and her nonmortality—as she is seducing an extragender couple that establish deceit as integral to her transgressive bisexual figuration. Without it, her subterfuge cannot manifest.

In the cinematic vampire, bisexual potentialities abound. For Jeffrey Weinstock, "the vampire is the cinema's most potent instantiation of sexual excess. . . . The vampiric body . . . courses with polymorphously perverse sexual energy."[3] With a pertinent reference to Freud's infant, the vampire is characterized by a drive toward a variety of objects regardless of gender. Curiously, discursive connections between bisexuality and vampirism are even present in Richard von Krafft-Ebing's sexological research, in which he reports on the necrophiliac "Sergeant Bertrand" that "the sex of the bodies is said to have been a matter of indifference to . . . this modern vampire."[4] In the cultural imagination, the vampire's targets are desired objects whose seduction via the sexually suggestive act of bloodsucking changes them irrevocably, both in the lapsarian fall from innocence to experience and through an ontological transformation, either from living to dead or from mortal to vampire.

Though this chapter centers queer female vampires, queerness has also been a quality, if a more implicit one, in literary and cinematic male vampires. Among the earliest cultural articulations of male vampires in the West are George Gordon Byron's unfinished novella "A Fragment" (1819) and the novel it inspired: John Polidori's *The Vampyre* (1819). Both texts detail close bonds between a mortal man and a suspected male vampire, replete with homoeroticism.[5] That Polidori's vampire, Lord Ruthven, bears stark similarities to Byron himself further buttresses a bisexual reading of this seminal vampire tale: The famously promiscuous Byron enjoyed relationships with both women and men.[6] Around a century later, F. W. Murnau's *Nosferatu: A Symphony of Horror* (1922) would invoke these implicit associations. After Thomas (Gustav von Wangenheim) nicks his thumb with a breadknife, Count Orlok (Max Schreck) proceeds to suck the bloody digit. This suggestive point of contact in Count Orlok's obsessive pursuit of Thomas is followed, notably, by that of his wife, Ellen (Greta Schröder), a bisexual array of targets. Homoerotic forms of tactility and bloodsucking between men also feature in two of late twentieth-century Hollywood's most successful vampire films: *Bram Stoker's Dracula* (Francis Ford Coppola, 1992) and *Interview with the Vampire* (Neil Jordan, 1994). Generally, the queerness of male vampires has taken these more muted forms; however, there are some notable exceptions.[7] All-male hardcore films sometimes look to vampire narratives in ways that are, obviously, explicitly queer; these include Tom DeSimone's *Sons of Satan* (1973) and Roger Earl's *Gayracula* (1983). A compelling iteration of queer male vampirism can also be found in Lucio Fulci's Italian sex-comedy-cum-vampire-film *Dracula in Brianza* (1975). After factory owner Costante (Lando Buzzanca) enjoys a night of debauchery with Count Dragulescu (John Steiner) and his entourage of bawdy women, he wakes up the next day naked in bed with the Count. Following this episode, Costante finds himself not only craving blood but also with a newfound desire toward men. Whereas *Dracula in Brianza* attests quite explicitly to associations between vampirism and bisexuality through a male figure, this connection has been exploited with greater clarity and regularity in female figures.

This chapter focuses on the female vampires of 1970s European and American cinemas, whose menace is rooted in the indiscrimination of their seductive ploys. Yet the common terminology used to describe these cinematic vampires—in both popular and scholarly discourses—elides this foundational quality in the appellation of *lesbian vampire*. As Ellis Hanson argues, "Many of these vampires are not really lesbians at all; in a truly omnivorous fashion, they happily forgo the taste of a woman when an adventurous red-blooded man stumbles onto the scene. . . . Bisexual would be a more useful term, I suppose, since it still enjoys, however improbably, a reputation for sexual indeterminacy."[8] Rather than incidental, this vampire's "sexual indeterminacy"—her bisexual capacity—is prerequisite to the execution of her schemes. This is a clarification that warrants deeper consideration as to the centrality of bisexual specificity for articulations of sexuality within vampire cinemas.

These vampires' sexual capacities carry epistemological implications that, as Andrea Weiss argues, effect a critique of heterosexuality in their signification of "the instability of the heterosexual social order."[9] Yet, for Weiss, these figures still constitute failures of lesbian representation. As figures that enact a critique of heterosexual hegemony while remaining not quite lesbian, a bisexual recalibration of terms allows us to consider them as destabilizers not only of heterosexuality but also of monosexuality more broadly.[10] To foreground this aspect of these vampires, an amendment to their designation is warranted. I propose the term *les(bi)an vampire*—its syncopated *bi* at once accenting and veiling the bisexuality of this figure who is both a glamorous spectacle and a doyenne of disguise.

This chapter foregrounds *Vampyres* (José Ramón Larraz, 1974), a British-made exploitation horror film, which I analyze alongside other films of 1970s les(bi)an vampire cinema. *Vampyres* follows a young couple—Harriet (Sally Faulkner) and John (Brian Deacon)—whose countryside caravanning holiday is disturbed by the presence of two mysterious women, Fran (Marianne Morris) and Miriam (Anulka Dziubinska). These women, who inhabit a country house adjacent to the couple's caravan, are vampires who use the ruse of hitchhiking to lure men back to a grand estate before having sex with them—and sometimes each other—and drinking the men's blood. *Vampyres* welcomes bisexual analysis in three distinct ways: its explicit and inventive depictions of sex acts, which work to degender sites of carnal exchange; its images of dissimulative femininity, which draw upon notions of bisexual female unknowability; and the racial-national ambiguity of the film's vampires—metaphorized in their awry navigations of cinematic space—which can be explored with reference to ideas of bisexual "primitivity" and nonlinearity. I begin with a consideration of how contemporary discourses around sexuality affect the les(bi)an vampire film and how the formal configuration of sex acts works to convey extensible bisexual possibilities. I then spotlight the les(bi)an vampire's femininity—a preoccupation of queer and feminist engagements with this corpus—in relation to theoretical work on cinematic femininity, particularizing and transforming these discussions through critical approaches to bisexual femininity. Central to both phenomena is dissimulation and the anxiety-ridden uncertainty occasioned when things do not appear as they seem. This fear of dissimulation also relates to the les(bi)an vampire's racial-national ambiguity. A return to the late nineteenth-century discursive contexts, in which tales of foreign vampires and supposedly uncivilized cultures both circulated, reveals the assignation of a so-called underdeveloped bisexuality to purportedly primitive peoples. The regular uncertainty around the les(bi)an vampire's roots introduces xenophobic fears around an unrecognizable Other—fears that are figured in her preternatural confoundment of spatial borders. I thus trace the interplay between the les(bi)an vampire's transgression of cinematic space and her interstitial figuration as between spaces. Cinema's les(bi)an vampires—gorgeous and lethal, inviting and immuring, titillating and repulsive—constitute paradigmatic figurations among cinema's iterations of bisexual transgression.

Exploiting Hybridity: Les(bi)an Vampire Genealogies

Throughout the 1970s, les(bi)an vampires proliferated in a sanguineous swarm across horror, exploitation, hardcore, and art cinemas. This figure has disparate filmic antecedents: the manipulative Countess Zaleska (Gloria Holden) of *Dracula's Daughter* (Lambert Hillyer, 1936), who spellbinds male and female victims alike; the deceptive Giselle (Gianna Maria Canale) of *The Devil's Commandment* (Riccardo Freda and Mario Bava, 1957), whose thirst for young women is matched by her ability to seduce male investigators; the envious Carmilla (Annette Strøyberg) of *Blood and Roses* (Roger Vadim, 1960), whose desires toward her female friend and male cousin lead her on a killing spree. Between the 1930s and the early 1960s, these films communicated the female vampire's indiscriminate threats through her indiscriminate bisexuality. After the 1970s les(bi)an vampire boom, this figure has continued to surface, albeit fitfully, with *The Hunger* (Tony Scott, 1983), *Nadja* (Michael Almereyda, 1994), *Lesbian Vampire Killers* (Phil Claydon, 2009), and *Bliss* (Joe Begos, 2019) attesting to her enduring transnational allure.[11] A milestone in the history of cinematic vampires was the arrival of HIV/AIDS, a context in which the vampire's queer sex, blood exchange, and murderousness could not but evoke parallels with the unfolding epidemic. Yet the pre-1980s influx of queer cinematic vampires reminds us that the alignment between vampires and queerness precedes HIV/AIDS and, while queer men would become scapegoats around fears of HIV transmission, bisexual vampires before HIV/AIDS are predominantly female. Such examples can be found across the oeuvres of some of 1970s popular film's most prominent directors, including Luigi Batzella (*The Devil's Wedding Night*, 1973), Jesús Franco (*Vampyros Lesbos*, 1971; *Daughter of Dracula*, 1972; *Female Vampire*, 1973), Jorge Grau (*The Legend of Blood Castle*, 1973), León Klimovsky (*The Werewolf Versus the Vampire Woman*, 1971), Jean Rollin (*The Rape of the Vampire*, 1968; *The Nude Vampire*, 1970; *The Shiver of the Vampires*, 1971; *Requiem for a Vampire*, 1971; *Lips of Blood*, 1975; *Fascination*, 1979), Stephanie Rothman (*The Velvet Vampire*, 1971), and Joseph W. Sarno (*The Devil's Plaything*, 1973). Attention to these films reveals close links between queerness, vampirism, and femininity exploited across a number of national contexts between the late 1960s and mid-1970s.

The female vampire has been linked to a variety of cultural myths, with influences ranging from the Jewish Talmud, to Greek mythology, to Malay folklore, and eighteenth- and nineteenth-century Romantic and gothic literature.[12] The figure circulating across these disparate discourses involves a dangerous woman whose femininity masks a darker core: often, a rampant libido, a desire to kill men, and a thirst for power. The most prominent influences on the Western female vampire film can be found in the history of and mythologies around Countess Erzsébet Báthory and in *Carmilla*, the 1872 novella by Irish writer Joseph Sheridan Le Fanu. Countess Báthory was a Hungarian noblewoman accused of murdering up to three hundred young women between 1590 and 1610.[13] Almost a century after her death, Jesuit priest László Turóczi introduced the myth that Báthory had bathed in her victims' blood to retain her beauty, an addendum that inspired vivid cinematic interpretations in *Countess Dracula* (Peter Sasdy, 1971), *Immoral Tales* (Walerian Borowczyk, 1973), and *The Legend of Blood Castle*.[14] The novella *Carmilla* presents a first-person account from the perspective of Laura, an aristocratic Austrian girl who is seduced by the family's foreign visitor, Carmilla. After Carmilla's arrival, Laura develops a close friendship with her guest and experiences "vague and strange sensations . . . [a] peculiar cold thrill" in her sleep.[15] One night Laura is bitten on the breast by a "beast," a metamorphosed Carmilla who is revealed to be the 150-year-old vampire Mircalla Karnstein. The tale of *Carmilla* inspired erotically charged adaptations that invoke the dangers and erotics of close friendship between young women, including *The Vampire Lovers* (Roy Ward Baker, 1970), *Daughter of Dracula*, and *The Blood Spattered Bride* (Vicente Aranda, 1972). Both the Báthory legend and *Carmilla* provide narrative foundations for films in which sexual contact between women is yoked to terror but also, importantly, in which such relations are interwoven with sexual contact between women and men.

The portrayal of dangerous desire observable in les(bi)an vampire films, alongside their depictions of bloody violence, speaks to the characteristics of their production mode: exploitation. The exploitation marker describes a twofold set of attributes: an industrial practice characterized by modest budgets, small crews, and limited distribution and a narrative investment in lascivious, morbid, or excessive subject matter. Naturally, exploitation film has itself been considered transgressive, a cinema predicated on the testing of boundaries of acceptability. However, the concept of exploitation cinema is broadly a demarcation determined by Anglophone reception practice. The continental European vampire films I discuss were produced and distributed within Europe as popular film, which drew upon elements of horror, fantasy, and sex film. The place of genre within this context can, therefore, be understood as more citational than purist, with the les(bi)an vampire film often invoking elements of both horror and softcore. While American exploitation cinema has been traced back to the early decades of the twentieth century, the late 1960s and 1970s saw the loosening of censorship codes in the United States and certain western European nations, allowing filmmakers greater explicitness in their renderings of illicit tales.[16] The preponderance of depictions of female queerness in the exploitation context can be linked to this liberalization, and the popularity of the female vampire genre here can be understood apropos the fertile ground it provided for exploring themes of sex and violence.[17] Les(bi)an vampire films can be grouped, therefore, under exploitation as a capacious category of organization in which the erotic and the macabre constitute transgressive attractions.

Vampyres is as a paradigmatic les(bi)an vampire text wherein tendencies in these films' treatment of gender, sexuality, sex, and violence converge in inventive ways that speak both to sexuality's excessive capacities and also to the interplays between violence and desire. These themes constitute familiar ground for José Ramón Larraz, whose early 1970s films display a recurrent interest in narratives of murder, rural settings, and explicit representations of sex—both between women and men and among women.[18] Larraz's propensity toward illicit subject matter did not confine his works to an exploitation context; his films circulated within both exploitation networks and those of European art cinema.[19] With his sixth feature, *Vampyres*, Larraz's auteurist interests were transposed to the vampire genre, inspired by the short stories of Belgian *fantastique* writer Thomas Owen.[20] The vampire myth's popularity in exploitation cinema—and in pulp literature—licensed Larraz to explore violence and sex more explicitly. Indeed, it was the explicitness of *Vampyres'* sex and violence, its marriage of graphic bisexual display with bloody acts of brutality, that precluded it from more respectable channels of distribution.

Vampyres was shot in March 1974 and premiered at the Cannes Film Festival in May of that year. While American distributor Cambist was convinced of the film's suitability to the American exploitation market, its British distributor, Fox-Rank, found its release more problematic.[21] In the United States, *Vampyres* was released uncut with an X rating.[22] As a distributor who specialized in sexploitation, the X rating was not a problem for Cambist but a point of spectatorial appeal, their promotional material promising "adult terror from Cambist."[23] In the United Kingdom, however, it would be a year after Fox-Rank's purchase of the film before it was released theatrically. A key hurdle delaying the film's release involved discussions between the film's production team and the British Board of Film Censors (BBFC).[24] Despite the connections with the BBFC professed by *Vampyres'* producer Brian Smedley-Aston, the film was required— after some negotiations—to cut almost three minutes, including moments of simulated bloodsucking and cunnilingus between women.[25] In a letter from a BBFC representative to someone from *Vampyres'* production team, the former expresses concern at the film's fusion of violence and sex: "We are more than a little worried about the close juxtaposition of sex to violence here. . . . I do agree that you have to have a little horror left in a horror film, and, of course, you also have sex in this picture: the two make rather unhappy bed-fellows."[26] Once these cuts had been negotiated (into a version Larraz sardonically called "the Vatican version"), *Vampyres* was released in the United Kingdom in 1975 under an X certificate, meaning it could be viewed only by people over eighteen.[27] The BBFC representative's assertion of the film's sex and violence being "unhappy bed-fellows" provides us with a clue as to the film's transgressive erotics and that of les(bi)an vampire cinema more broadly. The les(bi)an vampire film's juxtaposition of sex and violence appear dangerous or troubling in their compresence, while also demonstrating a bisexual kind of unpredictability regarding those with whom a bed is shared.

Vampyres displays multiple sites of hybridity—industrial, stylistic, generic, and representational. A film made by a Catalan director in the United Kingdom, fusing European horror aesthetics with a rural English setting, and augmenting the vampire myth's eroticism through softcore conventions, *Vampyres* is an inherently hybrid text. Hybridity's relation to bisexuality is explored by Jo Eadie, who writes of bisexuality's reminder that "deviance persists in the culture which is trying to expel it."[28] The les(bi)an vampire—neither mortal nor dead, neither heterosexual nor homosexual, of unclear cultural origins—reminds us of those hybridities that contest taxonomization. A preeminent site in which *Vampyres* makes such deviance known is the sex act, wherein boundaries of sexual explicitness, the singular directionality of sexual object choice, and the very limits of what constitutes the sex act are defied. Whether the les(bi)an vampire's bedfellows are happy or unhappy is debatable, yet what remains clear is that their presence, or perhaps more accurately their collocation, effects a bisexual kind of hybridization.

Fluid Exchanges: Sexuality, (Un)Death, and Vampire Coitus

Seduction and bloodsucking are central elements of the vampire myth and, while notions of sexual contact have always been implicit, the vampire figure's emergence within exploitation film allowed these connotations to be realized more literally than in its cultural predecessors. Sex between women was particularly visible within this context, a tendency that inspires Andrea Weiss to write that "outside of male pornography, the lesbian vampire is the most persistent lesbian image in the history of cinema."[29] Indeed, by the 1970s, adult film marketed toward heterosexual men had established sex between women as erotic spectacle, granting these queer sex acts a singular visibility. These representations of sex between women in straight pornographic film have tended to be presented alongside sex between women and men, a formal sequence that can be observed in early stag films like *At the Golden Crown, or The Good Inn* (anonymous, 1908). In the exploitation context, however, the latter could, generally, not be explored as graphically as the former. As Elena Gorfinkel elucidates, in the context of American sexploitation film, "bisexuality and lesbianism became an expedient way to present sexual content without the incriminations associated with full frontal male nudity, which remained . . . a forbidden zone of exposure."[30] The formal treatment of female bisexuality in the exploitation film thus diverges from hardcore film in a significant way: sex between women is afforded a greater visual prominence and explicitness than extragender sex. Although it is this comparative visibility that grounds Weiss's assertion of the female vampire's persistence as lesbian image, we should not lose sight of these moments' presentation alongside sex between men and women. Rather than discounting those less explicit visualizations of desire as inconsequential, as the "lesbian vampire" marker tends to, closer analysis reveals bisexual complexities at play in the les(bi)an vampire film's affinity for sexual variegation.

One kind of evidence that is insightful when considering these films' sexual politics is located extratextually: the les(bi)an vampire film's marketing materials. *Vampyres* was marketed by its distributors using sexually suggestive posters presenting tableaux of women in states of undress and sexual embrace with one another. As paratexts to the film, these posters—an important component in the exploitation film ecosystem—reveal the spectatorial attractions distributors sought to elicit. While we can, of course, observe the suggestion of sex between women via female bodies en déshabillé and in sexual proximity, it is notable that these are presented alongside renderings of male undress and suffering. The Cambist poster shows a man with his throat slit, covered in blood and screaming out; the Fox-Rank poster is bordered by a prone male body, his eyes closed, rendered in a deathly blue. These promotional materials' attraction thus involves the symbolic yoking of female pleasure to male displeasure, female ecstasy amid male suffering.

One common critique of the les(bi)an vampire film, postulated by Andrea Weiss and James Craig Holte, is that the representation of queer female sexual pleasure is contingent upon these characters' eventual so-called punishment through death.[31] But we should question the politics of representation such a critique espouses: the notion that the suffering or death of queer female characters—what has been termed, in recent years, the "dead lesbian syndrome"—is a political problem.[32] While I do not subscribe to this position, a survey of les(bi)an vampire films shows that the accusation against the les(bi)an vampire film—that it punishes or kills its les(bi)an vampires—is often unsubstantiated. In *Female Vampire*, for example, vampire hunter Dr. Roberts (Jesús Franco) is on a mission to kill Countess Irina (Lina Romay), but when he sees her luxuriating in a bath full of blood, he is too astonished to go through with it. In other examples, the les(bi)an vampire's death signifies not the end of her life but its transmigratory continuation. In *Daughters of Darkness*, Countess Elizabeth seems to die in a car crash—flung out of her vehicle and impaled on a tree. However, Elizabeth's vampire soul inherits the body of her apprentice Valerie (Danielle Ouimet), who now speaks with the Countess's voice. I use these examples to make a clarification: not that these films constitute positive representations because many les(bi)an vampires do not die, but that persistent invocations of *un*death establish the les(bi)an vampire's supplantation of mortal temporality. The les(bi)an vampire's superhuman perdurability, considered in tandem with her queerness, might therefore suggest the undying drive of female queer sexuality—the threat that anytime and anywhere, a woman's intragender desire might surface. Maria Pramaggiore makes a similar connection in her analysis of *The Hunger* when she observes that "the temporal pattern of vampire existence, stretching through the centuries, disrupts linear time measured in human terms. . . . Same and opposite sex desires

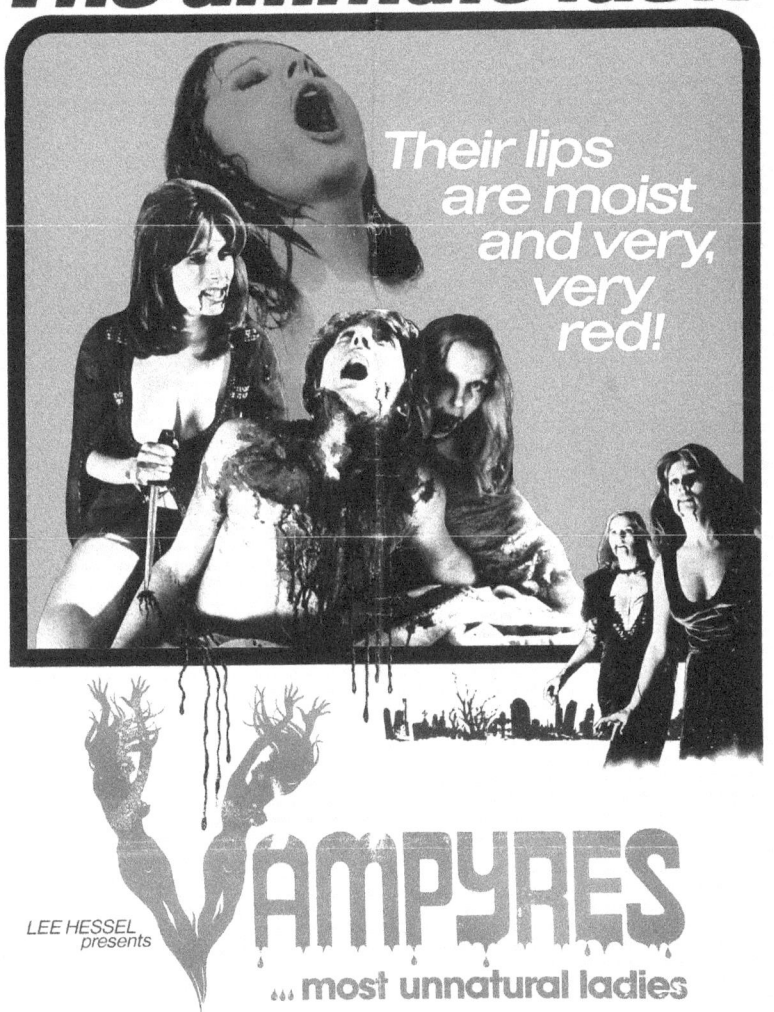

FIGURE 1.2 *Vampyres'* (José Ramón Larraz, 1974) one-sheet promotional poster, distributed by Cambist.

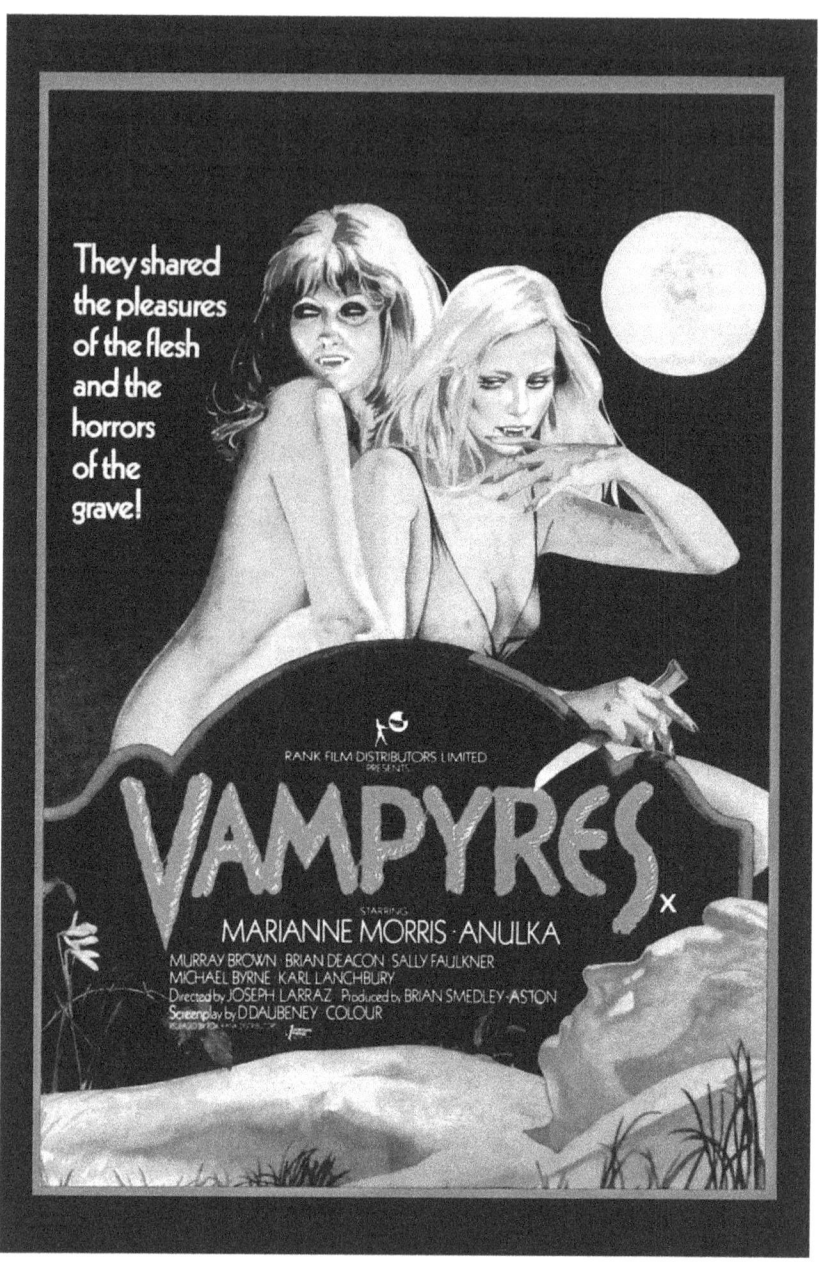

FIGURE 1.3 *Vampyres'* quad promotional poster, cropped from a double-bill with *The Devil's Rain* (Robert Fuest, 1975), distributed by Fox-Rank.

need not supplant one another but may oscillate over time or coexist simultaneously."[33] The desirous potential bisexuality elicits resists a temporal understanding of sexuality as linear. In the les(bi)an vampire film's temporal unpredictability, narrative milestones of wooing, coupling, the sex act, and even death cannot be trusted to indicate what they usually purport. *Vampyres* opens with a scene in which Fran and Miriam are lying on a bed naked, kissing and caressing one another; the door to the bedroom opens as Miriam begins to kiss Fran's nipple. When the women notice an intruder, they jump up startled, but it is too late. He shoots them and they lie dead, motionless, blood spattered across their bodies. In this opening, sex between women is met with murderous male retribution. However, these deaths signify not the end of Fran's and Miriam's lives but, as we will come to see, the beginning of their vampire reign.

Theirs is a reign teeming with an array of intense sexual encounters, which display a variety of carnal configurations. Fran's first seduction is Ted (Murray Brown), whom she invites into a country house after having hitchhiked with him. Their sex involves two consecutive positions: reverse cowgirl and missionary. While these terms are more commonly found in the pages of *Cosmopolitan* than in film analysis, I use them to underscore specific configurations of bodies and the attendant visual dynamics in their depiction. The reverse cowgirl position is notable for its nonexclusivity—the couple does not face one another—and, on film, for its exposure of the female body. As Fran rides Ted, it is the sensation of him that gives her pleasure, not necessarily him as a subjective other; her pleasure is not relayed back to Ted as a pleasure-giver but dispersed away from him.[34] This position recalls the mystical-religious figure of Lilith, identified in *The Alphabet of ben Sirach*, a medieval text that later became part of the Jewish Midrash, as the first wife of Adam.[35] The two of them argue about sexual positions, Lilith refusing to lie below Adam and Adam insisting he lie on top; this altercation leads Lilith to leave Adam.[36] Given the female vampire's mythological roots, this position can be interpreted as one of heterodox defiance. Sexual positions involving women on top are also pertinent when considering the contemporary feminist movement, in which sex between men and women was a site of extensive debate. The second-wave feminist cri de coeur "women on top," later popularized by Natalie Zemon Davis, is literalized in the reverse cowgirl position, a deviation from the "sexual position . . . now defined as 'standard'" famously lambasted by Anne Koedt.[37] The portrayal of Fran's riding of Ted can be understood in dialogue with both mythical and contemporary feminist discourses. Subsequently, however, Ted flips Fran—perhaps in a gesture of frustration—into the missionary position. Here, Ted embodies

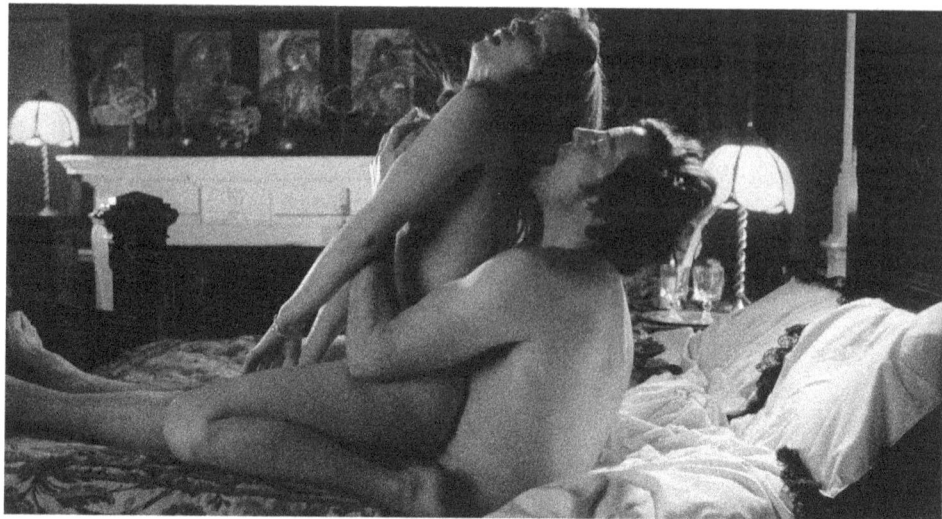

FIGURE 1.4 Fran rides Ted in reverse cowgirl. *Vampyres* (José Ramón Larraz, 1974). Digital screen capture.

the Midrashic Adam and the patriarchal figure of sexual domination, reasserting his position on top of Fran and manipulating her gaze back toward him. We will come to see, however, that this repositioning is short-lived.

Later in the film, after having been subdued with wine, Ted lies on the same bed in a daze while Fran and Miriam feed off his blood and kiss one another. Charged by the thrill of bloodsucking, the women proceed to have sex beside Ted, who reclines—impotent and feverish—gazing upon the women, a fast zoom into close-up conveying his horror. Ted's fearsome look as he gazes upon the women in coitus evokes Bonnie Zimmerman's observation that "the lesbian vampire . . . can be used to express a fundamental male fear that woman-bonding will exclude men and threaten male supremacy."[38] This fear is also realized by Miriam's date Rupert (Karl Lanchbury), here in a sadosexual paroxysm in which the half-dead Rupert serves as a conduit for the satiation of Miriam's and Fran's desires. Weiss understands these depictions of women in pleasure and men in peril as a symbolic response to second-wave feminism, in which "men understandably felt their dominant social position to be dangerously threatened."[39] Conversely, Zimmerman argues that these films' ability to render depictions of female power over men entertaining suggests how, between 1970 and 1973, men did not yet perceive feminism as a "fundamental threat."[40] These interpretations are complicated, however, by the fact that cinematic depictions of threatening women who endanger men had enjoyed a screen presence for many decades preceding second-wave feminism, from the *dive* of Italian silent cinema's golden age to the femmes fatales of Hollywood film noir. The divergence here lies more precisely in these fatal women's embrace of sexual pleasure either without men or without male control, a quality that Nina Auerbach also relates to second-wave feminism, writing, "Feminists in the 1970s were discovering, just as the vampire's lovers do, the multiorgasmic versatility of women's eroticism, which, despite the admonitions of male experts, requires no penis for arousal."[41] With emergent feminist discourses around female orgasms, a growing lesbian feminist movement, and an inchoate sex toy industry, the 1970s signaled a paradigm shift in relation to female sexual pleasure in which penetrative penile sex was more widely understood as inessential to women's erotic fulfillment.[42] Inessentiality marks a useful concept through which the les(bi)an vampire's relation to her male targets can be understood bisexually: She rarely eschews men entirely; instead, in a bisexual realignment, she regards them as perfectly desirable but not a necessity.

The inessentiality of men to the les(bi)an vampire is reflected in the tendency for her male targets to be killed, never to return, and for her female targets to become vampires themselves. Whereas Zimmerman claims that the les(bi)an vampire is a "vampire-rapist who violates and destroys her victim," Alexandra Heller-Nicholas is more precise, clarifying that "these seductions offer their female 'victims'—for better or for worse—a potential way out, be it of the tight hold of patriarchy or life itself."[43] The enticement of the les(bi)an vampire's female targets—from *Daughters of Darkness*'s Valerie to *Vampyros Lesbos*' Linda (Ewa Strömberg)—speaks more to a willing complicity. While sex between women is presented as a strong metaphysical bond, the attachments between the les(bi)an vampire and her male victims are more often a means to an end. Countess Carody (Soledad Miranda) of *Vampyros Lesbos* narrates this ethic to her female lover: "Men still disgust me. I hate them all." In *Vampyres*, Fran and Miriam shower together after their murder of Rupert. Under the water stream, Miriam relays her dread that Fran is getting too attached to Ted, entreating, "You're playing a dangerous game. Kill him before it's too late. Kill him! Kill him!" Miriam fears that by choosing to keep Ted alive, Fran may develop a romantic attachment to him. Miriam's anxieties prove unmerited; Fran is using Ted's body for sexual satisfaction and bloodsucking, killing him slowly in the process. Reading Fran's attachment to Ted through the romantic lens of patriarchal heteronormativity would thus be superficial. Closer attention to the nature of their sexual encounters reveals a subversive reconfiguration of the sex

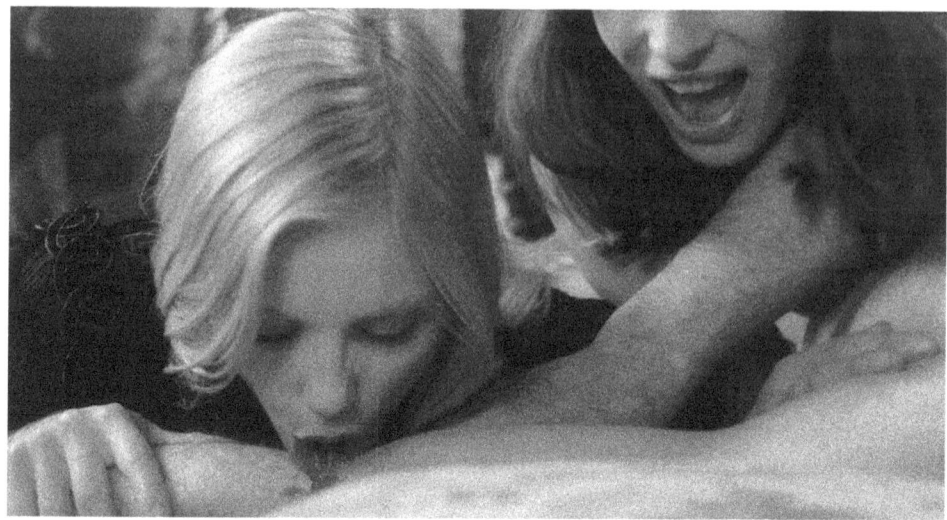

FIGURE 1.5 Miriam tongues Ted's wound as Fran watches on. *Vampyres* (José Ramón Larraz, 1974). Digital screen capture.

act, which—through an improvisation on a vampire motif—complicates their gendered relation.

After his first encounter with Fran, Ted wakes up alone with a wound in the fold of his inner elbow; the subsequent times they have sex, the wound gapes. This gash is the site of the vampires' feeding, an eschewal of the generic trope of the neck. Larraz explains his choice, saying, "I imagine my vampires turn almost to cannibalism, to eat somebody, to take the blood from anywhere, no matter if it is on the arm or on the balls!"[44] These remarks around the extensive voracity of Larraz's vampires echo Jo Eadie's analysis of *The Hunger*'s vampires: "Appetite transforms the body from an erotic object to the object of a less discriminate desire, the vampire's gaze offering an almost Whitmanesque democratic vision of all flesh as equally desirable, but equally undifferentiated."[45] In this sense, we can understand Fran's and Miriam's transfixed cathexis toward the wound as constitutive of their bisexual figuration. Bisexuality's indiscrimination regarding an object's genitals is rendered transgressively in what Eadie would term a bisexual *hunger*, a voracious desire (and ability) to turn any part of a body into a sexual organ.

Attention to the rendering of Ted's mutilation, the materiality of his wound, reveals additional sites of sexual reconfiguration. As Ted's laceration distends, it takes on a vulvic quality, the skin around the gash reddens and

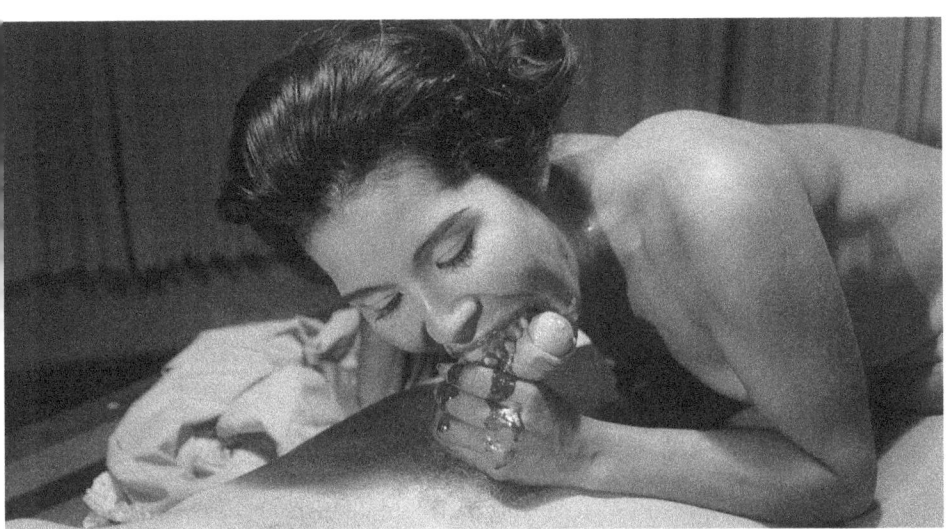

FIGURE 1.6 The Vampire Maid (Irene Best) sinks her fangs into John Stoker's (John Holmes) penis. *Dracula Sucks* (Phillip Marshak, 1978). Digital screen capture.

the fissure gapes; as a source of blood, connotations of menstruation are clear. When Ted reclines drunk and powerless, Fran and Miriam share the bloody feast his opening supplies, tonguing the wound and kissing one another. With this corporeal modification, Fred becomes the recipient of an ersatz form of cunnilingus from which he derives no pleasure; he is rendered penetrable, manipulable. If we are to explicate cispatriarchal heteronormative ideology to its most hyperbolic, penetrability and manipulability emerge as desirable qualities of the female body in coitus. The female vampires' manipulation of Fred's body thus constitutes an inversion of this structure. This inverted sexual threat is taken to perhaps its most literal conclusion in the hardcore film *Dracula Sucks* (Phillip Marshak, 1978), in which a vampire maid (Irene Best) sinks her teeth into John Stoker's (John Holmes) penis. Here it is the penis—one of American hardcore film's most celebrated penises—that is rendered penetrable by the female vampire's bite.[46] *Dracula Sucks* literalizes Barbara Creed's suggestion that the vampire "threatens to bite, to draw blood, and sever the penis. . . . Vampirism combines . . . the threat of castration [and] the feminization of the male victim."[47] For Linda Williams, however, these representations of women vampires sucking fluids from men are not simply fantastical metaphors but moments inspiring a reconsideration of penovaginal sex itself as "the female . . . milking the sperm of the male."[48] Williams underscores these films' potential to challenge the dominant idea of the male penetrator and female penetrated, a reconfiguration that recalls Bini Adamczak's term *circlusion*, an alternative to penetration, which describes the active engulfment of an object by an orifice.[49] The abstracted sites of sucking and penetration/circlusion observable in *Vampyres* might thus reconfigure other extragender sex acts away from cisgender, heteropatriarchal hermeneutics, offering queer possibilities that befit a bisexual sensibility.

The symbolic tendency observable here is one in which the genital associations of sex are radically realigned, which, in San Filippo's words, relocates "the primary erogenous zone from the sex-differentiated genitals to the sex-indiscriminate neck."[50] Yet, in *Vampyres*, the generic trope of the neck is also rejected, and the genitals displaced, in ways that speak to Tanya Krzywinska's contention that "the sexual power of the vampire leans on the notion that sexual ecstasy dissembles our 'normal' mappings of a unified and stable body."[51] Within this corporeal recalibration, the harmony between the sexed body and sexuality loses its hermeneutic congruence. In *Vampyres*' figuration of the les(bi)an vampire, hegemonic notions of gender and the sex act are radically recalibrated, destructively confused.

The close-ups of Ted's wound—once a smooth, contained surface, now a vulvic, bloody fissure—remind a spectator of the abject plasmaticity of the carnal body. Articulated by Sergei Eisenstein as "freedom from ossification, an ability to take on any form dynamically," *plasmaticity* is a useful term through which to understand figurations of the body that attend to its capacity to be radically reconfigured.[52] In *Vampyres*' representation of the wound-as-sex-organ, sexual desire is redirected away from the genitals-as-object-choice toward nongendered body parts in ways that are both celebrated in vampire lore and illuminative of bisexual desirous possibilities. Consider Christopher Craft's evocative description of eroticism in vampire texts:

> Luring at first with an inviting orifice, a promise of red softness, but delivering instead a piercing bone, the vampire mouth fuses and confuses . . . the gender-based categories of the penetrating and the receptive. . . . With its soft flesh barred by hard bone, its red crossed by white, this mouth compels opposites and contrasts into a frightening unity, and it asks some disturbing questions. Are we male or are we female? Do we have penetrators or orifices? And if both, what does that mean? And what about our bodily fluids, the red and the white? What are the relations between blood and semen, milk and blood? Furthermore, this mouth, bespeaking the subversion of the stable and lucid distinctions of gender, is the mouth of all vampires, male and female.[53]

Craft gestures toward the idea that the vampire genre's deliciously dangerous sensuality carries with it a desubjectivizing threat to the extent that, as Judith Butler famously argues, gender produces "the intelligible field of subjects."[54] In this fantasy space, necks and wounds usurp traditional sexual orifices, becoming preeminent sites of sexual aim.[55] Vampire coitus, in its sexuality beyond genitality, offers a form of pleasure for which the monosexual structure of single-gendered object choice cannot account.

The wound inflicted by the vampire, which often appears with visual prominence, is constituted by the skin having been ruptured. Let us reflect here on the significance of the skin breaking and the wound's conspicuity. While the skin has come to signify the body's very boundedness, its rending contests this circumscription, bringing with it values of untruth, illness, and unnaturalness. For Steven Connor, "The skin is the vulnerable, unreliable boundary between inner and outer conditions and the proof of their frightening, fascinating intimate contiguity. . . . In films such as *Videodrome* [David Cronenberg, 1983] and the *Alien* series [Ridley Scott, 1979; James Cameron, 1986; David Fincher, 1992; Jean-Pierre Jeunet, 1997], the skin betrays what is its function to guarantee, the integrity of the distinctions between internal and external, depth and surface, self and other."[56] The skin's vulnerability to puncture reveals the very instabilities of the binaries it precariously manages. In Connor's science fiction film examples, the skin fails in its function of division with the transgressive crossing of its divide. These examples recall Michel Foucault's account of transgression, which, he writes, "forces the limit to face the fact of its imminent disappearance."[57] In the skin's breakage, we glimpse the possibility of body-without-limit. Here, we might recall Eugenie Brinkema's comparative radical formalist reading of Ovid's *Metamorphoses* (8 CE) with Pascal Laugier's *Martyrs* (2008) in which the flaying of Marsyas and Anna (Morjana Alaoui), respectively, involve their becoming "nothing *except* one continuous raw wound."[58] In these accounts, Brinkema writes, "the body becomes the site of the violent transformation of a limitation, transfixion, and modification"; it demonstrates "infinite formal reconfigurability."[59] In this sense, the wound reminds us of the fleshy form lurking beneath the veneer of skin; the transformation of skin into wound begets further transformations, reminding us of the body's infinite capacity to change.

But what of the wound becoming an object of desire in and of itself when what is desired is not the ostensive surface but the fleshy fissure?[60] In Parveen Adams's discussion of *Crash* (David Cronenberg, 1996), she suggests that sexual desire toward the wound signals "the moment when libido passes beyond representation," when desire can no longer be said to be directed toward an Other.[61] For Adams, this image "represents a dissolution of otherness itself, a dissolution which is lethal. . . . [The wound] is not a kind of writing on the body so much as an unwriting of the body. It is already the other side of representation."[62] The wound dissembles the body insofar as it unwrites the fiction of corporeal containment. When a wound is rendered the (non)object of desire on film—in examples as disparate as *Flesh for Frankenstein* (Paul Morrissey, 1973), *In My Skin* (Marina de Van, 2002), *My Mother* (Christophe Honoré, 2004), and *L.A. Zombie* (Bruce LaBruce, 2010)—carnal bodies are abjectly rearticulated. The sexual cathexis to the wound observable in *Vampyres*, and in the examples above, suggests a phenomenon in which cinematic bodies are rendered plasmatic in ways that trouble their status as desirable objects.

In dominant structures of object choice, objects tend to take two interrelated configurations: the gendered person or the sexed genitals; desire toward the wound, however, takes neither. The ostensive, whole bodily surface, read according to codes of gender, is eschewed in favor of an ungendered part of the body. Here, we might recall Lou Andreas-Salomé's argument that, before ego formation, "sexuality . . . once embraced the whole body, such that any and every organ could be a site of pleasure."[63] The wound's unwriting of the body, described by Adams, is at once a reminder how sexuality and desiring can exceed the genital focus of cisheterosexist accounts thereof. Let us also recall that myths of a stable physiological sex binary are buttressed by a faith that the body's form can be ordered into categories of "male" and "female" that are often purported to be immutable. Here, we cannot forget the formal nature of sex's taxonomical designation: concerned as it is with the shape of genitals, the pitch of voice, the levels of steroid hormones, the structure of chromosomes. The wound, in its transformation of skin to fissure, in its attestation of the body's plasmaticity, undoes bodily myths of sexual dimorphism and immutability— myths that trans and intersex theories have, similarly, undone.[64] It is, therefore, not only that the wound, like the asses from this book's introduction, has no gender but that the wound attests to the body's capacity to be otherwise in ways that trouble dominant notions of bodily immutability vis-à-vis sex. With these correspondences in mind, parallels might be drawn between the vulvic appearance of Ted's wound and trans theoretical accounts of the trans vagina as, in Eva Hayward's words, "a regeneration of my bodily boundaries. . . . My cut is *of* my body, not the absence of parts of my body. . . . My tissues are mutable in so far as they are made of me and propel me to imagine an embodied elsewhere."[65] Let me clarify that to put Fred's vulvic wound in conversation with Hayward's account is not to perform a reading of the trans-vagina-as-wound, which, obviously, risks recirculating cissexism's pathologization of trans bodies and its mythologization of the unchanging and unchanged body.[66] Instead,

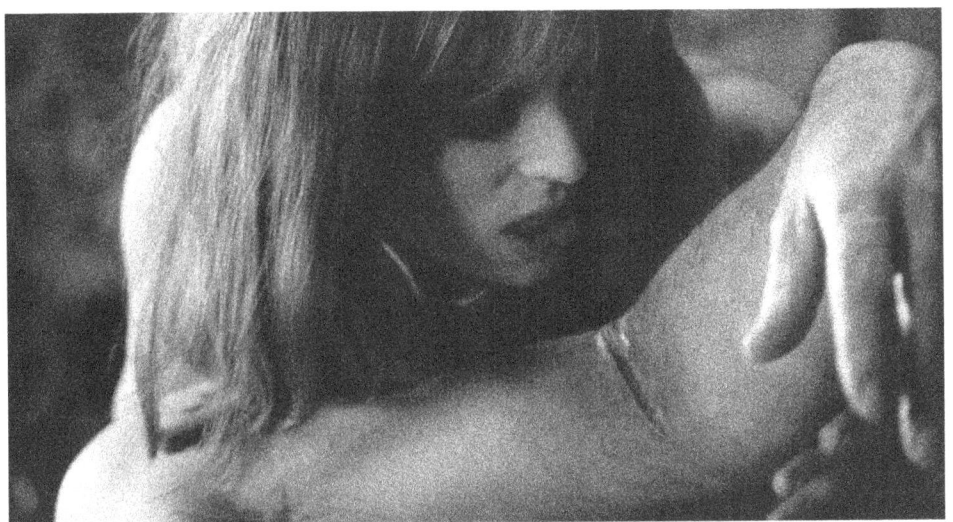

FIGURE 1.7 Fran stares voraciously at Ted's bloody, vulvic wound. *Vampyres* (José Ramón Larraz, 1974). Digital screen capture.

it is to foreground the significance of the vampire film's wounds vis-à-vis queer practices whereby the body's mutability is made manifest in the genitals' reconfiguration, a reconfiguration, as Hayward stresses, that occurs through the body, not in opposition to it.

Adams, in her discussion of *Crash*, highlights how in the film's presentation of sex with the wound, "gender, object choice, sexual aim, all these fundamental marks of identity began to fade into the background. The relation to the wound is what insists."[67] It is pertinent that among those marks of identity that, Adams contends, become diminished in this process are object choice and sexual aim. Because the wound has no gender, and because it attests to the capacity for physiological change, desire toward it necessarily involves monosexuality's evanescence. It is germane, therefore, that *Vampyres* visualizes the carnal wound as an extensible abstraction of its vampires' bisexualities: an awry figuration of transgressive desire undetermined by gendered object choice.[68]

Glamour, Aesthetics, and Bisexual Femininity

The magnetism that draws Fran and Miriam toward the wound is paralleled in the ineluctable magnetism they wreak over their targets that, similarly, transgresses gender. Toward the beginning of *Vampyres*, when the caravanning couple John and Harriet are driving through the Berkshire countryside, Harriet eyes the vampire women lingering at the edge of the woodland, Miriam hiding behind Fran. This image will come to visit Harriet in her dreams, inducing a suspicious curiosity, or perhaps a desire, that leads, ultimately, to her death. Yet for this parochial, demure wife, the curious desire toward these glamorously feminine figures—whose opulence presents a striking contrast with the dreary English countryside—proves too strong to resist.

Suspicion toward femininity has a long-standing cultural history, a symptom of misogynistic discourses that seek, at once, to eroticize feminine mystique and to denigrate it as deceptive. In film studies, a regularly cited incarnation of this ideological myth is the femme fatale: a seductress whose most striking characteristic, argues Mary Ann Doane, "is the fact that she never really is what she seems to be. She harbors a threat which is not entirely legible, predictable or manageable."[69] Later, Doane continues: "The seductive power attributed to the figure of the femme fatale . . . exemplifies the disparity between seeming and being."[70] Doane's arguments are part of ongoing critical debates within feminist film theory that grapple with representations of women's femininity as dissimulative. Here, an important intervention comes from Rosalind Galt, who identifies a tendency toward iconophobia in some of feminist film theory's approaches to images of women. In these accounts, Galt finds a conflation of the critiqued patriarchal axiom that "the woman lies by definition" with the critically espoused axiom that "the image lies by definition."[71] This conflation, Galt argues, constitutes an iconophobic approach to the image: "a rejection of spectacle per se, deploying it only as a totalizing category that can stand for patriarchal image culture . . . [thus] underwriting the political analysis of patriarchal culture by means of a patriarchal rhetoric of the image."[72] Rather than espouse patriarchal accounts of spectacle, we can instead, following Galt, understand prettiness, masquerade, and femininity as polyvalent phenomena carrying implicit threats to patriarchal aesthetics' accounts of the signifier's relation to the real. Donna J. Haraway's account of figuration is particularly useful in navigating the feminine image's meanings and functions as, for Haraway, the figure is neither truthful nor deceptive but a performative image that brings about knowledge, "producing both what can count as real and the witnesses to that reality."[73] Thus, we can speak of dissimulation as the fragility of the ostensive qua signification, it being, at once, that upon which we must rely to garner knowledge and that which cannot be trusted entirely to convey knowledge. Within this framework, dissimulation need not allude to a lying image but, instead, allude to a radical challenge to the logic of seeing-as-knowing.

While critiquing the misogynistic functions cinematic representations of dissimulative femininity can perform, feminist and queer scholarship has formulated considerations of femininity not simply as a product of patriarchal culture but as a complex and polyvalent set of signification practices that can operate in tandem with, against, and outside of this culture. To read the les(bi)an vampire simply as a vector of patriarchal visual codes is to ignore how her figuration often renders incoherent these very same codes. Representations of dissimulative femininity also engender a more fundamental cinematic uncertainty evoking that tension between artifice and reality André Bazin calls "the conflict between style and likeness."[74] With her polysemous signifiers, the les(bi)an vampire's threat lies in the inability for her stylizations—performance, costume, makeup, and the ways in which she is framed and edited—to coalesce in verisimilitude. The les(bi)an vampire's conflicts obtain.

The conflict between the les(bi)an vampire's hegemonic femininity and her queerness is significant. While, of course, femininity and queerness often coexist, I am discussing how, socially, these terms have been understood as incompatible insofar as they break with what Judith Butler terms "a causal continuity among sex, gender, and desire."[75] When Monique Wittig offers the provocation "Lesbians are not women," she highlights the symbolic yoking of the category of "woman" to female heterosexuality.[76] As a hegemonically feminine yet (often secretively) queer figure, the les(bi)an vampire's figuration unyokes femininity and heterosexuality, yet through her retention of desire toward men, she cannot be said to have eschewed heterosexuality in the same way as a lesbian figure. This quality of the les(bi)an vampire signals the bisexual nature of her transgressions: that which is supposedly contradictory is often only such insofar as it contradicts the logics of monosexual normativity, both in what Butler calls the "heterosexual matrix" and in relation to dominant ideas of what it means to be a lesbian.[77] Additionally, the fantastical elements that preclude the les(bi)an vampire's worldly verisimilitude are presented in concert with a feminine queerness also deemed short of verisimilar within hetero-monosexual logic. As the logic of mortality stumbles in the face of the vampire, the logic of monosexuality stumbles in her bisexuality.

Cinema's les(bi)an vampires have tended toward certain kinds of embodiment and certain styles of adornment. The 1970s les(bi)an vampires were played by many of the decade's most celebrated female stars, including Ingrid Pitt in *The Vampire Lovers*, Ewa Aulin in *The Legend of Blood Castle*, and Delphine Seyrig in *Daughters of Darkness*. These actors conform to a typical look: feminine, svelte, white. With *Vampyres*, Larraz worked with veteran casting director Miriam Brickman to find lead vampire women of this description. The appearances of Marianne Morris and Anulka Dziubinska were paramount to their casting, with Larraz remarking churlishly, "We made the correct decision to go with beauty over thespian ability."[78] Morris, who was twenty-four at the time of production, had appeared in advertisements, theater, and four bawdy comedy and horror films prior to *Vampyres*.[79] Dziubinska began her career in modeling, appearing as a "Page Three girl" in British tabloid *The Sun* in 1970, photographed for a controversial nude advert in *The Times* in 1971, featured in *Playboy*'s "Girls of Munich" pictorial in 1972, and appearing as *Playboy*'s Playmate of the Month in May 1973.[80] *Vampyres* was Dziubinska's first acting role, at the age of twenty-three. The looks of *Vampyres*' lead actors aligned with contemporary hegemonic notions of feminine beauty, and their agreement to appear in the film nude ensured the delivery of one of exploitation cinema's central spectatorial promises.

The vampires' wardrobes were designed by Dulcie Midwinter, whose garments endowed them with an air of Gothic, refined sophistication.[81] Regarding *Vampyres*' costumes, Mary Ann Caws writes, "These loving/slaying heroines so interestingly dressed, in and out of the castle, in their black and red garments, are clearly opposed to the readily dressed couple who appear, normally outfitted . . . dull against elegant, unremarkable against remarkable and unusual."[82] Caws highlights the sharp contrast between the looks of Fran and Miriam and those of John and Harriet. The latter couple's drab turtlenecks and densely woven overcoats betray a utilitarian approach to dress befitting a parochial English couple.[83] In this sense, John's and Harriet's clothing can be understood synecdochally *as* their characters: simple, unsophisticated, earnest. With them, the ostensive is transparent. Fran and Miriam, however, sport garments that dazzle and allure, belying their destructive urges. Harriet's short haircut, trousers, and high-necked garments signify her unadorned knowability; Caws recognizes her as a "boring, staid, regular old trailer wife."[84] Conversely, it is Fran and Miriam's femininity that hinders their knowability; their adornment constitutes spectacular feminine glamour. In Elizabeth Wilson's exposition of glamour, she notes "the sense of casting a sheen, that is to say dazzling or blinding the spectator . . . the dangerous secret of those outside respectable society. . . . Glamour depends on what is withheld, on secrecy, hints, and the hidden. . . . It is an *appearance*, including the supernatural magical sense of that word—as in apparition. . . . Its end result is the sheen, the mask of perfection, the untouchability and numinous power of the *icon*."[85] Glamour involves a bedazzling visual performance, staging dramatic conflicts between visible and invisible, suggestion and concealment, worldliness and magic. Importantly, glamour is often performed by those whose secrets are socially transgressive;

in this sense, the vampires' processes of glamorous adornment might be understood as labors of self-preservation. Wilson cites vampire cinema of the twentieth and twenty-first centuries as examples of how "the forbidden and the dangerous were always saturated in glamour."[86] The cinematic vampire's allure is a glamorous one, their stylized concealment of social transgression is characteristically bedazzling, and their figuration on-screen involves cinematic systems that, similarly, play with the concepts of visibility, truth, and fantasy.

Harriet's fascination with Fran and Miriam is animated by a desire to know who they are. Doane suggests, in comments relating to femmes fatales that are equally expository for les(bi)an vampires, that masquerade might "situate them as privileged conduits to a—necessarily complex and devious—truth."[87] Might we interpret Harriet's draw toward the vampire women as a desire to become privy to this truth, a yearning to be initiated into their realm of knowledge? There is an intriguing moment in which Miriam and Fran approach Harriet while she is outdoors painting a canvas. Fran approaches Harriet and runs a finger across her forehead, in a gesture Larraz intended to mirror the Christian sign of the cross, saying, "I always knew we'd find each other. By this sign I'll recognize you."[88] This comment suggests Fran's preternatural knowledge: She knows Harriet, but Harriet does not know her. The sign Fran performs resembles a kind of secret handshake, one which, if Harriet recognizes, she might understand. However, this recognition does not take place, and Harriet ultimately dies in the film's denouement, abducted by Fran and Miriam as she mourns the death of John, before having her throat slit by the women. Harriet's incomprehension ultimately leads to her demise.

Yet there are further clues as to the differences in the women's approach to seeing and knowing, suggesting an aesthetic chasm between them. That Harriet is crept up upon while she is painting invites a consideration of the formal layers of signification at play. The focus of Harriet's painting is the country house that has fascinated her, as she has been fascinated by Fran and Miriam. Rendering it in watercolor, Harriet mediates this house, whose mystery has wracked her, turning the worldly referent into an iconic, naturalistic representation contained within the borders of her canvas. Mid-painting, Harriet turns, sensing something might be behind her, before returning to the canvas. In medium close-up, we see Harriet from behind, perhaps from the point of view of someone who is watching her. She turns again, and we cut to her point of view: just desolate woodland. Back in medium close-up, Harriet wanders tentatively toward the woodland then, suddenly, two close-ups in quick succession: Fran, then Miriam—walking with pace. The contrast between the empty woodland and the tight close-ups refuses continuity editing's naturalization of space. With the naturalist style of Harriet's painting and the discontinuous editing style of the film, *Vampyres* stages a conflict between two forms of representation. While Harriet's aesthetic promises verisimilitude, recognizability, and containment, *Vampyres'* conveys precisely the opposite. Points of view shift, characters appear out of nowhere, spatial logic is contested. The clash between the scene's sylvan setting and the vampires' feminine glamour is uncanny. In the context of these formal conflicts, we can understand Fran's words and mysterious gesture in reference to aesthetics. "By this sign I'll recognize you" would now suggest a bid for Harriet to relinquish her tie to naturalism—the ruse of representing things as they appear—and, instead, to recognize that which is deemed unnatural, artificial, feminine. Yet Harriet remains dumbfounded by the vampires' feminine glamour, unable to adjust her perspective or perhaps to change her aesthetic sensibilities, to be granted *supra*natural understandings.

The relation between femininity and recognizability is a key problematic in Weiss's reading of the les(bi)an vampire vis-à-vis lesbian representation. Weiss observes, "The lesbian vampire fits the stereotype, not of the mannish lesbian, but of the white, feminine heterosexual woman."[89] It is this embodiment of hegemonic femininity, Weiss later continues, that troubles a lesbian reading of cinema's les(bi)an vampires: "They lack the lesbian verisimilitude that would enable them to 'pass' as lesbians."[90] While Weiss is discussing lesbian recognizability insofar as it relates to common stereotypes about lesbians, in doing so, she establishes a critical bind whereby femininity and appearing heterosexual are anathema to lesbianism. Weiss's siloing of femininity and lesbianism precludes the possibility of lesbian representation beyond depictions of butch women.[91] Yet, Weiss's limited framework illuminates something important: the precarity of categories of sexual recognition. As Butler writes, in response to an essay on bisexual femininity, "These categories that cross, such as the bisexual femme, expose the impurity of categorization itself. . . . The gesture by which [identity] differentiates itself becomes the border through which contamination travels, undermining differentiation itself."[92] For Butler, the bisexual femme's exposition of categorization's boundary-crossing impurities undermines those very categories of differentiation. Weiss's suggestion of the les(bi)an vampire's inability to pass as lesbian, despite her definitional queerness, reveals the ways in which this figure's bisexuality muddies the waters of monosexual recognizability.

In Clare Whatling's critique of Weiss's argument, she admonishes the foreclosure of the possibility of feminine lesbian representation on screen and, further, suggests that productive inquiry may lie in that which Weiss has abjured: in how the les(bi)an vampire "dissimulates right into the heart of hetero-patriarchy."[93] Taking up Whatling's call, I suggest that the les(bi)an vampire's bisexual femininity is precisely the conduit through which her dissimulations can be realized. Les(bi)an vampire figures lay bare the short-comings of structures of signification that claim to produce knowable sexual subjects. In the les(bi)an vampire film, performance, costume, makeup, and editing play with codes of sexual signification to produce a figure who resists intelligibility equally qua lesbian and heterosexual. Weiss briefly gestures toward this possibility, writing that the cinematic lesbian vampire "is doubly disturbing, as she appears 'normal' by society's standards for women and yet is not."[94] However, Weiss stops short of a consideration as to how appearing as one is not might function, what challenges this phenomenon might pose the logic of sexual representation, and which queer figural possibilities lie herein.

The ability to blend into society is an advantageous quality for vampires to possess. Fran and Miriam's unthreatening, feminine appearance enables them to hitch car rides from unsuspecting men. It is only after their male targets have been subdued via feminine seduction that the women's vampirism can be revealed and their bisexualities displayed. What might a focus on the im-perceptibility of bisexual femininity reveal about the les(bi)an vampire? Hem-mings is useful here in her consideration of the bisexual femme, positing that although the lesbian femme might be read as heterosexual, she is able to retain her queerness through a repudiation of extragender object choice. The bisexual femme, however, is unable to perform such a move of queer authentication as she refuses to repudiate both femininity and extragender object choice. Hem-mings suggests that these obstacles of intelligibility might be repurposed to effect a parody of heterosexuality via the bisexual femme's visual proximity to its images. She asks, "What might the implications for parody be if we consider the almost perfect copy . . . [the bisexual femme] can make of heterosexual-ity?"[95] As a seemingly heterosexual yet unintelligibly queer figure, we might understand the les(bi)an vampire as a kind of simulacrum whose ability to be read as the original refutes the readability of the original itself. Accordingly, the les(bi)an vampire is not simply a counterfeit imitation but a simulacrum of heterosexual femininity.

The les(bi)an vampire can thus be understood as the feminine that negates the eternal feminine, the heterosexual performance that negates compulsory heterosexuality, the appearance of mortality that negates the boundary be-tween living and dead. Under this framework, the ability to read femininity as heterosexual loses its hermeneutic power not through the oppositional terms of being homosexual but through the bisexually disruptive terms of being outside the heterosexual-homosexual binary. The glamorous feminine bisexual figure exposes shared investments between misogynistic, monosexist, and iconophobic accounts of film, embodying a threefold threat: the misogynistic axiom that the feminine is deceptive, the monosexist axiom that the bisexual is deceptive, and the iconophobic axiom that the image is deceptive. Yet, to refuse the legitimacy of these logics is to understand the les(bi)an vampire—in her femininity, bisexuality, and glamour—as a figure of polysemous significations and hermeneutic disruption. The les(bi)an vampire, in her leveraging of unintelligibility, wages multipronged attacks on logocentrism itself.

Racial-Cultural-National Imperceptibility, "Primitive" Bisexuality, and Cold War Anxieties

TED.	Are you English?
FRAN.	What makes you ask?
TED.	You don't look English.
FRAN.	Hmm.
TED.	Well, what are you then?
FRAN.	If I told you, you wouldn't believe me.

There is a subsequent matrix of intelligibility that the les(bi)an vampire confounds rooted in another aspect of her (non)identity: the inability of others to read her origins. In the European and North American les(bi)an vampire films I have surveyed, ostensibly nonwhite vampires are almost nonexistent.[96] Yet despite le(bi)an vampires' overwhelming whiteness, Richard Dyer notes how vampirism is often ascribed to "those who are not mainstream whites . . . those who are liminally white."[97] The les(bi)an vampire who appears white carries with her suspicions as to her murky origins, a phobic wariness of an unreadable national, cultural, or racial identity. When Haraway writes that "vampires are vectors of category transformation in a racialized, historical national unconscious," she underscores the racial-national anxieties this figure occasions.[98]

Vampyres' lead actors possess connotations of foreignness: Dziubinska, who has Polish ancestry, is credited only by her enigmatic non-English first name, Anulka; Morris—who is English but was born in Belgium—suggests that she was cast, in part, because "they wanted somebody who looked slightly foreign."[99] *Vampyres* establishes its vampires' sexual unreadability as it, simultaneously, raises questions around their origins. Here, the les(bi)an vampire's sexual boundary crossings intersect with those around race, culture, and nationality in ways that typify San Filippo's "bi-textuality."[100] In *Vampyres*' portrayal of the ambiguity around Fran and Miriam's origins—their "slight foreignness"—a bi-textual relation is forged between these vampires' sexualities and their unclear origins. An obvious analogy that emerges here is that of passing: As the les(bi)an vampire passes as heterosexual, she is not quite heterosexual; as she passes as mortal, she is vampire; as she passes as white and English, she remains "slightly foreign."

Vampyres' director José Ramón Larraz knew what it felt like to be a stranger in a foreign land. Larraz was born in Barcelona to a left-wing family that, under the authoritarian regime of Francisco Franco, was subject to surveillance.[101] Frustration with Francoist suppression led Larraz to emigrate at the age of twenty-two, moving to Paris in 1952, where he worked first as a comic strip artist and then as a fashion photographer, before moving to England in 1967.[102] The decision to credit himself as "J. R. Larrath" in his films *Whirlpool* and *Deviation*, and "Joseph Larraz" in *Vampyres*—truncated and anglicized versions of his forenames José Ramón—speaks to a strategic decision to conceal his nationality. With *Vampyres*, this strategy of concealment is foregrounded as a constitutive element of his vampires' chicanery, a feature that draws upon mythological alignments between vampires and a hidden otherness.

Early figurations of literary vampires were informed by antisemitic ideas about Jewish people, transposing notions of blood libel, the Wandering Jew, and conceptions of purported Jewish physiognomy onto the figure of the vampire.[103] The pertinent aspect of these ideas for my investigation is how antisemitic discourses imagine the Jew as a racialized figure who is able to inhere in European societies, how the Jew's imperceptible otherness—save some potential physiognomic clues—allow him to pass. Dale Hudson argues that "a defining feature of vampires is their ability to mutate and migrate. . . . The [Hollywood] vampire was white but not quite white. . . . The vampire's unnatural whiteness, thus, unsettles our assumptions about race."[104] The interactions between the les(bi)an vampire's not-quite-whiteness and her femininity can be elucidated further in relation to the figure of the Jewess.[105] Iterations of the Jewess's deviant, amoral core were popular in mid-nineteenth-century literature and theater with the archetype of the *belle juive*, under whose feminine masquerade depravities supposedly lay.[106] As Daniel Boyarin, Daniel Itzkovitz, and Ann Pellegrini elucidate, "The *belle juive* was a dangerous seductress who might lead [Christian] men to their doom: a kind of fifth columnist, infiltrating the enemy camp. . . . In her sexual aggressiveness and deceit, the Jewess's femininity was all show."[107] Like the les(bi)an vampire, the doom to which the *belle juive* leads her unsuspecting gentile victims is sexually aggressive and involves the revelation of a racially other core beneath the masquerade of white femininity.

Fears around racial-national ambiguity are also discernible in one of les(bi)an vampire cinema's most informative texts: Le Fanu's *Carmilla*. The eponymous character is described by the narrator Laura as having strange origins with which she is unfamiliar: "[Carmilla] sometimes alluded for a moment to her own home, or mentioned an adventure or situation, or an early recollection, which indicated a people of strange manners, and described customs of which we knew nothing. I gathered from these chance hints that her native country was much more remote than I had at first fancied."[108] Clues as to Carmilla's origins can also be found earlier, when Laura's governess, Madame Perrodon, describes the woman who delivered Carmilla in a carriage: "a hideous black woman, with a sort of colored turban on her head, and who was gazing all the time from the carriage window, nodding and grinning derisively towards the ladies, with gleaming eyes and large white eyeballs, and her teeth set as if in fury."[109] These suggestions around Carmilla's mysterious, exotic roots—twinned with the anti-Black, Orientalist, animalistic language used to describe her guardian—strongly evoke contemporary nineteenth-century ideas around so-called primitivity.

To understand the import of *Carmilla*'s allusions to its eponymous character's origins, and those of the films it inspired, we must briefly turn to contemporary discourses around race and sexuality. Neville Hoad outlines how—in naturalist, anthropological, and colonial travel writing, which circulated across Europe during the nineteenth century—"the presence of 'homosexuality' amongst 'the savage races' is engaged by ideologies of empire and the imputed national/racial otherness of it can be hierarchised by the evolutionary narrative."[110] Hoad argues that these texts' preoccupations with the sexual practices of Indigenous Peoples were instrumental in the formulation of European homosexual identity, effecting the discursive delineation of a lesser sexual species.[111] While Hoad presents convincing evidence to support these historical claims, a return to the major texts of colonial travel writing on sexuality reveals descriptions not of what would come to be understood as homosexuality but of a "primitive" bisexuality. Orientalist Richard Francis Burton, for example, makes the claim in 1886 that "the Vice" (any nonreproductive sexual practice) is more prevalent in areas with certain climates: the "Sotadic Zone."[112] Burton writes that "within the Sotadic Zone the Vice is popular and endemic, held at the worst to be a mere peccadillo."[113] Burton's claim is a suggestion not of an exclusively intragender sexuality but of the popularity, permissibility, and scope of nonreproductive sex. Burton goes on to claim, in his characteristically purple language that, in the Sotadic Zone, "there is a blending of the masculine and feminine temperaments, a crasis [mixture] which elsewhere occurs only sporadically. Hence the male *féminisme* [effeminacy] whereby the man becomes patiens [enduring] as well as agens [doing]."[114] Writing at a time in which gendered temperaments described not only gendered expression but object choice, Burton's claim is that there is a crasis—an amalgam—of sexual acts present in these "zones," both reproductive and nonreproductive. Further, his description of male effeminates who both *do* and *endure*—read: penetrate and circlude—speaks to the same claim of sexual versatility. Burton is most evocative in his description of racial others' expansive sexualities in his coining of the word *omnifutuentes* to describe Chinese sexuality, combining the Latin terms *omni* (all) and *futuēns* (the present participle of *to fuck*).[115] The sexual practices described in Burton's fantasies of both China and the Sotadic Zone are thus not specifically homosexual; instead, these are the settings in which he imagines a bisexual synthesis of "primitive" excess.[116]

Carmilla was published the same year as Charles Darwin's *The Descent of Man*, which explored evolutionary theory in relation to humans.[117] An evocative part of Darwin's account claims that "in utterly barbarous tribes the women have more power in choosing, rejecting, and tempting their lovers."[118] Similarly, we observe in Burton's comments regarding "primitive" women a contention of unnatural sexual dominance, underpinned here by allusions to queerness. For Burton the "primitive" woman is "a tribade, a votary of mascula Sappho, Queen of Frictrices or Rubbers."[119] This description teems with allusions not only to sex between women but to a masculinity among "primitive" women. The term *mascula Sappho* originates in Horace's comments on the purported masculinity of her meter, yet Burton explicates this term in a footnote as alluding to Sappho's "over-development of clitoris . . . which enabled her to play the man."[120] In both Darwin's and Burton's accounts of the sexualities of "primitive" women, we find an interplay of masculine and feminine, both desirously and, they argue, physiologically. For Burton, these women's tribadism is linked to a physiological masculinity (the large clitoris), yet Sappho's "votaries" also include "Frictrices": a word that can connote both "lesbian" and "prostitute."[121] These descriptions of female "primitive" sexuality, therefore, propose not an exclusive lesbianism but, again, a bisexually hybrid mixture of sexually transgressive attributes.

Considering Le Fanu's text in relation to this spate of anthropological inquiries into sexuality and gender among so-called primitive peoples reveals stark connections between Carmilla's peregrine cultural background, her sexual forwardness, and her bisexuality.[122] Intertextual investments between these

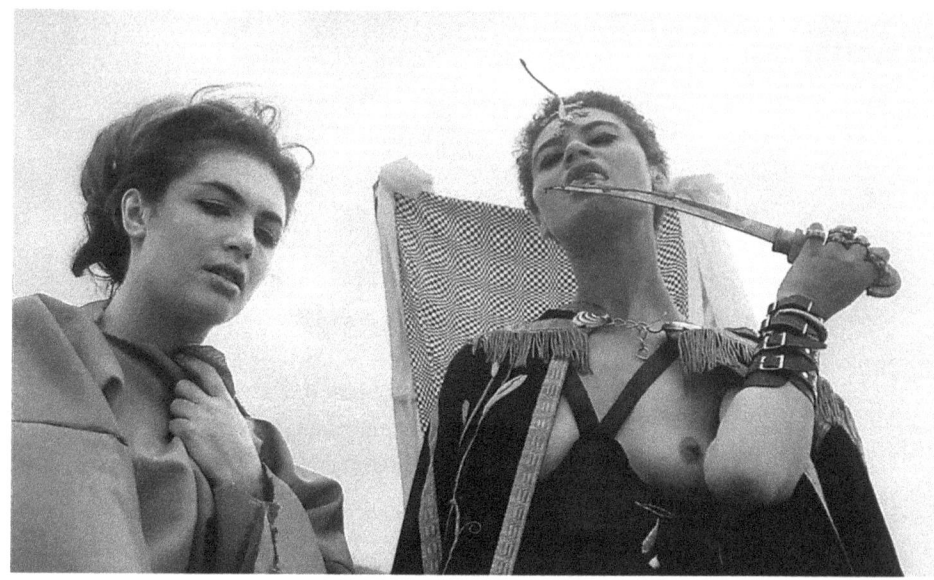

FIGURE 1.8 The Vampire Queen (Jacqueline Sieger) licks blood off a dagger beside an acolyte (Ariane Sapriel). *The Rape of the Vampire* [*Le Viol du vampire*] (Jean Rollin, 1968). Digital screen capture.

formative writings and the les(bi)an vampire films they inspired are traceable. The stylization of the Queen of the Vampires in *The Rape of the Vampire*—one of the few examples of a Black les(bi)an vampire—is perhaps the most explicit example thereof. The Vampire Queen's ornate headdress and breast-exposing regalia betray a colonialist fashioning of Native dress. This visual presentation recalls Rizvana Bradley's account of "the colonial imagination of the benighted native, to be deemed incapable of the aesthetic judgement required to recognize such a condition of deprivation as shameful."[123] Bradley finds in depictions of Black nakedness an anteriority—both a temporal-developmental beforeness and a being-before qua subjection—in relation to Western aesthetics and metaphysics. These observations share insightful parallels with colonialist-developmentalist understandings of sexual evolution toward a monosexual telos. In Jacqueline Seiger's Black les(bi)an Vampire Queen, the colonialist presumption of Black ignorance to the shame of nakedness (an anteriority to colonialist aesthetics and metaphysics) is invoked alongside colonialist ideas of supposed savage sexual excess (an anteriority to a colonialist episteme of sexual development). This example, however, is uncharacteristically explicit in its rendering of these associations. More commonly, there are subtler suggestions of racial, cultural, or national alterity observable across les(bi)an vampire cinemas.

In a moment of rhetorical sparring, one of Fran and Miriam's targets proves fatally uninformed when it comes to spotting the signs of their origins. Their victim—credited simply as "the Playboy" (Michael Byrne)—is invited back to the country house where they pour him a glass of wine, part of their seductive ritual. Fran and Miriam take on a blasé air when a topic of conversation arises that might reveal their origins:

MIRIAM.   It's a vintage of our own. My friend and I are rather proud of it.

PLAYBOY.   And yet I could tell you everything you wanted to know about this wine.

MIRIAM.   Oh, yes? I don't believe you.

PLAYBOY.   My dear young lady, you are sitting in front of a true connoisseur. First, I'll tell you the country of origin— shouldn't be too difficult to judge.

FRAN.   You'll never guess. I'll bet you anything you like.

PLAYBOY.   Don't be too sure. I'm an expert and I've recognized some very obscure wines in my time.

The Playboy proceeds to sip at the wine, making several incorrect guesses as to its origin, all regions of France. Fran informs him that the wine, in fact, comes from "a remote part of the Carpathian Mountains." This comment hints toward Fran and Miriam's vampirism—the Carpathians being the home of Báthory and the fictional location of Stoker's Castle Dracula. But, further, it is an unspecific geographical descriptor, a "remote part" of a mountain range spanning seven different countries across central and eastern Europe. In this moment, the Playboy's bravado is admonished by Fran and Miriam, who reveal enough to prove him wrong but not enough to divulge their exact origins.

Like the Carpathian Mountains, the myths that inform the les(bi)an vampire film have roots in central and eastern Europe: Báthory lived in Čachtice in what was then the Kingdom of Hungary and is now Slovakia; *Carmilla* is set in Styria in what was then the Austro-Hungarian Empire and is now split between Austria and Slovenia. At the time of *Vampyres'* production, these areas belonged, in part, to Socialist states: Čachtice to the Czechoslovak Socialist Republic, a Soviet satellite state, and Styria located partly in the Socialist Federal Republic of Yugoslavia (and partly in democratic-socialist Austria). It was in western Europe, however, that the les(bi)an vampire image circulated most persistently during the 1970s. During this time, the European Economic Community was exclusively composed of Western states, with much of central and eastern Europe constituting the Soviet Union and its satellite states. Three months prior to *Vampyres'* production, the United Kingdom became a member of the European Economic Community, with Prime Minister Edward Heath promising the benefits of a "great cross-fertilisation" among European nations.[124] This was, therefore, a historical context in which questions of transnational relations—interestingly expressed by Heath through reproductive terminology—were at the forefront of British politics. Within this geopolitical landscape, the influx of vampire films in western Europe might be interpreted as a reflection of Cold War anxieties around Socialist and Communist states. The frequency of characters with the surnames Karnstein, Karlstein, and Báthory signal an influx of interlopers with a cultural heritage to the east. Just as the les(bi)an vampire typifies Fritz Klein's "bisexual spy" and Clare Hemmings's "bisexual double-agent," those whose figurations allude to eastern Europe also evoke the contemporary KGB spy.[125] Steven Angelides makes similar connections in his analysis of Cold War discourses of sexuality: "Cold War hysteria concerning national security pivoted around oppositions such as sameness/difference, inside/outside, familiar/foreign, conformity/dissent, patriotism/subversion, normal/abnormal . . . during this period. . . . Bisexuality itself was the epistemic border between the heterosexual and the homosexual, the normal and the abnormal, the patriotic citizen and the subversive communist."[126] In this context, the les(bi)an vampire—in her foreignness, her unknowability, and her bisexuality—betrays potential allegiances to multiple fifth columns. Geopolitically, we can come to understand 1970s western Europe as a locale in which diplomatic cross-fertilization among western European states was positioned against and threatened by cross-contamination by eastern European Communists. A sip of wine one assumes to be French might, in fact, originate from a sovkhoz vineyard.

Spatial Transgressions, Bisexual Orientations

These observations around 1970s les(bi)an vampire films' geopolitical associations might inspire us to look beyond discursive hints of racial-cultural-national alterity and toward how vampires' bodies negotiate cinematic space. The transgression of spatial boundaries is observable in the visual motif of the les(bi)an vampire invading the bedrooms of mortals. In *The Vampire Lovers*, Emma (Madeline Smith) awakens to find Carmilla (Ingrid Pitt) has entered her bedroom; in *The Shiver of the Vampires*, Isolde (Dominique) emerges from a grandfather clock, startling the naive Isle (Sandra Julien); in *The Velvet Vampire*, Diane (Celeste Yarnall) watches an unsuspecting couple have sex in their bedroom through a two-way mirror; in *Daughters of Darkness*, Elizabeth and her secretary, Ilona (Andrea Rau), peer through a balcony window to watch a newlywed couple have sex. The les(bi)an vampire is, at times, able to appear in private space in unexpected ways—as with *The Vampire Lovers* and *The Shiver of the Vampires*—and, on other occasions, she gazes into private space through a screen that secures her position as voyeur: the two-way mirror of *The Velvet Vampire*, the translucent voile of *Daughters of Darkness*. The les(bi)an vampire is figured with reference both to a geographical history of boundary crossing and through her invasive approach to space.

Though *Vampyres'* locations are limited and contained, these settings convey a symbolically rich spatial politics. The film takes place exclusively in the country house, its grounds, and the area's surrounding woods and roads. Shot in two nineteenth-century buildings, *Vampyres'* country house harks back to vampire lore's Gothic roots, while simultaneously abiding as symbols of English aristocratic wealth.[127] Whereas Fran and Miriam are oriented toward the grand country house, John and Harriet's temporary home is their modest caravan, located on the perimeter of the house's grounds. Like the contrasts in the couples' dress, the vampires' locale is abundant and spectacular, the mortals' is modest and utilitarian. To reflect further on the import of John and Harriet's caravan, consider the following observation from a sociological investigation into British caravanning holidays, which characterizes their appeal as involving "the desirable balance between the perpetuation of daily routines and the imperative to change at least some of these upon entry into a potentially liminal zone of holiday-making; the predictable management of feelings of insecurity or anxiety which arise from being in temporary and unfamiliar surroundings."[128] Caravanning is a form of vacationing in which one is able to retain the familiarity of home comforts while venturing somewhat into the dangers of the unknown. Such a description harmonizes with the behavior of Harriet, who finds herself negotiating the countervailing pulls of her curiosity and anxiety toward the space beyond the caravan. It is through the caravan's window that Harriet gazes upon the vampire women. In the caravan's quasi-domestic space, Harriet peers into a world unfamiliar to her, like the cinematic spectator who, through the mediatory screen, can encounter unfamiliar worlds.[129] In contrast with the centuries-long foundations of the country house, the caravan suggests a modern approach to the home: mechanical, compact, functional. It is through these juxtaposed spaces, and the characters aligned to them, that we can begin to read the spatial politics that map *Vampyres*. Whereas the house's opulent mise-en-scène and the bisexual explorations that take place within it signify excess, the caravan lies in contrast as a symbol of hetero-monogamous containment, the security of its homely familiarity carrying the hope of it being an amulet against exterior threats.

Fran and Miriam's alignment with the luxurious country house, however, is importantly not one of ownership but one of transient residence. Though this is the building to which they most often return—and the site of their sexual and murderous endeavors—they are not its owners but its interlopers. When Ted asks Fran if the house belongs to her, she responds, "I'm only a guest." In the film's final moment, a real estate agent (Gerald Case) leads a prospective couple (Bessie Love and Elliott Sullivan) up to the house, dismissing the legend that "the ghosts of these poor women haunt the building." This statement confirms that Fran and Miriam are not simply vampires but specters haunting—as we might recall from the opening scene—the site of their murder. In this sense, it would seem the les(bi)an vampire shares a relation to space that prior queer film scholars identify in cinematic figures they describe as "lesbian." Patricia White's "lesbian specter" describes the "ghostly presence of lesbianism in classical Hollywood cinema"; Terry Castle's "apparitional lesbian" lays "in the shadows . . . a wanderer in the dusk, a lost soul . . . a pale denizen of the night."[130] On the one hand, the les(bi)an vampire's connection to these figures is clear: Be their desires bisexual or lesbian, these figures constitute a sapphic sisterhood of cinematic spectrality haunting heterosexual spaces. On the other hand, however, the lesbian specter as negated image functions as heterosexuality's repudiated opposite in ways a bisexual figure cannot. As Mandy Merck describes in her glossing of Castle's arguments, "The homosexual phantom gains entry to representation by virtue of its deniability: its ghostly appearance allows the culture both to register and to refuse its existence."[131] Yet the les(bi)an vampire's bisexual movement between spaces of intragender and extragender sexuality speaks not to an oppositional negativity but to a transgressive compresence that inheres across spaces delimited as separate, thus refuting the logic of the spatial delineations themselves. The les(bi)an vampire's spectrality is rooted not in absolute negation but in her crossings of multiple boundaries between that which is normative and that which is negated.

The les(bi)an vampire's boundary crossings parallel those of Hemmings's bisexual double agent. She describes this figure as "the 'outside' (which is also 'inside'), and the 'inside' (which is also 'outside'). . . . A double-agent appears to be part of one camp but is also strongly identified with another. . . . [They are] a link between the two worlds (heterosexual and homosexual), yet actually disrupts the very boundaries of the worlds we assume to be separate."[132] This rich description of bisexuality's spatial politics is echoed elsewhere in Hemmings's writing when she calls bisexuality an "abstract and curiously lifeless middle ground."[133] The spatial language of "inside," "outside," "camps," "worlds," "boundaries," and "ground" is particularly germane here, as is the lifelessness with which Hemmings characterizes the "middle ground." The unpredictability of the bisexual figure's movements—their lack of singular aim—poses a spatial threat. What Hemmings describes as the disruption of boundaries of "worlds we assume to be separate" speaks to Maurice Merleau-Ponty's perspicuity that "space is not the setting (real or logical) in which things are arranged, but the means whereby the position of things becomes possible."[134] The les(bi)an vampire affects the position of things through her nonlinear positionality; her transgressions into space change those very spaces, as well as those who share them. As with Fran and Miriam's defiance of the rules of continuity editing—appearing, without explanation, behind Harriet—the les(bi)an vampire's surprise transgression into the frame signals a realignment of cinematic space. By venturing into disparate spaces—often with aplomb, ease, impunity, and sometimes via preternatural means—the les(bi)an vampire proffers positional possibilities that resist monosexual demarcation while also disrupting a prior sense of cinematic space through her intrusions.

Yet these perpetual crossings, while radical in their undoing of spatial difference, simultaneously mark the les(bi)an vampire as a figure unable to lay claim to a home. In Fran and Miriam's wanderings between country house and caravan, roads and woods, they insinuate themselves, yet they remain homeless. Even the country house is not their home but the site of their death to which they are ceaselessly drawn. While we can read the les(bi)an vampire's transgression of spaces as a radical means through which borders are contested, we might also interpret her as a figure doomed to alienation. Like the bisexual, whose places in the straight world and gay community have been equally contested, the les(bi)an vampire is forever out of place. Sara Ahmed suggests that "to become straight means that we not only have to turn towards the objects that are given to us by heterosexual culture, but also that we must 'turn away' from objects that take us off this line. The queer subject within straight culture hence deviates."[135] Within Ahmed's formulation, *queer* is presented as synonymous with *gay*: a subjective position whose orientation deviates from extragender normativity toward intragender object choice. How does the bisexual become oriented stably in such spaces? They cannot. The bisexual is fated to exist in spatial flux, turning toward and away, closer then awry, in proximity then at distance, in a ceaseless dance that transgresses multiple lines. This spatial experience is what Hemmings describes when she terms the bisexual a "subject of dislocation," questioning to what extent "one can form any sense of belonging on the basis of temporary [spatial] identifications and alliances."[136] In this sexual geography, the les(bi)an vampire's relationship to space takes on a different hue: She transgresses to evade capture, she seems out of place because she has none to which she can lay claim.

The les(bi)an vampire troubles notions of space just as spaces trouble her. As a foreigner trying to acculturate, she often blends in, but, at times, the marks of her origins are discernible: Fran and Miriam's glamorous outfits, for example, appear out of place in the English countryside—creating unease in others upon the suspicion that this body might not belong in its surroundings. Yet the les(bi)an vampire body passes as one that *might* belong; as it passes through space, it parses the very notion of spatial belonging. As this body's navigation of space threatens others, so too does it threaten the logics that demarcate it as threatening. In patrician quarters, the les(bi)an vampire insinuates herself, the ornamented walls a safeguard against those who wish her harm, entombing her in a shelter where an opulent, queer excess can manifest. In these spaces we find Fran and Miriam's borrowed bedroom where carnal excesses unfold, the ornate bathrooms where *Countess Dracula*'s Elisabeth Nádasdy (Ingrid Pitt) and *Immoral Tales*' Erzsébet Báthory (Paloma Picasso) take baths of blood, the lush cubbyhole where *The Velvet Vampire*'s Diane satiates her voyeurism, the candlelit dungeon where *The Devil's Plaything*'s vampire women enjoy corybantic orgies. Yet the les(bi)an vampire is not confined to these recesses of erotic excess; she travels into worlds anew where others' perceptive shortcomings grant her license to roam untrammeled. Yes, she is homeless, but might her destitution signify a freedom in space, a freedom unshackled by spatial organization? To where shall she wander? The les(bi)an vampire's seamless vacillation between spaces, like the fluctuations of the bisexual's object choices, renders her future destinations unknowable.

The Allure of Unintelligibility

TED.	You're not easy to understand.
FRAN.	That's the way I have to be accepted: with no questions and no explanations.

Writing in the 1920s on the development of suspense film, Béla Balázs proposes that "a vampire is more frightening than a murder. . . . The surprise caused by a new unsuspected danger can never seem as uncanny as one that keeps recurring, that we continually expect, that is therefore really present all the time and that turns into a vengeful, implacable, mysterious fate."[137] For Balázs, the cinematic vampire's potential for omnipresence, recurrence, and undetectability is infinitely more terrifying than a sudden paroxysm of violence committed by a figure of recognizable alterity. The threat that always lurks but which cannot always be seen elicits suspenseful terror. Balázs's observations speak to the alignment between the figure of the vampire and a kind of threatening unintelligibility, later crystallized in the generic motif of the vampire's nonreflection. The revelation of Elizabeth's lack of reflection in *Daughters of Darkness* is paralleled in *Vampyres* in a moment when Ted discovers a papered-over mirror in the postcoital bedroom. Tearing back the sheet, he reveals the mirror, ostensibly covered up by Fran to avert the eyes of mortal visitors who might encounter her reflective absence. The interplay between the visible and invisible is not only a foundational tool of meaning creation in the cinema but also a means through which sexualities are made intelligible. The les(bi)an vampire's failures in symbolic intelligibility transgress the terms of recognition through which sexual types are made knowable.[138] However, for the les(bi)an vampire, these negations or reversals of subjective-symbolic coherence mean not a negation or reversal of a semiotic function but a polysemous plethora of signs whose relationship to their supposed referents is revealed to be incoherent, dissimulative.

What is remarkable about the les(bi)an vampire is how her refusal to signify monolithically does not negate her bisexual allure but rather constitutes it. Any character, and any spectator, might find in her something symbolically strange but seductively disruptive. This allure speaks to what San Filippo identifies as "the fascination and anxiety the vampire provokes [stemming] expressly from her liminality and (in)visibility."[139] The cinematic les(bi)an vampire's transgression of monosexist logic is both enthralling and terrifying. Rather than decry the polysemous cinematic image of the les(bi)an vampire, we can instead consider the import of her alluring disruptions along the lines Sue-Ellen Case proposes: "Her bite pierces platonic metaphysics and subject/object positions; and her fanged kiss brings her the chosen one, trembling with ontological, orgasmic shifts, into the state of the undead. What the dominant discourse represents as an emptying out, a draining away, in contrast to the impregnating kiss of the heterosexual, becomes an activism in representation."[140] Here, the les(bi)an vampire's preclusion from the symbolic is fashioned as a quality from which to build a politics of representation uninvested in the ruse of linear signification. Such are the fundamental bisexual erotics that structure the les(bi)an vampire's figuration, her interstitiality conveying not a lesbian oppositionality or a radically separate form of sexual alterity but that which threatens social orderings in its multiple heterotopies. Yet further, the draw of the les(bi)an vampire threatens to render others bisexual: to turn women away from their husbands, to render men penetrable. As in Gilles Deleuze and Félix Guattari's characterization: "The vampire does not filiate, it infects. The difference is that contagion, epidemic, involves terms that are entirely heterogeneous."[141] As the les(bi)an vampire infects via bisexual seductions, so too does she contest the monosexual singularity of her target, their tapered homogeneity. The les(bi)an vampire brings to bear that which monosexuality repudiates: a heterogeneous bisexual excess that—ineluctably—will recrudesce.

CHAPTER 2

TREACHERY IN LESBIAN CINEMA

She Must Be Seeing Things (1987)

Whereas the les(bi)an vampire films I discussed in the previous chapter emerged in the context of exploitation and popular cinemas, this chapter considers a radically different creative locus: lesbian cinema. This is a context in which issues around gender and sexuality were addressed directly in the formulation of a counterhegemonic cinema expressly influenced by lesbian theory, politics, and activism. This chapter asks how figurations of bisexual transgression function in these films in relation to contemporary debates around the bisexual woman in both lesbian politics and lesbian community. Disparate though popular les(bi)an vampire film and political lesbian cinema may be, contiguities can be traced in their figurations of transgressive bisexuality that speak to shared tendencies across divergent industrial and ideological contexts. As a means of navigating from les(bi)an vampire cinema to lesbian cinema, let us consider *The Mark of Lilith* (Bruna Fionda, Polly Gladwin, and Zachary Nataf, 1986), which offers a compelling critical bridge by virtue of its mutual investment in both lesbian feminist politics and the figure of the les(bi)an vampire. A British medium-length film made by three filmmakers studying under Laura

Mulvey's tutelage, *The Mark of Lilith* fuses moments of lesbian and feminist political and theoretical inquiry with fictional narrative.[1] The former comes in the form of didactic moments of direct address to camera, and the latter comprises a series of encounters between Zena (Pamela Lofton), a scholarly Black lesbian feminist activist, and Lillia (Susan Franklyn), a white les(bi)an vampire torn between the world of patriarchal mythology and an inchoate political awakening.[2] In Lillia's exchanges with Zena, we find an encounter between not only mortal and vampire but also Black and white, activist and apolitical, lesbian and bisexual.

The Mark of Lilith outlines various points of social contradistinction that map issues animating lesbian and feminist activism and theory: women's relations to cultural myths, the intersections of racism and misogyny, the politicization of apolitical women, and the frictions between bisexual and lesbian women. Lillia is presented as symbolically coextensive with the les(bi)an vampire figure I have traced: She is heavily made-up, feminine, white, bisexual; importantly, she is yoked to a fantastical realm structured by patriarchal myth. Zena, however, emanates from contemporary social reality: A Black woman engaged with antiracist politics, she wears casual outfits donning activist badges; as the film's only direct addressor, her voice is presented as that of a pedagogue. By establishing this dichotomy, Lillia is figured in relation to that which is dominant, normative, and unenlightened, while Zena's figuration conveys that which is marginal, antinormative, and critically minded.

In one scene, the two women share a bed together, and Lillia tries to bite Zena's neck as she sleeps. When Zena awakes, startled, she hurries to the other side of the room, before Lillia tries to justify her actions.

LILLIA.   Can't you see what I am? I thought you knew. . . .
                 It's not me that wants to do this to you, it's my
                 instincts. . . . I'm changing. I've been on the edge
                 of something for a long time now.

. . .

ZENA.   Why should I trust you, Lillia?
LILLIA.   Can't you understand how hard it is to change? I do
                 respect you, but I don't want to lose myself.

. . .

ZENA.   You don't have to accept their expectations.

In this exchange, the centrality of desire as a point of contestation mirrors contemporary debates in lesbian politics as to whether desire constitutes an unassailable drive, resistant to change by political persuasion, or, conversely, whether it is *the* personal-political locus that a politically conscious woman must interrogate and, ultimately, transform.[3]

The depiction of Lillia as bound to patriarchy, femininely embodied, apolitical, and resistant to change reflects, more precisely, attitudes toward female bisexuality in certain areas of lesbian politics—what I later term *bi-exclusionary lesbian ethics*. In presenting Lillia's eventual decision to reject her vampire bisexuality in favor of a new life with Zena, director Bruna Fionda reflects that the filmmakers wanted to suggest a "subtle positive choice implied by rejecting her male lover in favour for her female lover."[4] Zena's moments of direct address ask us to consider the appropriative power of mythological figures emanating from patriarchal contexts for a lesbian feminist politics. In *The Mark of Lilith*'s mobilization of the figure of the les(bi)an vampire, it enacts such a process, taking the les(bi)an vampire's extant sexual and transgressive associations and repurposing them in ways that chime with contemporary lesbian debates around bisexual women. Here, the bisexual woman's trustworthiness, her relation to men, and her political commitments take on dangerously transgressive associations, marking a recurrent tendency observable across much lesbian cinema. But rather than simply buttressing or consolidating ideas of the bisexual woman's dangerousness, this cinema has engaged with these ideas in a more critical fashion. In lesbian cinema, we find, at once, figurations that correspond to the circulation of ideas around bisexual transgression within lesbian cultures and sharp critiques of these ideas that deploy film aesthetics and form to explore the inconsistencies, contradictions, and ideological ramifications of these characterizations.

This chapter concerns invocations of female bisexuality in narrative cinema that circulated as lesbian film between the late 1970s and the 1990s. My central focus is Sheila McLaughlin's *She Must Be Seeing Things* (1987), which—in its explicit engagement with the dynamics between a lesbian-identified woman and a woman with bisexual desires—enjoins critical bisexual reappraisal. Between these decades, overlapping feminist and lesbian political movements flourished across western Europe, North America, and Australasia. This was a time when many women filmmakers undertook the knotty, expressly feminist, or lesbian feminist project of articulating an antipatriarchal or antiheterosexist cinema. Although these films were industrially marginal, they have proven historically significant in the various formal, stylistic, and representational approaches they deployed to effect a cinema that challenged the reproduction of patriarchal and heterosexist norms. The 1970s saw the emergence of women's film festivals, a cultural component of second-wave feminism's championing of female creative autonomy.[5] Against this backdrop of investment in female film authorship, specifically lesbian feminist film organizations champion- ing the work of lesbian filmmakers were founded in the United States.[6] Many of these filmmakers were as involved with emergent lesbian feminist com- munities as they were engaged with developments in feminist film theory, wherein questions of cinema's relation to gender, sexuality, desire, voyeurism, the body, and the gaze animated publications, conferences, and classrooms in- ternationally.[7] Here, a central question emerged for feminist filmmakers as to how to express female desire outside of patriarchal cinematic paradigms; for lesbian filmmakers, this question carried the additional burden of how to fig- ure desires toward women differently to the heteropatriarchal tendencies that feminist critics were scrutinizing.

Given that patriarchal ideology is, perhaps, most clearly discernible in clas- sical narrative cinema (and that this style was the focus of early feminist film theorists like Sharon Smith and Laura Mulvey), the eschewal of narrative form spelled, for some, a divestment from patriarchy.[8] Others, however, were less convinced of narrative's irreparability. When Annette Kuhn asks, "What are the implications for feminism of a classic realist cinema which is 'affirmative' of women?" she underscores the conflict between hegemonic form (narra- tive classical realism) and counterhegemonic ideology (feminism).[9] The 1970s film scholarship addressing gay representation displays a similar wariness of narrative cinema, with Richard Dyer's "Gays in Film" highlighting how spe- cific films' narrative frameworks "implicitly reinforce the heterosexual, sex- role norms."[10] Yet, as Edith Becker, Michelle Citron, Julia Lesage, and B. Ruby Rich outline, there is, for lesbian filmmakers, a "tension between creating new forms and maintaining contact with the audience they serve," wherein nar- rative constitutes both an efficient mode of communication and a source of spectatorial pleasure.[11] Discussing her decision to move from avant-garde to narrative filmmaking, Sheila McLaughlin recalls, "We had to think about pleasure and there is a kind of pleasure in narrative. . . . I like a story."[12] Al- though avant-garde and documentary film were the preeminent modes of les- bian filmmaking from the 1970s onward, narrative fiction film continued to be made by lesbian women, many of whom lived and worked in the context of lesbian community and politics.

The task of articulating a lesbian narrative cinema has not been approached monolithically, and, in many cases, the line between narrative and nonnarra- tive cinema is murky. Nevertheless, we can observe between the 1970s and the 1990s an international array of filmmakers who have been discussed in relation to lesbian cinema (although not all of them identify, or have always identified, as lesbians), including Lizzie Borden, Nicole Conn, Catherine Corsini, Donna Deitch, Cheryl Dunye, Cheryl Newbrough, Midi Onodera, Ulrike Ottinger, Léa Pool, Pratibha Parmar, Yvonne Rainer, Patricia Rozema, Monika Treut, and Rose Troche. These filmmakers' corpora maintain an investment in narrative, albeit not always exclusively. My turn to lesbian narrative cinema is guided by a curiosity toward how, in a cinematic mode predicated, to varying degrees, on comprehension and identification, bisexuality is made meaningful through figures who trouble set notions of identity. Becker, Citron, Lesage, and Rich stress that "lesbian films cannot be considered outside the context of the lesbian community . . . [and its] daily contradictions. . . . The recognition and working through of conflict."[13] These films, which have typically been discussed in relation to notions of lesbian, feminist, lesbian feminist, and queer cinema, also offer a unique set of approaches toward bisexuality. Attending to these aspects of lesbian film responds to Amy Villarejo's call for "investigations into specific visualizations of what we condense in the term *lesbian* in order to understand the slippages those visualizations struggle to contain, the limits at which representation functions."[14] It is here that the slipperiness with which certain lesbian discourses have characterized the bisexual woman effects representational slippages that trouble what Villarejo identifies as the demand to render *lesbian* static in the image.[15] These bisexual figures can be seen to threaten conventions of narrative intelligibility as they simultaneously complicate notions of lesbian politics, culture, or subjectivity predicated on exclusion.

Cultural Circulations of Bi-Exclusionary Lesbian Ethics

> If a lesbian has sex with a man, her whole life choice becomes suspect.
> —Daria (Anastasia Sharp) in *Go Fish* (Rose Troche)

Political and cultural connections between lesbianism and feminism have been articulated across a range of interpenetrating social justice movements from the 1970s to the 1990s, including lesbian feminism, political lesbianism, revolutionary lesbianism, radical lesbianism, and lesbian separatism. In the 1970s, the first decade of lesbian politics' proliferation, Jed Samer observes how the term *lesbian* "maintained an amorphous shape. How and why one became a lesbian and even what being a lesbian entailed varied greatly."[16] Despite this conceptual breadth, key individuals, organizations, and publications proposed more didactically expressed, more narrowly defined, and more exclusively circumscribed articulations of lesbian feminist politics in which female bisexuality came to signify a problem.[17] Consider lesbian activist Robin

Morgan's controversial revelation at the 1973 West Coast Lesbian Conference that she was in a relationship with a man. After professing her male partner's atypicality as a man (his membership of the men's antisexist groups the Flaming Faggots and the Effeminists), she goes on to distance herself from bisexuality, castigating "people who have used the word [*bisexual*] as a coward's way to avoid dealing with homosexuality. . . . We all know that ploy."[18] Morgan's eschewal of bisexuality, despite her own relationship with a man, is useful in establishing a cultural landscape in which female bisexuality constituted, in certain lesbian spaces, a cardinal bad object. This is a phenomenon I will term *bi-exclusionary lesbian ethics*. Importantly, the identification of this phenomenon should not suggest that all lesbian communities, or even lesbian feminist politics per se, are necessarily monosexist or biphobic, nor does it mean that lesbians or lesbian feminists should be considered as such. Indeed, some of the most potent critiques around the treatment of female bisexuality in lesbian feminist spaces has come from lesbian feminists themselves, including Amber Ault and Sharon-Dale Stone.[19] Instead, it names a persistent antibisexual axiom—sometimes presented as a coherent political credo, sometimes expressed as a general feeling of social suspicion, distrust, or disparagement—that is discernible in certain expressions of lesbian thinking, politics, or culture.

In calling this phenomenon an "ethics," I am inspired by the dialogue between Sarah Lucia Hoagland and Elisabeth D. Däumer. Hoagland, writing in 1988, is critical of an expression of lesbian ethics—a set of lesbian moral principles—informed by the desire to control external forces and either to praise or to blame others dependent on choices deemed to be either good or bad.[20] Däumer's intervention into Hoagland's discussion explores how bisexuals' being "both inside and outside a diversity of conflicting communities" poses important challenges to forms of lesbian ethics predicated on aversion to external threat and the adjudication of moral choice.[21] Bi-exclusionary lesbian ethics thus names the set of moral principles devaluing female bisexuality as a bad choice that must be controlled against and against which a lesbian ethics of exclusion is positioned.

In discursive expressions of this ethics, female bisexuality is regularly demarcated as troublesome, threatening, and treacherous. As Lillian Faderman summarizes: "In the '70s and '80s, radical lesbian-feminists were vociferous in their anger against women who said they were bisexual. It seemed to them treacherous and incomprehensible that women who had fought side by side with them on the battleground of feminism and who understood both the political significance and the pleasures of lesbianism would desert lesbian-feminism to sleep in the enemy camp."[22] The existence of a bisexual problem can be found in lesbian texts from the early 1970s up until the 1990s. While the term *les-bian feminism* had mostly fallen out of favor by the mid-1980s, bi-exclusionary lesbian ethics persisted in various aspects of lesbian culture. These assertions continued most fervently in British and Australian writing circulating in con-texts of radical feminism, lesbian separatism, and political lesbianism. In the United States, these conflicts are documented in anecdotal writing in which we find painful accounts from women whose bisexualities resulted in their os-tracism from activist and community life, a form of excommunication that Elizabeth Armstrong describes as being "cast into the outer darkness."[23] Writ-ing by women who once identified as lesbians but later developed relationships with men attests to the agony of these expulsions.[24] Lilith Finkler reflects, "The woman I had quietly mocked before was the very woman I now faced every morning in the mirror."[25] Although the lesbian communities that bur-geoned in the 1970s often embraced a broad church of women under the term, the bisexual woman continued to resurface in the decades that followed as a figure susceptible to ostracism.

The cause of these exclusions is rooted, most fundamentally, in the tenets of political lesbianism, which generally refers to the idea that lesbianism, or "woman-identification"—directing one's social, romantic, and cultural atten-tions toward other women—is prerequisite to the practice of feminist liber-ation. Bisexual women's retention of attraction toward men thus falls short of this credo. Political lesbianism conceives of lesbianism as a choice that all women are capable of making. It contends that, because relations between men and women are plagued—insuperably—by patriarchy, lesbianism is the praxis through which to eschew men and, ergo, patriarchy in a woman's per-sonal and community life. Sheila Jeffreys is perhaps the most extreme example in her articulation of this politics, contending that "the choice to love only women resists a fundamental principle enforced by male supremacy . . . that of man-loving. Gay men, heterosexual women, bisexual women, heterosexual men, all love men. They are conformists. Only lesbians are resisters and reb-els who put women first and refuse to love men against all the pressures of the male-dominant, man-loving culture."[26] In this framework, desire toward men is always already subject to patriarchal corruption. Thus, a heterosexual woman (some preferred the term *pre-lesbian*) was simply a woman who had yet to come to terms with the fact of her oppression.[27] Many lesbian feminists ad-vocate the Marxist term *false consciousness* to describe this state, out of which one could be delivered by efforts in lesbian feminist consciousness-raising.[28] Elizabeth Reba Weise explains that, in this ideological outlook, bisexual women "were merely women who hadn't yet overcome the false consciousness of thinking they *chose* to be with men."[29] As Jill Johnston's foundational lesbian feminist text puts it, in no uncertain terms: "Bisexuality is a state of political oblivion and unconsciousness."[30]

The monosexual imperative that one must fall on one or the other side of the gay-straight binary is, in some ways, complicated by political lesbianism, which considers a woman's sexuality prior to consciousness-raising to be mutable. After consciousness-raising, however, the monosexual imperative takes a specifically political lesbian form in which only two options are available: lesbianism being the politically necessary choice, heterosexuality being the politically retrograde one. Writing in the American lesbian feminist magazine *Furies* in 1973, Loretta Ulmschneider contends that "lesbians represent that part of every woman that male supremacy has destroyed or suppressed.... Women who practice bisexuality today are simply leading highly privileged lives that do not challenge male power and that, in fact, undermine the feminist struggle."[31] In Ulmschneider's characterization, bisexual women have not made adequate sacrifice—have not sufficiently challenged male power—to embody the lesbian feminism she envisions, which involves severing sexual (and sometimes friendly) relations to men. Sharon-Dale Stone highlights how female bisexuality was often conceived of as a perfunctory attempt at political lesbianism, reflecting that "lesbian feminist ideology held that by choosing to sleep with men, [bisexual] women were demonstrating their essential lack of commitment to women."[32] In these strands of political lesbian ideology, the political choice of centering women necessitates a correspondent decentering of men. For groups like Berkeley's Gutter Dyke Collective, bisexual women's failure to repudiate men was taken as proof that "male approval and identification is still primary to their existence."[33] For these lesbian feminist thinkers, the presence of men among a woman's object choices reveals a commitment to patriarchy, a threat to lesbian feminism, a mark of inauthenticity. This position is taken to what is perhaps its logical end by Marilyn Murphy, who proposes that "women who call themselves 'bisexual,' not because they are in transition or are afraid of their lesbianism, but because they choose to relate sexually to both women and men, are the only women who are really heterosexual. They are the only women who choose to relate to men after having known and experienced a non-compulsory alternative."[34] Unlike the "pre-lesbian" women who have not yet undergone consciousness-raising, Murphy contends that bisexual women—in their retention of desire toward men, despite their full knowledge of the subjugation of women through heterosexuality—are the real heterosexuals.[35] Bisexual women's desire toward men spells heterosexual complicity.

This disparagement toward female bisexuality not only invokes bisexual women's supposed partial commitment to lesbianism and feminism but also ideates them as both attached to male ascendency and larcenous in their partaking in lesbian feminist life. Murphy's characterization of bisexual women's involvement in lesbian communities invokes ideas of theft, describing bisexual women's involvement with the movement as "a way of profiting from their inclusion in the camaraderie and richness of the lesbian community, in addition to the joys of women-loving, without accepting the individual and societal penalties that 'real' lesbians suffer."[36] In this economic metaphor, the lesbian community's richness, camaraderie, and joys are positioned as bounties to be earned through the endurance of social and interpersonal experiences of lesbophobia. Because, according to Murphy, bisexual women do not experience the latter, they are conceived of as pillagers of the former. Here, we might consider the economic rhetoric that animates Clare Hemmings's description of the anxiety induced by bisexual women in certain lesbian cultures, when she writes: "I think that to a large degree the fear of bisexual women is . . . the fear that the secrets of a lesbian subculture will be sold to the dominant heterosexual culture at the price of a one-night stand."[37] This is also the conception from which Hemmings develops her idea of the bisexual double agent, a figure harmonizing with characterizations of bisexual women as spies (also see the New York City–based C.L.I.T. Collective, who describe bisexual women's being in lesbian communities as a "Reconnaissance Mission").[38] Here, the bisexual woman is cast as an infiltrator into lesbian space whose underhanded dealings and purportedly inevitable return to heterosexuality threatens the lesbian herself. Across these lesbian discourses we thus find a range of reprobative characterizations of the bisexual woman, who is made meaningful through an array of transgressive figures: the traitor, the Laodicean, the interloper, the thief, the spy, the mercenary. Here we find the bisexual woman cast as a figure to whom ideas of political or moral dishonor were imputed.

Allusions to bi-exclusionary lesbian ethics can be found in some key examples from 1990s American lesbian cinema, which provide wry commentaries on the previous decades' lesbian thinking while attending to the persistence of contemporary suspicions toward bisexual women in lesbian communities. Films like Cheryl Dunye's short *The Potluck and the Passion* (1993) and Rose Troche's feature *Go Fish* (1994) play on their status as reflexive lesbian independent films, featuring recognizable lesbian archetypes, community in-jokes, and esoteric points of cultural reference. In a memorable scene in *Go Fish*, Daria (Anastasia Sharp)—who identifies as a lesbian—has sex with a male friend of hers. Following this, she daydreams of being kidnapped by a group of women who bring her to a kangaroo court where she is put on trial for her transgression. This hyperbolic presentation of Daria's interrogation and defense works to parody the stringency and intensity of prohibitions against female bisexuality in certain lesbian cultures. A similar critique of antipathy toward bisexual women can be found in *The Potluck*, which portrays an interracial group of women as they meet for a potluck dinner. Here, one of the guests, Evelyn (Pat Branch), reveals that she fell in love with a man while vacationing in Liberia. As the night continues, another guest, Meaghan (Nora Breen), becomes jealous that her date, Tracy (Shelita Birchett), is building a rapport with Evelyn. As Meaghan and Tracy wash dishes, they discuss Evelyn:

MEAGHAN.   I think she's arrogant and self-centered. She's not even a lesbian.

TRACY.   How do you know what she isn't? You don't even know her.

. . .

MEAGHAN.   (*To camera.*) I really don't get what's up with her. She meets this Black woman for a total of three hours, a woman who doesn't even identify as a lesbian, and starts ignoring me.

While the dynamics at play between these characters obviously explore tensions around race—Evelyn and Tracy are Black, Meaghan is white—these also intersect with issues of sexuality. Meaghan sees in Evelyn's past extragender relationship a means of discrediting Evelyn to Tracy. Dunye, in her humorous portrait of the fissiparity of queer female social life, shows how a woman's bisexuality can be used to cast aspersions on her character, a phenomenon that is also referenced in one of Yvonne Rainer's more narrative films, MURDER and murder (1996). In a postcoital conversation between Mildred (Kathleen Chalfant) and Doris (Joanna Merlin), Doris chides Mildred that her lesbianism has never been called into question. Mildred retorts, "My old girlfriend always said I wasn't the real thing because I'd had sex with men." Doris, who has only recently started calling herself a lesbian, is despondent: "Oh, Christ. They'll never let me into the club after my lifetime of copulation." Later, Doris dreams she attempts sex with a man (Gordon Synn) but resolves not to tell Mildred that she had desired him. Rainer's metacommentary offers a sardonic meditation on the verboten status of extragender desire in certain lesbian spaces, while attesting to its enduring existence—in past and present alike. Like *The*

Potluck's Tracy, who asks not "How do you know what Evelyn is?" but "How do you know what she *isn't?*," *MURDER and murder* critiques a repudiative model of lesbian being. In their engagements with the persistence of bisexuality in lesbian spaces, Troche's, Dunye's, and Rainer's films question the monosexist imperative to taper one's desires as they question the ability for any one relationship, any one desire, to have a totalizing effect over sexual identity.[39]

With films like *Go Fish*, *The Potluck*, and *MURDER and murder*, which teem with garrulous, politically engaged characters, engagements with and critiques of bi-exclusionary lesbian ethics can be analyzed through dialogue. But this is just one route of inquiry into the question of how bisexual transgression comes to be figured in lesbian cinema.[40] Turning to questions of visuality and form opens up different avenues as to how bisexuality affects the lesbian film. Weise writes that "to be a bisexual-feminist woman means to live an intensely examined life."[41] The forms of this intense examination in lesbian cinema can only be understood with reference to bi-exclusionary lesbian ethics, a set of principles that is, at times, cogent and logically systematic but, at others, paradoxical and incoherent. It is within these latter spaces of instability that the bisexual figure effects formal instabilities in lesbian cinema, her transgressions carrying with them the threat of razing the very foundations of a bi-exclusionary conceptualization of lesbian being, politics, or culture.

Indices of Extragender Desire: She Must Be Seeing Men

In July of 1988, excerpts of *She Must Be Seeing Things* were screened at a plenary session of London's Lesbian Summer School. This screening, facilitated by instructors Cherry Smyth and Campbell X, polarized the school's participants. Rumors circulated that the film contained "brutal scenes of lesbian sado-masochism . . . heterosexual rape . . . violence against women."[42] When the screening began, some participants tried to rip the film from the projector.[43] Unsuccessful in their attempts, a group of women, including Sheila Jeffreys, set up what Susan Ardill and Sue O'Sullivan recall as a "safe space for lesbians to come to if they were distressed by the film."[44] Smyth remembers this space being demarcated a "Porn-Free Zone," an inference that *Seeing Things* was itself a pornographic film.[45] Seven months later, strong reactions to the film showed no signs of waning upon the announcement that *Seeing Things* would be screened at the Manchester movie theater the Cornerhouse. In the two weeks prior to the British release, the theater's director received phone calls with threats to discredit her to funders and, on three occasions, the cinema's fire alarms were set off in a series of hoaxes.[46] When the film began its run, the Cornerhouse was met with pickets and ambushes of the stage. In Bristol, women's venues were flyered by activists warning not to see the film; at a theater showing *Seeing Things* in Bradford, cement was poured down a toilet in protest.[47] These virulent protests reached their apotheosis when a fake bomb was left in the Cornerhouse, leading to a panicked evacuation.[48] What was it about *Seeing Things* that precipitated such impassioned reactions? The whisperings Ardill and O'Sullivan recall—that the film depicted brutal sadomasochism (S/M), heterosexual rape, and violence against women—prove either false or exaggerated. Given the insubstantiality of these rumors, I propose a return to the text itself. Upon closer inspection, the embellishments the film inspired can be traced, I contend, to a searing epicenter: the film's treatment of female bisexuality.[49]

Seeing Things is the third film by American director Sheila McLaughlin, who had previously made the experimental short film *Artificial Memory* (1976) and the feature-length *Committed* (1984), with codirector Lynne Tillman, a biopic of the life of actor Frances Farmer.[50] McLaughlin was part of the New York avant-garde artists' cooperative the Collective for Living Cinema, where she worked alongside Lizzie Borden, Heinz Emigholz, and Yvonne Rainer.[51] *Seeing Things* was shot in New York in coproduction with the West German Zweites Deutsches Fernsehen, which emerged in the United States as an ally to independent filmmakers after its support for Jim Jarmusch's *Stranger than Paradise* (1984). *Seeing Things* tells the story of Agatha (Sheila Dabney), a Black human rights lawyer of Brazilian heritage, and her lover Jo (Lois Weaver), a white American filmmaker.[52] Agatha is staying at Jo's New York apartment while Jo is out of town when she finds an old diary chronicling the men with whom Jo has had sex. While Jo attends a screening of a film of hers, she is invited to dinner by a man (Ed Bowes); she accepts this invitation and the two eat together, but Jo turns down his proposition to stay overnight. Agatha's discovery of Jo's diary compels her to suspect that Jo is cheating on her with a man. As Agatha's suspicions grow, she thinks she sees Jo acting romantically with men—kissing a man in the street, holding a man's hand, visiting a diner with a man (a date?)—but she cannot be sure. Agatha changes her appearance to become more butch, donning a suit and slicking back her hair. Meanwhile, Jo is directing a film dramatizing the life of Antonio de Erauso (referred to in the film by their birthname, Catalina), a Spanish nun who spent the early years of the seventeenth century traveling the world under a male identity.[53] Agatha enlists the help of the couple's gay mutual friend Eric (John Erdman) to find out if Jo is being unfaithful; Eric can find no basis for Agatha's suspicions. As Jo finishes editing her film, Agatha sits next to her; the two then leave the apartment late at night to have dinner.

The aspects of *Seeing Things* that garnered the most opprobrium among lesbian audiences were points of contention already polarizing 1980s lesbian politics. As Ardill and O'Sullivan explain: "Many of the issues around lesbian sexuality which have been simmering and occasionally boiling over for the past few years—butch/femme; domination and submission; who's a real lesbian (or feminist) and who isn't; and a relatively new entry to the rostrum, the relationship of heterosexuality to the sexuality of committed lesbians—have been sparked off again in lesbian discussion of this film."[54] In the 1980s, certain articulations of lesbian feminist doxa, formulated in 1970s theory and politics, met with challenges from heterodox dissidents within lesbian communities, an internecine conflict that was later termed the "lesbian sex wars." The film's depiction of butch-femme and domination and submission are the foci of much critical discussion around the film. Although I return later to how the film's presentation of butch-femme intersects with discussions around bisexuality, it is not necessary to rehash these debates. It is relevant, however, to note that both butch-femme and S/M were understood by some of the more dogmatic lesbian feminist thinkers as indexing heterosexuality or maleness. For Janice G. Raymond, these constitute "male power modes," and for Sheila Jeffreys "a sexual desire that eroticises power difference" is always heterosexual.[55] Although Raymond's and Jeffreys's arguments operate in a dichotomized schema wherein phenomena are demarcated as either lesbian feminist or patriarchally heterosexual, the process they describe spells less the threat of patriarchal heterosexuality than the presence of phenomena deemed patriarchal and heterosexist among queer women. This contamination is characteristically bisexual in its sexual compositeness. What is threatening for Raymond and Jeffreys is not simply heterosexuality's invasion but a bisexual breakdown of the boundaries between *lesbian* and *heterosexual*, which confounds the very terms upon which their articulation of lesbian feminism is predicated.

Beyond the film's depictions of butch-femme and sexual powerplay, *Seeing Things*' most clearly heterosexual impulse was to be found, for its detractors, in its depiction of a queer woman's desire toward men. These reactions would not have surprised McLaughlin, who, in fact, sought to explore this dangerous ground, saying: "What I wanted to do in this film was to foreground the relationship between the two women and then have that act in relation to male culture . . . to try to confront and be iconoclastic towards what have become lesbian and feminist taboos. . . . I was trying to deal openly with the ultimate lesbian horror, the fantasy of having sex with a man."[56] *Seeing Things* did, indeed, horrify some lesbian spectators. When Teresa de Lauretis screened the film on multiple occasions, she recalls that "lesbians especially were disturbed by the heterosexual fantasies."[57] McLaughlin remembers the film's extragender sex scenes being booed at some American screenings.[58] The *Pink Paper* reviewer Caz Gorham echoes these reactions, lamenting, "It is disappointing and perverse to discover that a film with lesbianism at it's [*sic*] heart has heterosexuality in its libido."[59] *Seeing Things*' depiction of the recurrence of desire toward men in a woman who desires women notably diverges from tendencies in American lesbian cinema that would become established by the end of the 1990s. In films such as *Desert Hearts* (Donna Deitch, 1985), *The Incredibly True Adventure of Two Girls in Love* (Maria Maggenti, 1995), and *But I'm a Cheerleader* (Jamie Babbit, 1999), a woman's heterosexuality is eschewed in favor of female object choice. The discomfort of *The Incredibly True Adventure*'s Evie (Nicole Ari Parker) and *But I'm a Cheerleader*'s Megan (Natasha Lyonne) around their boyfriends serves a proleptic function, establishing them as always-having-been lesbian, even before knowing it themselves. In *Seeing Things*, however, Jo is suspected not to have eschewed her extragender desire; her figuration resists a teleological narrative of lesbian becoming. The verboten status of desire toward men within contemporary lesbian cultures thus rendered the film's engagement with this topic disturbing, objectionable, and even perverse for some spectators.

Yet it was certain articulations of lesbianism as oppositional to or outside of heterosexuality that frustrated McLaughlin, who saw in these positions an erroneous denial of heterosexuality's social power over everyone. As she elaborates:

> Heterosexuality is the dominant code of the society that we live in, and it defines and in a sense creates our own sexuality, whether we choose to participate as literally heterosexual or not. I think it's somehow inescapable, that we're inextricably bound up with that. We've gone through a long time of trying to deny that, and yet it's important, if we ever want to get beyond that stage, to find a "new language" or whatever you want to call it, to work through that in some sort of discourse before we can . . . figure out what our desire is or is about.[60]

Writing *Seeing Things*, McLaughlin conceived of a woman who has participated in heterosexuality through her extragender desires and a woman who has not participated in it yet feels paranoid at the threat of heterosexuality through her partner's past desires. *Seeing Things* confronts head-on the pervasiveness

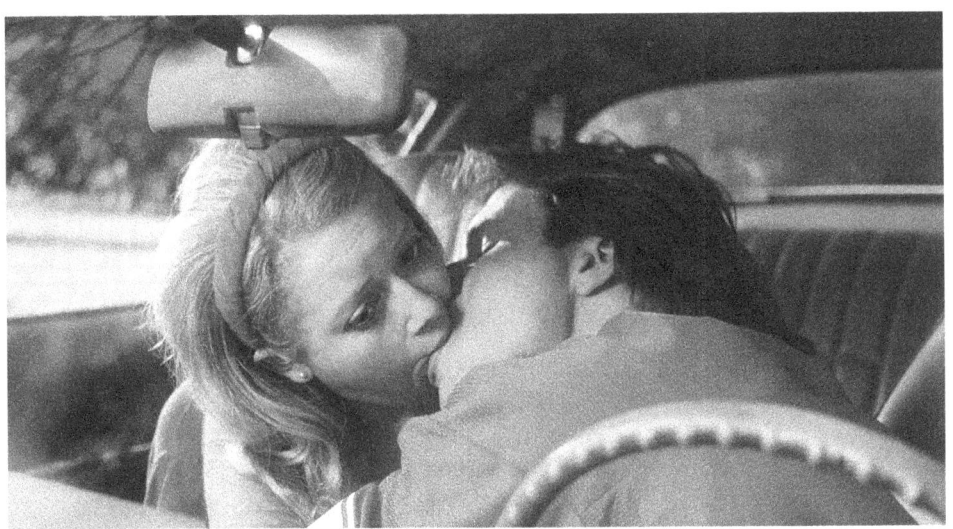

FIGURE 2.1 Megan (Natasha Lyonne) bungles a kiss with her boyfriend Jared (Brandt Wille). *But I'm a Cheerleader* (Jamie Babbit, 1999). Digital screen capture.

of extragender desire. In one of the pivotal texts of lesbian activism, Del Martin and Phyllis Lyon write that "fear, at some time or another, plays a big part in the life of every Lesbian. For the most part her fears are real; only rarely do they slip over into the realm of imagined fear, of paranoia."[61] This latter lesbian paranoia—distinct from the fears of lesbophobic oppression—can be seen in Agatha discovering Jo's past extragender relationships. However, rather than theorizing this paranoia as related to heterosexuality per se, I will resist a monosexist hermeneutic to attend to how it is, more accurately, Jo's bisexuality that incites Agatha's paranoia.

A key way in which *Seeing Things* indexes Jo's bisexuality is through a symbolically rich cinematic object: her diary. As Agatha tidies Jo's apartment, she attempts to organize an overflowing bookshelf. In the process, Agatha notices a Polaroid that has fallen on the floor. The photograph shows a man reclining in bed—naked, save a duvet. Agatha picks up the photograph and looks to Jo's bed beside her, recognizing it as the bed in the picture. She scoffs and mutters: "Slut." She returns the photograph to a book on the shelf before rummaging further, finding another Polaroid. Agatha then discovers a black book, a diary with appendages overgrowing its pages. As she begins to leaf through it, we watch in close-up as Agatha turns page after page filled with men's names, handwritten entries, and instant photographs. "Tom, David, Ned, John, Paul."

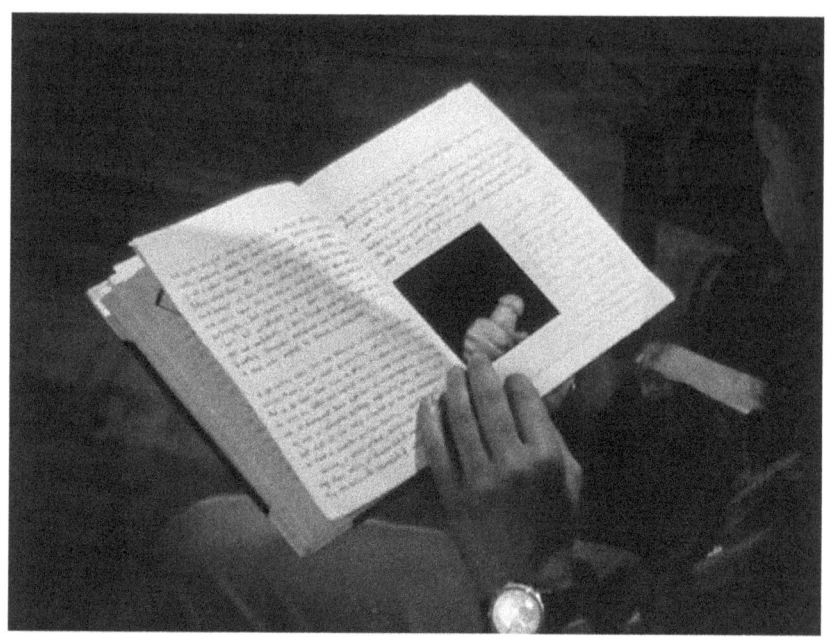

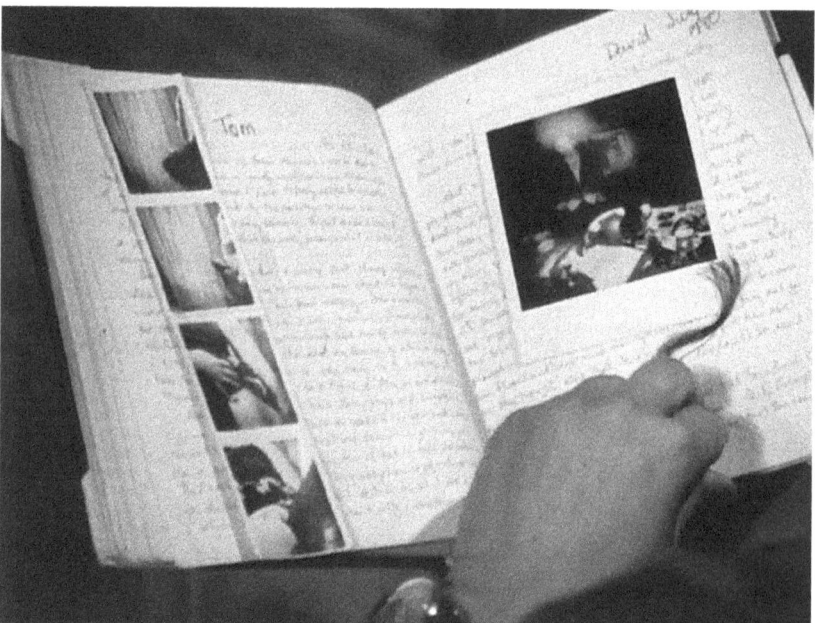

FIGURES 2.2–2.3 Agatha (Sheila Dabney) flips through Jo's (Lois Weaver) diary. *She Must Be Seeing Things* (Sheila McLaughlin, 1987). Digital screen captures.

Later in the film, Agatha reads again: "Chris, the guy from California prison, Sam, Robbie, Steve and Henry, Ed, Richard, Tony, Paul." The Polaroids are varied: a man in a photo booth, a man at a table, a man in a shower. One simply depicts an erect penis held in a fist. On two pages, lockets of hair are pasted.

We can parse precisely how *Seeing Things* invokes bisexual disruption through this diary through four considerations: of the reading modes engendered by the written word on film, of the form of diaries more broadly, of the idiosyncrasies of this particular diary, and of the formal mechanisms through which Agatha's discovery of it is structured. Francesco Casetti writes that "on the screen we can celebrate the becoming-things of objects."[62] Later, he suggests how these things' aesthetic treatment can affect their significance: "Things strike us but also implicate us. This occurs above all when they are shot in close-up."[63] It is through a prolonged close-up that *Seeing Things* announces Jo's diary as a cinematic object of import, a compelling thing possessing meaning in relation to Jo. This diary is a text within the text that the spectator is invited to read. Cinematic objects that contain writing demand a unique kind of cinematic reading, outlined by Belén Vidal in relation to the cinematic letter: "Due to [the] polysemic ambiguity between material object, text and sign, the [cinematic] letter . . . *literally* demands of the spectator to 'read' the cinematic image and to 'see' (and hear) writing embedded in the aural and visual textures of film."[64] An object of writing, the revelation of Jo's diary ushers a spectator's closer attention; it is a call to read, to interpret.

The nature of this writing is private and prurient: qualities with which diaries already share association.[65] As a record of Jo's sexual encounters with men, entries proceed without a sense of narrative arc or teleology. Rebecca Hogan reflects on the diary's narrative and temporal form that "what [diaries] have in common is their accumulation of discrete entries . . . their capturing of a series of 'present moments' in the diarist's life, their unfinishedness. . . . Diaries embody 'life as *process*, not *product*.'"[66] Diary form is unmoored from the narrative and temporal conventions to which most published prose is beholden. This feature of the diary is particularly significant in relation to sexuality's narrativization. Whereas narratives that naturalize monosexuality have been understood to deploy linear structures—heterosexuality's arc of coupling, marriage, and childbearing and the closeted-to-uncloseted journey of homosexuality—these teleological narratives of sexuality are incommensurate with the diary's unedited and unpremeditated form. This form is better suited to presenting sexual accounts that resist organization into a linear structure, and it is here that an affinity with bisexuality is discernible.

The bisexuality of Jo's diary is thus apparent not simply in the sexual acts to which it attests but through the diary's amenability to what have been theorized as bisexual reading modes. Frann Michel contends that reading bisexually "involves neither, on the one hand, just a reading of a static moment outside its history . . . nor, on the other hand, simply a teleological reading of narrative, in which the ending determines the significance of particular moments that have come before. It involves, instead, reading the tensions of an ongoing construction."[67] This nondeterministic approach to sexual narrative allows for a text's compositeness—its oscillations and inconsistencies—to remain unsystematized, an account of sexuality that need not signify along monosexual lines. For Agatha as reader, such a presentation of sexual history proves troubling. The surfeit of sexual encounters, structured in a chronicle of presents and recent pasts, poses a threat that seems at once excessive and immediate. Diary form presents the nowness of each of its entries while paradoxically telescoping a large stretch of time for its reader. This presentation of Jo's sexual past thus induces a reaction in Agatha as if Jo's sexual encounters are all happening in the present, attesting to the coincidence of her intragender and extragender desires.

Jo's diary also contains Polaroids and lockets of hair, additions carrying their own symbolic pertinence. Peter Buse remarks how "it is something of an open secret that Polaroid, by eliminating the darkroom and taking the professional photo-finisher out of the equation, turned countless of its users into amateur pornographers or erotic artists."[68] The Polaroid provides a means through which Jo memorializes each man, sometimes with explicit images that need not have been mediated through a third party. The Polaroid also possesses a unique material significance. As Buse continues, "Polaroid . . . added an extra dimension to the privately-made erotic image. There was a special kind of sensuality about the image itself . . . one whose charge was increased by appearing in the very scene in which it was made."[69] While all photographs have a close relationship to reality predicated upon their indexicality, the Polaroid carries an additional dimension of indexicality insofar as the photograph is created at the very site where the image it depicts existed. If, as Roland Barthes suggests, "photography's inimitable feature (its *noeme*) is that someone has seen the referent . . . *in flesh and blood*, or again *in person*," then an axillary noeme of Polaroid is that it, as object, has shared propinquity with the referent.[70] Agatha's recognition of Jo's bed in one of the Polaroids, a bed to which she is in spatial proximity, attests to the referent's material existence, endowing the other photographs with an eerie closeness. The diary's lockets of hair multiply this effect, providing Agatha with a slice of the realities the diary chronicles. Neither symbol nor index, the locket of hair is the referent itself, a part of the men in question. Through its incorporation of prose, Polaroid, and hair, Jo's diary combines discursive reflections and indexical representations with material cuttings. In the context of the diary's revelations—Jo's past relationships with men—this object must be understood as more than a record of Jo's past: It is a discursive-indexical-material repository of male sexual partners.

In a later scene, Agatha reads the diary (speaking its words in voiceover) as she and the camera pivot around a fulcrum, the apartment moving around her as she is centered in the frame.[71] This moment signals the film's first and most defamiliarizing break with classical style: The 180-degree rule is broken and the contrast between a stationary foreground and moving background highlights the shot's artifice. This formal abstraction produces a disorienting effect just as Agatha's perception of Jo's sexuality is being disoriented. Sara Ahmed's work on queer phenomenology is useful here in her argument that becoming lesbian involves a kind of reorientation: "While lesbians might have different temporal relations to 'becoming lesbians,' even lesbians who feel they were 'always that way,' still have to 'become lesbians,' which means *gathering such tendencies into specific social and sexual forms.* Such a gathering requires a 'habit-change,' to borrow a term from Teresa de Lauretis: it requires a reorientation of one's body such that other objects, those that are not reachable on the vertical and horizontal lines of straight culture, can be reached."[72] In Ahmed's theorization, the reorientation required to gather lesbian tendencies into the social and sexual forms of "being lesbian" is a reorientation of oneself away from the axes of straight culture. This process speaks to what Clare Hemmings describes as a "repudiative model of gendered and sexual subjectivity" in which the repudiation of one or the other gendered object constitutes the intelligible monosexual subject.[73] If we consider this reorientation or repudiation as a constitutive element in lesbian being, then Agatha's discovery of Jo's extragender objects might be said to produce a *disorienting* effect. Whereas "specific social and sexual forms" are achieved through the lesbian process of reorientation toward women and repudiation of men—most immovably in the context of bi-exclusionary lesbian ethics—these forms are troubled by the haunting return of extragender objects through Jo's portentous repository of desire. Agatha's encounter with the diary's photographs, in fact, recalls Barthes's conception of the photograph as having a spectral quality.[74] Agatha witnesses a resurrection of extragender objects in a subject who was assumed to have been reoriented toward intragender ones. In *Seeing Things*, this spectral rupture produces both hermeneutic and formal disorientations. As Jo's lesbian intelligibility is disoriented, so too is the film's treatment of space and perspective. An object attesting to bisexual desire produces a formal cinematic disruption.

Monosexual cinematic signification depends upon certain formal conventions. This relation is observable from the siloing of monogamous desire in shot-reverse shot editing patterns and the visual ovalization of couples in framing, analyzed by Cüneyt Çakırlar and Gary Needham in relation to gay cinema, to the postclassical convention Karl Schoonover and Rosalind Galt term "heterosynchrony," in which a narrative brings together disparate forces in a sequence of events that naturalize heterosexuality's fatedness.[75] These theorizations demonstrate how form can work to secure homosexuality's and heterosexuality's naturalized recognizability. Stanley Cavell argues that a cutting out of the world in favor of that which is photographed is ontological to a camera's mechanism, that this "explicit rejection" is "as essential in the experience of a photograph as what it explicitly presents."[76] A homology can be fostered between this ontological photographic quality and the cinematic forms through which monosexual monogamy is maintained. That which is cut out of the latter is the space of bisexual possibility. Beyond the lover's gaze or the couple's containment in-frame lie desirous alternatives. Beyond the narratives of synchronicity that render the couple's love fated lie asynchronous phenomena that speak, instead, to an aporic chaos. As the import of Jo's diary reveals itself to Agatha, there is not only a narrative revelation but a formal splintering wherein classical style ruptures. Up until this point, frames have contained bodies and objects. Now, however, the camera spins, producing a dizzying 360-degree panorama of space that has, heretofore, been cut out. *Seeing Things* undoes its adherence to classical style in concert with Agatha's discovery of bisexual possibilities. *Seeing Things* troubles the supposition of Jo's lesbianness as it rejects those formal mechanisms through which monosexuality has been naturalized.

Figuring Bi-Exclusionary Paranoia: Forms of Perception

Agatha holds Jo's diary as she sways in a rocking chair. Jo walks around the corner of a city street where she is met with machine-gun fire; she convulses and falls, her abdomen spattered with blood. An off-screen scream. Jo lays in front of a car; it is night, she has been run over. A bedroom lit in chiaroscuro: Jo lies dead, her lips a crimson red, her blond hair splayed, a phone cord wrapped around her neck; a howl tone rings out. Agatha looks concerned, then returns the diary to the shelf. In this sequence, we witness the murderous fantasies inspired by Agatha's reading of Jo's diary, a notably cinematic salvo of deaths. Chronologically, genre markers can be assigned to each of these tableaux: the gangster film, the thriller, the film noir. These cinematic citations recall the fates of cinema's wayward women: the stylized demises of sexually transgressive coquettes, vamps, and femmes fatales. This sequence, however, is one of the few moments in *Seeing Things* in which the fantastical nature of the images is clear. At other times, Agatha's paranoia is positioned in relation to images whose diegetic veracity is more ambiguous, evoking the titular question of whether or not Agatha "must be seeing things."

This title, *She Must Be Seeing Things*, serves as a critical springboard for Teresa de Lauretis, who proposes that the "must" in the title refers not to Agatha's perceptive shortcomings but to an assertion that "she can't help seeing things the way she does."[77] De Lauretis's interpretation points to a consideration of how Agatha's perception, like all perceptions, is reregulated by a hermeneutic. This phenomenon is, in fact, a central tenet of philosophical hermeneutics, which stipulates, as Hans-Georg Gadamer outlines, that "all understanding inevitably involves some prejudice."[78] Prejudice—which, for hermeneutics, connotes not necessarily untruth but the more general phenomenon of anticipatory judgment—is central to the process of interpretation. Interpretation requires judgment with limited knowledge. *Seeing Things* opens with a close-up of Agatha's eyes as they widen, then dart from one point of focus to another, before her head leaves the frame entirely. The prominence of Agatha's suspicious eyes suggests their being understood as the hermeneutic frameworks through which parts of this diegetic world might be mediated. Yet Agatha's position as visual mediator is most discernible in moments of diegetic incongruity, suggesting inconsistencies in her perception. I contend that Agatha's paranoid perceptions are structured by a hermeneutic that relies upon bi-exclusionary ideas around lesbian veracity. These constitute its prejudices, its anticipatory judgments. Such a hermeneutic depends upon a fatalistically monosexual binary wherein that which is seen *must* be ordered.

An illustrative moment of diegetic incongruity occurs when Agatha is shown working in her office. Distracted, she wanders toward a window. As she looks out, Agatha sees Jo walking along the street with a man; the two pause and then begin to kiss up against a record store. Agatha rushes down to the street to find that the woman in question is not Jo but a woman who looks similar to her (Sheila McLaughlin). In this scene, Agatha's hermeneutic affects her perception in ways that draw upon two cultural phenomena: first, the discursive lesbian feminist trend Amber Ault describes whereby a lesbian in a relationship with a bisexual woman occupies the subject position of the cuckold and, second, the generic tendencies Mary Ann Doane identifies in the "paranoid woman's film." With the former, Ault observes how, in some lesbian discourses, fear around being left for a man "moves the lesbian into a subject position similar to the cuckolded heterosexual husband and the bisexual woman into the subject position of the adulterous, hyper-femme wife."[79] These are the subject positions occupied in Agatha's paranoid fantasy, wherein Agatha becomes cuckold and Jo becomes adulterous wife. Let us compare this moment to those in contemporary films outside of lesbian cinema that also invoke notions of cuckoldry in their dramatization of relationships between women. In *A Woman like Eve* (Nouchka van Brakel, 1979), *Entre Nous* (Diane Kurys, 1983), and *Softly . . . Softly . . .* (Lina Wertmüller, 1984), a male character can be understood as being cuckolded by a female character, an inversion of the classic cuckoldry genre. Rather than one man emasculating another by having sex with his wife, a woman usurps the man. In *Softly . . . Softly . . .* , when husband Oscar (Enrico Montesano) suspects his wife's infidelity with another woman, he despairs, "There's no tradition. No rules for dealing with it. . . . Am I a cuckold or not?" Whereas these films' sexual dramas involve the transgressive inversion of the cuckoldry genre, *Seeing Things* presents a double-inversion: The lesbian is cuckolded by a man. Pertinent here is that rather than subverting the myth of male sexual dominance, this scene of double-inverted cuckoldry expresses the fear that a lesbophobic axiom might be realized: the notion that a woman requires a man for sexual satisfaction.

In this scene, Agatha's pained visage contrasts with the titillated and ostentatious couple she observes flaunting the social acceptability of their public embraces. A similar moment takes place in Nicole Conn's *Claire of the Moon* (1992), in which lesbian psychiatrist Noel (Karen Trumbo), who "never get[s] involved with women who straddle both sides of the fence," looks through a window at her roommate Claire (Trisha Todd), who is "into whatever feels good at the moment," as she kisses a man (Damon Craig). The lesbian women's spatial separation from the extragender couple marks an insuperable lacuna of difference. Similar fears of the bisexual woman's return to men play out in Australian filmmaker Ann Turner's medium-length film *Flesh on Glass* (1981). Following a heated affair between Kate (Penelope Stewart) and Aggie (Lisa Dombroski), Aggie goes on to have a relationship with Kate's brother Hall (Ian Scott). When Kate visits the now-married couple's blissfully bourgeois home, she proceeds to smash their decorative ornaments, her fury at Aggie's marriage meted out in shards of glass. In these instances, Noel, Kate, and Agatha witness an encounter with what Maria San Filippo calls the charge of "bisexual privilege," the accusation that bisexuals are able to "enjoy the thrill of sexual transgression while maintaining the option of a recourse to heterosexual

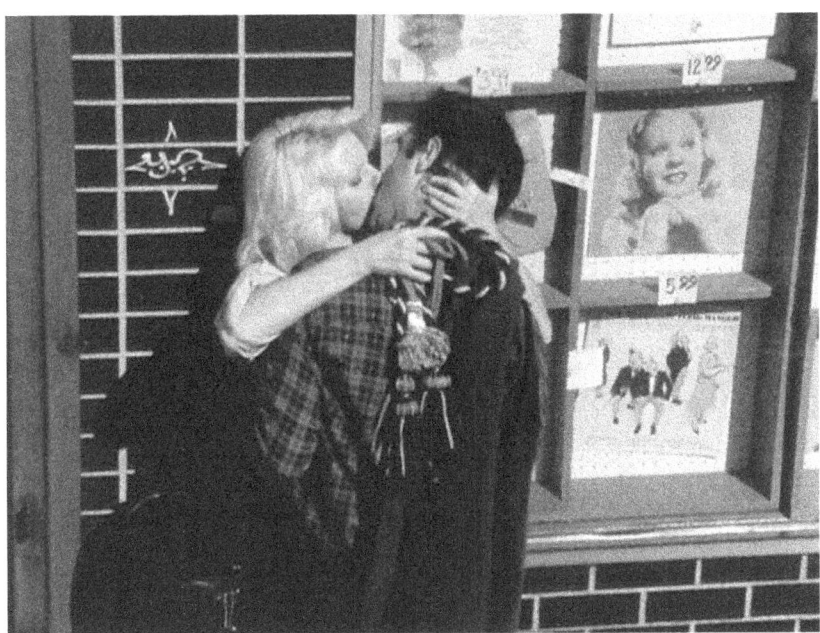

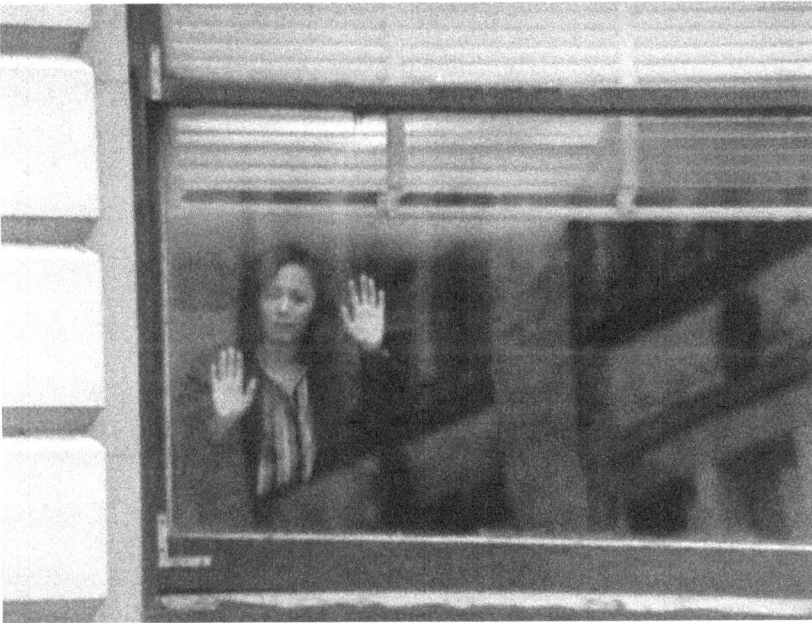

FIGURES 2.4–2.6 Agatha thinks she sees Jo with a man, but when she looks again, it is a different woman (Sheila McLaughlin). *She Must Be Seeing Things* (Sheila McLaughlin, 1987). Digital screen captures.

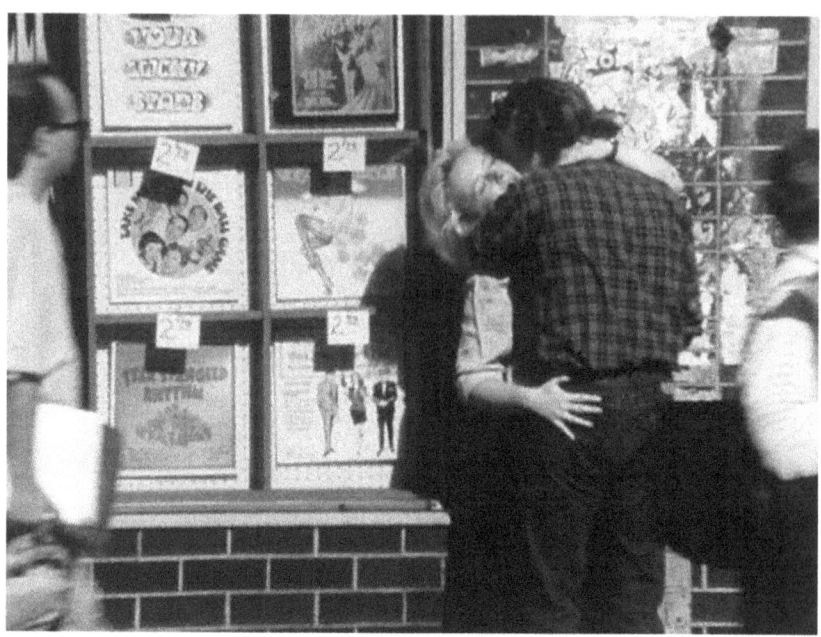

privilege."[80] It is through this double-inverted cuckoldry fantasy that Agatha expresses her fears around Jo's bisexual infidelity, imagining her to be the privileged bisexual parading her access to heterosexual public space.

Here, Agatha also corresponds in pertinent ways to the newly married wives of what Doane terms the "paranoid woman's film." This female archetype is defined by the delusions she begins to have in response to the mystery of her husband's past. In Agatha's discovery of Jo's past sexual encounters, a discovery that precipitates her own delusions, she operates analogously to the wives Doane discusses. Doane argues that, in these paranoid woman's films, the wife's suspicions are realized through cinematic form: "A crucial premise of the films [suspicion of the wife toward the husband] is thus aligned with the very signifying material of the cinema and manifests itself as a crisis of vision in relation to sexuality. . . . There is, therefore, something about the filmic representation of paranoia, female paranoia in particular, which foregrounds and even, at points, interrogates a fundamental semiotic mechanism of the cinema."[81] In the paranoid woman's film, the paranoia of the woman affects the film's semiotic mechanisms themselves. A similar treatment can be seen in this sequence of *Seeing Things*, where Agatha's paranoia produces a disruption of continuity. Doane's citation of Alfred Hitchcock's *Rebecca* (1940)

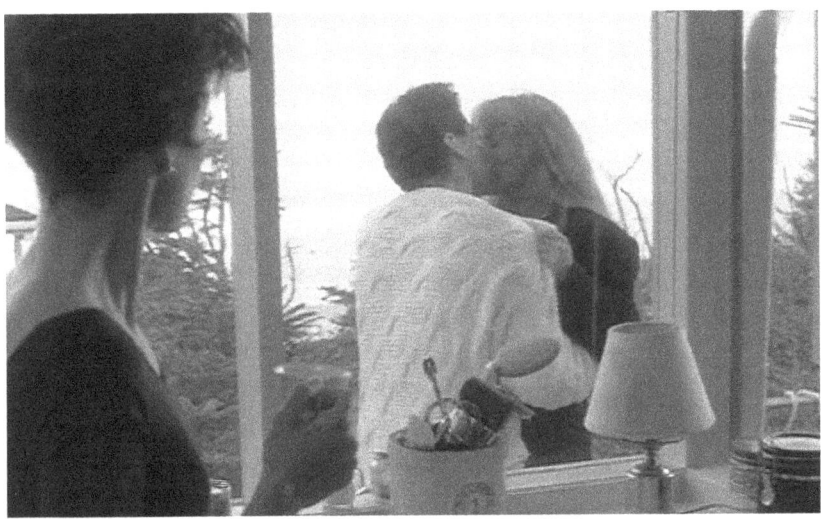

FIGURE 2.7 Noel (Karen Trumbo) watches Claire (Trisha Todd) kissing Brian (Damon Craig). *Claire of the Moon* (Nicole Conn, 1992). Digital screen capture.

as an example of a paranoid woman's film is relevant here, as this sequence of *Seeing Things* is notably Hitchcockian. The indeterminate identity of a blond woman evokes the Madeleine/Judy (Kim Novak) character(s) of *Vertigo* (1958), and McLaughlin's appearance in this moment recalls Hitchcock's signature cameos.[82] In the Hitchcock film, a spectator initially misrecognizes Madeleine and Judy as two different characters before they are revealed to be the same person. *Seeing Things*, however, uses an inverse yet isomorphic form of spectatorial misrecognition: We are set up—through Agatha—to recognize Jo before the revelation that this is someone else. This revelation induces a kind of visual paranoia in the spectator: "Did I see Jo kissing a man? Is Agatha imagining this? Should I trust what I am shown?"[83]

This spectatorial response is coaxed through specific formal phenomena, the first being the film's subversion of classic continuity editing. *Seeing Things* imitates this editing style, which usually maintains bodies and spaces across cuts in ways that cohere, rendering, instead, something incoherent. This scene also uses découpage in its movement from distance to closeness but, rather than revealing greater clarity or detail (as classical découpage usually does), a spectator is faced with aporia. Here, the film instrumentalizes a distinct quality of cinematic fantasy outlined by Cavell: its troubling nearness to reality. As Cavell elucidates: "It is a poor idea of fantasy which takes it to be a world apart from reality, a world clearly showing its unreality. Fantasy is precisely what reality can be confused with."[84] The tensions between fantasy and reality occasioned by film have been long debated in discussions of cinematic ontology, but the relation of this interplay to paranoia is explored most extensively by Jacqueline Rose. Challenging theorizations of "the spectator's subsumption into an imaginary totality," Rose proposes that "paranoia could be said to be latent to the structure of cinematic specularity in itself, in that it represents the radical alterity of signification . . . the potential splitting of [an imaginary totality] within the moment of its constitution."[85] For Rose, it is the not-quite-reality of cinematic signification itself that induces paranoia. But what kinds of images illuminate Cavell's understanding of fantasy's capacity to be confused with reality and Rose's conception of the latent paranoia in cinema's systems of signification? The moment of Jo's recognition/misrecognition functions as such because of its interplay between systems of perspective and those of diegetic signification, in ways that further speak to Doane's observations around the paranoid woman's film. Doane discusses a moment in *The Spiral Staircase* (Robert Siodmak, 1946) in which "paranoid woman" Helen (Dorothy McGuire) experiences a daydream-cum-nightmare: "There is a sense in which its level of reality cannot differ from the rest of the film. . . . Helen's subjectivity unwittingly becomes an objectivity."[86] Both *The Spiral Staircase* and *Seeing Things* establish formal registers in which the distinctions between diegetic reality and a character's perception of the world are difficult to distinguish.[87] Doane's analysis points to the potential for a character's perception to affect the film's presentation of a diegetic world in ways that complicate distinctions between fantasy and reality. When McLaughlin reflects, "I wanted the fantasy scenes to seem as real as the rest because it *is* very real, often stronger than reality," she speaks of a volition to render the paranoid fantasy's nearness to reality in form.[88]

Although this scene does provide a kind of hermeneutic resolution, with its revelation that Agatha was seeing things, it is complicated by the fact that so too was the spectator through the assumption of Agatha's perspective. It is not that we were mistaken but that Agatha's mistakenness is constitutive of the film's very signifying material. The first woman Agatha recognizes as Jo is, in fact, played by Weaver, while the woman Agatha sees on the street is played by McLaughlin; the men each woman embraces are also played by different actors. As a director discussed as a lesbian filmmaker, and whose films circulated in lesbian exhibition contexts, the decision to portray herself kissing and caressing a man is bold. It is likely that a spectator would not recognize McLaughlin in her brief cameo, rendering this decision fascinatingly furtive. Consider a similar gesture of bisexual subversion in Midi Onodera's experimental film

The Basement Girl (2000), which follows a woman (Kate Ashley) reflecting on a recent breakup. Here, the narrator (Linda Blom) speaks in French, and the woman's ex-lover is referred to with male pronouns; the film's English subtitles, however, refer to the ex-lover with female pronouns. Onodera reflects, "It was my little subtle (subversive) statement on bisexuality."[89] In the subversive subtleties camouflaged in McLaughlin's and Onodera's films, the filmmakers gesture toward sexuality not being what it initially seems, a reflexive vindication of the possibility of extragender desire lurking in a figure once assumed to be lesbian. Just as San Filippo argues that bisexuality's polysemy can lay bare the mutability and contingency of desire, film's formal capacity to effect polysemy works here to contest monosemous conceptions of sexuality.[90]

Following this scene, a spectator cannot but be wary of the veracity of the images with which they are presented, especially when signaled as mediated through Agatha. When Agatha and Jo speak over the phone, Jo informs Agatha that she is going to be meeting up with her assistant director, Tom (Uzi Parnes), to give him advice on editing. Agatha's suspicions are sparked once again, and she tracks Jo through New York to a diner where Jo and Tom sit. Agatha gazes at them, her reflection emerging between the two in the window. She stands stoic as the camera zooms slowly. First, a triptych is established: Jo, Agatha's reflection, and Tom. But the camera zooms further, until Jo and Tom are off-screen, leaving Agatha's mirrored image, a lone portrait. Although Agatha surmises that the meeting between Jo and Tom is romantic in nature, her encounter with them is presented in a way that contradicts her interpretation, establishing Agatha's paranoid perceptions to be more rooted in herself than the objects of her suspicion. This visual treatment of paranoia recalls Sigmund Freud's claim that paranoiacs "love their delusions as they love themselves."[91] Peering into the window, through Agatha's eyes, the zoom leads a spectator to a confrontation with Agatha herself; she is gazing at her own delusion. In the following scene, Agatha follows Jo and Tom to a parking lot, where the two enter a car and begin kissing passionately, prone on the backseat. Agatha looks up at the diner's empty window. She has been daydreaming; the couple she is tracking have now left the diner. Karin Quimby interprets this sequence as a refracted kind of engagement with heterosexuality: "This position [of gazing] indicates the degree to which [Agatha] is outside the hetero economy, but her voyeuristic gaze . . . also signifies how she is experiencing (or interjecting) this heterosexual existence through Jo."[92] It is through Jo, and Agatha's paranoid fantasies of her infidelity, that Agatha can confront the threat of extragender desire. The Freudian conception of paranoia is, once again, useful here, as, for Freud, "the purpose of paranoia is . . . to fend off an idea that is incompatible with the

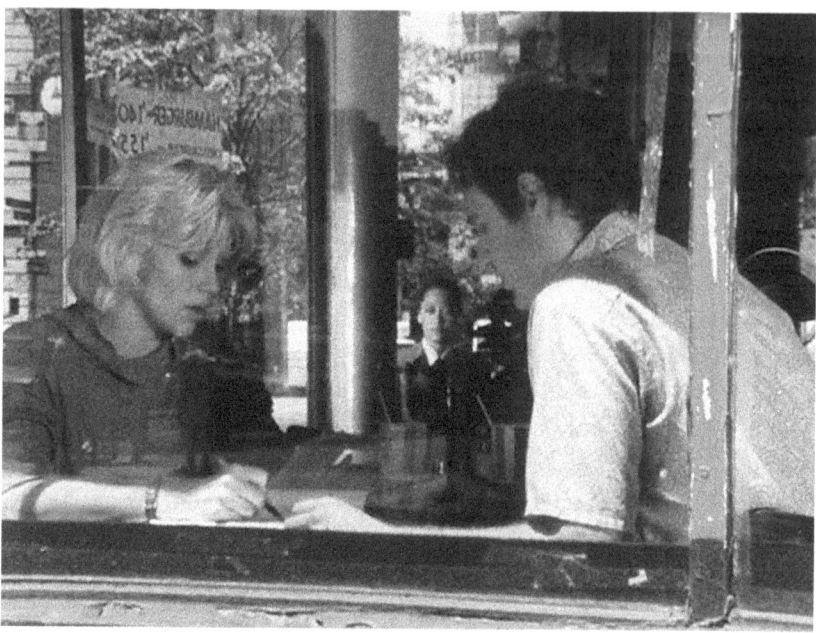

FIGURE 2.8 Agatha's surveillance of Jo and Tom (Uzi Parnes) transforms into a gaze at her own reflection. *She Must Be Seeing Things* (Sheila McLaughlin, 1987). Digital screen capture.

ego, by projecting its substance into the external world."[93] The incompatibility of extragender desire with lesbian identity—a line toed with fervor in expressions of bi-exclusionary lesbian ethics—leads Agatha to project extragender desire externally, through paranoid delusions. Seeing things in this way, imagining Jo's adulterous bisexual transgressions, enables a shoring up of Agatha's own lesbianness.

The constitutive differences between these fantasies might be elucidated through de Lauretis's proposition that it is not only Jo who is making a film in *Seeing Things* but Agatha, too.[94] Jo's and Agatha's differences in perspective and desire affect the fantasies they create, the things they must be seeing. Consider Quimby's interpretation of a scene in which Agatha and Jo watch extragender couples kissing on a beach. Here, Agatha expresses annoyance at their "being everywhere," while Jo retorts, "It's no big deal, they all come here to make out." Quimby observes that "rather than sharing a common fantasy here, their vastly different interpretations of *this* scene point out the very uncommonality of their sexual histories and identities. . . . While they may be looking together at the same scenario, what they actually see is different, and this is a difference that matters."[95] Quimby finds this moment of the film instructive as it suggests that the differences between Agatha's and Jo's sexualities affect their perception. There is another moment when Agatha views an extragender couple that shares similarities with her gaze here. When Agatha is staying at Jo's apartment, she switches on the television and watches the legal program *Divorce Court*. In the dramatized case, a painter husband is frustrated at his wife's implausible demand to have him sketch her as they have sex. Agatha cackles at the ludicrousness of the dispute on-screen and switches off the television after thirty seconds. In this scene, like Agatha's gazing through windows, her encounter with an extragender couple is separated by a screen; however, the differentiation this screen maintains provides a partition that is securing rather than alienating. This moment shares similarities with a section of Jan Oxenberg's *A Comedy in Six Unnatural Acts* (1975), in which a lesbian DJ (Alice Bloch) plays music for a dance filled with extragender couples. Oblivious to the skipping record, the DJ holds a 7-inch single to her eye, peering through its aperture at the heterosexual ritual in front of her, the record a mediator securing her difference from these antics. As with Agatha's television screen, these mediatory objects demarcate a divide between risible heterosexual capers and a lesbian spectator, whose partition secures her difference. While Agatha can be understood as making her own film, we must also account for her regular positioning as a spectator. Watching carefree extragender couples on the beach and a divorcing couple on television, Agatha is able to maintain a distance from that which she views, a distance whose safety is secured by its express heterosexuality.

In one scene, however, in which Agatha visits Jo on the set of her film, we find a moment in which Agatha is invited to see things in a way that is aligned most pronouncedly with a recognition of bisexual possibility. Agatha watches as Jo directs her actor Claudia (Kyle deCamp), who plays Catalina. In this scene of Jo's film, Catalina is watching furtively as a man and a woman have sex. The positions set up in this scene are strongly redolent of what Freud terms the "primal scene," in relation to his patient the Wolf Man's recollection of witnessing his parents having sex.[96] In Freud's analysis, he stresses that "it was not only a single sexual current that started from the primal scene but a whole series of them. . . . His libido was positively splintered up by it."[97] In Freud's characterization of the primal scene, we find a libidinal splintering that gives rise to a series of sexual currents, an opening up of multiple libidinal, positional, and relational possibilities. Similarly, in Jo's directions to Claudia, she cues her actor to emote curiosity, jealousy, confusion, recognition, pain, and pleasure. Agatha

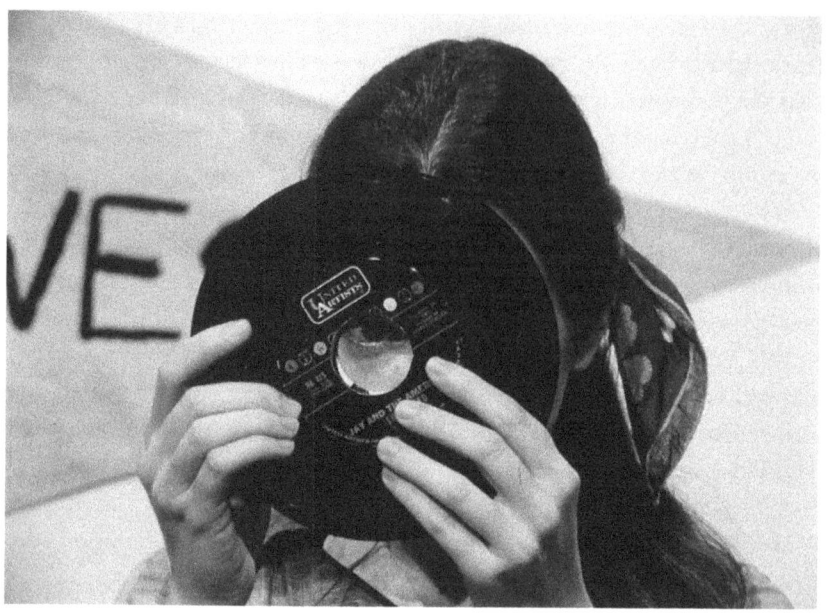

FIGURE 2.9 The DJ (Alice Bloch) peers at extragender couples dancing through a record's aperture. *A Comedy in Six Unnatural Acts* (Jan Oxenberg, 1975). Digital screen capture.

watches Jo as she narrates this sequence of affects, which suggest splintering variations of attraction and repulsion. This is an affective sequence in whose syntagmatic collocation we find bisexual possibility. In this sense, this scene's mise en abyme puts Agatha face-to-face with a performance, first, of a bisexual range of possibilities and positionalities and, second, of sexuality's very mutability. That these cues are directed toward Kyle deCamp (an androgynous actor) playing Catalina (a historical figure noted for their gendered transgressions) situates a performance of desirous unfixity in a figure of sexual unfixity. Wandering onto Jo's set, Agatha finds an improvisation on Freud's primal scene whose inherent capacities for sexual splintering Jo's direction amplifies. Throughout *Seeing Things*, we find a number of perspectival shifts that attest to an interplay between the perception of reality and the means of making sense of it, the import of fantasy and its nearness to reality, and the capacity for more classic sites of textual performance—from the television screen to the film set—to transform the ways things are seen. Yet the perceptive differences between Agatha and Jo, the "films" they make and what they see, cannot be fully grasped without attention to how they, in turn, are seen.

Femme Negotiations, Butch Navigations

Two months after the 1988 Lesbian Summer School fiasco, Cherry Smyth and Campbell X showed the film in its entirety at a sold-out women-only screening, where they were joined for a discussion with actor Lois Weaver and scholar Mandy Merck. There, Weaver responded to claims that, at the Lesbian Summer School, one spectator shouted, "She's not a lesbian, that blonde one!" Weaver clarified that she is, in fact, a lesbian, "not a blonde actress trying to make her fortune doing lesbian movies."[98] Campbell X reflected on how Weaver had been read: "White and blonde equal heterosexual unless your hair is really cropped, but another type of look is allowed to be lesbian. Still using those definitions, we're not being radical enough."[99] This part of the discussion around *Seeing Things* speaks to one of the central issues regarding lesbian intelligibility: that, by themselves, it is difficult for femme lesbians to signify "lesbian" unequivocally. Often, for a femme to be read as lesbian they require positioning in relation to what Clare Hemmings calls "their butch chaperones."[100] In relation to film, Jack Halberstam observes that "if femme reads as lesbian only in the presence of a butch partner, then femme becomes a wholly dependent category, borrowing an aura of authenticity from the masculine woman."[101] The only intelligibly queer image of a woman that does not depend on situatedness for authentication is the butch woman; she is the figure to whom the lesbian femme must be related lest she be read as heterosexual. The lesbian femme thus embodies a uniquely visual problem with which lesbian cinema has had to contend in its visual approaches toward lesbian specificity and lesbian verisimilitude.[102] This problem is complicated further when the question of the femme's desire toward men is left open.[103]

While the demarcation of Weaver as nonlesbian as a result of her femmeness in *Seeing Things* is obviously misguided—Weaver is not her character, lesbians can be femme—the spectator who shouted out, "She's not a lesbian," is not necessarily wrong. Taken as a response to the character of Jo, it is reasonable to conclude that, through her evidenced desire toward men, Jo is not a lesbian. I am interested, instead, in how, in the context of a crisis of intelligibility in which femme lesbians are often precluded from lesbian signification, *Seeing Things'* portrayal of the femme with bisexual desires muddies this crisis of intelligibility further. In the previous chapter, I discussed how representations of dissimulative femininity on film evoke what André Bazin calls cinema's "conflict between style and likeness."[104] The interplay between a feminine exterior and that which it conceals draws upon the cinematic tension between what something appears to be and what it is. The lesbian femme is caught up in a similar conflict, having to assert what she is against that which she appears to be.

The performative gesture necessary to render the lesbian femme qua lesbian is, therefore, a repudiation of heterosexuality or bisexuality. As Hemmings writes, "The [lesbian] femme becomes a contemporary subject by insisting on her absolute difference from the bisexual."[105] But when the femme desires bisexually, as in *Seeing Things*, the repudiation of extragender desire fails to take place, confirming, as the fear dictates, that the femme always retained her attraction toward men. Further, as Hemmings continues, "the bisexual femme makes real the fear that female/femininity craves male/masculinity for its fulfillment, settling for a butch only when a man is unavailable."[106] A femme who has not repudiated her desire toward men cannot necessarily rely on her "butch chaperone" to authenticate her queerness. Expressions of femme bisexuality can thus spark suspicions of heterosexual etiology. Let us remember that, in the most extreme political lesbian discourses, butch-femme itself is considered etiologically heterosexual, that, in the words of Sheila Jeffreys, it constitutes "the idealisation of precisely the power dynamics that keep women subordinate and abused within heterosexual relationships."[107] Among proponents of butch-femme, however, the lesbian femme is able to challenge what she appears to be (heterosexual) with attestations of what she is (lesbian). On the contrary, the bisexual femme must challenge both what she appears to be (heterosexual) and the associations tied to what she is (bisexual) by protesting that neither renders her heterosexual.[108] This answer is not intelligible within a monosexual model of sexual epistemology. *Seeing Things*' troublesomeness lies in its refusal to perform the requisite repudiation that would make Jo an intelligible lesbian femme. Her sexual ambiguity obtains.

Jo's femme pièce de résistance comes in the form of a striptease she performs for Agatha. In this scene, Agatha has surprised Jo with a present: a satin babydoll dress. "You're crazy!" Jo exclaims, before pausing and uttering a seductive, "You go sit in there." She changes into the babydoll dress behind a curtain. This style of dress, often worn as a negligee, fuses ideas of girlhood innocence with sexual suggestiveness, at once concealing the body's form through its puffiness and revealing it through its thin fabric and high hem. Agatha's (and McLaughlin's) choice of the babydoll dress as a present for Jo is striking as an item of clothing that exudes girly hyperfemininity. Teetering on the borders of acceptability in its reference to the Lolita archetype, it invokes the sexual infantilization of women in ways that would have been controversial for a 1980s feminist audience. Jo performs a striptease for Agatha, incorporating a translucent curtain, a feather boa, gloves, a fan, and a lollipop into her performance. These objects render Jo's performance a classical strip-tease, shot from the similarly classical perspective of Mulvey's scopophilic "in-visible guest" and harkening Rita Hayworth's performance in *Gilda* (Charles Vidor, 1946).[109] Yet the film undermines this visual paradigm both with cho-reographic mistakes (Jo rips her stocking by accident) and the incorporation of an incongruent operatic soundtrack that gets stuck on the record player.[110] It is through this confluence of feminine performance, failure, and incongruence that, I contend, the film stages a bisexual conflict between Jo's perception as either feminine heterosexual or lesbian femme.

To some extent, *Seeing Things'* depiction of feminine performance as a site of play works to unyoke femininity from patriarchal heteronormativity. Ag-atha's position as the butch voyeur is, similarly, a playful one; she is instructed to sit by Jo in order to create a scene of seduction in which conventions of het-erosexual performance are played with. This setup speaks to Sue-Ellen Case's contention that butch/femme roles "are played in signs themselves and not in ontologies. Seduction, as a dramatic action, transforms all of these seeming realities into semiotic play."[111] With her subversive performance, Jo can thus be seen to ironize those heterosexual norms in which Agatha fears she is par-ticipating precisely by performing them exaggeratedly. Correspondingly, we can comprehend the positioning of Jo's femininity toward the gaze of Agatha as an effort in performing a femmeness intelligible to lesbian culture. As Hem-mings articulates, "The feminine woman is structurally positioned as object of both a heterosexual *and* a homosexual gaze. . . . While her femininity is con-ferred upon her through the masculine gaze, it is also true that one cannot tell, just by looking, which gaze she will return. Femininity (in women), then, could be said to be the thorn in the side of a heterosexual/homosexual opposi-tion."[112] Jo's striptease undoes the aporia produced by the image of the feminine woman and the question of to whom her femmeness is directed. By returning Agatha's gaze, Jo tweezes, albeit momentarily, the thorn in her side—the ques-tion as to where Jo's loyalties lie. Jo successfully participates in what de Laure-tis identifies as "that space between the fantasy scenario and the self-critical ironic lesbian gaze."[113] She is thus somewhat successful in asserting her lesbian belonging via participation within ironic lesbian semiotics, yet the suspicion around her feminine image endures.

In the context of Agatha's suspicions around Jo's extragender adultery, this performance could also be considered an attestation not simply of Jo's lesbian authenticity but of her fidelity. This layer of meaning is discernible in the soundtrack to which Jo performs. It is, of course, uncommon for a striptease to be performed to opera, and this uncanniness renders the performance consistent with lesbian irony. But the soundtrack to which Jo strips is starkly germane to the film's narrative. The aria that plays is "Ah! Non Credea Mirarti" from the second act of Vincenzo Bellini's *La sonnambula* (1831). The opera tells the story of Amina, who is engaged to be married, when she sleepwalks into the bedroom of a man who is not her fiancé, leading others to believe that she has been unfaithful. In "Ah! Non Credea Mirarti," Amina affirms her love of her fiancé and attests to her virtue.[114] If Jo's striptease is seen as asserting her lesbian authenticity against accusations of bisexual infidelity, there are striking parallels with Bellini's Amina, a figure also wrongly accused of adultery. While Jo is not aware of these accusations, the meanings present in this choice of soundtrack persist, suggesting the striptease be considered a dance of defense against accusations of infidelity, an attestation of her authenticity, her virtue.

As Jo positions her bisexual femininity toward both lesbian irony and monogamous fidelity, Agatha's gendered expression—its journeying in and out of butchness—operates in a similarly dense semiotic landscape. Agatha's transformation into her recognizably butch look comes in the aftermath of the phone call in which Jo informs her that she is meeting up with Tom. After the call, Agatha wanders into a curtained-off side room and talks to herself, imitating Jo intermittently: "Bitch. 'I like him.' I bet you like him. 'He's nice. I'd like to get to know him better.' You'd like to add him to your list perhaps. 'He's gonna work for free; I'm teaching him editing.' Slut." Agatha emerges from behind the curtain, physically transformed into a suave butch look. She wears a suit, shirt, and tie and walks up to a mirror, where she runs her hand over her slicked-back hair. At first glance, it would seem that *Seeing Things* makes the troubling suggestion that Agatha's butchness involves her imitation of a man. Agatha's physical transformation is positioned, ostensibly, as her response to the threat of Jo's desire toward men. Quimby suggests that this transformation might be read as Agatha's desire to become that which Jo desires: "[Agatha's] appearance in drag at this instance genders the terms of her jealousy or of her psychic struggle with the difference in Jo's sexual orientation. Her change into butch attire, in which she dons the signifiers of (heterosexual) male privilege, could signal her wish to be someone she thinks Jo desires."[115] Embodiment of that by which one is threatened has, in fact, been conceptualized as a feature of paranoia. Developing and explicating Melanie Klein's theory of the paranoid-schizoid position, Eve Kosofsky Sedgwick paraphrases one of paranoia's propositions: "Anything you can do (to me) I can do first—to myself."[116] This is the sentiment that grounds Agatha's response to her paranoid fantasies: to dress up as their aggressor. Another notable aspect of this transformation is its accompaniment by Agatha's off-screen voice, which not only imitates Jo but also berates her with misogynistic quips. By calling Jo "bitch" and "slut," Agatha not only wears masculine attire but also becomes the emblematic male misogynist. In an earlier scene, Agatha and Jo are having a postcoital conversation in which Agatha says, "You know I'm a misogynist. The church taught me to hate women. Now . . . I hate women." In this instance, Agatha's statement is ironic, coextensive with the powerplay in which they have been engaged, and accompanied by knowing smirks. In her butch transformation, however, no such irony is present. Through her deployment of misogynistic language, Agatha seems to suggest, "I can also be a misogynist. Isn't that what you want?"

This representation of butchness is certainly provocative. Accusations of butch lesbians wanting to be men have long been leveled by heterosexist ideology just as accusations of butches being misogynists have been leveled by certain anti-butch-femme lesbian thinkers. I do not wish to advocate either of these positions, nor do I believe that this is what the film does. Instead, I suggest that what we see in Agatha's transformation is, first, a paranoid response to the threat of female bisexuality that enacts the threat itself and, second, an attachment to butchness as a means of securing her lesbian authenticity. With the first, the butch transformation is not the effect of misogyny but, instead, the form taken by the embodiment of a paranoid fear. For butchness to function in this way may be no less controversial than typically lesbophobic representations of butches, but it is more complex. Second, it is pertinent that this transformation is not only a "disguise," as McLaughlin notes, or, as Quimby suggests, "drag" but a form of *lesbian* dress.[117] The outcome of Agatha's transformation is not that she becomes a man but that she becomes more recognizably lesbian. This is Quimby's second interpretation of Agatha's transformation, that "she may also be visibly claiming her already acknowledged identification as a lesbian."[118] Newly donned in her butch attire, Agatha signifies as lesbian. Given, as Sally R. Munt argues, that "butch is *the* recognisable public form of lesbianism," Agatha's transformation into a butch look can be understood as a shoring up of her lesbian recognizability.[119] In this sense, Agatha's embodiment here might be understood as more typical of what Jackie Stacey terms "butch noir": "a relational dynamic by which queer subjects are generated through their anticipation of other people's reading of them. . . . The having-already-been-read-ness of this anticipatory dynamic might be characterized . . . in the following way: my vulnerability arises in your capacity to wound me, but my queerness defies this wounding power, since it has already embraced and incorporated your derision."[120] In Stacey's theorization, an embodied queerness—a performative butchness—functions as a kind of amulet: The embrace of intelligible queerness blunts its reader's derision in its refusal of shame around having-been-read-as-queer. When Agatha goes to observe Jo and Tom's meeting, she is met with an unintelligible image. However, this image gives way, through a zoom, to an intelligibly lesbian Agatha, whose reflection in the window becomes the frame's privileged focus. The reflective symbolic power of the butch lesbian image endures. Whereas Jo's bisexual femininity is a site of an arduous negotiation of meaning, Agatha's draw to the image of butchness involves both an acting-out of her paranoia and a comfort in a singular image of lesbian intelligibility.

Racial Difference and Catholic Afro-Brazilian Cultural Identity

Beyond the butch-femme dynamic—or, as I will argue, animating this dynamic—is another site of contrast between Agatha and Jo: their racial difference. For a number of the film's commentators, however, this aspect of the film is alleged to be depthless: For de Lauretis, the film "does not . . . lend itself to an understanding or examination of racial difference"; for Richard Fung, people of color are "simply inserted to legitimate the liberal credentials of the film"; for José Esteban Muñoz, *Seeing Things* typifies queer films whose "mode of diversification is incidental because the characters of color never articulate their ethnic and cultural location. . . . [They are] multicultural window dressing."[121] Although the film does not foreground racial difference as explicitly as it does gender and sexuality, closer textual analysis finds more allusions to racial-cultural specificity than these critiques do justice. Agatha's Blackness is inextricable from a specific cultural history of Catholic Afro-Brazilian identity: She refers to a Catholic upbringing, a Brazilian father, and watches a Brazilian telenovela alone at home. These details are important in their indexing of a particular culture and history wherein notions of race, creed, and culture converge.[122] When de Lauretis comments that *Seeing Things* collapses questions of racial difference "into questions of cultural or ethnic difference," she misses how, for an Afro-Brazilian like Agatha, race, culture, and ethnicity are bound together.[123] Further, we might consider what we see of Agatha in her professional world, working as a lawyer at what seems to be an NGO investigating human rights abuses. At a board meeting, Agatha, alongside her Black colleague Julia (Elizabeth Cunningham) and white colleague Jonathan (Bob Dannin), advocates that her organization respond to Indigenous Guatemalans' call for their help in the face of displacement, enslavement, and massacre by an American corporation. Here, a Latin American anticolonial politics makes itself known in Agatha's insistence on working in solidarity with Indigenous resistance to American imperialism. Allusions to racial difference do appear, therefore, in pertinent ways in the film, including in two scenes—one in a sex shop and one in a bar—that I analyze later in this chapter. Their articulation, however, is culturally specific, with the specificity and hybridity of Agatha's Catholic Afro-Brazilian heritage precluding some of the film's readers from reading allusions to it qua race.

These racial aspects of the film also interface with questions around sexuality. Notably, in casting the roles, McLaughlin entertained the possibility of casting Dabney as Jo and Weaver as Agatha, but she was wary of having a Black Jo invoke the stereotype of the "sexy black bitch."[124] Here, it is bisexuality's associations with hypersexuality that risked perpetuating notions of Black female hypersexuality—specifically the Jezebel stereotype. Yet, casting Dabney as Agatha could still, in McLaughlin's words, "be read as racially problematic."[125] Ling-Yen Chua, for instance, reads the film's depiction of the Black butch as hypermasculine, contrasted with Jo's idealized white Hollywood femininity.[126] This double bind reflects Zakiyyah Iman Jackson's perspicuity that "the black body is characterized by a plasticity, whereby raciality arbitrarily remaps black(ened) gender and sexuality."[127] Black gender and sexuality's hyperbolization to what Jackson calls "the border of the sociological" reflects the impossibility of disambiguating the sexual from the racial, an interrelation that I explored in chapter 1 of this book to consider the import of race in historical genealogies and contemporary discourses of sexual epistemology.[128] With these considerations in mind, we must acknowledge that, although racial difference is not announced by the film as explicitly as the preeminent issues it addresses, it is erroneous to conclude that this issue is absent from the text.

In Agatha's Blackness—in her Catholic Afro-Brazilianness, more precisely—we find a culturally specific iteration of racial-national-religious positioning. This positioning informs her professional life and its underlying political commitments, with an anticolonial politics discernible in her call for solidarity with Indigenous struggle. Her Blackness and Jo's whiteness cannot but animate the two's butch-femme dynamic, where stereotypes of Black masculine virility and white feminine beauty are enmeshed in the relation. In this sense, the relationship perhaps recalls my analysis of *The Mark of Lilith* that opened this chapter, where a politically conscious Black lesbian is positioned in contrast with a white feminine apoliticality. This neat divide, however, is complicated in a key scene that finds Agatha in the most culturally Black space she navigates in the film, a blues bar, in which she invokes the stringency of one aspect of her cultural identity, Afro-Brazilian Catholicism, as she begins to reject biexclusionary lesbian ethics, accompanied, all the while, by a soundtrack from a uniquely Black bisexual tradition: the blues. I return to this undertheorized scene in this chapter's conclusion, but before I do so, it is worth revisiting a more widely discussed moment in the film wherein the dynamics of butch-femme and racial difference converge in a symbolically rich object: the dildo.

The Polysemous Dildo

As Jo and Agatha lie in bed, Jo asks her, seemingly out of nowhere, "Do you really want a cock?" The two of them laugh, giving way to a pause. Agatha responds, "Hm, no. Sometimes, maybe. I don't wanna be a man." Jo then pretends to masturbate Agatha's "cock." "Stop it!" Agatha retorts, and they laugh again. Agatha then proceeds to play along, offering an ambiguous comment: "Anyway, you got it wrong. I have two." In this exchange, Jo and Agatha broach what is, again, a controversial topic in lesbian culture: the relation between lesbians and the penis. Heterosexist-cissexist ideologies purport two interrelated lesbophobic ideas: first, that butch lesbians (who are already assumed to want to be men) wish they had a penis; second, that sex without a penis is less authentic or fulfilling. The dominant lesbian response to the question of whether a lesbian wishes she had a cock would be an unequivocal "no." Agatha's response, however, is ambivalent; she sees herself as relating somewhat to the idea of having a cock. Her suggestion here is that there is something in the idea of the penis that is, conceptually, a desirable asset, but only insofar as it is divorced from the idea of being a man. Within this context, Agatha's comment that she has two cocks suggests a relation to the idea of "cock" that differs from the cisgender man's penis, of which there is strictly one per person. A similar relation to the penis is observable in Cheryl Newbrough's lesbian erotic drama *Such a Crime* (1998), in which Cal (Mary-Kate Stoever) remarks of swashbuckling ecoterrorist Skip (Heather King), "She can't keep her cock in her pants." Skip's cock, like Agatha's, exceeds the cisgender penis.

Elsewhere in the film, however, Agatha's paradoxical investment in the cock-as-cisgender-penis is made apparent. In a much-discussed scene, Agatha visits a sex shop looking to buy a dildo. She asks the shop assistant (David Hofstra) for "something very realistic," to which he responds, "That depends on what you think is realistic." Agatha peruses the array of dildos—all of different shapes and sizes—some penis-like, some not, but all of a white flesh tone. She picks out a large strap-on dildo that resembles a penis, with testicles to match. As Agatha inspects the strap-on dildo, she overhears a customer (Ron Vawter) who wants to buy a Judy doll (an inflatable sex doll) suggest that he take the display doll as the shop is out of stock. The disgruntled butch woman shop

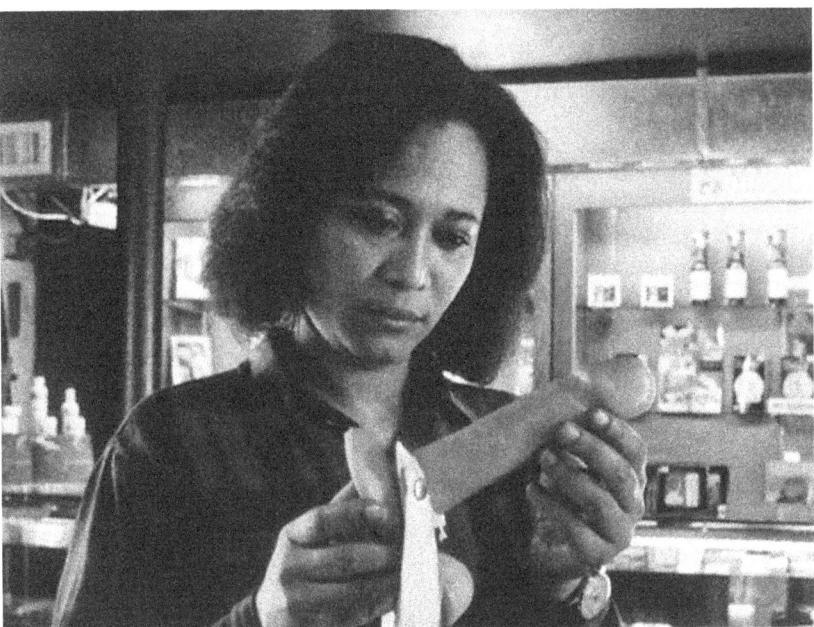

FIGURE 2.10 Agatha assesses the strap-on dildo. *She Must Be Seeing Things* (Sheila McLaughlin, 1987). Digital screen capture.

assistant (Diane Jeep Ries) retrieves the doll and deflates it on the counter, the Judy doll's body contorting on the surface. Agatha puts the strap-on back on the counter and excuses herself, leaving the sex shop. This scene, in concert with the scene of postcoital conversation, evokes debates that took place within lesbian feminist communities in the 1980s around the dildo and the penis. Heather Findlay writes that the opposing sides of this debate can be "divided roughly into two camps. On the one hand, some lesbians have debunked the dildo and its notorious cousin the strap-on, calling them 'male identified.' . . . On the other hand, some lesbians have argued that dildos do not represent penises."[129] Findlay characterizes this second camp's defense of the dildo as "downplaying its referentiality."[130] Agatha's visit to the sex shop is motivated by her suspicion of Jo's infidelity with a man. Her desire to find a "very realistic" dildo is presented as an affirmative desire to find an object that resembles a penis, something she believes Jo desires. In this sense, Agatha's intentions are verboten on both sides of the lesbian dildo debate, as she initially desires that which anti- and pro-dildo lesbians similarly disavow: a dildo that imitates the penis.

However, as the scene progresses, a disavowal does occur. The comic, twisted deflation of the Judy doll embarrasses the male customer. After seeing this take place, Agatha rejects the strap-on dildo she has picked out, eschewing its purchase as a reactive route for her paranoia to take. In Paul B. Preciado's critique of this moment, he argues that "dildos and sex toys appear in the film as transitional objects that allow the lesbian protagonist to deromanticize and denaturalize the heterosexual stage."[131] Preciado is instructive here in his suggestion that the sex shop is presented in the film as a retailer of heterosexual objects. Through the comic display involving the Judy doll, heterosexuality is stripped of its social power, yet, with this stripping, so too are all sex toys in the shop. Preciado continues, "In the film's heterosexual imagination, the inflatable doll is correlative to the dildo."[132] It is, therefore, the very cisheteronormative terms upon which Agatha initiates her inquiry into dildos ("very realistic") that allow for a renunciation of sex toys in toto. This dynamic is complicated, however, by racial politics also at play in this scene. The dildos the shop has to offer are all of a white flesh tone and, consequently, it is possible to read Agatha's rejection of the dildo as a frustration at the shop's lack of suitable options for her as a Black woman. Inherent here would be a critique of the whiteness of the sex toy industry's commodities.[133] Agatha's rejection of the dildo is thus positioned, through cross-cutting, as a response to the straight white man's antics, her sexual, gendered, and racial difference from him spelling the dildo's incommensurability to her, while aligning what she surmises to be Jo's desires in the world of white heterosexuality. This formal dynamic supports Preciado's reading that the rejection of the dildo signifies an eschewal of the sex toy as a heteropatriarchal object, despite the fact that this understanding of the dildo was, paradoxically, Agatha's initial draw to it.

Some lesbian scholars, including Heather Findlay and June L. Reich, theorize the dildo as both in reference to and in excess of the penis, as a denaturalization of essentialized understandings of the body.[134] Such treatments of the dildo can be observed in a number of erotic films made by lesbians. Dildos are used in Cheryl Newbrough's Such a Crime and Goodbye Emma Jo (1998), and they also populate a number of dyke porn films—lesbian-made video pornography—including Debi Sundahl's Shadows (1985), Clips (1988), Hungry Hearts (1989), Suburban Dykes (1990), and Safe Is Desire (1993).[135] In Newbrough's and Sundahl's films, the dildo appears neither as narrative obstacle nor as metonym of heterosexuality; it is, instead, part of a lesbian semiotics of eroticism. Agatha's relation to the dildo in this scene, however, is mediated by the male penis and, in a broader sense, the heterosexual symbolic. As might be expected, this is a characterization of the dildo with which Preciado takes umbrage. Preciado contends that, rather than being an imitative object of cisheteronormativity, the dildo "suggests that the organs we interpret as natural (male or female) have already suffered a similar process of plastic transformation."[136] Agatha's perception, charged with paranoia, is plagued by a monosexual, heterosexual symbolic that demands a binary hermeneutic. This hermeneutic precludes the possibility that the dildo might be something other than an imitation penis and Agatha thus eschews it as a symptomatic object of patriarchal heterosexual culture.

Accordingly, this scene can be seen to explore one of the thorniest critiques of bi-exclusionary lesbian ethics: that it enacts the very phallocentrism it purports to disavow. Consider the moment from *Go Fish* in which Daria imagines herself on trial for having slept with a man. When Daria tries to reason with her accusers, "Maybe we just need to . . . ," she is interrupted by a juror who jibes, "What? Go out and get some dick?" Later, a different juror responds to Daria's declaration of love for women with, "But you just can't stay away from that dick." The misogynistic and lesbophobic idea that sex with someone with a penis would "cure" women of their lesbianism is obviously rooted in patriarchal and cissexist ideologies invested in myths of phallocentrism.[137] Yet, to consider a woman's bisexuality as evidence of this claim, however, reflects a reification of phallocentrism on the part of the accuser, in which the penis is mythologized as phallus. This exchange offers a pertinent example of Amber Ault's perspicuity that "lesbian antipathy toward bisexual women recirculates a larger cultural discourse that lesbian feminists have theorized as misogynist when it has been deployed against them. . . . The sense that bisexual women eventually always choose men reflects not bisexual phallocentrism but the phallocentrism of this lesbian discourse, which attributes to the phallus the power to define the bisexual woman's life."[138] The line of interrogation used by *Go Fish*'s jurors signals the same conception of the penis that undergirds Agatha's relation to the dildo, a paradox whereby the value system of patriarchal heteronormativity is adopted to discredit female bisexuality in a lesbian context.

As a vector for lesbian fears, Agatha's response to the dildo belies an investment in phallocentrism that is elucidated further by Preciado: "Separatist lesbian theory and transphobic feminism, which criticize dildo use because of its complicity with the symbols of male domination, still believe in the ontological reality of the penis as hegemonic genitalia. In this naturalistic erotica, the absence that structures the body, faithful to a monocentric, totalizing anatomical chart, mourns the vestiges of the very phallocentric system it criticizes."[139] In these discourses' aggrandizement of the penis, we can observe a recapitulation of patriarchy's naturalization of the penis as the ontologically hegemonic sex organ. The conception of a dildo as realistic is predicated on an investment in the penis as the dildo's ontological referent. But, as the employee reminds Agatha, "that depends on what you think is realistic." *Seeing Things* thus proffers two divergent engagements between the lesbian and the penis. In the first—Agatha's postcoital ruminations—the idea of the penis is played with, imaginatively appropriated beyond its heteropatriarchal symbolic status. However, in the second, Agatha's encounter with the dildo is determined through a heteropatriarchal phallocentric logic as an encounter with the penis, a logic precluding her from seeing things differently. What is glimpsable here, however, is the bisexual possibility of a conception of desire akin to what Preciado proposes as "countersexuality," wherein the matter of sexual desire is decoupled from the ruse of ontology, where sexuality's semioticity does not preclude pleasure but, rather, is constitutive of it.[140] *Seeing Things* suggests the impossibility for Agatha to reconcile the fantastical with her mediation of reality, becoming a conflicted subject who entertains, through fantasy, a relation to the penis beyond monosexual heteropatriarchal meaning yet is persecuted, in her perceptions, by this very hermeneutic. Yet perceptions, like desires, can be mutable.

The Bisexual Skeleton: Lesbian Cinema, Reverse Discourse, and the Blues

JULIA.   Listen, Agatha. I don't mean to sound negative, but what do you expect getting involved with a woman whose sexual history has been mostly with men?

AGATHA.   Look, all my life, I've been told what's right and what's wrong—from my father, by nuns, by priests—and finally I discover something that gives me great pleasure and there's another ideology telling me that it's wrong. Do you wanna know what I think about that?

This chapter has explored a film made within the context of lesbian cinema in which the invocation of female bisexuality deracinates the foundations of bi-exclusionary lesbian ethics. The revelation of Jo's bisexuality induces a suspicious, paranoid reaction in Agatha, affecting her perception, which, in turn, affects the film's form. With the latter, *Seeing Things* abstracts systems of cinematic sexual signification to explore the anxieties and instabilities female bisexuality occasions when perceived through a bi-exclusionary lens. By at times adhering to and at others breaking the rules of classical narrative realism, the film's approach to form is transgressively dissimulative. This formal approach works to expose the mechanisms upon which the intelligibility of sexuality on film is contingent. The incensed reactions the film inspired can, thus, be traced back to its cinematic permeation of the strict divide between lesbianism and heterosexuality. As I established in this book's introduction, dominant formations of heterosexuality and homosexuality are made meaningful by their mutual repudiation of one each other. *Seeing Things*' terror lies in its figuring the lingering presence of an unrepudiated heterosexuality in the body assumed lesbian. Judith Butler observes how "crafting a sexual position, or reciting a sexual position, always involves becoming haunted by what's excluded. And the more rigid the position, the greater the ghost."[141] The film's figuration of the haunting presence of bisexuality in a rigidly demarcated lesbian space speaks to some of the reactions to *Seeing Things* de Lauretis remembers hearing: "They thought it shouldn't be made public on film but kept as the proverbial skeleton in the lesbian closet."[142] *Seeing Things*' provocation involves the release of the bisexual skeleton from the lesbian closet. This is an opening out of which the bisexual skeleton crawls, carrying with her the disturbing debris of butchness and femmeness, masculinity and femininity, sadism and masochism, penises and dildos.

McLaughlin is not alone in her status as a lesbian feminist director whose work troubled monosexist lesbian feminist ideology. German director Monika Treut (with whom McLaughlin collaborated as an actor) is another filmmaker whom, while often being discussed as a lesbian filmmaker, Marcia Klotz describes as challenging "the utopian assumptions that have been connected to the radical lesbian movement."[143] In *Seduction: The Cruel Woman* (1985), dominatrix Wanda (Mechthild Großmann) oversees a house of sexual deviance in which people of different genders participate in s/m play—a space where monosexual categories have become superfluous; in *Virgin Machine* (1988), Dorothee's (Ina Blum) journey from relationships with men to relationships with women involves an encounter with female masculinity, of drag kings and dildos; in *My Father Is Coming* (1991), Vicky (Shelley Kästner) flits between a relationship with her hapless lesbian coworker (Mary Lou Grailau) and a brooding transgender man (Michael Massee); in *Taboo Parlor* (1994), couple Claire (Priscilla Barnes) and Julia (Camilla Søeberg) seduce a straight man, Victor (Michael Carr), coercing him into getting pegged before murdering him, a sadistic depiction of sex between a man and two queer women that resists being understood as heterosexual.[144] Similar to some of the lesbian feminist reactions to *Seeing Things*, Treut's work has been accused of being "excessively heterosexual," and Treut herself is alleged to have "betrayed the label of lesbian filmmaker."[145] What *Seeing Things* and these examples of Treut's work share is a draw toward bisexual possibility, representations that trouble the dominant notion of submissive female heterosexuality while also destabilizing the oppositional notion of a monolithic lesbianness.[146] As they erode the divide between lesbian and heterosexual, these films give way to a sexual-symbolic morass where the dominant monosexualities' foundations become unmoored.

While questions of what constitutes lesbian cinema have been the subject of ongoing critical debates, it is clear that certain films are able to shore up more exclusionary forms of lesbian identity through specific narrative and formal devices that elide bisexual potentialities. This cinematic concretization of meaning is achieved by constructing *lesbian* in relation to discursive and symbolic forms that are already intelligible, what Clara Bradbury-Rance calls, in relation to the notion of lesbian visibility, "the fixing of a set idea in the image."[147] This kind of lesbian cinema can thus be understood as characteristic of the process Michel Foucault calls "reverse discourse," whereby "homosexuality began to speak in its own behalf, to demand that its legitimacy or 'naturality' be acknowledged, often in the same vocabulary, using the same categories by which it was medically disqualified."[148] In *Seeing Things* and many of Treut's films, dominant notions of lesbianism, as a category with knowable meaning, are complicated. That which looks lesbian is not, the oppositional binary between heterosexuality and homosexuality does not hold, a film authored by a lesbian does not promote exclusionary forms of lesbian ideology but, instead, exposes fissures therein. In the films I have discussed, the limits of lesbian visibility are tested and, in doing so, they illustrate the precarity of sexuality's signification through reverse discourse. Bisexuality's lack of historical medicalization qua bisexuality has precluded it from the strategy of reverse discourse.[149] These films' figurations of bisexuality can, thus, be understood as encouraging strategies of figuring queer sexuality beyond reverse discourse's stronghold over established codes of queer representation. Rather than reify dominant notions of lesbianness within preexistent discursive and symbolic economies, the figuration of bisexual possibility allows for a disruptive interrogation of these systems and the monosexual binary that governs them. Such a process need not involve a disappearance of the image of the lesbian per se but may instead be a process of what Shane Phelan calls a "presencing" of lesbianism "detached from the temptation to present icons of lesbianism" and attesting to "the instability of lesbian identity."[150] Such a process, Phelan continues, "includes acknowledging that many women who have loved women also love(d) men or will love them in the future; it means acknowledging 'bisexuality' . . . at the center of lesbian existence."[151] In McLaughlin's and Treut's films, the ruse of what Phelan calls "icons of lesbianism" is refused, as is the allure of a stable reverse discourse, to reflect, instead, the always-having-been-there-ness of women who desire men in lesbian spaces.

Toward the end of *Seeing Things*, Agatha sits in a predominantly Black blues bar with her Black colleague Julia as she reflects upon the distress occasioned by her discovery of Jo's bisexual past. In response, Julia rehearses the mantra of bi-exclusionary lesbian ethics: the bisexual woman is not to be trusted. Agatha's rebuttal to this comment, however, shows a verbal disavowal of this doxa, which she names as an ideology akin to the patriarchal Catholicism with which she was raised. It is through Agatha's identification of this ideology as ideology that she can begin to escape the maddening hold it has had over her perspective. The camera cuts, intermittently, to singer Princess Pamela, who performs on a stage. Pamela sings a classic twelve-bar blues song that recalls the music of Ma Rainey and Bessie Smith. Notably, these icons of Black American blues music expressed desire toward both men and women, attested to in historical accounts and in both implicit and explicit references to bisexual desire in the songs they authored.[152] Pamela's performance of the sounds and styles of 1920s Black women blues musicians can be understood, in the context of the scene, as invoking the sexual politics of these queer figures whose lives transcend monosexual interpretation. Pamela's singing offers a metacommentary on the conversation taking place in the same room. Associatively challenging the alignment of female bisexuality to whiteness—what is perhaps a subtext to Julia's words—Pamela's music hearkens a history of Black bisexual cultural production. As Julia criticizes Agatha for having entered a relationship with a woman who has a bisexual history, Pamela's words echo the trouble female bisexuality wreaks for bi-exclusionary lesbian ethics: "Yes, everybody's worried since I came to town."

CHAPTER 3

AMBIGUITY, MASCULINITY, AIDS

Savage Nights (1992)

In Bertrand Blier's *Ménage* (1986), the unpredictable desires of an enigmatic visitor uproot the foundations of a heterosexual couple's life of staid domesticity. This visitor is Bob (Gérard Depardieu), a petty criminal who insinuates himself into the unhappy marriage of Antoine (Michel Blanc) and Monique (Miou-Miou), cajoling them into burglarizing houses together. In front of the first house in their spree, Bob spits on a bump key, declaring: "A keyhole needs lubrication, like all orifices. You start with some saliva and wait till it yields." Inside, Bob attempts to seduce Antoine, dressing him in women's finery and looking into his eyes amorously. Antoine runs out of the room, scandalized, to find Monique, warning her that Bob is "a fairy" (*une tante*). The couple tries to leave when Bob spots Monique and admires her body, adorned in a black negligee. As he kisses her arms, she remarks, "This guy's not a fag [*un pédé*], it's not possible." She grabs Bob's erection, visible through his leather pants, exclaiming, "If all fags were like you, there'd be fewer unhappy women!" Bob then proceeds to wreak a particularly bisexual variety of chaos.[1] He has sex with Monique in front of Antoine before taking Antoine as his lover, relegating Monique to sleeping on a stool as he fucks her husband. Bob then arranges for Monique to be seduced by a man who ends up coaxing her into sex work. Meanwhile, Bob dresses Antoine in women's clothing, renaming him Antoinette. The film ends with the three of them as sex workers, Bob and Antoine cross-dressed, looking for clients on the cold streets of Paris. A once-traditional couple has been transformed beyond recognition by the arrival of the bisexual transgressor.[2]

Previous chapters have observed how cinematic figures of bisexual transgression can transform various status quo antes, from the mortal societies infiltrated by the les(bi)an vampire's preternaturality to the lesbian spaces in which efforts to purge bisexual women effect an unremitting paranoia. As we move toward male figurations of bisexual transgression, this transformational potential endures, but it is articulated differently. Similar to his female counterparts, this bisexual figure flits between the normative and the subversive, the dominating and the submissive, the harmful and the healing, yet the dynamics of these oscillations cannot be understood without attention to their relation to codes of masculinity and structures of patriarchal power. Central to many of these figurations, from the 1980s onward, is the threat of HIV transmission, insofar as discourses around AIDS brought the figure of the male bisexual to the fore as a specter of disease transmission. Whereas previous chapters have considered the metaphorical contaminations performed by the bisexual figure—in the les(bi)an vampire's pernicious bite and the bisexual woman's sullying of lesbian space—the male bisexual's infectiousness here harnesses a literal social referent. Although the literal/metaphorical distinction has a limited bearing on figuration—Donna J. Haraway's examples involve composite "material-semiotic processes"—the figure of the male HIV transmitter is made meaningful via a citation of contemporary epidemiological danger, imbuing him with a sense of sociopolitical reflexivity and immediacy.[3] These figures of bisexual transgression are thus marked by two distinct qualities: their constitution vis-à-vis (patriarchal) masculinities and their embodiment of a contemporary social figure of contagion whose bisexual proclivities spell the viral vulnerability of all.

This chapter analyzes Cyril Collard's 1992 art film *Savage Nights*, in which the French director stars as a bisexual HIV-positive cameraman, Jean. Collard was a musician, novelist, poet, and actor and a director of music videos, television, and film; he also worked as an apprentice for Maurice Pialat on his sexually charged art films *Loulou* (1980) and *To Our Loves* (1983). Collard first became known in France with his novels *Love Condemned* (1987) and *Savage Nights* (1989).[4] The eponymous film adaptation of the latter follows Jean, who returns from a work assignment in Morocco back to Paris, where he discovers that he is HIV-positive. At an audition for a television advertisement, Jean meets the seventeen-year-old Laura (Romane Bohringer), with whom he begins a relationship. Meanwhile, Jean begins to have sexual encounters with his friend Samy (Carlos López), a macho rugby player. When Jean reveals to Laura that he is HIV-positive, she is initially angry, but they reconcile soon thereafter. Later Laura visits her aunt in Nice, and Jean and Samy move in together, which enrages Laura upon her return to Paris. Jean breaks up with Laura, but she telephones him incessantly, telling him that he has given her HIV. Laura is institutionalized at a clinic, where tests reveal that she does not have HIV. Jean grows distant with Samy, who joins a neofascist street gang; Laura enters a relationship with another man. Jean then drives from Paris toward Europe's remotest edges, in southwest Portugal. There, he reflects that life is something in which he participates.

Savage Nights exemplifies how male bisexuality's conceptual ambiguity and mutability—values that have precluded it from social recognition—are rendered, in art cinema aesthetics, criterions of metaphysical truth. It is in this context that we find an affirmative treatment of male bisexuality's capacity to illuminate masculinity's mutability. In the wake of the HIV/AIDS pandemic, growing awareness of male bisexuality had ramifications on-screen. In the French context, films addressing HIV/AIDS tended not to affirm a gay male identity (as was the tendency in contemporary American independent film), exploring instead how HIV/AIDS troubles notions of sexual identity in ways that could not but contend with bisexuality's presentness. Central to these portrayals of male bisexual possibility are questions of sexual space—the exigencies of which dominated discourses around HIV transmission—and the ways bisexuality troubles these spaces' discreteness. These spatial dynamics also highlight the function of relationality in exploring bisexuality on film: how bisexuality's multiplicity of gendered objects is made manifest in varied modes of relation to others and how these irregular relations are figured in form. Whereas my other chapters work through relatively distinct contexts of genre and mode of production, this chapter's critical context is more capacious. Art cinema, insofar as it constitutes a set of aesthetic conventions, is this context, as is the social, cultural, and cinematic landscape of 1980s and 1990s France, where art cinema enjoyed sustained engagement. The breadth of these contexts is evident, but what marks their unique relation to conveying male bisexuality is precise: These are contexts in which ambiguity—as an aesthetic and even philosophical value—has been afforded affirmative treatment.

Art Cinema, Ambiguity, and Bisexual Authorship

Art cinema champions ambiguity.[5] In David Bordwell's enduring neoformalist conception, he contends that art cinema "defines itself . . . against the cause-effect linkage of events . . . [with] psychologically complex characters . . . [lacking] defined desires and goals."[6] This nonlinear complexity is also reflected in the art film's approach to narrative, with Bordwell later asserting that "the story will often lack a clear-cut resolution . . . leav[ing] causes dangling, questions unanswered."[7] Bordwell identifies certain textual qualities that typify art cinema: Its narratives favor a more episodical than causal presentation of events, its characters often lack aim, and its endings tend not to resolve narrative problems. These are some of the central ways in which art cinema has distinguished itself from classical film aesthetics. Whereas the latter privilege intelligibility in their communication of singular meaning, Kalling Heck outlines how it is ambiguity that serves as art cinema's "major structuring principle."[8] This is an aesthetic principle that harmonizes in important ways with certain philosophical traditions' embrace of ambiguity. Whereas Aristotelean logic is suspicious of ambiguity's capacity to obscure reason through fallacy, other approaches have sought not to dismiss ambiguity so swiftly. In Diogenes Laërtius's account of Stoic thinking on ambiguity, he describes the necessity, in understanding certain utterances, to comprehend multiple *pragmata* at once.[9] The need to understand things in their multiplicity is reflected in later invocations of ambiguity in the existentialist tradition with, for instance, Søren Kierkegaard's emphasis on maintaining the "elastic ambiguity" of human psychology or Simone de Beauvoir's ethics of ambiguity, which involves a refusal "to deny *a priori* that separate existants can, at the same time, be bound to each other."[10] For the Stoics, Kierkegaard, and Beauvoir alike, ambiguity is conceptualized divergently from its characterization in Aristotelean logic as, instead, signaling a composite, truthful, or ethical relation to the world.[11] Art cinema makes a similar contention insofar as, in Maria San Filippo's words, it "embraces ambiguity and illogicality as truthful rather than obfuscating."[12] Art cinema's presentation of ambiguous, heterogeneous, or even seemingly contradictory phenomena is made meaningful through its reflection of ambiguity, compositeness, and contradictoriness in the world. In other words, we might say that for art cinema, ambiguity carries the criterion of truth.

Art cinema's aesthetic qualities can also be put into meaningful dialogue with conceptions of bisexuality in relation to a number of shared structuring principles. Let us recall that the etymological roots of the word *ambiguous* lie in the Latin *ambi-* (go round) and *agere* (drive).[13] The orbital movements of the former and determined thrusts of the latter chime evocatively with bisexuality's own winding drives around and toward differently gendered objects. Maria Pramaggiore writes that bisexual reading strategies are particularly compatible with European art films "which focus on the episodic quality of a nonteleological temporal continuum across which a number of sexual acts, desires, and identities might be expressed."[14] Insofar as, in Traci Carroll's words, "bisexuality implies its own nonteleology," there are stark affinities between bisexual temporalities and art cinema's resistance to teleological narrative structures and neat conclusions.[15] San Filippo expands upon Pramaggiore's hypothesis, arguing that art cinema, "with its willingness to probe the dilemmas of desire," has regularly "mounted a substantial critique of compulsory monosexuality."[16] Bisexuality's unintelligibility within a monosexual symbolic economy is thus refashioned in art cinema as reflecting the messy vicissitudes of life; a representation of bisexuality against the dominant logic of the monosexual binary takes on a realist claim. As we watch Rainer Werner Fassbinder's *Katzelmacher* (1969), for example, Paul (Rudolf Waldemar Brem) being in a relationship with Helga (Lilith Ungerer) and occasionally sleeping with Klaus (Hannes Gromball) does not constitute a narrative event per se; it does not necessitate a cathartic moment of coming out. In art cinema, the presence of phenomena that are incongruous with monosexual logic need not be explained away; indeed, univocal explanation would be anathema to a persistent ethical suggestion in art cinema that univocality obscures the messier, necessarily polyvalent nature of truth.

Art cinema, characterized by Rosalind Galt and Karl Schoonover as "impure" insofar as it is routinely "frustrating to taxonomy," provides fertile ground for male bisexuality's own taxonomy-frustrating impurities.[17] Examples of male bisexuality's capacity to transform, sully, or render precarious social structures can be found in some compelling cinematic figures emanating from the art cinema tradition. In Pier Paolo Pasolini's *Theorem* (1968), a mysterious Visitor (Terence Stamp) seduces each member of an Italian bourgeois family, leaving the lives of each in tatters, save a maid whose encounter with him transforms her into a pious saint. In Péter Tímár's *Before the Bat's Flight Is Done* (1989), Hungarian single mother Teréz (Erika Bodnár) begins a relationship with an imperious police officer, László (Gábor Máté), who later molests her teenage son, Robi (Róbert Csontos); László's increasingly destructive and obsessive antics eventually push Teréz to suicide. In these examples, the figure of the bisexual man exerts a transgressive force—sometimes politically radical, sometimes destructively violent. In each case, the bisexual man transforms those he encounters. Vitiating heterosexuality with intragender desire, subverting

hegemonic masculinity with a mutable compositeness, warping spatiotempo-
ral modes of sexual situatedness and teleology, the figure of the male bisexual
transgressor finds, in art cinema, an accomplice in impurity.

The idea that a film is or should be guided by an individual creative force—
the auteur—has been central to notions of art cinema, especially in France
where the concept was developed by Alexandre Astruc, André Bazin, and
François Truffaut, among others.[18] Insofar as the work of auteurs is positioned
as an extension of their identity or personality, it is common for these films to
be considered informed by and representative of their director. *Savage Nights* is
both an adaptation of Collard's own eponymous novel and a film in which he
stars, establishing both his authorial role and his alignment with the protagonist pronouncedly. Like Jean, Collard was bisexual, HIV-positive, a cameraman, a musician; these parallels encourage a hermeneutic approach in which
the director and his character are thought of together, as when a *L'Express* journalist writes, "Between Cyril and Jean there is no screen."[19] The bifaceted figure
of Cyril/Jean dominates critical writing on *Savage Nights*. Carolyn A. Durham
writes that Collard's untimely death "turned the man into a myth and his life
and career into a social and cultural phenomenon," resulting in an "abrupt as-
cension to the stature of a mythic figure."[20] *Savage Nights* achieved tremendous
commercial success upon its release, with a reported 2.8 million admissions in
France in 1993; at the end of 1992, *Cahiers du Cinéma*'s readership voted it the
best film of the year.[21] Contemporary French press around *Savage Nights* often
call it a cult film, not in the generic sense of the term but in relation to the way
it galvanized the passions of young people, sometimes referred to as "la généra-
tion Collard."[22] Collard died from AIDS-related illnesses just three days before
his film would win four Césars, the first film in the French awards ceremony's
history to win both Best Film and Best First Film. The 1993 ceremony was dominated by hagiographic tributes to Collard by his co-collaborators, in mourning, as they were, just three days after his death. Fabienne André Worth likens
"the parallel deaths of the film's hero and its auteur" to "the death of Christian
martyrs," a kind of secular sacrifice.[23] It is telling that Worth misremembers
Savage Nights as featuring Jean's death, which does not take place. This conflation between the auteur and the character is not incidental but symptomatic
of the film's reception, which blurred the textual and extratextual. At Collard's
funeral, his fans gathered to pay respects. Speaking to a France 2 reporter, one
fan reads aloud Jean's final lines in *Savage Nights*, a printed frame from this moment in his hand.[24] For this fan, Jean's words—written by Collard, spoken by
Collard—take on commemorative value, filmmaker and character coalescing
in a singular Jean/Collard figuration.

Between the 1980s and 1990s, the figure of the homosexual auteur had begun to gain ground in France.[25] The oeuvres of directors including Patrice Chéreau, Guy Gilles, Diane Kurys, François Ozon, André Téchiné, and Paul Vecchiali can be understood as consistent with the auteurist values of thematic consistency and personal inflection. The latter quality carries with it the queer valence of what Sam Bourcier identifies as the "political self-expression" typical of queer filmmakers in France.[26] By making films inspired by their own queer lives, these auteurs could not but contend with the political import inherent in their authorial voices, but this was mainly understood in France in relation to the idea of specifically homosexual culture. Collard was open about his bi-sexuality in various interviews, yet he expressed a feeling of alienation from both France's gay community and its homosexual culture, which I consider in greater detail later in this chapter. Collard's frustrations reflect Catherine De-schamps's observation that, in France's homosexual movements of the 1970s, "suspicions never entirely stopped hanging over both identified and identifi-able bisexuals."[27] Consider a moment in Carole Roussopoulos's 1971 documen-tary Le F.H.A.R., in which activist Anne-Marie Grélois addresses a meeting of the Homosexual Front for Revolutionary Action. Grélois declares: "Of course, we have bisexuals among us. So the issue has arisen . . . Why not rather de-fend bisexuality? Firstly, because bisexuality is easily redeemable for both boys and girls. If a guy can still fuck a woman sometimes, that proves he is still a male, right? If a girl can fuck a boy sometimes, that simply proves that she is a bit sluttier than others and therefore even more desirable for guys. So even those of us who do practice bisexuality should claim homosexuality, and noth-ing else!"[28] Disparaging attitudes like these toward bisexuals effected their so-cial, cultural, and political alienation among France's homosexual movements. This alienation was, in turn, repurposed in biphobic discourses attributing to the bisexual individualistic values like narcissism and egotism. French journal-ist Jean-Luc Hennig makes numerous declarations about the bisexual man to this effect at different points across his book-length diatribe against them: "A bisexual man does not love anything, *he lets himself be loved*"; "The bisexual is (like Narcissus) his own object of knowledge"; "The bisexual man never fully embodies his character but, rather, uses it to shield himself."[29] We can see, therefore, a rhetorical process at play in which the bisexual is first excluded from a gay body politic and then demonized for their individualized state.[30] Whereas the figure of the homosexual auteur could exploit their access to no-tions of homosexual culture and community, the ostracism of bisexuality from these spaces—twinned with understandings of bisexual people as narcissists divorced from homosexual life—precluded bisexual artists' incorporation into this culture. Yet this exclusion was precisely what Collard would leverage in his self-stylization as a bisexual outcast auteur.

In Collard's own reflections, we find clues as to the ethical dimensions of his self-professed sexual outlaw status. In an entry from Collard's journals from 1987, he inveighs against various social groups in a stream of invective that warrants extended quotation:

> You're all as bad as each other. You fags who have reproached me for sleeping with girls. They disgust you, and you don't think it possible that I have had pleasure with them. You think that I'm exactly like you. But I'm not exactly like you. I love to have sex with women and, unlike you, I can think of their genitals without vomiting. . . . And you, heteros . . . you are no better than them. You want to convert me, to cure me, to make me happy, to make me forget, to make me love. To make me love you. . . . You don't know about what I experience when I sleep beside certain boys, when they hold me in their arms. . . . For you, fags, I am a coward. I dodge the truth, I skirt around it by sticking with girls. You'd like to see me more militant, more proselytizing. . . . And you others, you get sad, you cry about my future. . . . I hate you all equally. . . . You live according to reflexes, you think according to formulas. . . . Selfish people are probably the only tolerable ones.[31]

The selfish person, for Collard, describes an ethical subject position that does not concern itself with others' desires and actions, a position from which others are not interpellated into dominant categories of sexuality. The fury with which he speaks of others in this passage is rooted in their tendency to ascribe to him attributes or ideals rooted in formulaic thinking—read: the logic of the monosexual binary. If, as Godfrey Cheshire claims, "many gay men reportedly bristle at [*Savage Nights'*] recurrent emphasis on bisexuality," it would seem that making them bristle was precisely Collard's intention.[32]

Bisexual Masculinities and the Bisexual HIV Transmitter

The Best Way to Walk (Claude Miller, 1976) is set at a French boys' summer camp, where bullish patriarch Marc (Patrick Dewaere) prides himself as the alpha male among the youth leaders. After Marc catches his colleague Philippe (Patrick Bouchitey) dressing in women's clothing and applying makeup, Marc tries to blackmail him, with Philippe offering Marc sexual favors to stop the torment. Eventually, Phillipe chooses to refuse the rules of Marc's game. He joins forces with his fiancée, Chantal (Christine Pascal), facilitating a costume party where, wearing a dress, Philippe flirts with Marc in front of the partygoers, embarrassing him while Chantal watches from the side as her fiancé's knowing accomplice. Here, Philippe's flexibility with his own masculinity—its correlativity with his own femininity, his embodiment of a searing, self-assured masculinity-in-a-dress—precipitates the uprooting of a patriarchal pecking order. Further, Philippe harnesses the support of his fiancée in undoing this structure; Chantal attends the costume party dressed in drag herself, wearing a suit and sporting a fake mustache. For Sergei Eisenstein, artistic depictions of cross-dressing remind us of our "androgynous being," of a "unitary bisexual element" existing as a capacity in us all.[33] *The Best Way to Walk*, in its depiction of a bisexual man and his female partner's cross-dressing, produces such an effect, engendering rearticulations of extragender desire beyond the constraints of patriarchal heteronormativity.

Art cinema has allowed for a particular kind of mutability around masculinity on screen, exemplified in *The Best Way to Walk*. Following György Kalmár, I contend that we can find more regularly in the European art film reflections of "the ways our contemporary ideological fantasies fail to materialize in some men's lives . . . men who do not live the (ideological) dream, who did not make it, who cannot incorporate the dominant fantasies."[34] European art cinema has, not exclusively but more habitually, granted narrative space for male characters' failures in the face of patriarchal masculinity's demands. This is not to suggest that art cinema offers an egalitarian treatment of gender free from the constraints of patriarchal culture.[35] Nevertheless, art cinema's investment in the ambiguous does offer greater flexibility in its treatment of male bodies and masculinity. This flexibility is not ipso facto antipatriarchal; instead, it holds the potential to challenge patriarchal standards of masculinity. As bell hooks reminds us, the general notion of masculinity need not be conflated with patriarchal masculinity: The masculine can be cleaved from the patriarchal.[36] Whereas representations of men's extragender desire on film have tended toward patriarchal heterosexual masculinity, art cinema's portrayals of male bisexuality have the potential to complicate these alignments precisely through their embrace of multiplicity and ambiguity.

In *Savage Nights'* Jean, we find a composite masculinity featuring variegated textures of gendered expression. *Sight and Sound* critic Amanda Lipman comments that "what is remarkable about Collard's performance is the way he transforms a number of male clichés into a credible, even sympathetic character."[37] At times, Jean displays a tender softness—a jocular routine he performs for Laura involves his imitating a possum—but elsewhere he is aggressive, at times berating Laura with misogynistic quips. Jean may wear leather jackets and drive a fast car, but his masculine exterior is undermined by his ill body, dotted with Kaposi's sarcoma, made vulnerable under the medical professionals we see prodding and biopsying him. In sex, Jean displays versatility: Sometimes he penetrates others, sometimes they penetrate him. In one scene, he lies down in a cruising ground and asks to be urinated on. The bisexual capacities of *Savage Nights'* Jean are conveyed through a plastic masculinity whose meaning is not fixed. This stylization of male bisexuality as composite and changeable speaks to conceptual qualities with which male bisexuality has been aligned. Yet, conversely, it is these very qualities that have produced a disqualifying effect toward male bisexuality epistemologically: How can something composite and changeable exist in an economy of sexual signification that values singular and stable meaning?

In this book's introduction, I established how the purported nonexistence of male bisexuality is posited by determining all men who desire men as putatively homosexual; the concurrence of desire toward women herein is deemed unthinkable. Such assertions can be found as regularly in heterosexist culture as in gay culture and have even, in the psychoanalytic and psychological cases I discussed earlier, been reified in some parts of the medical sciences. A notable disturbance of this cultural trend, however, occurred in the United States with the 1948 publication of an influential study led by sexologist Alfred Kinsey, *Sexual Behavior in the Human Male* (1948). The conclusions of this study report that 46 percent of the men interviewed had reacted sexually "to persons of both sexes."[38] Kinsey's findings were troubling for societies, both within and beyond the United States, that had assumed the predominance of heterosexuality among men. Despite the study's well-documented methodological limitations, its discursive impact should not be underestimated. Unlike fin de siècle sexologists, for whom bisexuality marked underdevelopment or "primitivity," *Sexual Behavior in the Human Male* purports to provide evidence that men's desires among the general population were less heterosexual and more flexible than had once been assumed. As the report concludes, "Males do not represent two discrete populations, heterosexual and homosexual."[39]

In France, male bisexuality has occupied a similarly contentious position in two national surveys on sexual behavior comparable to Kinsey's in the United States: the Simon Report (1972) and the Spira Report (1992). While the first report mainly focuses on heterosexual couples, it also found—through more than 2,500 interviews—that 5 percent of men surveyed had had a sexual partner of "the same sex."[40] Twenty years later, the Spira Report found that "those who report having had at least one sexual relation with a person of the same sex also report, in large numbers, having had sexual relations with people of the opposite sex (4% of men). . . . This 'bisexuality,' of which there are apparently high levels, is sometimes due to people having had sexual relations with individuals of both sexes, sometimes heterosexuals having had an occasional homosexual relation, and, reciprocally, homosexuals having had an occasional heterosexual relation."[41] The rhetorical acrobatics here are remarkable. A testament to bisexuality's disruption of sexual taxonomy, this anomalous 4 percent troubles the linear explanations found elsewhere in the report. Male bisexuality, which can only be written in scare quotes, lacks a uniform behavioral pattern or a stable notion of identity with which to align it. Instead, it is conceived here as an aberrant kind of either heterosexuality or homosexuality, this aberrance threatening to disrupt the distinction altogether.

Despite Kinsey's warning that "the world is not to be divided into sheep and goats," France's subsequent studies faced difficulties in trying to bifurcate their research participants as such.[42] Curiously, goats also come to the fore in an obsolescent French term used to describe bisexuality: "être bique et bouc" (literally, to be both a nanny goat and a billy goat).[43] It is notable that, in this vernacular phrase, bisexuality is characterized as being two things at once, combining maleness and femaleness in a nonhuman configuration that speaks to Alan Sinfield's articulation of bisexuality as "a blatant disturber of neatly gendered models."[44] This idea of multiplicity is conceptually inherent to male bisexuality given its disquieting presence beyond dominant monosexual logic and masculine singularity. In art cinema, male bisexuality's multivalence finds an aesthetic tradition that holds the potential to grant male bisexuality that which a dominant social order denies it: an affirmative treatment of ambiguity. However, it is this ambiguity that would, in the wake of the AIDS pandemic, spell male bisexuality's threat. Here, male bisexuality emerged as a problem for the very reasons some art cinema has embraced it: its imperceptibility, its indeterminateness, its enigmatic allure. How would the pullulating sociocultural discourses, which stigmatized male bisexuality as an epidemiological threat, affect art cinema?

In the West German–French coproduction *AIDS: Love in Danger* (Hans Noever, 1985), one of the first European films to engage with AIDS, Tamara (Claudia Arnold), who suspects that the boyfriend of her friend Jessica (Géraldine Danon) is sleeping with men, reads her a warning from a newspaper: "Today many homosexuals maintain intimate relationships with women. . . . They behave extremely irresponsibly and endanger everyone."[45] A film produced in the first years of knowledge about AIDS, this moment reflects the intensity of media discussions around sexuality in the wake of inchoate knowledge around a deadly sexually transmitted virus. The June 1993 issue of the French edition of *Marie Claire* carries a headline on its front page: "Secretly Bisexual Husbands: AIDS Danger?" Inside, we find the story of Mina, a woman who contracted HIV from a husband who had hitherto hidden his bisexuality from her. The article's author, Tessa Ivascu, writes: "The man must understand that in lying to his wife . . . he is implicitly taking the decision, alone, to assume the risks of the couple's contamination."[46] This French magazine invokes the fears around the bisexual male contaminator similarly to contemporary Anglophone publications: A 1987 front-page *New York Times* headline reads, "AIDS Specter for Women: The Bisexual Man"; a 1988 article in Black American magazine *Ebony* proclaims, "The Hidden Fear: Black Women, Bisexuals, and the AIDS Risk"; a 1992 *Los Angeles Times* headline warns of "Hidden Dangers: Worried by AIDS Threat, Experts Focus on Bisexual Men Who Put Themselves, Families at Risk"; a 1994 article from British newspaper *Daily Express* is titled "How to Cope When Your Man Is Bisexual," with the subtitle "Secret Passions Can Prove Deadly."[47] The discursive figure of the secretly bisexual man transmitting HIV to women proliferated in media discussions of AIDS on both sides of the Atlantic, with his purported threat to women in particular taking center stage.

In the wake of the AIDS crisis, it is the male bisexual—difficult to identify, tricky to trace—who became what Jan Zita Grover called in 1987 "the epidemic's new bête noir."[48] In the early years of AIDS, both medical and journalistic discourses discussed "high-risk" populations, which included gay men, sex workers, intravenous drug users, and hemophiliacs. By the latter half of the 1980s, however, it was clear that women outside of these groups were contracting the virus, signaling its diffusion beyond supposedly high-risk populations. Writing in 1986, French medical practitioner Ghéorghiü Grigorieff tries to grapple with the dissemination of HIV outside these populations, concluding that "the liberalization of social mores has revealed a latent bisexuality . . . one of the principal factors in the infiltration of the AIDS virus [*sic*] outside of high risk groups."[49] In order to explain these avenues of transmission, the figure of the male bisexual transmitter became both uniquely visible (considering bisexuality's regular discursive elision) and threateningly *in*visible, insofar as the bisexual man was routinely characterized as nondescript. For Jonathan Dollimore, bisexual men were imagined as "carriers of AIDS into the straight community"; for Grover, the bisexual man is understood in these discourses as "a homosexual posing as a heterosexual—acting as the secret conveyor of the diseases of the former to the healthy bodies of the latter"; for Martin S. Weinberg, Colin J. Williams, and Douglas W. Pryor, "the bisexual [man] stands as a secret agent spreading a deadly disease to the unsuspecting public."[50] Transnationally, the bisexual man thus arose as a powerful discursive and symbolic figure whose infection of heterosexuals was deemed symptomatic of his own clandestine transgressions.

This problem of appearances symptomized a larger issue around contemporary HIV/AIDS prevention: that sexual behavior does not always align neatly with sexual identity. The first cases of AIDS in France appeared in 1981, the same year that the first reports on the infection came out of the United States.[51] By the end of 1990, France had the second largest number of AIDS cases in Europe, with over three times the amount of cases per capita than the United Kingdom as a point of comparison.[52] France's disproportionate levels of infection have been linked to various political factors, including frequent changes of government throughout the 1980s, the structural separateness of medical and social policy bodies in public administration, and a ban on the advertisement of condoms, not lifted until 1987.[53] Exacerbating this unsteady political climate were cultural factors in France, where notions of sexual identity and sexual minority community were often considered culturally unbefitting. David Caron observes how, in France, "the notion of a gay community threatens the boundary between public and private spheres, a boundary on which individual freedom rests. The (hypothetical) gay community is perceived as a factor of increased social fragmentation because it relies on a difference rather than on a unifying political will."[54] Jean-Pierre Boulé relates these foundational political principles to traditions of French republicanism, which is regularly positioned against the "communitarianism" of countries like the United States.[55] Boulé argues that these ideological factors influenced France's AIDS policy: "In this context, the socialist government treated a *public* health emergency, the AIDS crisis, as a *private* matter for individuals."[56] When it became clear that certain groups were at higher risk of contracting HIV, France had to contend with ideas around sexual identity and community that had hitherto been considered inappropriate for the French context. While the notion of "the homosexual" had some social import in France—with its history of homosexual activism, gay magazines and radio stations, some gay districts and venues in cities—bisexuality had no such cultural capital with which to ground itself. As Catherine Deschamps writes about France in the 1980s, "Homosexuality was defined by both customs and culture . . . bisexuality only by behavior."[57] In the wake of the AIDS crisis, however, male bisexuality was illuminated as a troubling behavioral phenomenon, illustrated by Jean-Luc Hennig's reflection on it: "We have been forced to admit (by AIDS) that desires have been circulating much less wisely than one would have hoped."[58] In Hennig's assessment, it is the revelation of this purportedly unwise circulation of desire that demanded France contend with male bisexuality. The male bisexual thus found a unique cultural prominence in the wake of AIDS, less as an identity type but more as a figure whose perceived character did not align with his sexual practices.[59]

Central to the threat of the male bisexual transmitter is the infection of the heterosexual woman, often characterized as the wife or mother, and of their children, a notion invoked by a warning from *Newsweek* in 1987 that "bisexual husbands and bachelors can spread the infection that ultimately affects their wives and children, or their straight girlfriends."[60] Elizabeth Grosz describes the heterosexual anxiety during this time that while populations already considered perverse were stigmatized in the wake of AIDS, fears around a husband's or father's "clandestine bisexuality or drug use" served as a reminder of the possibilities of certain perversions' existence within the family.[61] In the French context, Eric Lamien writes that ideas around bisexual men are enmeshed in a "fantasy of dangerousness which, in turn, designates certain lifestyles or practices . . . detrimental to the integrity of a mysterious 'heterosexual identity' that is *a priori* necessarily safe."[62] This threat to heterosexual identity is rooted in a clear underlying question: How might we identify a queer threat that looks like a heterosexual man? The figure of the bisexual man thus emerged as the answer to the mystery of sexually and morally normative populations contracting HIV: They had been infiltrated by a sexual dissident.

Fears around the secretly bisexual husband in the home come to the fore in Ivascu's *Marie Claire* article, which is, notably, accompanied by images from two French films that explore male bisexuality in relation to AIDS: *Savage Nights* and *The Lie* (François Margolin, 1993). The positioning of these films as illustrative suggests how, in the French context—where public messaging around the prevention of HIV transmission was belated and limited—cinema offered some of the most direct engagements with AIDS. Explorations of male bisexuality in relation to AIDS can be found in a set of French films released between 1985 and 1993. Whereas American AIDS melodramas of this time, such as *Buddies* (Arthur J. Bressan Jr., 1985), *An Early Frost* (John Erman, 1985), and *Longtime Companion* (Norman René, 1989), center expressly gay men

FIGURES 3.1–3.2 Illustrating the danger of the bisexual husband in *Marie Claire*. Above the frame depicting Nathalie Baye, Christophe Bourseiller, and Didier Sandre in *The Lie* [*Mensonge*] (François Margolin, 1993), the caption reads: "How a blood test—seropositive—can blow up one family's seemingly happy life." Above the frame depicting Corine Blue, Romane Bohringer, and Cyril Collard in *Savage Nights* [*Les Nuits fauves*] (Cyril Collard, 1992), the caption reads: "The reproach is not so much that of infidelity, or bisexuality, as that of the imposed danger of contamination." My translations. Document scans.

«Mensonge», de François Margolin (1993):
comment un test sanguin – séropositif – peut faire exploser la vie
apparemment heureuse d'une famille.

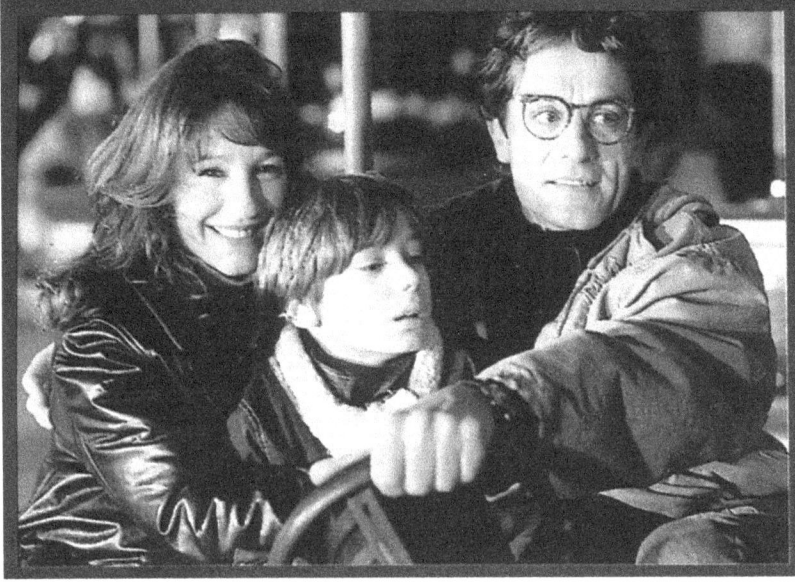

«Les Nuits fauves», de Cyril Collard (1992): le
reproche n'est pas tant celui de l'infidélité, ou de la bisexualité,
que celui du danger, imposé, de la contamination.

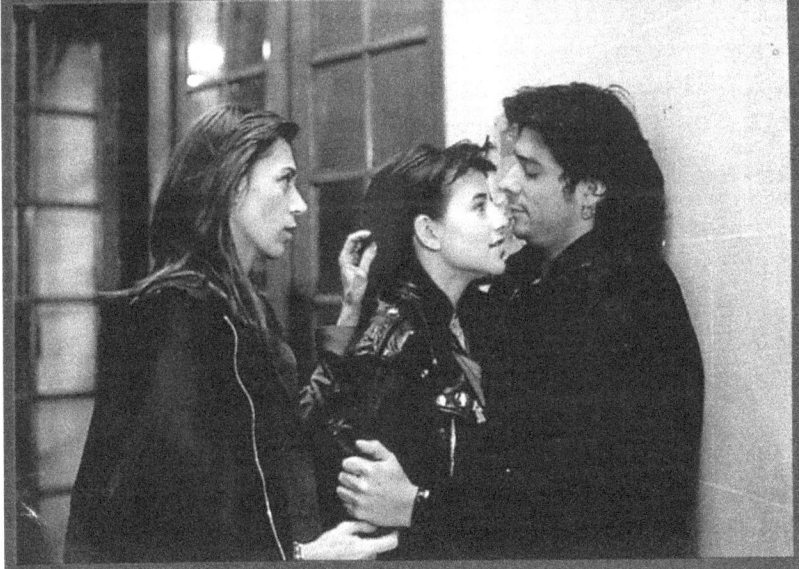

in tales equally sentimental and didactic, French cinema's approach to deal-
ing with AIDS took less proscriptive forms and was also less exclusively gay.
There is evidence to support Mark Nash's claim that "French (as opposed to
Anglo-American/queer) AIDS narratives emphasize bisexuality."[63] A survey of
French-produced films from the mid-1980s to the early 1990s reveals a number
of examples of the trend Nash describes, with male figures with bisexual desires observable in *AIDS: Love in Danger* (1985), *Once More* (Paul Vecchiali, 1988),
I Don't Kiss (André Téchiné, 1991), *Savage Nights* (1992), and *The Lie* (1993). The
persistence of male bisexuality in these films in comparison with American
AIDS melodramas' assertions of gay identity might be linked to the French
cultural skepticism toward sexuality-as-identity, in contrast with American
social justice traditions of politicizing identity. Less beholden to notions of gay
minority identity, French cinema was perhaps freer to explore sexuality's plasticity beyond monosexual identity frameworks in its AIDS narratives, a freedom aided by art cinema's embrace of the ambiguous.[64]

These aspects of French cinema's treatment of AIDS proved troublesome,
however, for contemporary AIDS activism, which critiqued certain French
novels and films as evading AIDS's sociopolitical dynamics. Collard faced these
accusations directly: Act Up–Paris, for example, alleged that Collard and HIV-
positive writer Hervé Guibert do not understand "that the disease touches, first,
marginalized minorities, because neither of them . . . feel part of a marginalized category: it's only about their individual destinies as creatives."[65] In a similar vein, André Glucksmann criticizes what he terms "le syndrome de Collard,"
describing "the denial which simultaneously blocks the awareness of dangers
and the implementing of safeguards."[66] Indeed, *Savage Nights* can be seen to
forgo a reckoning with the sociopolitical import of AIDS: It does not engage
explicitly with issues of governmental inaction or community activism.[67] In
an interview, Collard explains: "I don't deny the monstrous character of AIDS,
but I chose to talk about it from the angle of life . . . to shatter taboos, to
render seropositivity unsensational, in the good sense of the term."[68] Collard's
decision to play Jean was, he claims, a result of not being able to find an actor
who could play an HIV-positive character with "frivolity" (*légèreté*).[69] Collard
thus defended his work's lack of engagement with contemporary politics on
both contextual and artistic levels. He insists that Jean's negotiation of AIDS
must be understood, first, in relation to its setting in 1986, "when a consciousness around the disease had not really come about," and, second, in relation to
its protagonist's "incapacity to recognize that [AIDS] is a part of him."[70] Here,
Collard makes a realist claim around his film's historical setting: His character's lack of political awareness or engagement reflects that of society at the

time. But additionally, Collard's artistic approach speaks to familiar terrain for art cinema: Rather than creating a work of political didacticism around AIDS (in one of Collard's rebuttals, he says, "My film is . . . not an advertisement for the Ministry of Health!"), he chooses to center the experiences of a character whose seropositivity engenders a more existential kind of chasm.[71] This art-cinematic treatment of AIDS speaks, for James N. Agar, to "the artful, humanizing, and original depiction of individual suffering and ultimate redemption through love [that] could be valued in France."[72]

French cinema's will to figure male bisexuality provided fertile ground for a number of films that, either directly or indirectly, invoke the figure of the male bisexual transmitter. We can observe this figure metaphorically, as Georgia Mulligan does, in *Parking* (1985)—the musical adaptation of the Orpheus myth directed by Jacques Demy, who had sexual relationships with women and men and would later die of AIDS-related illnesses.[73] Singer-superstar Orphée (Francis Huster) is married to Eurydice (Keiko Ito) and also in a relationship with a male lover, Calaïs. In a song, the singer laments his inability to choose between any two things: the fig and the grape, laughter and reason, or either of his two lovers.[74] In the song's final line, he concludes, "Why choose?" Following this jovial ditty, however, the film takes a darker turn. After an argument with Eurydice, Orphée goes out partying with Calaïs; Eurydice, at home on her own, overdoses and later dies. The formal presentation of this sequence, argues Mulligan, establishes a pernicious relation between the men's kiss and Eurydice's death, metaphorizing male bisexual contamination of women.[75] The danger of the bisexual man to women takes a more literal turn in Margolin's art film melodrama *The Lie*, which follows couple Charles (Didier Sandre) and Emma (Nathalie Baye) and their young son. While Charles is away on a business trip, Emma discovers that she is both pregnant and HIV-positive. Processing the news, Emma laments, "I've got a baby inside me and sickness in my blood." Charles's bisexual transgression transforms Emma's body into a perverse site of contradiction where heterosexual reproductivity coalesces with a foreign, queer disease.[76] It is in the body of the pregnant heterosexual woman that the horror of male bisexuality's potential for social contagion comes to bear.

These fears proved overblown, empirically speaking. In a 1998 survey of international epidemiological data, sociologist Christopher Hewitt concludes that "initial predictions that AIDS would spread rapidly from gays into the general population due to the large numbers of men who were behaviorally bisexual have now been falsified."[77] Nonetheless, the discursive tendencies around male bisexuality that came to the fore during this time speak to a characteristically spatial anxiety evident in Hewitt's invocation of "spreading."

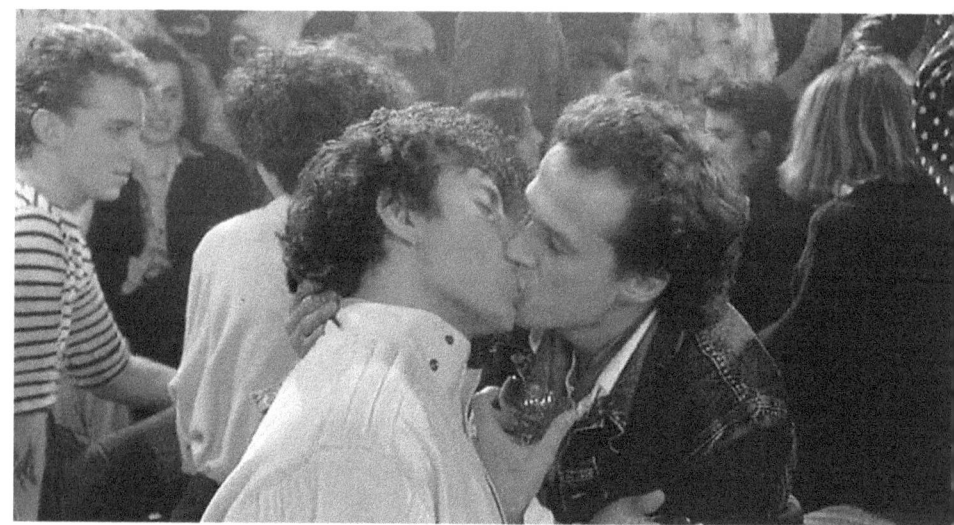

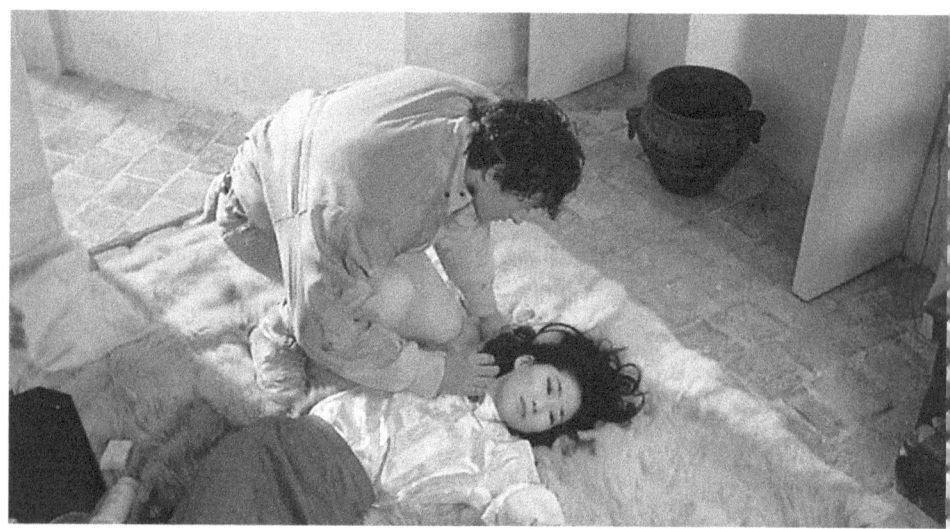

FIGURES 3.3–3.4 Orphée (Francis Huster) and Calaïs (Laurent Malet) kiss; Eurydice (Keiko Ito) dies. *Parking* (Jacques Demy, 1985). Digital screen captures.

The attendant fear here is that gay and straight spaces would be infiltrated by a bisexual transgressor carrying disease from one space to another, sullying the purity of each in the process. In European art films that figured male bisexuality after the arrival of AIDS, these issues of sexual space contoured the aesthetics of cinematic space.

Aller à voile et à vapeur: Tourism, Translocality, and Emplacement(s)

> I feel I go through life like American tourists go through the countries they visit, doing as many towns as possible.
> —Jean, *Savage Nights* (Cyril Collard)

> There is no bisexual world, only people who do tourism.
> —Jean-Luc Hennig, *Bi: De la bisexualité masculine*

In the early years of the AIDS crisis, the concept of "high-risk" and "low-risk" populations became spatialized: AIDS was located in fixed locales from specific cities to certain countries. However, toward the end of the 1980s, observes Lukas Engelmann, the cartographic models developed by epidemiologists made it clear that AIDS was "no longer just a disease of homosexual men confined to the territory of certain stigmatized districts."[78] To make sense of the movement of AIDS from perverse to normative spaces was to acknowledge the presence of a transgressor who navigated both.

In Jean's first line of dialogue, spoken in voiceover, he likens himself to an American tourist, "doing as many towns as possible." With these words, Jean announces himself as a traveler driven by wanderlust to see as much as he can, a declaration that carries obvious parallels with his character's bisexual promiscuity. The stereotype of the American tourist connotes a superficial engagement with places visited, but further, it recalls how, in the early years of the AIDS pandemic, some in France conceived of it as "a new plague brought from America."[79] The United States was not the only country tarred with the brush of contagion during this time. Grigorieff claims, in 1986, that 20 percent of Haiti's population "admit to practicing bisexuality," citing it as a factor in its high levels of HIV infection.[80] Grigorieff's suggestion reveals how racist and xenophobic ideas around an alleged cultural propensity toward bisexuality became territorialized in response to the pandemic nature of the AIDS crisis. Such assertions exemplify Clare Hemmings's observation of how, in developmental discourses around global sexuality, "bisexual behaviour" is both temporalized and spatialized as belonging to "premodern" geographical or cultural spaces.[81] One of the regions that has carried associations with male bisexuality in the Western imagination—and especially in France—is the Maghreb. Mehammed Amadeus Mack outlines how, in French culture, "bisexuality has long been associated with North African men in Orientalist and colonial representations as well as their modern extension," effecting "stereotypes of Arab bisexual secrecy."[82] It is apposite, therefore, that *Savage Nights* begins not in France but in Morocco, where Jean is on a work assignment and, as is often the case, on the prowl.

The opening scenes of *Savage Nights* establish Jean's bisexual desires through the visual treatment of his interactions with those he meets in Morocco. In the first instance, we take on the perspective of Jean's camera as he films young men on the street, the camera hovering around their faces as they register being filmed. This dynamic is voyeuristic, and the men's awareness of being watched accentuates a viewer's understanding of this gaze's desirous character. Later, we watch Jean navigate a labyrinthine ruin, where he exchanges glances with a woman (Maria Schneider) in shot–reverse shot. We then cut to the evening, where a desubjectivized camera shows Jean watching a fire-lit musical performance. The same woman approaches Jean from behind, he notices her and the scene ends. In this opening sequence, Jean's bisexual desires are established through a series of erotically charged encounters, shown in three different ways: subjectivized voyeurism, shot–reverse shot, and a frontal two-shot. This variety of shots, in quick succession, work to establish the variety of Jean's sexual interests. This sequence is also firmly grounded in Morocco: the young men he shoots are Arab, the mazelike structure he navigates suggests an ancient ruin, the musical performance is Amazigh, and features *zaghrouta* (vocal ululation) accompanied by a *bendir*, a North African drum.[83] It is in this Maghrebi locale, which carries associations of bisexuality in the French national imagination, where Jean's bisexuality can be both established and located.[84]

Jean's characterization of himself as a tourist draws upon ideas of a specific subjective approach to the world, combining a colonial register of looking at difference with broader notions of leisurely or pleasurable travel. Dean MacCannell stipulates that "the frontiers of world tourism are the same as the frontiers of the expansion of the modern consciousness with terminal destinations for each found throughout the colonial, ex-colonial, and future-colonial world where raw materials for industry and exotic flora, fauna, and peoples are found in conglomeration."[85] The entwinement of the colonial imagination in tourism is illuminated by *Savage Nights*' opening in Morocco (which was under French and Spanish colonial rule until 1956), where Jean observes local performances and navigates ruins from a European position of observation. For Mandy Merck, *Savage Nights* the novel foregrounds the wild (*fauve*) characterization of Jean's "Arab amours" and "reveals its bourgeois bottom to be a top, older, wealthier, and whiter than his sexual objects."[86] While Jean's relationships with Maghrebi men populate the novel, most are not depicted in the film, yet, in its opening, the dynamic Merck describes can be observed in Jean's cruisy-colonial Moroccan stint. These scenes also evoke John Urry and Jonas Larsen's description of the tourist's taking pleasure from difference: "Places are chosen to be gazed upon because there is anticipation, especially through daydreaming and fantasy, of intense pleasures, either on a different scale or involving different senses from those customarily encountered."[87] The centrality of looking in *Savage Nights*' opening sequence foregrounds the visual nature of Jean's tourist experience, his watching for pleasure. The term *tourist*, however, also often carries with it derogatory connotations of shallow engagement with foreign lands and cultures, often positioned against more supposedly authentic modes of travel. Jean's embodiment-as-tourist in this opening sequence thus marks him with a polysemous set of attributes: He is, at once, the colonial explorer, the hedonist, the superficial traveler. The compositeness of this characterization, and the ethical issues it raises, announces Jean's departure from notions of virtue. By naming Jean as tourist, *Savage Nights* rejects ideas around moral upstandingness, which were plaguing discussions of AIDS, establishing its positioning in spaces of ethical ambiguity.

The term *tourist* has also been used—in Anglophone and Francophone contexts alike—as a pejorative against bisexuals. Hennig declares that "there is no bisexual world, only people who do tourism."[88] David Bell parses similar accusations of bisexual tourism, which he sees as suggesting that bisexual people are "taking trips into 'gay' subcultures, having our fun, then going home with a few snapshots and some fond memories. . . . In this kind of discourse our true 'home' is [heterosexual society]."[89] The accusation of tourism establishes the bisexual as a heterosexual interloping in gay space in an uncommitted and temporary fashion. Yet, by embodying the bisexual tourist, both explicitly through dialogue and through his movements, Jean appropriates the pejorative in a way that resists reifying it, eliciting, instead, a consideration of the issues that undergird it: concerns around spatial belonging and leisurely pleasure-seeking.

Throughout *Savage Nights*, Jean travels: between Morocco, France, and Portugal; often he speeds across Paris in his convertible car. As suggested by one of French's slang terms for bisexuality, *aller à voile et à vapeur* (to go by sail and by steam), Jean travels in different ways and to different places.[90] Often he adapts to these spaces with ease, chameleonlike. It would be difficult to characterize any of these spaces as Jean's home—he displays multiple spatial attachments—and while he does have an apartment, its inhabitants and associations change throughout the film. Thierry Giaccardi observes one scene in Jean's apartment where the mise-en-scène reflects Jean's spatial proteanism: "Jean and Laura are pleased with how smoothly their life of coupledom has been going. . . . However, the shot, sharply divided vertically in two, seems to contradict the dialogue. . . . Jean goes from one room—meaning one side of the frame—to the other, to answer a phone call that we can presume is from Samy."[91] In Jean's movement from one room to another, one side of the screen to another, he travels between two romantic attachments. Giaccardi reads this scene as signifying Jean's bisexual nonmonogamy, which it does, but simultaneously it conveys Jean's multiple attachments spatially, transgressing two sides of what gives the illusion of a split screen. To account for this unique mode of spatiality, I propose a geographical term: *translocality*. Whereas *wandering, nomadism,* or *flânerie* might be said to lack attachment to the spaces journeyed through, *translocality* describes a spatial mode of being involving numerous attachments toward spaces and places.[92] Translocality involves "a mode of multiple emplacement or situatedness both *here* and *there,*" a multiplicity and simultaneity of spatial attachments.[93] Through translocality, we can comprehend Jean's easy acclimatization to disparate locales not as indicating intrusion or infiltration but as characterizing a wide network of spatial identifications.

The figure of the translocal bisexual shares some similarities with Maria San Filippo's bisexual-bohemian: "Typically a privileged white woman who straddles two worlds: her native Western culture, characterized as stifling and heteropatriarchal, and an alternative (usually non-Western) realm shown to be seductive and liberating yet potentially dangerous and perverse. . . . Art cinema's bisexual-bohemian literally inhabits a transcultural space and metaphorically inhabits a bisexual space."[94] Like the bisexual-bohemian, the translocal bisexual travels through and between different cultural spaces, some of which are aligned with normative sexuality, others of which are demarcated as perverse. Yet, not all of the spaces into which Jean ventures are as culturally monolithic as those described by San Filippo. While as a white man visiting Morocco and desiring its inhabitants, Jean occupies a position akin to the bisexual-bohemian venturing into "perverse" non-Western locales, his main extragender relationship, socially sanctioned within heteronormative society, is with Laura, who comes from a mixed white and Maghrebi background. Similarly, Jean's engagement with Samy's family cannot be demarcated strictly along Western/non-Western and normative/perverse lines: Theirs is a traditional family whose elders only speak Spanish—they are white but culturally

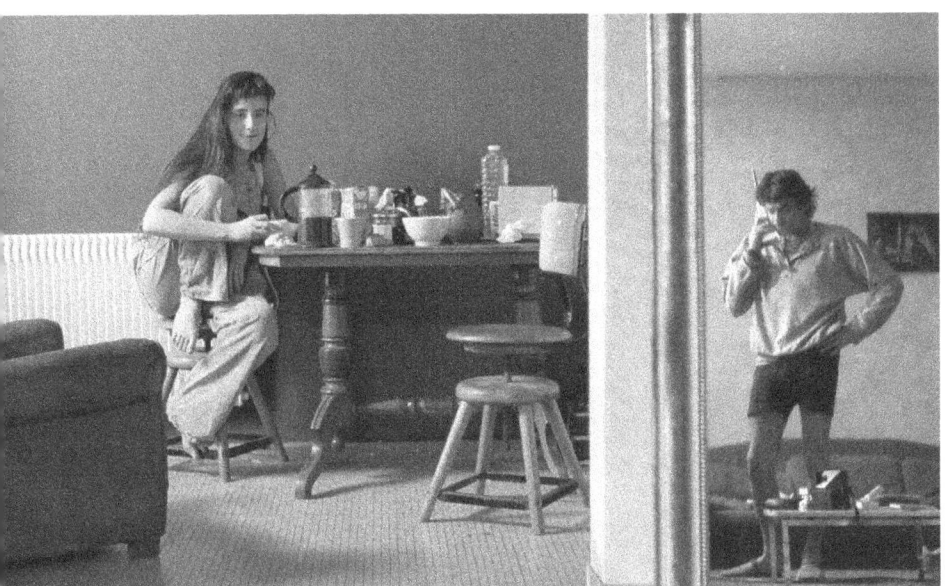

FIGURE 3.5 Jean's double alignments, conveyed through form. *Savage Nights* [*Les Nuits fauves*] (Cyril Collard, 1992). Digital screen capture.

Other—and Jean and Samy's relationship flits between that of heteronormative masculinity and homoerotics. Jean is, therefore, less the venturer between heteronormative Western space and perverse non-Western space and more a traveler through spaces of national, racial, and sexual polysemy.

In these spaces, Jean is both tourist and translocal: He journeys in pursuit of pleasure, of the new, but when he arrives in space he is emplaced, meaning the opposite of *displaced*, connected with one's physical and social environment.[95] In heteronormative spaces (the breakfast table he shares with Laura and the gourmet restaurant where he eats with her, the family home of Samy where he is a guest of this Spanish family) and gay or queer spaces (the bar where Jean's female impersonator friend sings Édith Piaf songs, the cruising ground flanking the Seine that he frequents), Jean is similarly emplaced, connected, attached. This emplacement is a central point of differentiation between the translocal bisexual and the bisexual-bohemian. Whereas the latter travels into spaces already holding sexual definition—stifled by heteronormative space, freed by the otherness of perverse space—the translocal bisexual is both attached to and formative of the spaces into which they venture. One of translocality's definitional tenets contends that "subject formation [is] a place-making process," that places are constituted by the subjects inhabiting them.[96] Spaces are thus transformed by those whose emplacement constitutes them. Jean's spatial attachments convey not only a bisexual transgression of space but a translocal approach to spatiality in which monosexual spaces lose their univocality through bisexual emplacements.

A germane example of how bisexual translocality complicates notions of monosexual space can be found when Jean and Laura visit a cruising ground together, where they have sex. Cruising is, typically, a gender-segregated practice. The history of cruising among men is not only a history of spaces but of codes in appearance and behavior, often undergirded by the security of the masculine body in public space even as this very same body is made vulnerable by the queer sex it seeks. Men's cruising involves male bodies that often articulate themselves through codes of masculinity. What happens when a woman not only enters this space but uses this space for extragender sex? Jo Eadie reads this scene as Laura's failed attempt to make a claim on Jean's sexuality. Eadie argues: "While Laura espouses her desire to colonise the queer space by having Jean where so many men have had him before, her impossible dream is undercut by the weight of associations which the space possesses, potently eroticised as it has been by the scenes of Jean having sex there at night."[97] I disagree with Eadie's assertions that, first, the sex between Jean and Laura constitutes a colonization of queer space and, second, that the space's associations undercut the fulfillment of Laura's desire. In keeping with art cinema's typically loosened narrative economy, the decision to have sex in the cruising ground is not explained by narrative. Instead, the camera pans from a *bateaumouche* traveling along the Seine to the cruising ground on its banks, where we see the two embracing. The camera encircles them as they engage in passionate sex. Eadie's framing of this moment as Laura's failed reclamation of queer space misses Jean's complicity in the act, evidenced most obviously by the logical conclusion that it is he who would have introduced Laura to the cruising spot. Ironically, Eadie himself stresses in a later article how "the carving of spaces into the heterosexual and the homosexual, serves largely to make those identities seem more distinct than in fact they ever have been."[98] *Savage Nights'* establishment of the cruising spot as a site of mutual desire between Laura and Jean undoes the exclusionary work of those carvings, undercutting the cruising space's myth of male sanctity, and instantiating Emiel Maliepaard's observation that, although certain spaces might be characterized by monosexual assumptions, they do not determine bisexuality's *"doing."*[99]

Similar scenes can also be found in a selection of films by François Ozon that, as Fiona Handyside argues, "offer a way of envisaging a queer cinema which is not predicated on individual bodies performing discrete acts, but which aims to offer a framework for constantly reconfiguring what queer forms and practices might be . . . [beyond] (hetero *and* homo) normative scripts."[100] In *A Summer Dress* (1996), a queer man (Frédéric Mangenot) has sex with a woman (Lucia Sanchez) in the cruising grounds by a beach as they are watched by a cruiser obscured by foliage. In *See the Sea* (1997), a woman (Sasha Hails) ventures into a wooded cruising ground where she observes men having sex; she rests up against a tree where a man (Nicolas Brevière) approaches before performing cunnilingus on her. These moments stand in contrast with a scene in *Once More*, in which the ex-wife (Florence Giorgetti) of the protagonist (Jean-Louis Rolland) visits him at a cruising ground to warn him of the danger of AIDS, her separateness from the space marked by the finery of her dress and the moralism of her words. Contrastingly, the transgression of the woman into gay cruising space in Ozon's films and *Savage Nights* is depicted as a titillating disturbance of space involving queer men's participation in sex with women. Samuel R. Delany reflects that the participation of women in male cruising settings "might certainly cause some problems" but that these would be "social problems to be socially solved."[101] The social problems engendered by such transgressions speak to Michel Foucault's conception of transgression as when "the limit . . . finds itself suddenly carried away by the content it had rejected and fulfilled by this alien plenitude which invades it to the core of its being."[102] A reminder of the eroticism inherent in transgression, here, the already verboten site of queer public sex is not rendered heterosexual but less delimited with the participation of a female recusant. In Ozon's films and *Savage Nights*, a woman is granted access to a male cruising locale through sex with a bisexual man and, through this act, that which the locale had rejected is transgressively embraced.

Just as Laura and Jean's bisexual transgression into monosexual space can be understood as altering the space itself, the spatialization of sexuality cannot hold when bisexual transgressions between spaces occur. Discussing the problem of locating bisexuality, Clare Hemmings contends that "the burning question is how one can become a subject of dislocation. . . . The problem may also be the way forward, may be the impetus to explore new ways of theorizing not just bisexuality, but all forms of sexual location."[103] One egress, I contend, is to theorize bisexuality not as dislocated but as translocal. In characterizing bisexuality as such, we can see how multiple bisexual emplacements render precarious a space's claim to monosexual meaning. In some scenes, *Savage Nights* presents a mass of male bodies at the Seine's cruising spot, but in the sex scene there between Jean and Laura, they are foregrounded, the silhouette of a cruiser discernible in the background. This formal layering allows for a palimpsestic kind of spatialization in which the space's plasticity is visualized through planes of

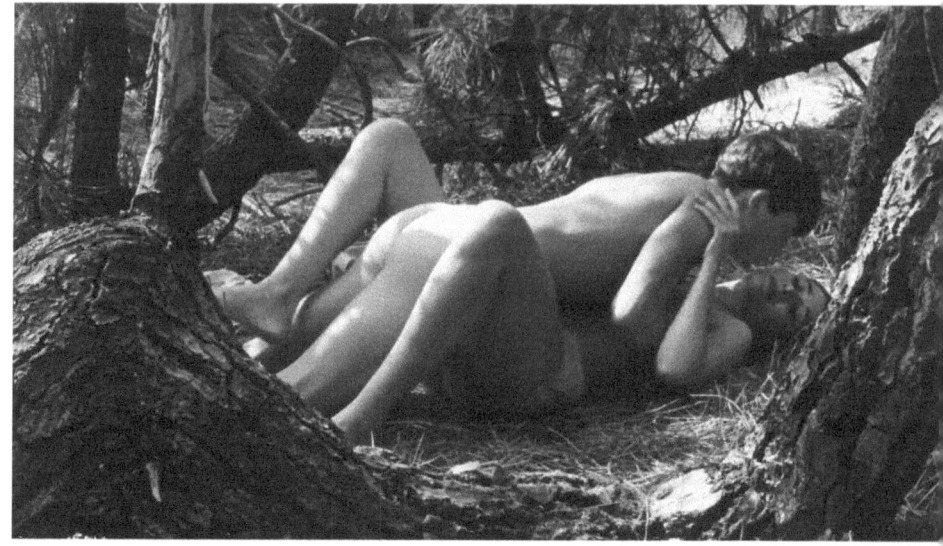

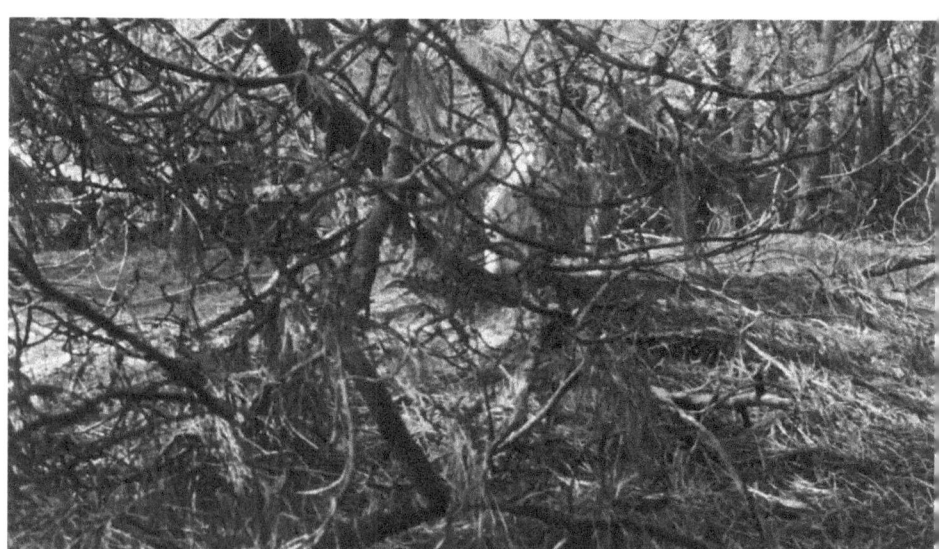

FIGURES 3.6–3.7 Luc (Frédéric Mangenot) and Lucia (Lucía Sánchez) have sex as a cruiser (uncredited) passes by. *A Summer Dress* [*Une robe d'été*] (François Ozon, 1996). Digital screen captures.

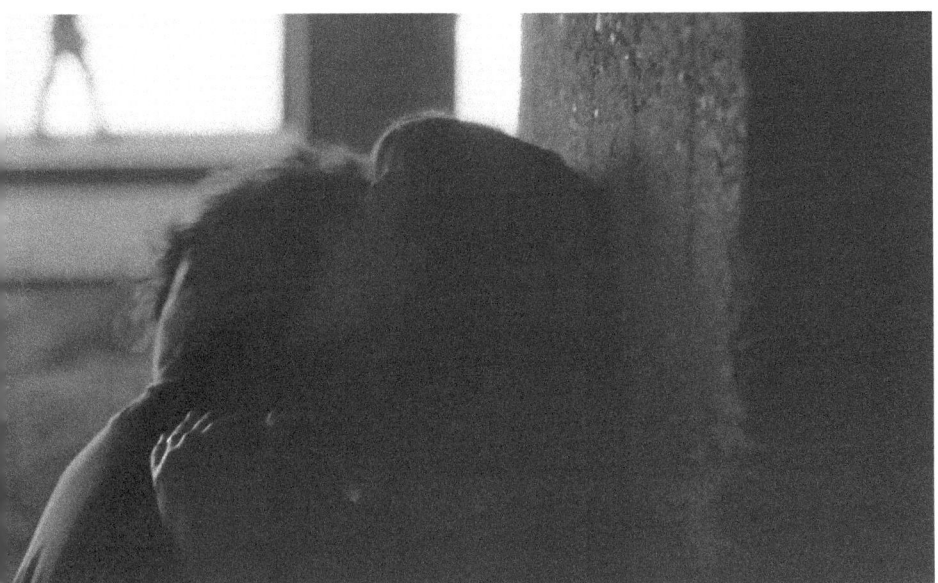

FIGURE 3.8 Jean and Laura have sex on a bank by the Seine as a figure cruises in the background. *Savage Nights* [*Les Nuits fauves*] (Cyril Collard, 1992). Digital screen capture.

meaning. Insofar as, in the context of the AIDS pandemic, so-called high-risk populations were initially aligned with certain spaces, bisexual transgressions therein reveal the instability of spaces and their potential for transformation. This is a realization to which epidemiologists were coming internationally: that identities and the spaces with which they are aligned are insufficient frameworks through which to understand a virus to which all are susceptible. By figuring bisexuality through translocal transgressions and multiple emplacements, *Savage Nights* reveals the plasticity of sexual space itself.

Bisexual Relationalities: Coupledom, Triangularity, Extensibility

Savage Nights showcases an array of relational modes in which Jean participates. I borrow the term *relational mode* from Foucault, who contends that subjects are constituted through their relations to people and things. A relational mode, for Foucault, thus describes *how* one relates, this conception crystallized in one of his final interviews where he advocates for the need for new relational modes.[104] In order to explore how cinematic bisexuality might be figured relationally, I consider three different relational modes observable in both *Savage Nights* and other European art films exploring male bisexuality: coupledom, triangularity, and extensibility. The cinematic construction of these relational modes is contingent upon deployments of form, notions of monogamy and nonmonogamy, the numerical and the geometric. Attention to these relational modes allows for an exploration of how bisexuality on film is constituted by the bisexual transgressor's relation to others, foregrounding the role relationality plays in the figuration of cinematic bisexuality.

COUPLEDOM

"Bisexuality," writes Robin Wood, "represents the most obvious and direct affront to the principle of monogamy and its supportive romantic myth of 'the one right person.'"[105] For Wood, the relation between bisexuality and the monogamous romantic couple involves a vehement disavowal of the latter on the part of the former. In the context of Hollywood film, about which he is writing, bisexuality is conceptualized as anathema to one of this cinema's enduring myths: monogamous love. Bisexual theory explores, similarly, the deconstructive potential bisexuality wields over notions of monogamous coupledom. However, an enduring assertion with much bisexual activism propounds the ability of bisexuals to practice monogamous coupledom. As Christian Klesse writes: "Non-monogamy is a troubling issue for many bisexuals, because dominant discourse constructs bisexuals as non-monogamous *by necessity*."[106] The bisexual responses to the discursive alignment of bisexuality with nonmonogamy—and its resultant incompatibility with coupledom—have been bidirectional: some have celebrated how bisexuality's ontological excess destabilizes conceptions of the couple, while others assert how coupledom is a relationship form to which bisexuals are just as amenable as monosexuals. Both these strands of thinking are relevant to *Savage Nights* insofar as the film stages a conflict between a bisexual figure and a coupledom in which he participates, which is, at once, a site of success and failure.

Conventionally, the couple cannot be read bisexually. The axiomatic assumptions that ground a monosexist, cissexist visual hermeneutic can be expressed algebraically:

man + woman = heterosexual/straight
man + man = homosexual/gay
woman + woman = homosexual/lesbian

Within these equations, the addition of one binary, intelligible gender to another equals a sexuality. Although these can be complicated by the addition of more than one desiring subject or object, for now, I want to stay with coupledom as a formulation that resists bisexual interpretation. The bisexuality of *Savage Nights'* Jean is made intelligible not through his coupledom with Laura but by a consideration of this relationship in the context of his other desires, evidenced by desirous gazes, sex with others, travel into gay space, and his own words. "I like boys too," Jean tells Laura on one of their early dates. "I know," she responds. "But you don't care?" asks Jean. "I don't not care," answers Laura. At this early point in the film, Jean's bisexuality presents itself as a potential problem for the couple. In monosexuality's calculus of coupledom, bisexuality introduces possible third terms that disrupt the equations.

S. Pearl Brilmyer, Filippo Trentin, and Zairong Xiang identify the figures that threaten the security of the couple as "shadowy thirds," examples of which include "the ex" and "the second husband."[107] They contend that "the couple almost always generates another one in its stead, producing and reproducing thirds that only momentarily disrupt, and ultimately only perpetuate, the totality of the One [meaning, the couple as a united 'One']."[108] In the authors' formulation, the couple is both haunted by a shadowy third and rendered whole by that third's repudiation; in a vacillatory dance, the couple is forever producing and eschewing shadowy thirds. The authors maintain that these thirds are queer figures because they are threateningly within the couple and must also be dispelled in order to secure it: These figures describe that which is "always *inside* the couple, [and] is constantly thrust *outside*."[109] Recall that when Jean and Laura have sex at the cruising ground, a cruiser is present in the image's background. Out of focus, literally shadowy, he is the queer third lingering behind the extragender couple's embrace. In this instance, Jean and Laura's coupledom can be seen to be haunted by a queer specter who portends Jean's being-seduced-by-another and the undoing of the couple's monogamous twoness.

The susceptibility of the bisexual male figure to unfaithfulness constitutes a familiar cinematic cliché. From *I Love You, I Don't* (Serge Gainsbourg, 1976), to *Coming Out* (Heiner Carow, 1989), to *Hamam* (Ferzan Özpetek, 1997), this figure's bisexuality is initially communicated through an act of infidelity. As I argue elsewhere, infidelity within a monogamous relationship constitutes a popular narrative event through which bisexuality is conveyed on film.[110] The dominance of monogamy as a social norm, twinned with the demand for sexuality's visual authentication, can thus be understood as the foundations from which images of bisexual infidelity are propagated in a monosexist system of visuality. Rather than take these representations at face value—as in, for example, the work of Wayne M. Bryant, who reads bisexual infidelity simply as a confirmation of social biphobia—we can come to understand bisexual infidelity as a symptom of both dominant structures of sexual signification and social anxieties around (hetero)monogamous coupledom.[111] Catherine Deschamps elaborates on the latter, writing that "bisexuality, insofar as it is associated with infidelity or instability in the couple, works to reveal a general will to normative integration and to harbor the seeds of many people's fears: of not being satisfied by social requirements."[112] Through Deschamps, we can understand cinematic representations of bisexual infidelity as useful representational clichés to the extent that they display the centrality of monogamy and visual authentication to the signification of sexuality on film, just as they dramatize the very human anxieties around that within us which exceeds these structures.

Leo Bersani, in his quintessentially provocative rhetorical mode, describes monogamy as "cognitively inconceivable and morally indefensible."[113] For Bersani, monogamy's impossibility is characterized by its "arrested deployment of desire's appetites and curiosities," constituting a "profoundly immoral rejection of our promiscuous humanity."[114] Even if we might question Bersani's claim of a universal promiscuous humanity, his highlighting of monogamy's arresting nature, its truncation of desire, is informative. Cüneyt Çakırlar and Gary Needham use Bersani's ideas around monogamy and promiscuity to theorize certain visual registers in gay cinema. A "monogamous optic" in film, they argue, can be seen in "an expressive aesthetic—operating through subjectivity—that presents the visual field of amorous connections by confining and stabilizing identities, psychologizing subject positions, and *settling beings* as personalities on screen."[115] In Çakırlar and Needham's argument, monogamy's curtailment of extensible desire is facilitated by formal cinematic qualities that work to contain the monogamous couple. The authors' contention that the stabilization of identities is a function of the monogamous optic is insightful when we consider one moment in *Savage Nights* in which editing destabilizes identity. Jean is driving Samy in his car, where they are edited in shot-reverse shot. We cut to the car speeding in an underpass, too fast to discern who is being driven. We then cut to Jean and Laura in two-shot. A perversion of continuity, the identity of Jean's passenger is rendered unstable through this metamorphic edit; as this character changes, so too does the gender of Jean's companion in an inventive visualization of bisexual desire. In this moment, *Savage Nights* bisexualizes conventions in cinematic form itself.

Similar moments are observable in Liliana Cavani's *Beyond Good and Evil* (1977) and Ilan Duran Cohen's *Confusion of Genders* (2000), in which a figure changes from one character to another—and one gender to another—through a continuity edit cut. In Paul de Lussanet's *Dear Boys* (1980), Wolfbroer (Hugo

Metsers), who professes his ephebophilic "zealotry for the Greek principles," seduces Tonny (Marina de Graaf), someone he believes to be a teenage boy. When the two return to Wolfbroer's bedroom and undress, he sees that the adolescent has breasts. After his initial stupefaction, Wolfbroer moves to have sex with Tonny, proceeding despite the misunderstanding. The surprise revelation of breasts in *Dear Boys* performs a similar function to the gender-changing continuity edits of *Beyond Good and Evil*, *Confusion of Genders*, and *Savage Nights*: an unexpected bisexual expansion of possibility through a subversive deployment of form. With these films, it is the doubling of couplings that produces a bisexualizing effect; the consecutive display of a character in romantic pairings with people of different genders denaturalizes cinema's formal conventions just as it denaturalizes monosexual monogamy.

Multiple couplings are presented in *Savage Nights* through its flexible approach to narrative temporality, which allows for Jean's relationships with Laura and Samy to develop side by side. This temporal approach to communicating bisexuality can be understood as what B. C. Roberts terms "concurrent": when a character "has relationships with men and women within a space of time," as can be observed, for example, in *Duffer* (Joseph Despins and William Dumaresq, 1971), *Sunday Bloody Sunday* (John Schlesinger, 1971), and *Once More*.[116] The unpredictable narrative movement between these couples speaks to the affinity for formal experimentation and dissident sexuality found in art cinema. The doubling of the couple image and the perversion of its formal methods of communication offer what Galt and Schoonover would identify as impure formal techniques that befit an impure bastardization of coupledom.[117]

Despite the fact that Jean enjoys romantic pairings with both Samy and Laura, it is the latter that constitutes a more traditional conception of coupledom, as a result of both its narrative predominance and its extragender configuration. However, the coupledom between Jean and Laura contains conflicting elements, which both support and dissent from conventions of the cinematic couple. One example of such rupture, given particular attention in the film's journalistic responses, occurs in the aftermath of Jean having unprotected sex with Laura without disclosing his HIV-positive status (though he chooses not to ejaculate inside of her). When Jean eventually reveals to Laura that he has HIV, she is initially angry that he had previously withheld this information from her, but, in the following scene, they begin to have sex again. Jean reaches for a condom and unwraps it, but Laura then removes it and places it in an ashtray; she proceeds to ride him, saying, "I want you to come." Laura's active desire to participate in unprotected sex with an HIV-positive partner speaks

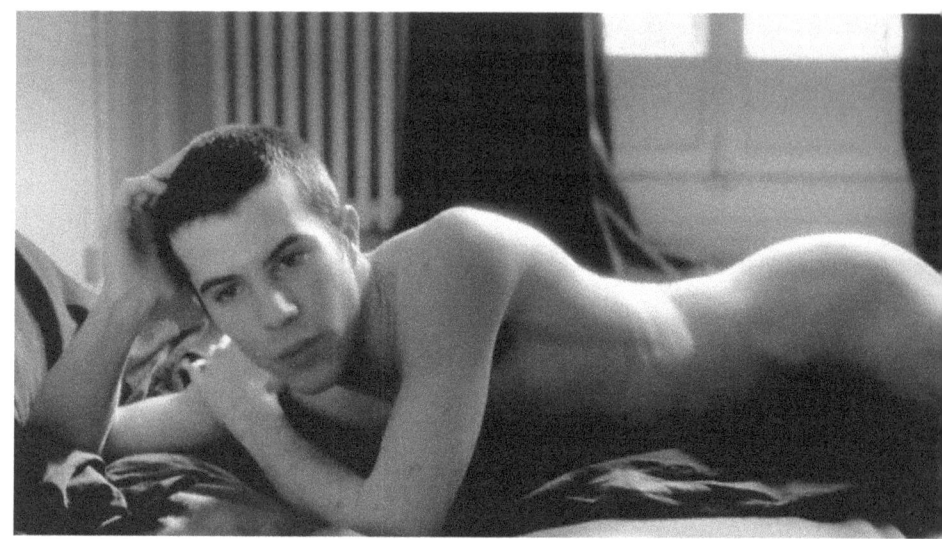

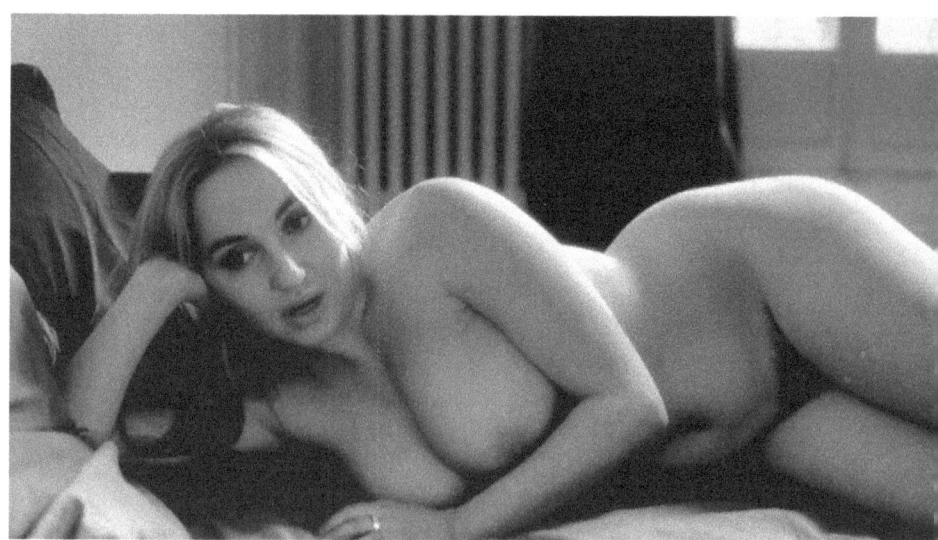

FIGURES 3.9–3.10 The lover to whom Alain (Pascal Greggory) is speaking changes from man (Samuel Perche) to woman (Chloé Mons). *Confusion of Genders* [*La Confusion des genres*] (Ilan Duran Cohen, 2000). Digital screen captures.

to a willful yearning toward Jean's unsheathed body, a sexual encounter with him in which Jean's HIV—here, an index of his queerness—is not repudiated by Laura but, rather, embraced.

The ethical import of this moment was first discussed in Anglophone critiques of the film: In the *Wall Street Journal*, Julie Salamon writes, "Once AIDS is introduced into the picture it becomes impossible to condone the unlimited pursuit of pleasure—even as a spectator sport."[118] This aspect of the film and its critical responses speak to the ethical ambiguities *Savage Nights* evokes, characterized by the conflict between the film as representational fantasy and as a reflection of sociopolitical reality. Although moral castigation of fictional characters risks ignoring the status of film as a representational medium, narratives around AIDS remain linked to sociopolitical contexts. These links came to the fore dramatically in 1993 in what came to be known as the Collard Affair, when it was revealed that Collard transmitted HIV to Erica Prou, who died that year of AIDS-related illnesses. Despite the fact that Prou contracted HIV from Collard in 1984, when information around HIV prevention was scarce in France, Rachel Gabara details how the Collard Affair was treated as "a concrete realisation of the consequences of Collard's romantic linking of love and AIDS."[119] Public knowledge of Collard's sex life thus allowed for the conflation of his art with his life and for a confirmation of the danger of male bisexual promiscuity to the extragender couple.

The film itself, however, paints a more composite picture of the relationship between Jean and Laura, which stresses the complicity of Laura in the act of risk-taking. The representation of Laura's active embrace of unprotected sex with the knowledge of Jean's HIV can be elucidated, I contend, in relation to what would come to be known in gay male subculture as "bug chasing," the active pursuit of HIV by seronegative men through unprotected sex. Tim Dean suggests that "bug chasers want to resist normalizing power, to express skepticism regarding mainstream ideals of health and risk-avoidance, and to learn how to live with mortality . . . taking on the fundamental limit of death that defines us all."[120] While, in some ways, bug chasing should be understood in relation to the gay male subculture in which it occurs and a historical period in which highly active antiretroviral therapy medications are prevalent, Dean's ideas can be extended beyond these contexts. Alan Hunt reminds us that "in late modernity *not* to engage in risk avoidance constitutes a failure to take care of the self," rendering risk avoidance consistent with centuries-long "techniques of moral regulation."[121] As a facet of self-governance then, failure to avoid risk is not an ethical problem per se but a problem for a moralizing politics seeking to instill a normative, morally self-regulating subject or citizen.[122] It is easy to read Laura's embrace of unprotected sex as a symptom of *amour fou*, heralding, as it does, a psychological downturn that eventually leads to her hospitalization. But we should pause to consider this moment as evidence not simply of self-destructive mental illness but of a passionate embrace of risk, which transgresses a moralizing politics' demands for moral self-governance.

In Laura's embrace of unprotected sex, she takes on the risk Dean describes in a way that can be read as confronting mortality and death. Unlike male cultures of barebacking, which have attracted complex critical considerations, women's unprotected sex is discussed most regularly in academic literature in relation to a supposed ignorance of risk. Yet to understand Laura's actions as an informed embrace of risk is to avoid the misogynistic suppositions upon which readings of her victimhood are predicated and that, admittedly, the film can be seen to, at times, support. Instead, we can take Laura's willingness in this moment seriously. Dean characterizes the dynamics of bug chasing (and its corollary, gift giving) as involving relations of kinship insofar as they constitute an act of solidarity that secures a social bond.[123] Seen in this light, Laura's desire to have unprotected sex with Jean can also be understood as a desire toward kinship with him, to instantiate a social bond between the two of them. Like French AIDS activist Isabelle Muller writes in her memoir, recounting the relationship with her HIV-positive partner: "I no longer wanted Xavier to wear a condom, but to make use of that which bore witness to his contamination, that which, during our relations, recalls—unremittingly—the presence of the virus."[124] Against the regime of moral self-governance, Laura, like Muller, embraces risk as a means of forging a selfless coextensivity with an HIV-positive lover.

Rather than providing a clear moral framework with which to approach AIDS, as some hoped it would, *Savage Nights* attends instead to these more existential concerns. As Michel Condé outlines: "*Savage Nights* commands a new attitude . . . which consists of suspending (at least temporarily) our moral judgements in aid of comprehending the more or less complex motivations of characters: the demand for truth—particularly the truth of the soul, of emotion, of the moment—carries more import here than atemporal principles of good and evil."[125] This moment gives space not only to a risky, ardent desire but to a formation of coupledom in which one partner's sex with others—indexed in Jean's HIV—is embraced. Laura's descent into psychological breakdown can be seen, in this context, not simply as a misogynistic portrayal of female hysteria but as communicating her character's failure to reconcile a heterosexual monogamous ideal with a bisexual nonmonogamous alternative.

Foucault argues that discourses of the eighteenth and nineteenth centuries produced "a centrifugal movement with respect to heterosexual monogamy," which became the "internal standard" for an "array of practices and pleasures."[126] This standard's reliance not only on heterosexuality but also on monogamy should remind us of the importance of the repudiation of both one's and the other's extensible desires to the concept of normative sexuality. Brilmyer, Trentin, and Xiang propose a model for the incorporation of a queer nonmonogamy into a couple structure where a queer coupledom must not repudiate shadowy thirds but stay with them.[127] In *Savage Nights*, however, Laura cannot but attempt to repudiate Jean's shadowy thirds. When she arrives at his apartment one morning, she is faced with a ménage à trois tableau: Jean asleep beside Samy and his ex-girlfriend, Karine (Laura Favali). Laura reprimands him: "Do you have to sleep with everything that moves?" Her prior openness to Jean's desires dissipates in the face of their materialization. This moment portends the eventual breakdown of Laura and Jean's coupledom but, simultaneously, it offers, albeit briefly, a potential alternative for the visual representation of bisexuality. In the image of three sleeping bodies, we find a relational alternative to the couple: the triangle.

TRIANGULARITY

Catherine Deschamps reflects that "it is hard to sum up bisexuality . . . other than by signifying the presence of three people."[128] The endurance of the image of the triangle in bisexuality's visualization is rooted in these exigencies of signification. As Clare Hemmings expands, "Most contemporary attempts at resolving the problems of bisexual representation have used the same paradigm to create images of threes—two men and a woman; two women and a man—through which to recognize bisexual behavior or identity."[129] The bisexual erotic triangle is one of the few images through which bisexuality can be definitively read. Consider an AIDS prevention campaign by France's Ministry of Public Health and Health Insurance, which directly addresses bisexual men.[130] Accompanying the words "When you have sex with Pierre, think about protecting Virginie" is a photograph of a chair draped with two pairs of pants. This is a triangulated image: The camera assumes the perspective of the bisexual man being addressed, the female partner is metonymized as a pair of jeans, the male partner a pair of chinos. This image conveys two differently gendered object choices at once.

The triangular visualization Hemmings describes is among the most unequivocally intelligible forms bisexual desiring can take on film.[131] Consider

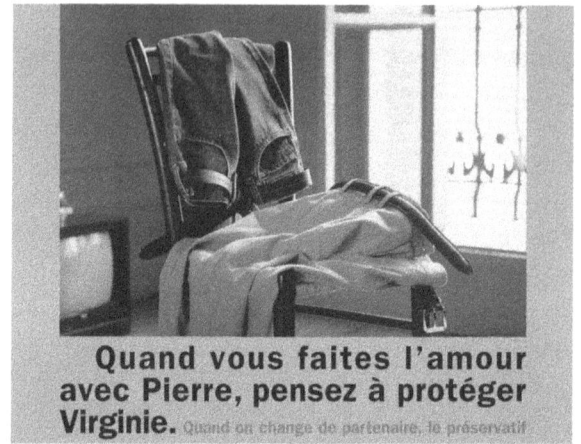

**Quand vous faites l'amour
avec Pierre, pensez à protéger
Virginie.** Quand on change de partenaire, le préservatif
est, bien utilisé, la meilleure protection contre le virus du sida
(VIH) et les maladies sexuellement transmissibles (MST). La
première fois et à chaque fois, avec un homme ou avec une
femme, à chaque pénétration. En cas de sécheresse vaginale
ou de pénétration anale, afin d'éviter tout risque de rupture
du préservatif, il est recommandé d'utiliser un gel à base
d'eau, en vente dans les pharmacies et dans certaines
grandes surfaces. Adopter le préservatif, c'est se protéger
soi et ses partenaires. Pour en parler, Ecoute
Gaie au (1) 44.93.01.02 et Sida Info Service
au 05.36.66.36. **Protégez-vous du sida.**

a scene in Claude Bernard-Aubert's *Adieu je t'aime* (1988), in which husband Michel (Bruno Cremer), wife Nicole (Marie-Christine Barrault), and lover Philippe (Stéphane Bonnet) take turns in kissing one another. These consecutive kisses establish each character's subject/object status, speaking to Pramaggiore's observation of the triangle's amenability to simultaneous subject/object positions: "Because the triangle offers the possibility for simultaneous desire and identification among its various positions, regardless of the gender of the figures occupying those positions, triangulation often highlights the both/and quality of bisexual desire."[132] As Marjorie Garber reminds us, in the common use of the term, most erotic triangles are not in fact triangles but Vs, in which two subjects desire the same object but not each other.[133] The unique triangularity of the bisexual triangle can be found in its multiple subject/object positions and the interchangeability of desires between each of the three.

This phenomenon is most pronounced in visualizations where touch between characters is not successive but simultaneous. In these examples, the

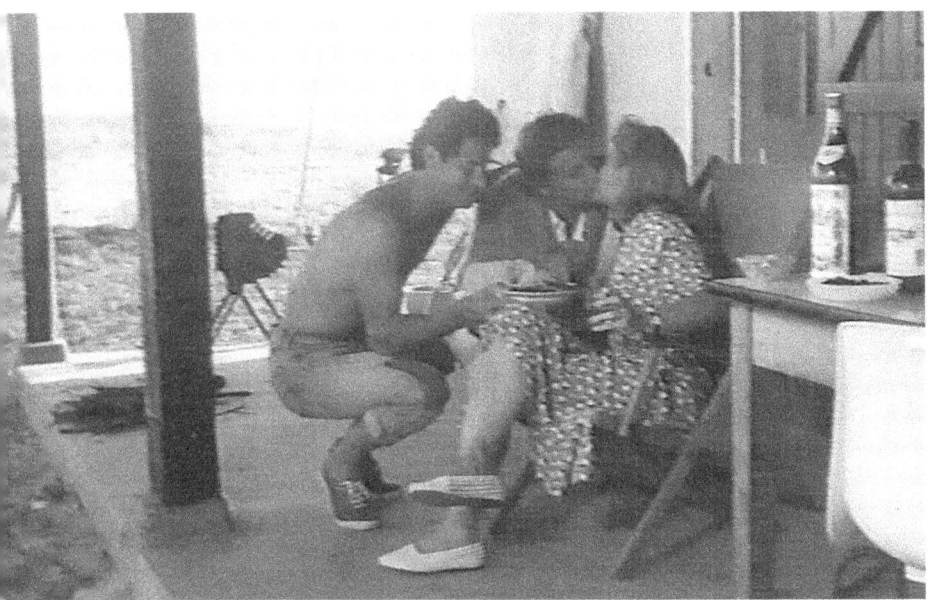

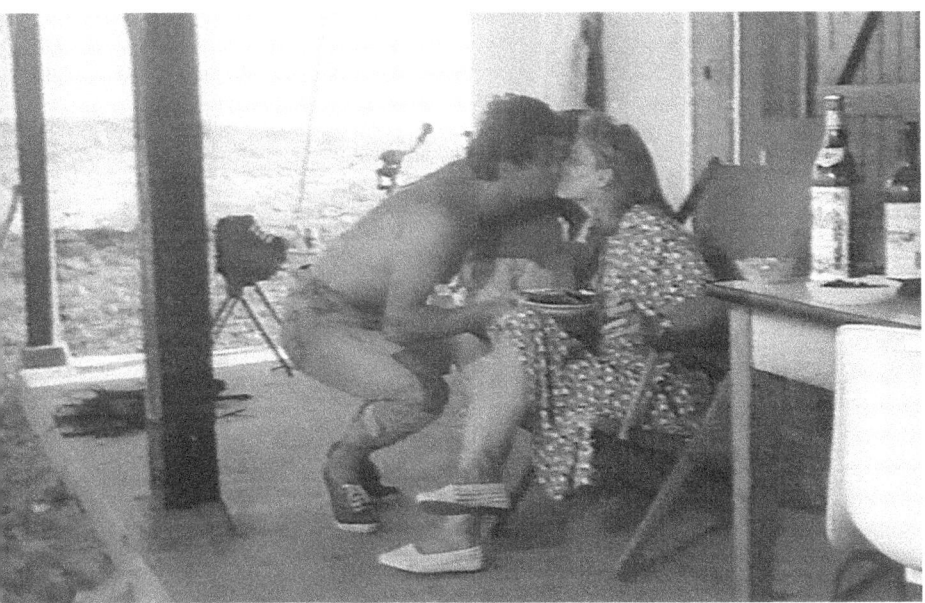

FIGURES 3.12–3.14 Philippe (Stéphane Bonnet), Michel (Bruno Cremer), and Nicole (Marie-Christine Barrault) take turns kissing one another. *Adieu je t'aime* (Claude Bernard-Aubert, 1988). Analog screen captures from a VHS cassette.

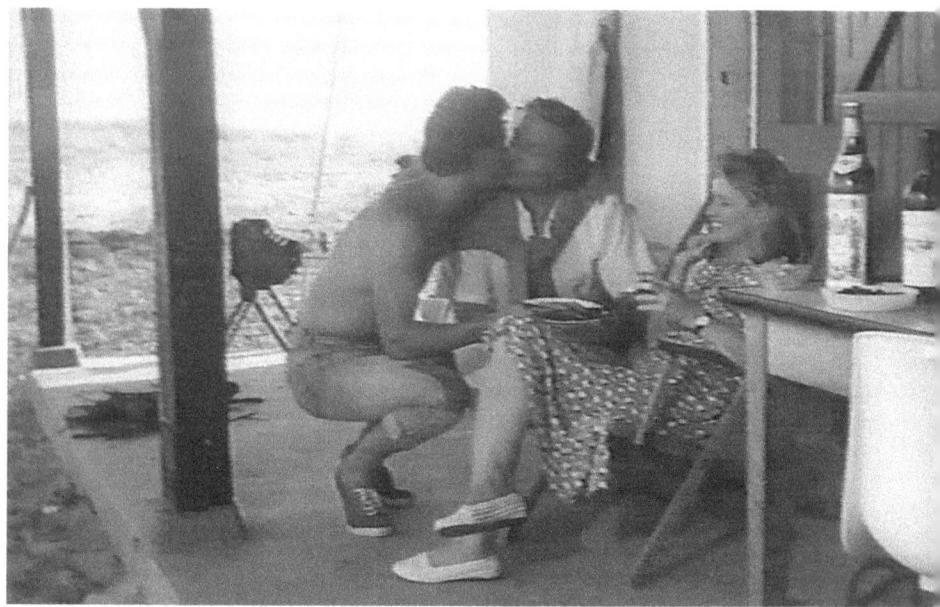

cinematic image contains structural similarities to the geometric triangle. In the geometric triangle, by definition, one side always touches the other two. We can theorize the points where these sides meet, the triangle's vertices, as haptic insofar as they form touching points between sides. In the filmic bisexual triangle, these vertices are anthropomorphized into points of convergence between characters, where fingertips, lips, or genitals might touch. For this chapter's focus, filmic bisexual triangles featuring two men and one woman (hereafter, MMF triangles) are of interest, given their suggestion of male bisexuality. In these examples, both men touch each other as they touch a woman—a representation of multiply gendered desire through tactile simultaneity. In a social context in which aspersions are regularly cast on a man's ability to desire both men and women—reified by scientific assertions of its physiological impossibility—these images provide an affirmative visual display of male bisexual possibility.

A variety of theorists have taken erotic triangles featuring two men and one woman as their object of inquiry. In Claude Lévi-Strauss's triangular model of kinship, marriage functions as a form of social relation between men in which the "exchange of women" from the bride's father to her fiancé constitutes a gift from one man to another.[134] As Gayle Rubin writes in her glossing of Lévi-Strauss: "If it is women who are being transacted, then it is the men who give and take them who are linked, the woman being a conduit of a relationship rather than a partner of it."[135] René Girard's literary analysis also proposes the triangular nature of desire, arguing that the male characters he discusses desire not the female object but, rather, to be like another man he admires and emulates.[136] Both Lévi-Strauss and Girard highlight how certain structures of desire between men and women fundamentally sublimate relations between men in which the woman is less the desired object but more the mechanism through which a different desire can be articulated. The desirous potential of this triangular configuration grounds the intervention of Eve Kosofsky Sedgwick, who uses literary examples to theorize "homosocial desire," meaning "the potential unbrokenness of a continuum between homosocial and homosexual."[137] By hypothesizing homosocial desire's continuous relationship to homosexual desire, Sedgwick proposes, first, that friendships between men operate in the field of desire and, second, that the (homophobic) disavowal of this desire secures a man's participation in patriarchal, heterosexist society. Sedgwick's analysis of the MMF triangle builds upon Girard's ideas to stress the triangle's asymmetricity: how "one gender [woman] is treated as a marginalized subset rather than as an equal alternative to the other [man]."[138] Sedgwick thus contends that desirous friendships between men can be enacted in erotic triangles through the marginalization of the woman.

How does the bisexual MMF triangle fare in relation to the theoretical scholarship that critiques the (heterosexual) erotic triangle? If Lévi-Strauss's triangle is characterized by the exchange of women, what happens when men are also the objects of exchange? If Girard's man sublimates his desire to be a different man onto the woman, can the same process be observed when the desire between men is expressly sexual? If Sedgwick's men must disavow their desire toward one another, what happens when the triangle's men do avow their desire, and what is the fate of the woman upon whose marginalization the men's bond was previously predicated? And, finally, how might cinematic form affect the construction of the MMF triangle in ways that differ to anthropological and literary theory? After Jean and Samy flirt with a young woman, Sylvie (Marine Delterme), in the street, she invites them back to her apartment. There, the three begin to embrace on a sofa: Jean kisses Sylvie's leg as Samy kisses her mouth and neck. Jean's and Samy's hands touch, and they move toward each other and begin to kiss. Sylvie is startled. "Are you kidding me?" she asks. Samy and Sylvie proceed to attempt to have sex without Jean, who leaves them. Samy joins Jean soon thereafter, saying, "Damn, she won't let me fuck her." While this failed attempt at a bisexual MMF threesome is short-lived, it is useful in exploring the dynamics of triangular relationality at play here. The failure of this ménage à trois is caused by a chasm between Sylvie's heterosexualized conception of the erotic triangle and Jean and Samy's bisexual openness to what it could be. Sylvie's affirmative desire to be the Lévi-Straussian gift is central to her threesome fantasy; by acknowledging each other as potential gifts, Jean and Samy reduce Sylvie's gift value, thus recalibrating the relational structure. The asymmetricity Sedgwick identifies as structuring the traditional erotic triangle is thus rendered symmetrical: the isosceles becomes equilateral. This transformation is also dependent upon an affirmation of that which Sedgwick's triangle repudiates: sexual desire between men. The desire between men need not be displaced, à la Girard, onto the woman but is, instead, coextensive with their desires toward her. The ménage à trois's failure is pronounced by its female heterosexual participant for whom the promise of the traditional erotic triangle is dashed by a bisexual recalibration.

Such recalibrations are also apparent in this scene's deployment of film form, which is harnessed or, perhaps more accurately, wrestled with to account for the bisexual erotics before the camera. The embrace between the three characters is first shown to us from an unorthodox angle: the camera points down, canted from above to display the three bodies intertwined. This shot type is akin to the bird's-eye view, but it is more angular; the camera must position itself to account for this unwieldy intermingling of three bodies. A similar shot can be observed in Eloy de la Iglesia's *Confessions of a Congressman* (1978), where a three-way kiss is shot from above in a spatially abstracting fashion. In these examples, a new perspective is introduced in order to capture an embrace that is unwieldy to a horizontal plane. This shot resembles the parallel perspective used in some Chinese and Japanese painting, and observed similarly in some East Asian cinemas, in which there is no illusion of a single vanishing point within the frame. This perspective, argues Hao Dazheng, "indicates that two vanishing points exist in infinity," the vanishing points extending beyond either side of the frame.[139] In Jean-Louis Baudry's influential account of Western classical cinema's debts to conventions in Western easel painting (which he also contrasts with Chinese and Japanese painting), he describes a regime of monocular vision "which corresponds to the idealist conception of the fullness and homogeneity of 'being.'"[140] To present a bisexual, triangular embrace that eschews monocular vision through parallel perspective thus works to figure a more fragmented and heterogeneous notion of being that is inherently relational. Here, the horizons of sexual possibility are

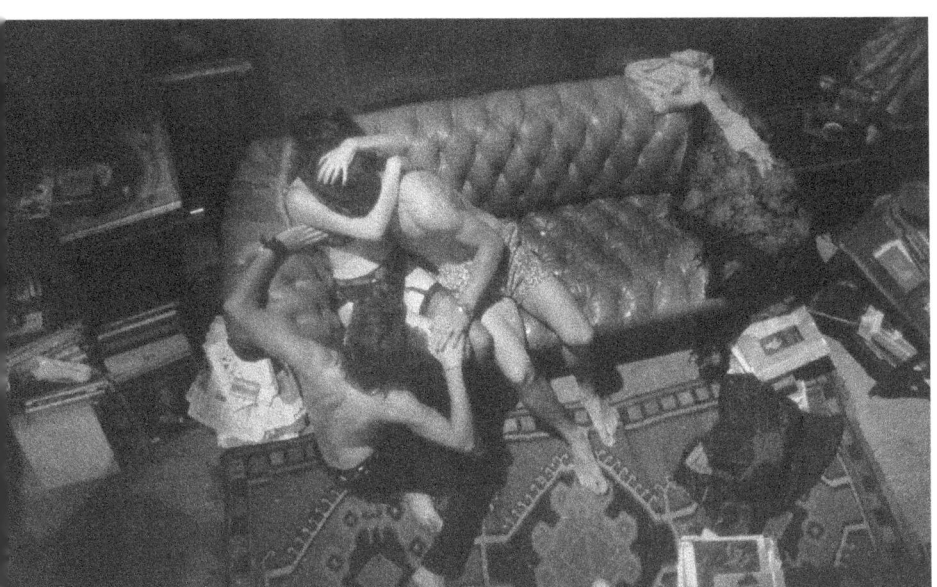

FIGURE 3.15 Jean, Sylvie (Marine Delterme), and Samy (Carlos López) embrace one another. *Savage Nights* [*Les Nuits fauves*] (Cyril Collard, 1992). Digital screen capture.

expanded with and through an expansion of perspectival horizons. The infinite vanishing points created by this angle signal a move from contained security to expansive possibility.

Analysis of the angles and framings through which the bisexual MMF triangle is shot shows that, instead of containing the trio, certain cinematic forms attend to the extensible potentials of such a configuration. To probe this phenomenon further, it is insightful to turn briefly to geometry to consider how triangularity gives form to extensible bisexual possibilities. Trigonometry's most basic contention—from its antecedents in ancient mathematics and astronomy to the development of Euclidean geometry—is that discrete parts of a structure are correspondent, interdependent.[141] Trigonometry recognizes relationality between seemingly discrete elements. The Euclidean triangle—which became trigonometry's prized object of study around the mid-sixteenth century—has three vertices.[142] These vertices contain not only interior angles but reflex angles formed outside of the triangle's borders. The term *reflex angle* was first used in eighteenth-century trigonometry, with *reflex* coming from the classical Latin *reflexus*, meaning "bent" or "curved back."[143] Attention to reflex angles alongside interior angles allows us to appreciate how a polygon's vertex both bears in on it and is, simultaneously, bent back, bearing out of it.

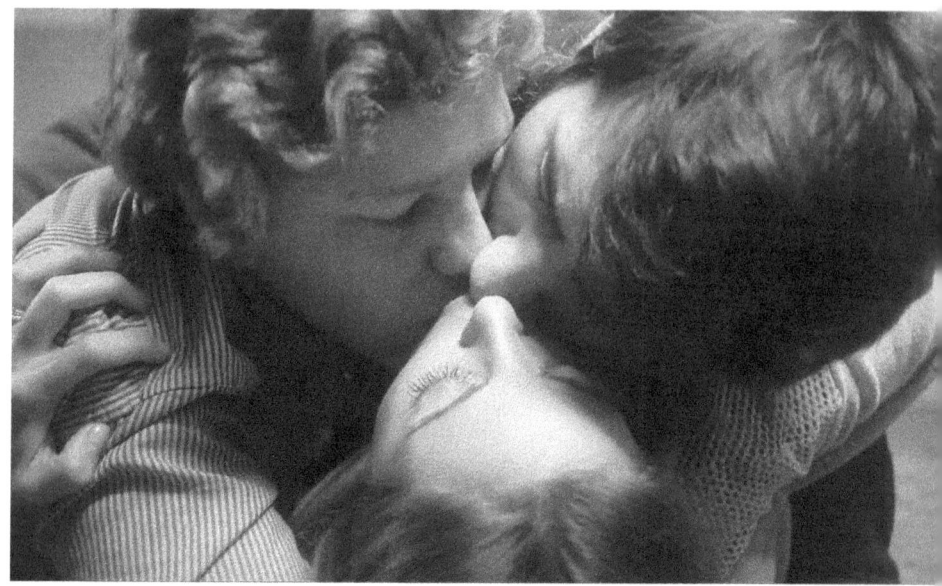

FIGURE 3.16 Roberto (José Sacristán), Carmen (María Luisa San José), and Juanito (José Luis Alonso) share a three-way kiss. *Confessions of a Congressman* [*El diputado*] (Eloy de la Iglesia, 1978). Digital screen capture.

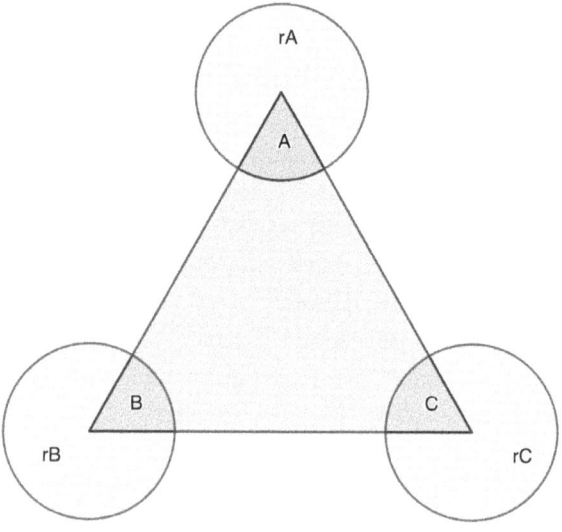

FIGURE 3.17 *A*, *B*, and *C* mark the triangle's interior angles; *rA*, *rB*, and *rC* mark the triangle's reflex angles.

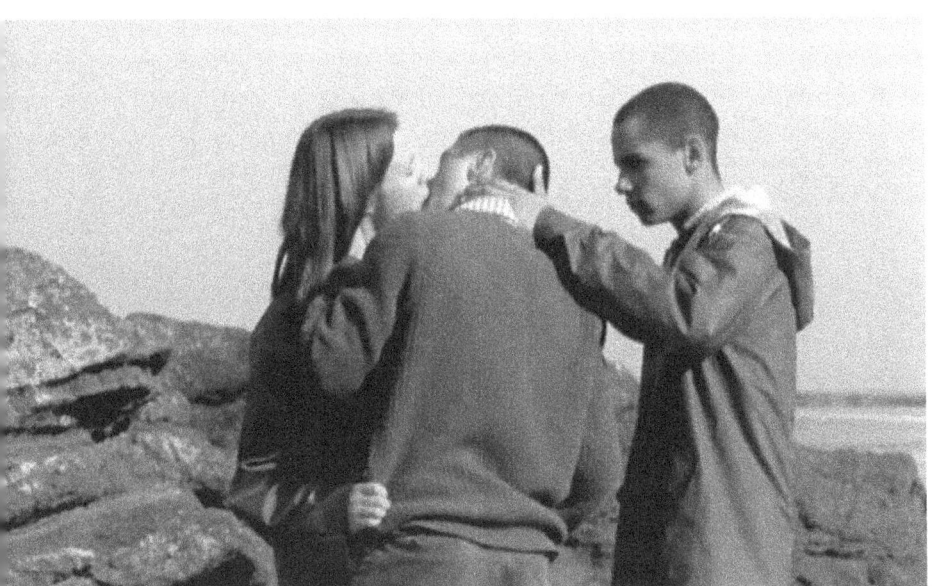

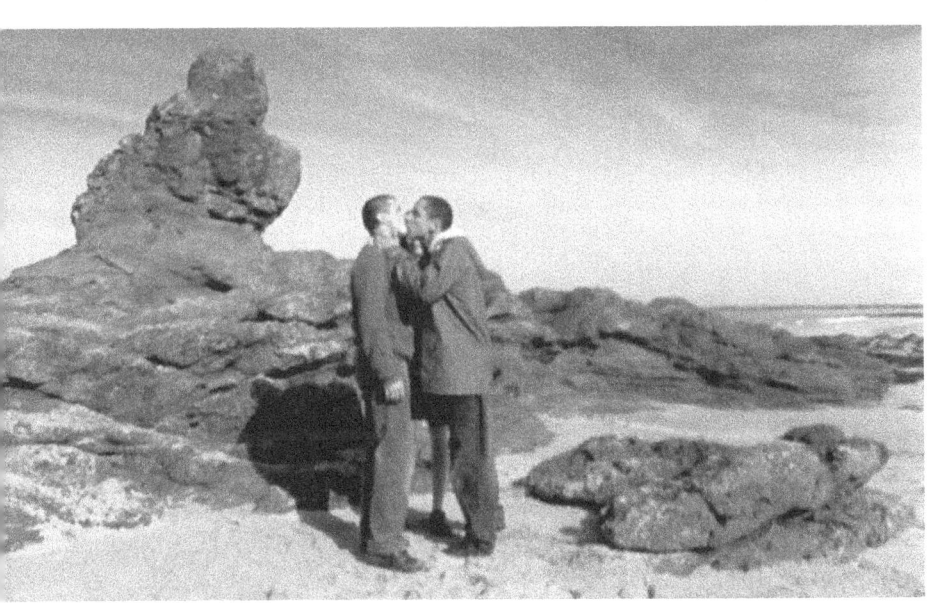

FIGURES 3.18–3.20 Ruby (Alison Mac), Billy (Daniel Newman), and Sammy (Fraser Ayres) embrace one another. *Speak like a Child* (John Akomfrah, 1998). Digital screen captures.

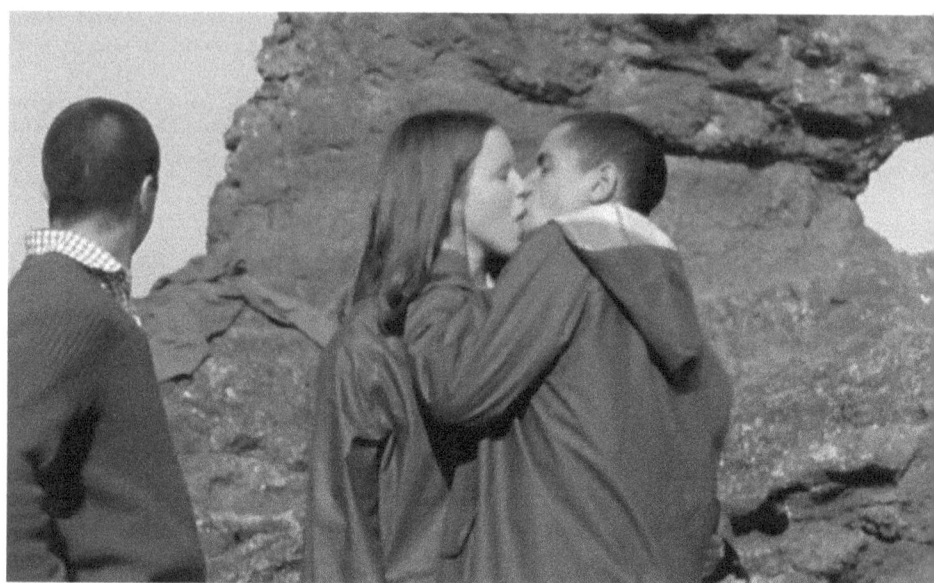

These qualities of the geometric triangle—its inherent relation to that beyond its edges—help us to comprehend bisexual cinematic triangles as nonexclusive forms, inherently extensible figurations of desire.[144]

Consider a moment in John Akomfrah's *Speak like a Child* (1998), in which a trio of friends run away from their Northumbrian boarding school to a rocky seaside, where they embrace their desire for one other. In this scene, the triangle presented is continually transforming. Its irregular angles—oscillating between acuteness and obtusity—suggest neither an isosceles nor equilateral triangle but a succession of scalenes.[145] These triangles' configurations are in flux, and their reflex angles are just as discernible as their interior ones. Sometimes the three characters are embraced inwardly but, at other times, two kiss while one looks on, looks through, or looks beyond the others. In one moment, Sammy (Fraser Ayres) and Ruby (Alison Mac) kiss as Billy (Daniel Newman) looks out to the sea. Just as his body forms a vertex of the triangle that looks inward (an interior angle), so too does it look out beyond it, forming a reflex angle oriented toward a vast landscape.

In Euclidean geometry, this reflex angle will always be greater than its adjacent interior angle.[146] To continue the metaphor whereby each vertex signifies a desiring subject/object, we can understand the triangle's interior angles as signifying desire toward the triangle's two other (remote) angles. Yet, inherent in this structure, we can also find the vertex's reflex angle, which bears out beyond the triangle's borders. We can, therefore, read the reflex angle as signifying an outward-facing, extensible desire, which, in Euclidean triangles, is always greater than the inward-facing angle. Here, I do not mean to suggest that we interpret this phenomenon axiologically, as if an angle's numerosity of degrees signifies its being better. Instead, I want to suggest that the reflex angle's greatness be understood as signaling a capacity or an abundance in the outwardly extensible. The alignment between bisexuality and the triangle, and its cinematic invocation, is thus not simply an affirmation of simultaneous desiring within the confines of a geometric structure. It suggests, in its very geometry, the greatness of extensible possibilities beyond its borders. This cinematic bisexual triangle not only visualizes an irregular relationship structure, it also figures a representation of desire that is nonexclusive, where extensible desires might stretch forth toward areas greater than that which the triangle contains.[147]

EXTENSIBILITY

In Bersani's consideration of the maxim that, in love, one desires that which makes one whole or complete, he suggests that the lover lacks "more of what he is," that "this is a lack based, not on difference . . . but rather on the extensibility of sameness."[148] In this theorization, an outward-looking, curious desire is conceived of as coextensive with the subject. What might it mean to understand *Savage Nights'* Jean as a figure drawn, in an extensible fashion, toward others in whose sameness he finds more of what he is? This disposition toward others is articulated by Bersani elsewhere as "a series of ejaculatory relays of the self through others . . . a generous outpouring of the self" exemplified in coital positions in which lovers do not face one another.[149] Similar configurations of openness can be found in Jean's experiences in the Seine cruising ground where masses of bodies intermingle, Jean's openness to others conveyed through overpopulated frames teeming with bodies. Or perhaps we can observe a similar kind of openness when Jean lies on the ground of the cruising spot and asks one man to urinate on him while he kisses another, his extensible desires figure in a simultaneous openness to urine and saliva, as he lays prostrate, vulnerable, open to all that could bear down on him. While it might be tempting to focus on Jean's trips to the cruising ground as emblematic examples of extensible relationality, such a focus would elide how his character's approach to desire in toto reflects an extensibility, an indeterminacy, in which the film does not allow one kind of desire to become ascendant. Toward the beginning of the film, the anonymous woman Jean sleeps with in Morocco tells him: "Open up to others. Expose yourself. Let go of yourself." Her words constitute an apt epigraph for the extensible relationalities that Jean will go on to model.

Giaccardi asks: "As Jean enjoys being sodomized by Samy, does he think about Laura and the child they could conceive together?"[150] To think of bearing a child with a woman he loves while being penetrated by a man he loves would suggest a bisexually extensible desirous potentiality, unmoored by the presentness of any sexual encounter. Giaccardi's question responds to the figuration of Jean's bisexual desire, wherein traditional configurations of love—unidirectional, oppositional, characterized by difference—cannot hold. Further, it instantiates a process Félix Dusseau observes whereby "bisexualities, by virtue of the multirelational potentialities they pose *in theory*, enable original reconfigurations among individuals."[151] Jean's ability to occupy different sexual positions in coitus can be understood, synecdochally, as representative of this bisexual multirelational extensibility. Giaccardi contends that "*Savage Nights* illustrates this very concrete idea that to be penetrated by a penis and to penetrate another body with yours refers, more subtly, to being *in oneness* [à l'unicité], likely more so than its being *singular* [à l'unique]."[152] Giaccardi reads Jean's positional versatility as characteristic of a plastic being-in-oneness with the other. Here, "being in oneness" can be understood as synonymous with Bersani's "extensibility of sameness." Through this lens, Jean's sexual versatility reflects not an individualized, Byronesque propensity toward sexual conquest but a figure in whom multiple relations with others allow for an expansion of the self.

As a point of comparison, we might consider the character of Samy, who, like Jean, explores his bisexual desires but who, unlike Jean, is reluctant to sacrifice his own masculine sense of difference. Samy, a muscular rugby player, has a girlfriend toward the beginning of the film and cheats on her with Jean. In one scene, Samy takes a job as a dom and is led up to an attic where an older effeminate man is restrained with hand shackles. Samy is visibly disturbed by this display and responds by meting out violence, which only arouses the man further. Recalling this encounter to Jean, Samy cries at the thought of how violent he had been: "Worst of all," he laments, "it gave me a hard-on." In the encounter between Samy and his client, we see a confrontation between an older queer man—dressed in BDSM attire, speaking with a queeny sardonicism—and a younger, hegemonically masculine *rugbyman*. Samy's horror at this encounter is rooted in how his erection betrays an extensible relation between him and his client: His hard-on dispels the illusion of a masculine oppositionality to an abject queerness. Following Jean and Samy growing distant with one another, Samy becomes involved with a neofascist street gang. Later, we see him accompanied by other young, white men as they beat up an Arab boy. In the context of Samy's resistance to extensible relationality, we can understand this movement toward racist violence as consistent with his attachment to oppositional difference.[153] Not only does the fascist gang provide Samy with a macho social sphere in which he can repudiate his queerness, it also allows him to violently maintain his difference from a racialized other and repudiate his own immigrant heritage. Remarkably, Jean's response to encountering this racist gang violence is to cut himself and threaten the white boys with his seropositive blood. Faced with figures of fascist, white, impenetrable masculinity, Jean renders himself extensible through the rending of his own flesh. The contrast established between Samy and Jean thus highlights one of *Savage Nights'* central ethical investments in a breaking down of the distinction between the self and the other. As Frédéric Strauss argues, *Savage Nights* constitutes "a forcefully impure message, made of heterogeneous images, . . . forcefully cacophonous, kindling the need to return a place to the Other. The Other who is also the stranger, the body of elsewhere."[154] This returning of a place to the Other occurs not only textually but through Jean's physicality and metaphysicality, a figuration that conveys what Collard calls "this multiplicity that I have in me."[155] The mode of being to which Jean arrives might be characterized as that which Jean-Luc Nancy calls "being singular plural," the recognition that "Being is being with," that it is "the 'with' that constitutes Being."[156] Through his openness to others—his desire toward them and identification with them—Jean finds not points of oppositional difference but an extensible sameness.

In *Savage Nights'* ending scenes, Jean has driven to the Setúbal district of southwestern Portugal, an area he explores alone. There, he looks out at cranes on the docks, he looks at boys on the streets, he listens to his Walkman. The final time we see Jean, he stands atop the Cabo Espichel, an awesome cape opening onto the Atlantic. In internal monologue, he reflects that he is alive and that, even if he dies of AIDS, life is something of which he is part. Following these final words, we cut to the perspective of an aerial camera hovering above Jean, which moves from long-shot to extreme-long-shot in a sublime expansion of the frame. Jean's openness to the world is figured in these moments through an overwhelming sense of expansiveness, a limitless extensibility. Here, the film suggests as its telos Jean's outward-looking receptivity to the world around him. In this image, the boundaries of the self are most vehemently contested: Jean's acknowledgment of his partaking in the world is affirmed in speech as the film presents his encounter with the sublime.

FIGURE 3.21 The sea's extensive, fragmented lines. *Savage Nights* [*Les Nuits fauves*] (Cyril Collard, 1992). Digital screen capture.

For Nathan Carroll, it would not be incidental that this moment of sublimeness occurs as Jean narrates his opening up to the world, insofar as "the contemporary sublime comes to represent our ... everyday desire for the Other: other parts of the self, other identities, other experiences, mysteries, spiritualities, sexualities."[157] Sublime aesthetics are deployed here to convey the sheer quantity of those othernesses beyond the self. From its place hovered above Jean, the camera nosedives toward a pelagic infinity.[158] The camera's speed turns the sea's blueness and its shimmers of spume into painterly strokes. These images are unsignifying, yet they suggest movement. The lines of oceanic texture point, like transgression, to a place beyond the limit. They exemplify Eugenie Brinkema's suggestion of "how joy might be figured as a release *into* form. . . . The approach of visual infinity . . . as line is an affirmation of every possible formal transmutation that has taken place, and that might also, in the future as the possible, take place."[159] Jean's extensible openness to the world is thus figured in form: splintered lines—dashes—whose fragmentation suggests not brokenness but porosity.

For André Roy, Jean is a "fragmented being," yet it is precisely this quality that allows for his transgressive style of relationality inflected by a bisexual transgression beyond the limits of monosexual relationalities.[160] Collard hints toward this quality of *Savage Nights* in response to a question about the role of bisexuality in the film: "What interests me is how bisexuality intervenes in relationships between the characters."[161] Bisexuality, for Collard, allows for an intervention into questions of relationality, where multiple, fragmented, nondeterministic relational modes coalesce. This coalescence is not as idealistic as it might seem theoretically—the film demonstrates the litany of conflicts that can arise therein—but it is, critically, counterhegemonic. *Savage Nights'* figuration of bisexuality offers a range of counterhegemonic relationalities: a coupledom in which queer, external desires might be embraced in an extragender pairing; glimpses of triangularity that draw upon the MMF triangle's bisexual readability and offer equitable alternatives to dominant heterosexual triangles; and an overarching affirmation of extensibility that contests the strictures of masculine oneness just as it rejects the self-other distinction. *Savage Nights* plays with a heterologous array of relational modes, rendered through an inventive approach to narrative and form. To witness this spectrum of relational modes is to feel—vicariously—the bisexual possibilities that outlie a hetero-monosexual monogamous norm.

Love, Plasticity, and Bisexual Utopia

When the words "I love you" are uttered on film, they often carry with them the baggage of a saccharine sentimentality, no more so than when they end a film. Associated with the heterosexual, monogamous couplings prized by Hollywood, these words, when spoken in a film's final moments, carry with them ideological import. "I love you" is one of the final phrases uttered by Jean; it is heard following a conversation with Laura, whom he telephones from Portugal, but the question of whether or not these words are uttered diegetically is equivocal. Corine Blue, Collard's partner, recalls him adding the words in postproduction as a voiceover: "This was the main thing he was never before able to say to anybody. . . . It was a very important thing for him. . . . And it came at the same time he was saying this to me."[162] Considering the ideological weight of the cinematic "I love you," it is unsurprising that some of *Savage Nights'* queer critics find in the film a capitulation to heteronormativity. Reflecting on the film's ending, Simon Watney remarks, "We do not need a catastrophic epidemic to teach men and women how to love," a reproval that echoes Mark Nash's characterization of the film's narrative as "dominated by a heterosexual romance" and Chantal Nadeau's inclusion of *Savage Nights* in a list of French films that purportedly depict "male bisexuality as heteronormative."[163] Even for Jo Eadie, a bisexual theorist, the film's ending "enables the relinquishing of the queer past in favor of the heterosexual future. Errancy has been corrected and the true path of salvation has been resumed."[164] For Eadie, Nadeau, Nash, and Watney alike, the film is cathected—insuperably—to heterosexuality.

What these critiques miss, however, is the context in which these words are spoken. Overwhelmed by the words' status as heteronormative cliché, they fail to account for the line being uttered at a point in the film in which Jean is at his farthest from Laura: his love, unlike that of the Hollywood couple, cannot be realized. His is a bathetic love; he comes to the realization of his love too late. We should also not forget that this moment is preceded by Jean watching Portuguese boys along the roads of Setúbal and followed by Jean opening himself up to the world atop a cliff. This formal presentation reminds us that "I love you" need not mean "I love *only* you." In the final images of *Adieu je t'aime*, couple Nicole and Michel bid farewell to their bisexual lover Philippe, Nicole leaving a message in the sand: "I love you" (*Je t'aime*). After watching the couple walk away, Philippe kneels down in the sand and amends the message to "I love both of you" (*Je vous aime*), a nonmonogamous, bisexual acknowledgment of love's nonexclusive potentials. With these potentials in mind, we can return to Jean's "I love you" not as indicating an investment in heteromonogamous coupledom but, more convincingly, as Jean's acknowledgment of his own capacity to love. For Judith Butler, "Love always returns us to what we do and do not know. We have no other choice than to become shaken by doubt, and to persist with what we can know when we can know it."[165] Butler's emphasis of love's insistence in an investment in the as-of-yet unknown harmonizes with Brinkema's radical formalist account of it: "Love requires more than what is possible because what it requires has not yet been asked of it (—this is infinite form)."[166] At the end of *Savage Nights*, Jean occupies this space of partial knowledge and partial uncertainty, love's "infinite form" figured in the sea's propulsive, fragmented lines. Jean acknowledges his desires as he acknowledges his illness, but he looks out, hopeful, at the potential for a world in which he can participate.

Perhaps this sounds a little utopian. Michael du Plessis is critical of how discursive deployments of bisexuality assign it "extreme values, so that it can be extolled . . . as a panacea, a fantasy, a promised land."[167] But, as José Esteban Muñoz reminds us, "hope is spawned of a critical investment in utopia, which is nothing like naive but, instead, profoundly resistant to the stultifying temporal logic of a broken-down present."[168] Thinking utopia can be a tool of imagining the world otherwise, a world radically different from the present. For Daniel Guérin, the French queer anarchist thinker, bisexuality suggests a means through which to overcome what he feels are tendencies toward puritanism, essentialism, and exclusionism in French homosexual politics.[169] "The society of the future," Guérin prophesizes, "will be a bisexual society."[170] To articulate utopia bisexually is to imagine a world without compulsory monosexuality and its attendant strictures. Nowhere are these fantasies of bisexual utopia more seductive than on film.

While *Savage Nights* is not explicitly aligned with a political vision of utopia or a particular school of political thought, there is something utopic in its radical reimagining of sexuality in the world. The film's French title, *Les Nuits fauves*, evokes the twentieth-century art movement Fauvism, which saw the use of striking colors and a rejection of impressionism's realist values.[171] Like the paintings of the Fauvists, Collard's film imagines a world that is somewhat recognizable but radically restructured, a plastic world in the sense that Catherine Malabou writes that "plasticity configures traces and erases them to form them, without however rigidifying them."[172] In Fauvist Henri Matisse's painting *Le Bonheur de vivre*, we can observe this plastic aesthetic, in which figures' bodies are recognizable as bodies but they have been altered. Some follow the contours of the landscape around them. They boast bright colors, some fleshlike, others not. The Fauvist plasticity of Collard's world might be found, if you look closely enough, in one of *Savage Nights*' final shots, where the sun seems to rise from the west to the east—an editing trick effecting a subtle, near-indiscernible, rendering plastic of the world. If Matisse invokes the bodily figure to render it plastic in *Le Bonheur de vivre*, *Savage Nights* limns, in a similar fashion, figurations of sexuality: the stylish boy racer, the submissive cruiser, the hopeless romantic girl, the macho *rugbyman*. Insofar as plasticity is understood in Kyla Schuller and Jules Gill-Peterson's words as "the capacity to be formed by outside pressure, yet to maintain internal coherence all the while," these figurations of sexuality can be understood as formed at once by their adherence to type and by their transgressive recalibrations beyond type.[173] As Giaccardi observes, "When [Jean] poses the question to Laura, 'What do you know about faggots?,' [he] delivers the same blow to the spectator," what do you know about this figure you thought you recognized?[174] Dashing sexual-epistemological logic, *Savage Nights* renders glimmers of bisexual utopia: nonexclusive queernesses in which queer men turn toward women desirously, the recognition and manifestation of bisexual potentiality.

These images work to illuminate the possibilities of bisexual utopia, albeit flickeringly so. We catch a glimpse of the possibility of a bisexual threesome between Jean, Samy, and Sylvie but are forced back into the ideological present through Sylvie's queerphobic jibe; Laura embraces Jean's queerness and his

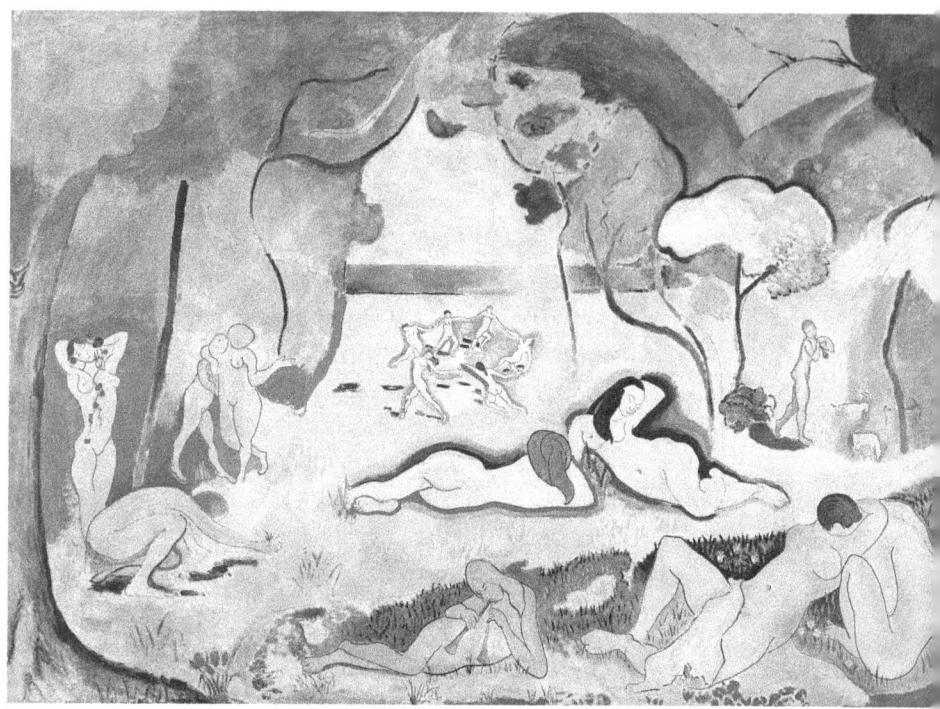

FIGURE 3.22 Henri Matisse, *Le Bonheur de vivre*, 1905–1906. Oil on canvas. © Succession H. Matisse/DACS 2024/The Barnes Foundation, Philadelphia, Pennsylvania. Photo © Barnes Foundation/Bridgeman Images.

virus, yet the laws of heteronormativity obtain in her, catalyzing her psychological breakdown. *Savage Nights* allows us to witness flashes of bisexual utopia, which are then painfully dashed by the ideological force of present.[175] If the film looks outwardly, hopeful, to utopian possibilities beyond the monosexual now, so too does it show us the brute forces that bear down on the present. But what if we stay with those utopic possibilities the film does glimpse? To gather them together as lightly traced blueprints of potential bisexual utopias. Might we see something akin to Matisse's *Le Bonheur de vivre*? Figures in an array of relational modes: singular, coupled, and grouped. A world that we recognize somewhat, yet a world whose difference from the now is unmistakable. Perhaps we see what Hélène Cixous calls *"the other bisexuality . . . the nonexclusion of difference . . . the multiplication of the effects of desire's inscription on every part of the body, and the other body."*[176] A world where configurations of gendered bodies are unpredictable and, in instances, unreadable. A world teeming with a bisexual erotics.

CHAPTER 4

THE EROTIC THRILLER'S
ALLURING CONFOUNDMENTS

Basic Instinct (1992)

In the fall of 1990, American activist group the Gay and Lesbian Alliance Against Defamation (GLAAD) was leaked the screenplay of a forthcoming Hollywood production, which would become one of their preeminent objects of protest: *Basic Instinct* (Paul Verhoeven, 1992). First formed in 1985, GLAAD had sought to highlight purported links between so-called negative representations of queers on screen and violence against queers in the world. For GLAAD, the *Basic Instinct* screenplay exemplified such a media object: In an advertisement they took out in *Daily Variety*, it is listed among a selection of films under the headline "Hollywood Images Fuel Gay/Lesbian Bashing."[1] Over the next two years, GLAAD's campaign against the film intensified. The group's May/June 1991 bulletin reads:

> *Basic Instinct* features the latest in man-hating killer lesbians. Roxy, the psycho lesbian, slashed her little brother to death when she was 14. She tries to kill the hero because he's involved with her bisexual female roommate. The roommate herself is an ice-pick man-killer. A third woman,

who is either bisexual or lesbian, is also apparently a murderer. The film contains no sympathetic lesbian, gay or bisexual characters. . . . The only representations of gays . . . or lesbians by major studios is as queer psycho killers or as objects of ridicule. Tell the studio that if changes are not made, loud protests, like those that greeted *Cruising*, will greet this movie when it opens.[2]

And GLAAD's protests against *Basic Instinct* were certainly loud. In collaboration with other gay and lesbian as well as with feminist groups, GLAAD activists disrupted its filming in San Francisco on numerous occasions, petitioning a venue owner not to lease his bar for the shoot, breaching temporary restraining orders with noisy protests, glitter-bombing the set, and blocking traffic during the filming of a car chase sequence.[3] Activists also met with representatives from the production on multiple occasions to ask that the film be rewritten, causing tensions between screenwriter Joe Eszterhas, who sympathized with their demands, and production company Carolco and director Paul Verhoeven, who did not.[4] *Basic Instinct*'s production proceeded with the activists' demands unmet.

That a film involving the narrative staples and stylish aesthetics of the erotic thriller came to disquiet gay, lesbian, and bisexual activists has some precedent. The most formative year in the erotic thriller's early history saw the release of three films—*Windows* (Gordon Willis, 1980), *Cruising* (William Friedkin, 1980), and *Dressed to Kill* (Brian De Palma, 1980)—each of which were protested in an organized and persistent fashion by lesbian, gay, and feminist groups across the United States.[5] In each of these films, which make up what Linda Ruth Williams terms the erotic thriller's "Golden Age," connections are forged between queerness and violence.[6] *Windows*' Andrea (Elizabeth Ashley) facilitates the sexual assaults of her neighbor Emily (Talia Shire) and watches them through a telescope for her own sexual gratification. The serial killer narrative of *Cruising* takes place in the underground queer milieu of New York's male leather bars. And in *Dressed to Kill*, the murderer of a series of female victims is revealed to be the female persona of psychiatrist Dr. Elliott (Michael Caine), who is established, by the film's denouement, as a transgender woman named Bobbi.[7] While the political dimensions of these films are subject to ongoing critical debate, the protests around them in 1980 share a specific political premise: that screen representations of amoral queers—whose violence coalesces with their sexual deviancy—function both as a symptom of and a catalyst for violence against queers beyond the screen.

In the introduction, I outlined how such approaches to representation misattribute a truth-value to texts, using poorly evidenced arguments around media effects to draw lines of causation between textual representations and violence in the world. The appeal of these approaches lies in their consolidation of social queerphobia into objectionable, repudiable, and protestable objects. In this process, the media object finds itself taking on wishful or convenient meanings that are harder to justify textually and that, I argue, close reading tends to undo. Rather than replicating existing social prejudices, the erotic thriller, in particular, offers remarkably ambivalent treatments of sexuality, gender, desire, and transgression. That none of these phenomena are presented univocally is, in fact, central to the erotic thriller genre, which stylizes the multiplication of meanings and an undoing of epistemological certainty. Further, as films that persistently suggest that desire might be dangerous or even deadly, erotic thrillers speak to a more universal notion famously theorized by Sabina Spielrein and Sigmund Freud: that the pursuit of pleasure can be a form of destruction.[8] The anxieties invoked here are thus less a phobic projection of a pathological sexual alterity but, more broadly, a reminder of what Zygmunt Bauman proposes in his discussion of Eros: "There is a thin boundary . . . between a soft and gentle caress and a ruthless iron grip. . . . The deeper and denser your attachments, commitments, engagements, the greater your risk."[9] It is this facet of Eros that is distilled in the erotic thriller's bisexual figures, who come to embody the genre's investment in the dangerous interplays between sexuality, risk, and power.

In the erotic thriller, the alliance between bisexuality and transgression takes on socially destructive and alluringly salacious forms. To trace the representational histories of the erotic thriller is to observe a persistent evocation of bisexual possibility—glimpsed in its films' narrative twists, erotic spectacles, and compelling figurations. That bisexuality is regularly figured in these dramas of dangerous desire and unreadable bodies is far from incidental: It is one means through which 1980s and 1990s cultures negotiated a changing landscape of sexual politics and the anxiety-inducing threat of that which risks collapsing structures of a gay-straight ordering. These tendencies are no more discernible than in *Basic Instinct*, whose central figure, the indomitable Catherine Tramell (Sharon Stone), became a prominent cultural reference, known for her skilled subterfuge, alluring unreadability, and wanton bisexual desires. *Basic Instinct*, like its erotic thriller contemporaries, catalyzes the relation between bisexuality and erotics while invoking contemporary debates around the sociopolitical status of (queer) femininities. I also propose that, with the repeated figuration of nefariously wealthy bisexuals, these films produce an anxious fever dream around the incorporation of queers into institutions of credit lending and wealth accumulation during the first decades of financialization. Finally, the erotic thriller's classically noir narratives of criminal investigation offer stirring probes of the relations between sexuality, gender, visuality, and epistemology. In the erotic thriller's shadowy milieux, in which investigators are both allured by and flummoxed in the face of sexually ambiguous suspects, bisexuality's compelling polysemy effects a reckoning with the very certitude of epistemological and taxonomical organization.

Bisexuality's Dangerous Thrills

> The inner experience of eroticism demands from the subject a sensitiveness to the anguish at the heart of the taboo no less great than the desire which leads him to infringe it.
> —Georges Bataille, *Death and Sensuality*

The transgressive pleasures of the erotic thriller can be found in the alluring concoction that constitutes its generic formula: sex + social deviance. In this potent pairing, the erotic thrills of sexiness and sex acts are presented both alongside and as implicated by the socially deviant thrills of immorality, dissidence, and criminality. These elements' interrelation and interdependency mark the erotic thriller's recognizability. Yet the suggestion that transgression is central to eroticism predates the genre. It is precisely this implication of the transgressive in the erotic, and vice versa, that characterizes the aphorism from Donatien-Alphonse-François de Sade's Madame de Saint-Ange, explored in this book's introduction, as well as Georges Bataille's later writing on the erotic.[10] Bataille's description, quoted in this section's epigraph, gives us a framework through which bisexual transgression might be understood as typically erotic. If eroticism is constituted by a taboo and its infringement, then bisexual transgression can be understood as a form of eroticism in which it is the law of compulsory monosexuality that is broken. This suggestion echoes those of Marjorie Garber and Tim Dean (which I discuss in this book's introduction), who propose that eroticism is a form of sexuality that either looks beyond a single gendered object or de-emphasizes gender in its realization, speaking to a bisexual structure of desiring (or perhaps a desirous structurelessness) in eroticism.[11] The transgression of compulsory monosexuality can produce an erotic thrill characterized by the breaching of social rules, the alluring exposure to new sexual knowledge. These are the bisexual erotics with which the erotic thriller regularly plays: In a social order structured by a heterosexual-homosexual binary, bisexual transgression offers thrills at once criminal and carnal.

The genealogy of the erotic thriller has been constructed retrospectively. Although this genre marker has not been applied exclusively to American films, an overwhelming majority of its corpus emanates from the United States, with Hollywood producing its most watched and discussed titles. Erotic thrillers owe a clear debt to the aesthetics and narrative preoccupations of film noir and share some generic investments with the American sexploitation roughie and the Italian *giallo*.[12] Linda Ruth Williams identifies the 1970s films *Play Misty for Me* (Clint Eastwood, 1971) and *Looking for Mr. Goodbar* (Richard Brooks, 1977) as establishing the erotic thriller's "basic formula."[13] These films foreground a number of qualities that would come to characterize the genre: narratives involving crime (especially murder), sexually promiscuous protagonists, the return of the femme fatale in *Play Misty*'s Evelyn (Jessica Walter), and the figuration of a murderous bisexual in *Mr. Goodbar*'s Gary (Tom Berenger). In Williams's extensive study of the genre, she adumbrates its definitional traits: "Erotic thrillers are *noir*ish stories of sexual intrigue incorporating some form of criminality or duplicity, often as the flimsy framework for on-screen softcore sex."[14] Later, she traces the genre's promise to the spectator and its unique mode of transforming the generic staples of film noir: "The erotic thriller should thrill its viewers in a uniquely two-edged way, through narrative suspense and engagement, and through sexual delivery. . . . *Film noir* was and is centrally about sex anyway, but the erotic thriller . . . also shows *noir* to be at the heart of a certain form of (increasingly mainstream) pornography, albeit one overlit with the bright opulence of Californian primetime soap."[15] These evocative definitions situate the erotic thriller and its generic appeal at an intersection between the thrills of both sexual and social dissidence. That these thrills might be said to characterize all film noir speaks to the importance of this generic genealogy for the erotic thriller, which itself overlaps with what has been termed "neonoir." Broadly speaking, neonoir is a genre marker used in reference to a body of films produced from the 1960s onward that invoke the formal style of classical noir cinema (chiaroscuro lighting, canted angles, off-center composition) as well as its thematic preoccupations (moral ambiguity, crime, violence, alienation, paranoia) and its staple characters (femmes fatales, fall guys, ethically compromised protagonists).[16] These films are also less beholden to the strictures of censorship codes, allowing for criminals to go unpunished and for the transgressions of flawed protagonists to be more egregious.[17] Although the erotic thriller can be considered part of the tradition of neonoir, the latter does not necessitate sexual "delivery," as Williams terms it.[18]

Neonoir shares the erotic thriller's themes of criminality, dissimulation, and unknowability, but the erotic thriller carries with it a generic promise of sexual explicitness. There are many films that fall into contested territory between these genre markers, and there will likely be films I address that others deem better suited to the broader umbrella of neonoir. Nevertheless, what interests me here is not to offer a deterministic approach to genre classification but to discuss those noirish films from the twentieth century's final decades that engage questions of sex and sexuality with relative explicitness. It is precisely this infusion of a noirish landscape—criminal, morally ambivalent, mysterious—with explicit sexuality that signals the erotic thriller's singularity.

Significantly less restrained by censorship than noir films of the classical era, the erotic thriller's history is, crucially, coterminous with that of video pornography. In the United States, adult home video first appeared in a legal marketplace context in late 1977, although it circulated in private, illegal, and semilegal contexts throughout the 1970s.[19] The erotic thriller emerged at this paradigm-shifting cultural moment, when the availability, consumption, and market success of video pornography was increasing.[20] However, the term *erotic* in *erotic thriller* belies this connection. As Williams observes, sex in these films rarely connotes the more respectable "erotica," understood as "'loving' . . . tender and respectful . . . aesthetically subtler or more suggestive"; instead, the erotic thriller "prefers contextless and often consequenceless sexual display, anonymous encounters, a variety of sexual scenarios."[21] That is to say, the erotic thriller's textual treatment of the sex act is more typical of pornographic film. It is under the aegis of the term *erotic* that these films widen their market appeal toward, in Williams's words, "those who would avoid the top shelf," particularly a heterosexual female viewership encouraged to "join their (male) partners on the viewing-sofa."[22] The promise of the sex act's visibility is, like pornography, central to the erotic thriller's appeal. Although the sex portrayed in these films is often heuristically called "simulated" or "softcore," Maria San Filippo observes how "the erotic thriller . . . both flaunts and disavows its adjacency to porn."[23] These representations might, therefore, be understood in a more complex fashion as teetering on the boundary of what is and what is not considered "real" sex, between notions of eroticism and pornography, between soft- and hardcore. Tanya Krzywinska reminds us that it is the explicit visualization of ejaculation and penetration that tends to authenticate images as hardcore, but where does that leave instances of sexual bodily contact between actors that do not fall within these categories of authentication?[24] While unsimulated penetrative sex does not take place in these films, unsimulated portrayals of frottage and breast-licking, for example, are commonplace. These are interstitial acts of screen sex that may or may not be considered real. The sense in which the erotic thriller can, in Williams's words, "openly flirt with pornography" marks this genre's aesthetic territory, a space on the borders of acceptability, explicitness, and simulation, a mode of erotic tease that winks to a viewer with the knowledge of its own liminality.[25]

The erotic thriller's links to pornographic film also carry import in relation to its depictions of queerness, particularly insofar as pornographic film, since the earliest extant stag films, has incorporated images of sex between women as a mainstay. These performances were a feature of straight theatrical hardcore titles, like *Behind the Green Door* (Artie Mitchell and Jim Mitchell, 1972), and continued to be featured regularly in straight video pornography.[26] Fairly explicit depictions of sex between women would also migrate into the erotic thriller's generic territory with relative seamlessness. That these sex acts need not involve penetration means that the criteria here for what constitutes real sex—a notion historically tied to cissexist and heterosexist norms—are murkier. In a generically nonpornographic space that forbids explicit penetrative sex or erect penises, sex between women devoid of these features is thus not necessarily considered real and is subsequently permissible.

Although we cannot, of course, lose sight of the address of these scenes—positioned, as they are, toward what is imagined to be heterosexual male fantasy—these intentions need not determine their wider significance. As Jennifer Moorman highlights in relation to pornographic film, to interpret images of sex between women as heterosexual or inauthentic is to reify a normalizing framework that adjudicates what queer women and queer sex between women *should* look like.[27] Instead, an alternate mode of interpretation might consider how scenes of sex between women—in both pornographic and nonpornographic contexts—display carnal images that might, at once, offer pleasures typical of straight sex films and pose queer threats that destabilize heteropatriarchy's sexual myths. With the erotic thriller, Williams underscores how "the spectacle of female pleasure, particularly pleasure which excludes men, is central."[28] The potential here for reading queerness against the grain of its heteropatriarchal nullification is strong. The erotic thriller's treatment of sex between women, in fact, provides a fitting example of the genre's dangerous allure: The image of sex between women, likely to arouse many who view it, carries with it the antipatriarchal threat of women's sexual self-sufficiency. Similar to the scene I discuss from *Vampyres* in chapter 1, in which the impotent and dazed Ted watches in horror at Fran and Miriam having sex without him, these are carnal images that foreground women's desire for each other while decentering their desire toward men. As in the les(bi)an vampire film, this figuration of sexuality is not simply an oppositional denial of men's desirability. Instead, a bisexual alternative is at play. Men are neither undesirable nor are they necessarily unwanted; instead, they are inessential, nonobligatory. When *Secret Games'* (Gregory Dark, 1992) new brothel employee Julianne (Michele Brin) informs her colleagues that her first client was a woman, her colleague Greta (Kimberly Williams) reflects, "Men don't understand how to please a woman, you have to train them like pets." To a male viewer of *Secret Games*, Greta utters simultaneously a provocation and a threat.

Sex between men, however, is depicted less regularly in the erotic thriller. Notable exceptions to this tendency include *Cruising*, in which a variety of sex acts between men are displayed, and *Crash* (David Cronenberg, 1996), whose protagonists' polymorphous perversity takes many forms, including an intimate scene of anal sex between James (James Spader) and Dr. Vaughan (Elias Koteas). It is instructive that, in both of these instances, sex between men is presented in contexts of sexual fetishism, appearing as one among many deviations from sexual norms that populate the erotic thriller genre. The obvious explanation for the paltry amount of images of sex between men in the erotic thriller (in comparison to their female counterparts) is rooted in the incongruity of these images with dominant conceptions of heteropatriarchal fantasy. Unlike fetish sex practices, power play, or even sexual violence, sex between men is, more often than not, a transgression too far for the erotic thriller. However, the relative invisibility of images of sex acts between men in the erotic thriller belies the array of queer male figures who slip in and out of the genre. From protagonists like *The 4th Man*'s (Paul Verhoeven, 1983) incandescently libidinous Gerard (Jeroen Krabbé), to the central object of a film's erotic fascination, such as *Apartment Zero*'s (Martin Donovan, 1988) dissolute hustler Jack (Hart Bochner), and *Dark Harbor*'s (Adam Coleman Howard, 1998) mysterious and duplicitous Young Man (Norman Reedus), we can trace male figures who interweave desires toward men and women in a bisexual figuration that often perplexes those around them.

Consider *Looking for Mr. Goodbar*'s Gary, who is introduced in the film's final fifteen minutes, dressed in drag for a New Year's Eve celebration. Fed up with his overbearing male lover, Gary dedrags and escapes to a bar. There, he rebuffs male attention with homophobic jibes but welcomes the advances of the film's sexually liberated protagonist, Theresa (Diane Keaton). The two return to Theresa's apartment, where they attempt to have sex, but Gary cannot achieve an erection, despite his attempts to do so with the aid of amyl nitrate. When Theresa tries to console Gary, he misinterprets her words as her construing him as gay. He responds violently, attacking her. Newly aroused by the violence he has inflicted, Gary is now able to become erect and rapes Theresa. Mid-coitus, he produces a knife from his back pocket and stabs Theresa to death. This unexpected ending is characterized by a gruesome outburst of violence in which a queer figure's sexual turmoil is meted out onto the body of the film's protagonist. But further, this ending's unexpectedness is itself constituted by Gary's unreadability. We have witnessed him in drag, heard him uttering homophobic insults, and seen him pursue a sexual encounter with Theresa. The unpredictability of Gary's outburst of violence, which ends the film, is inseparable from the polysemous signifiers he displays. Bisexuality thus functions here both as constitutive of and as metaphor for the unknowability of the other, the anxiety produced by the knowledge that the signifiers through which people are conventionally read are themselves unreliable.

The construction of narrative intrigue through characters' sexual unreadability would come to typify the erotic thriller genre. *Basic Instinct* arrives toward the beginning of the 1990s, in which Hollywood's Big Six studios were beginning to innovate their business models to maintain their influence in a rapidly changing media landscape.[29] Although the Big Six had—to varying degrees—become subsidiaries of conglomerates with reach far beyond cinema, the blockbuster remained at the center of their industrial practice.[30] *Basic Instinct* would become one such blockbuster. Produced by the independent Carolco and distributed by Sony Pictures' TriStar, directed by Hollywood's hottest émigré, Paul Verhoeven, starring Michael Douglas in the heyday of his career as Nick, and making a successful investment in star-in-waiting Sharon Stone, as Catherine, *Basic Instinct* would go on to gross a mammoth $352.7 million internationally.[31] *Basic Instinct*'s screenwriter, Joe Eszterhas, had, by 1990, authored the screenplays of some of Hollywood's highest-grossing blockbusters, including erotic thriller *Jagged Edge* (Richard Marquand, 1985), which made a not-insignificant $40.5 million.[32] By 1990, Hollywood's erotic thrillers had already proven some of its highest earners, with *Dressed to Kill, Body Heat* (Lawrence Kasdan, 1981), *Jagged Edge, 9½ Weeks* (Adrian Lyne, 1986), and *Black Widow* (Bob Rafelson, 1987) all surpassing $20 million at the box office internationally and *Fatal Attraction* (Adrian Lyne, 1987) making its mark as the highest-grossing film of 1987 worldwide at $320.1 million.[33] The erotic thriller was profitable business.

In June 1990, Eszterhas was released from contract with the Creative Artists Agency and was now free to auction his *Basic Instinct* screenplay independently.[34] A bidding war ensued between all of the Big Six and three independents.[35] This war would be won by Carolco, an independent production company that Jim Hillier characterizes as a "distinctively new breed of independent . . . sufficiently well capitalised to be able to produce on their own, without recourse to

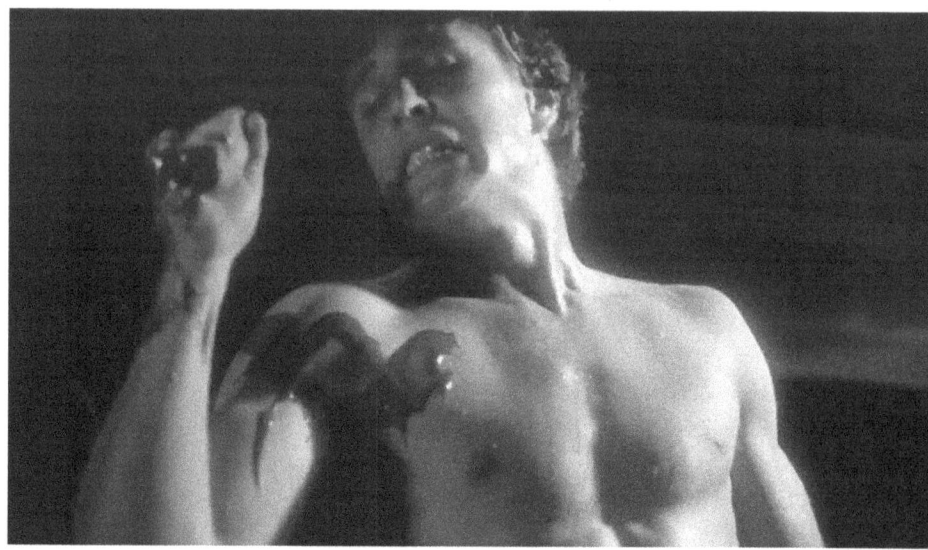

FIGURE 4.1 Gary (Tom Berenger) kills Theresa (Diane Keaton). *Looking for Mr. Goodbar* (Richard Brooks, 1977). Digital screen capture.

studio finance, but generally with an established relationship with a studio for domestic theatrical release."[36] During the 1990s, such independents produced some of Hollywood's most successful blockbusters, using negative pickup deals with the Big Six and its subsidiaries for distribution.[37] Carolco's unique approach within this emergent system involved making a small amount of savvy investments in projects that promised sizable returns.[38] In *Basic Instinct*, Carolco eyed a lucrative investment, buying Eszterhas's screenplay for a record-breaking $3 million, the highest amount ever paid for a screenplay at the time.[39] This sizable investment and its subsequent payoff cannot be understood without accounting for the erotic thriller's potential for profitability: This genre had proven success, and Eszterhas's screenplay promised to deliver the goods.

The actions of Carolco and Verhoeven over the period of preproduction suggest that part of what attracted them to the project was its daring potential for sexual explicitness and, for Verhoeven, a narrative incorporating female bisexuality. Verhoeven imagined he would make a "sexually explicit thriller" that would be "the first mainstream film to include a shot of an erect penis."[40] Whereas Eszterhas's screenplay called for sex scenes to take place in the dark, Verhoeven wanted "graphic and visible" nudity, causing Eszterhas to fear that his work would be "turn[ed] into porn."[41] Verhoeven and Carolco, however, shared a vision of an erotic thriller that pushed the boundaries of the images of sex and sexuality acceptable for Hollywood cinema, a film that would test the limits of the erotic thriller formula. Central to this vision was an investment in the transgressive power of visualizing bisexuality through images of sex. After Eszterhas quit the project later in 1990, citing "philosophical and personal differences," Verhoeven set out to rework the screenplay, with one of his central concerns being to flesh out the relationship between Catherine and Roxy (Leilani Sarelle).[42] Verhoeven's investment in bisexual erotics was already evident in the depiction of male sexuality in his Dutch films *Spetters* (1980) and *The 4th Man* (which he later called *Basic Instinct*'s "prequel").[43] Later, these themes would also be revisited among women in *Showgirls* (1995) and *Benedetta* (2021). Additionally, it is insightful, given Verhoeven's status as an auteur, that he discusses bisexuality in relation to both himself and his work. In interviews, he shares his view that "we are probably born bisexual," disclosed an adolescent crush toward another boy, and recounted a sexual tryst with Dutch actor and screenwriter Jan van Mastrigt.[44] These personal accounts work—perhaps through ideas of a European sexual liberalism inherent in his auteur image—to establish him as a figure possessing both a personal openness to bisexual possibility and an aesthetic investment in bisexual erotics. These are the erotics *Basic Instinct* would mobilize and that would contribute toward the film's superlative success within the erotic thriller canon.

What Carolco saw in *Basic Instinct*'s screenplay was not simply a recognition of the market value of Eszterhas's story or of the erotic thriller but the marketability of images of female bisexuality. Yet these images also carried with them the troublesome threat of bisexual transgression—a threat both seductive and smarting. Hollywood's late twentieth-century imag(in)ings of bisexuality speak to this potential to be, at once, profitable and pernicious, desirable and destructive, hegemonically produced yet subversively deracinating. It is in the figurations of *Basic Instinct*'s Catherine, Roxy, Beth (Jeanne Tripplehorn), and Hazel (Dorothy Malone) that we can observe the erotic thriller's efforts toward and failures in managing female bisexuality, a phenomenon that, toward the beginning of the 1990s, could be found in the very heart of mainstream cinema.

Sharon Stone, Postfeminism, and Bisexual Marketability

On April 11, 1992, Sharon Stone hosted *Saturday Night Live* (SNL) and, in her opening monologue, re-created the now-famous interrogation scene from *Basic Instinct*. Sporting her character's white sleeveless turtleneck minidress, she sits smoking with her legs crossed and thigh exposed. With this reflexive mise-en-scène in place, Stone delivers a sultry monologue about her week with the SNL cast, pausing to take drags of her cigarette. "Leaving here is gonna be sad because I'll miss all the pleasure they gave me," she reflects wryly. "Especially the men, because they're so *funny.*" We cut to enraptured cast members Chris Farley and Phil Hartman, who gawk at her. "But you know what?" Stone teases, "The women are funny too. Very funny. That's right, the *women* make me laugh too." This time, we cut to a mesmerized Victoria Jackson, who licks her bottom lip, just as spellbound as her male colleagues. Central to this self-reflexive performance are two contentions: first, that Stone's star persona is yoked to Catherine Tramell in ways with which she plays and, second, that inherent in this dualistic figuration is her potential to desire and to be desired bisexually.

Basic Instinct's interrogation scene would become renowned for a moment in which Catherine uncrosses her legs and crosses them again, exposing her uncovered vulva for a beat. Three decades after the film's release, the ethics of Stone's exposure would come under scrutiny in the wake of the #MeToo movement, which encompassed, in part, a reckoning with the sexual abuse and harassment of women in Hollywood. While Verhoeven alleges that Stone had full knowledge of the frontal nudity the scene entailed, Stone alleges that she did not and was told, "We can't see anything."[45] After viewing the film in a private preview, Stone recounts, "I did have choices. So I thought and thought and I chose to allow this scene in the film. Why? Because it was correct for the film and for the character."[46] Stone's personal reasoning behind allowing the shot to remain in the film despite her misgivings provides us with a clue as to its germaneness to Basic Instinct: It announces the transgressiveness of both Catherine and the film. This moment would become cemented in film history, paid homage to by various figures in disparate media texts. These have included, to name just two among many, the kilt-wearing Scotsman Groundskeeper Willie in a 1995 episode of The Simpsons and musician Beyoncé in the music video for her 2006 song "Ring the Alarm." In each of these instances, this scene from Basic Instinct and the Catherine figure herself are used to convey defiance against an interrogating authority. This theme is played to comedic effect in The Simpsons when the unabashed Scotsman Groundskeeper Willie stuns his interrogators with the revelation he is wearing nothing beneath his kilt. In the "Ring the Alarm" video, the interrogation room is where Beyoncé stages a provocation around her love interest's suspected infidelity. Basic Instinct's interrogation scene is an eminently citable point of cultural reference across the landscape of American visual culture and beyond.

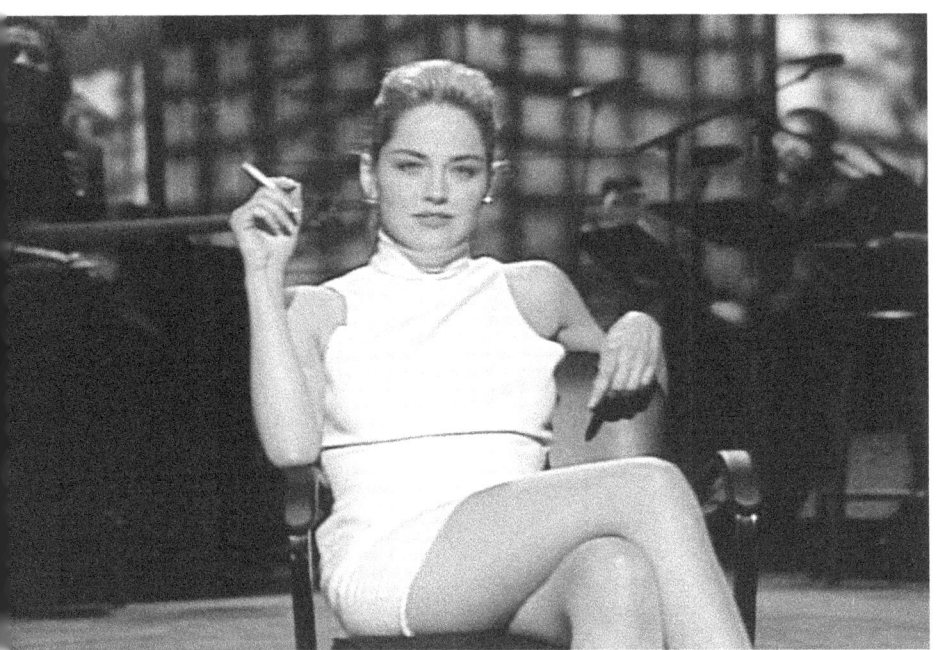

FIGURE 4.2 Sharon Stone hosts *Saturday Night Live*. "Sharon Stone/Pearl Jam" (NBC, 1992). Digital screen capture.

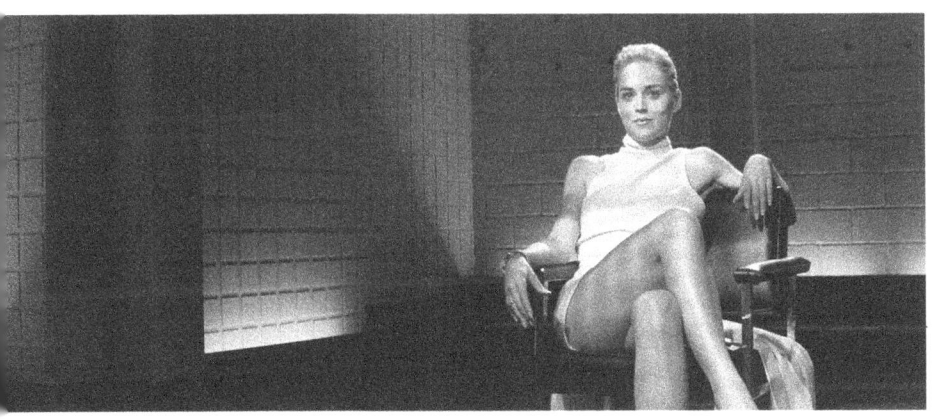

FIGURE 4.3 Catherine's (Sharon Stone) interrogation. *Basic Instinct* (Paul Verhoeven, 1992). Digital screen capture.

Catherine's demeanor, movements, and words in this scene are careful and deliberate; against a multipronged interrogation, she maintains a confident and wry disposition. She waives the right to an attorney, she parries with her male interrogators, she undermines the men's authority. The apotheosis of this scene—the brief exposure of Catherine's vulva—beckons a classically Freudian reading: The men are confronted by castration anxiety, akin to that of the boy seeing his mother's vulva and fearing the loss of his penis. This confrontation is made by a phallic femme, adorned with the concomitant accoutrements of heels, a tubiform dress, and, of course, a cigarette.[47] In such a reading, these phallic adornments' failure to assuage castration anxiety would be rendered all the more threatening through the vulva's revelation. But this moment is also remarkable due to the atypicality of frontal images of vulvae in Hollywood film, imbuing it with the shock of the unexpected and the verboten on a spectatorial level. The film's surprise of the viewer works to establish its own transgressiveness: A cinematic rule has been broken, as have the laws that govern what is expected of a Hollywood actress. Here, *Basic Instinct* and Stone alike announce their dangerous audacity, confronting the spectator with a double-edged symbol from the misogynistic imaginary that fuses the horror of the castrated mother with the exhibitionism of the whore. That this figure displays herself openly particularizes her figuration: Her paradoxical phallic lack and plenitude mirrors her capacity for both intragender and extragender seduction.

Prior to *Basic Instinct*, Stone had appeared in a disparate selection of Hollywood-produced films as character parts, few of which granted her serious critical recognition but some of which gave her experience in performing seductive, feminine danger. Spanning a range of genres, many of Stone's film roles were defined solely by their relation to male characters.[48] Of particular interest, however, are the multiple instances in which Stone depicts powerful, deceptive, and alluring women. Such examples can be found in Stone's early television acting career, where her characters are revealed as the unsuspected murderer in episodes of *Remington Steele* ("Steele Crazy After All These Years," 1983), *The New Mike Hammer* ("Shots in the Dark," 1984), *Magnum, P.I.* ("Echoes of the Mind, parts 1 and 2," 1984), and the television film *Calendar*

FIGURES 4.4–4.5 Homages to Catherine's interrogation: Beyoncé Knowles-Carter in the music video for "Ring the Alarm" (Sophie Muller, 2006); Groundskeeper Willie in *The Simpsons*, "Who Shot Mr. Burns? Part Two" (Wes Archer, 1995). Digital screen captures.

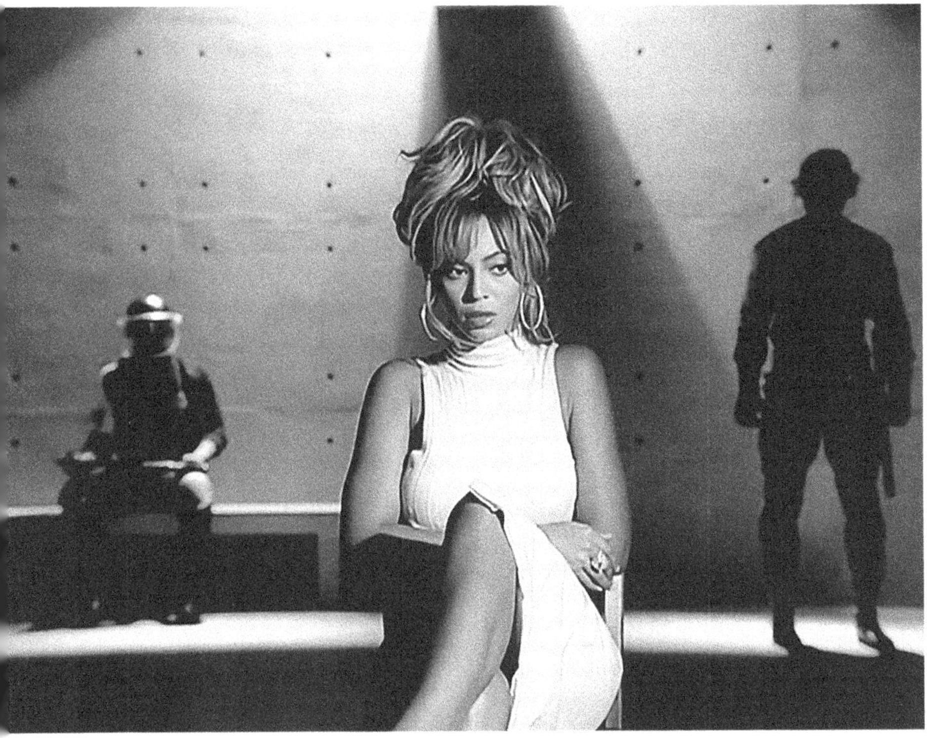

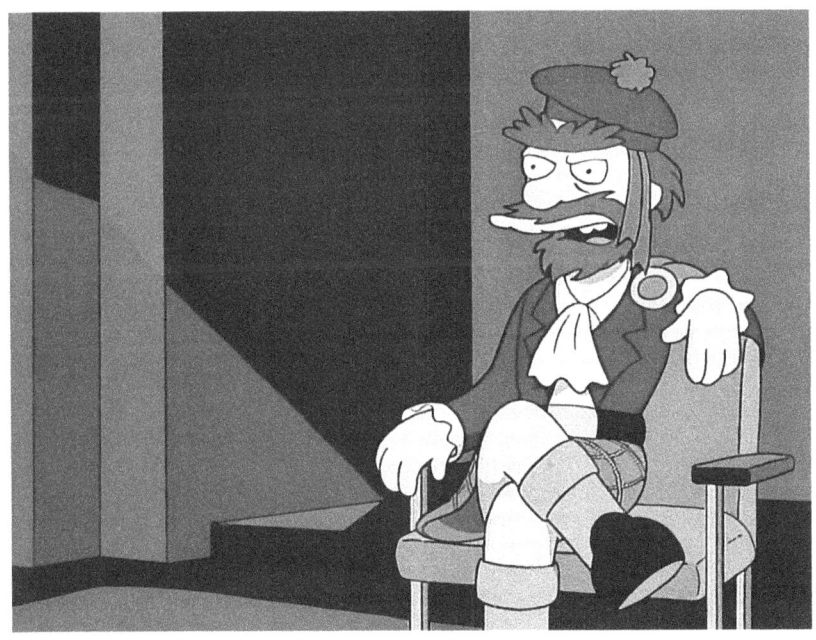

Girl Murders (William A. Graham, 1984). In theatrical films, Stone also had a number of roles that married allure and danger, here in neonoir, thriller, and erotic thriller contexts. In *Cold Steel* (Dorothy Ann Puzo, 1987), she plays a femme fatale who seduces a man she believes murdered her brother; in *Blood and Sand* (Javier Elorrieta, 1989), she plays a sexually forward, cocaine-snorting landowner; in *Total Recall* (Paul Verhoeven, 1990), she plays a double agent pretending to be the brainwashed protagonist's wife; in *Year of the Gun* (John Frankenheimer, 1991), she plays a photojournalist who seduces a novelist in the hope of stealing evidence from him. While Stone's career prior to *Basic Instinct* was by no means limited to a certain character type, we can observe across this period multiple occasions in which she gained experience playing dangerous, seductive women. These are the character qualities that would prove central to her career-defining role in Catherine Tramell.

Stone would become symbolically inseparable from Catherine.[49] Though she went on to enjoy a moderately successful career in Hollywood, with three subsequent Golden Globe nominations, the character of Catherine lingered, even in media discourses around Stone's philanthropic work.[50] At times, Stone exploited her association with the character, referencing it in her SNL appearance and resurrecting it for the genre film parody *Last Action Hero* (John McTiernan, 1993), as a brief cameo, and for the sequel *Basic Instinct 2: Risk Addiction* (Michael Caton-Jones, 2006). While Stone sometimes resisted attempts to yoke her to Catherine in interviews, she recalls how, after watching *Basic Instinct*, she took inspiration from her character's tough exterior in her public life: "It wasn't that I vowed to be this character from now on, but I *would* be less weak on the outside."[51] Stone saw in Catherine the qualities of resilience and imperviousness of which she could make use navigating her newfound fame. These qualities were buttressed by notions of sexiness and allure that beckon attention while simultaneously securing a sense of starry unreachability. This concoction of femininity and power is central to figurations of bisexual women in the erotic thriller and cannot be understood without reference to two emergent critical concepts that circulated in discourses around women in nineties popular culture: postfeminism and bisexual marketability.

I use *postfeminism* here to describe a cultural sensibility, which emerged toward the end of the twentieth century in the Anglophone world, that championed a depoliticized, feminine, capitalism-friendly articulation of female empowerment. The postfeminist sensibility, Rosalind Gill argues, is politically guided by neoliberal notions of female individualism, subjectivity, and choice; visually preoccupied with images of the feminine body, measured through heteropatriarchal economies of value; and ontologically invested in resurgent ideas of natural sexual difference.[52] The postfeminist sensibility sees itself, in turn, as against, beyond, or subsequent to the project of feminism, yet simultaneously, it discursively recirculates certain ideas associated with feminism. Gill parses some aspects of this contradictory paradigm: "On the one hand, young women are hailed through a discourse of 'can-do' girl power, yet on the other their bodies are powerfully re-inscribed as sexual objects; on the one hand women are presented as active, desiring social subjects, yet on the other they are subject to a level of scrutiny and hostile surveillance that has no historical precedent."[53] The postfeminist sensibility works, simultaneously, to render the feminist struggle obsolete and to reinterpret extant feminist credos of self-determination and freedom as neoliberal values. In the postfeminist sensibility, the broadly defined aspiration of greater power for women becomes synonymous with individual women's power within capitalist frameworks, and ideas around sexual freedom become synonymous with women's ability to perform feminine aesthetics championed by heteropatriarchal culture.

In important ways, Stone's star image is characterized by this marrying of unabashed feminine erotic performance with a self-professed seriousness and ambition as an actor. This typically postfeminist amalgam is parsed by Rebecca Feasey, who writes that "Stone's image is shaped in relationship to discourses of femininity and the ways in which these are ranked and valued within cultural hierarchies. . . . She represents the lowest of the low within the hierarchies of Hollywood femininity, the 'nudity-friendly' dumb blonde. . . . However . . . in other contexts the actress is privileged as a female star who is sharp, intelligent and in control of her own career. Unfortunately, this presentation also involves an othering of the 'dumb blonde.'"[54] Feasey's analysis identifies how the contradictions in Stone's star image—typical of a postfeminist visual culture—both cite and undermine patriarchal conceptions of womanhood. However, we should not lose sight of the rupture inherent herein. When we read these postfeminist images, we can certainly find evidence of patriarchal culture's managing of female power within its own aesthetic frameworks, but we also witness the anxiously unmanageable images that pose a threat to a patriarchal social order. Similarly, though the erotic thriller's femmes fatales can be seen to embody what Katherine Farrimond calls "postfeminist rhetoric about the empowering nature of heteronormative display and performance," there are noteworthy filmic examples in which such a performance belies both a queerness and a criminality that lurk beneath it.[55] The erotic thriller's femme fatale does not simply embody the contradictions of the postfeminist sensibility; it mobilizes the image of the postfeminist woman as a means of projecting patriarchal culture's very fears.

The early 1990s also saw a proliferation of images of desire between women in public visual culture. Although these titillating images had long been commonplace in adult and exploitation film, their particular propagation in mainstream media, and particularly advertising, signaled a shift from margin to mainstream. The terms *lipstick lesbianism, lesbian chic,* or *bisexual chic* abound in contemporary discussions of this tendency. These terms name a cultural alignment among hegemonic femininity, female queerness, fashionability, and marketability. The term *bisexual chic* had, in fact, been used two decades prior, in ways that cited a range of bisexual phenomena in the 1970s: the hangover of sixties cultures of sexual liberation, bisexual swinging among married couples, the sexualities of rumored or openly bisexual stars in film and popular music.[56] The difference between the discussions of fashionable bisexuality in the 1970s and in the 1990s lies in their purported cultural positioning. Whereas seventies bisexual chic was to be found in countercultural scenes like swinging and glam rock, nineties bisexual chic circulated in the mainstream: glimpsed in the frames of billboards and the pages of fashion magazines. This nineties iteration of a bisexual trend was less about bisexuality as a dissident form of rebellion and more about the deployment of bisexuality as tool of marketing.

The question as to why female bisexuality became susceptible to being deployed in marketing is addressed by Katie King, who contends that "bisexuality has currency in a globalized economy of niche markets where the most circulated objects are those that can be viewed within the greatest range of divergent local markets as 'like-us.' . . . A highly commodified version of bisexuality can be exploited as differently important in a local and distinctive reception by a wide range of markets, especially media markets."[57] The ability of images suggesting bisexuality to appeal to a large number of niche markets provides media producers with a tool to maximize a product's desirability. Bisexuality can be seen at play, for instance, in the 1995 marketing campaign for Calvin Klein's unisex fragrance CK One. In one advertisement, couples kiss on either side of the frame and, though the shirtless figures are intelligible as men, the figures they kiss are androgynous, perhaps most recognizable as women in butch attire: braless in tank tops. Here, the spatial arrangement of similarly and differently gendered figures mingles with polysemous signifiers of sexuality to effect tableaux of bisexual indeterminacy. The accompanying tagline, "A fragrance for a man or a woman," winks similarly toward bisexuality: The fragrance itself will take a man or a woman. Yet these are not representations that evoke notions of queer radicalism. As Danae Clark writes with reference to nineties "commodity lesbianism" in advertising, these images are

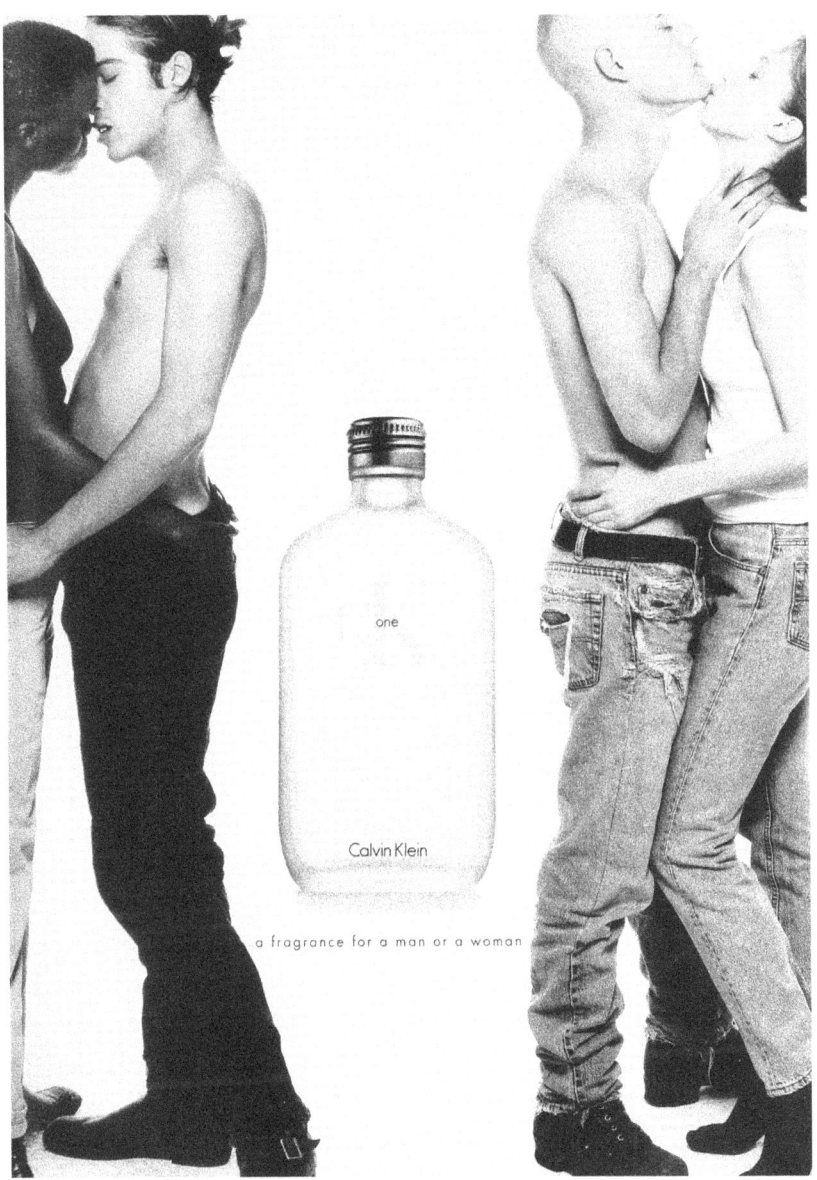

FIGURE 4.6 CK One advertisement (1995). Scanned document.

"cleansed" of their association with identity or politics.[58] Instead, these images' bisexual erotics position themselves as a widely cast net of consumer allure.

In conversation with King, Maria San Filippo relates this trend to cinema, calling it "a mode of queer commodification that mobilizes bisexuality to appeal to a queer audience without threatening straight spectators."[59] Among San Filippo's examples of this cinematic mode at play is *Basic Instinct*, which she calls "compromised" and "sensationalized."[60] But to what extent can the concept of bisexual marketability be transposed from advertisement media to cinema, and can this claim be made specifically with respect to the erotic thriller? Though erotic thriller films trade in alluring images of (mostly female) bisexuality, it would be inaccurate to suggest that this mode of representation acquiesces straightforwardly to a patriarchal, heterosexist erotic economy. Rather than taking images of queerness and depoliticizing them for straight consumption, *Basic Instinct*, like a number of its erotic thriller contemporaries, does something more dissimulative. In a sequence in which Nick is following Catherine, he tracks her down to a raucous nightclub, where house music blares and lithe partygoers—with looks akin to those contemporary Calvin Klein models—let loose. On the dance floor, Nick spots Catherine's girlfriend Roxy, who wanders into the men's bathroom, where a multigender array of bodies sprawl. Roxy finds Catherine in a stall snorting cocaine with an unnamed man (Keith McDaniel); Roxy straddles Catherine and proceeds to lean in for a bump the man is preparing for her. Meanwhile, Catherine catches Nick watching them. She makes eye contact with him, established through shot-reverse shot, and gives Nick a sultry grin. Then, maintaining her gaze, Catherine uses her leg to shut the stall door with a forceful slam. As Katherine Farrimond observes here, "Catherine's physical disruption of the male gaze points towards a more complex version of bisexual representation than accusations of pandering to straight male fantasy can account for."[61] How, instead, should we account for it?

Central to this moment's resistance to classical taxonomies of spectatorship is Catherine's simultaneous drawing in and pushing away of both Nick and the spectator. Catherine solicits Nick's and our gaze before blocking it abruptly, denying us access to her stall of bisexual erotics. Here, the spectacle of bisexual excess—signified classically with a bisexual triangle, evoking the transgressions of interracial desire (the unnamed man is Black, Catherine and Roxy are white), and demarcated as dangerously hedonistic by the narcotic indulgence on display—lures a curious, inquisitive gaze. Yet the pleasure Nick is able to take from this tableau is suddenly blocked, as is the spectator's scopophilia: a perverted game of *fort/da* or, perhaps more accurately, *da/fort*.[62]

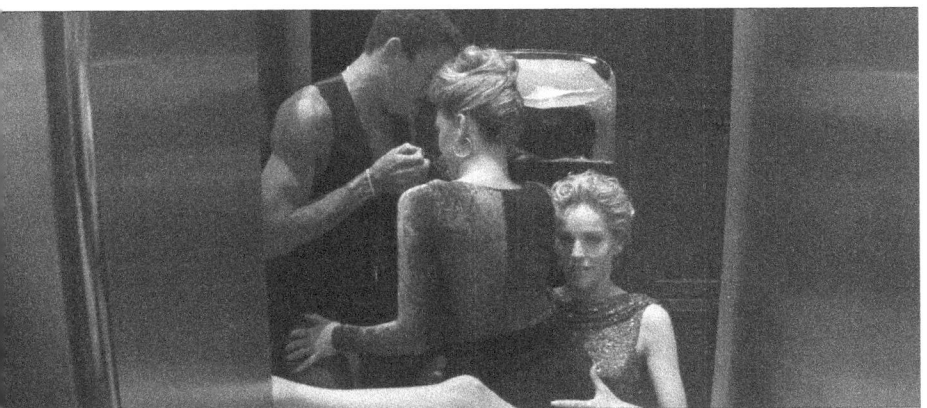

FIGURE 4.7 Catherine shares her stall of bisexual erotics with Roxy (Leilani Sarelle) and an unnamed man (Keith McDaniel). *Basic Instinct* (Paul Verhoeven, 1992). Digital screen capture.

This paradoxical enticement-exclusion evokes an ontological cinematic quality Christian Metz observes: "The cinema manages to be both exhibitionist and secretive. . . . The rectangular screen permits all kinds of fetishisms, all the nearly-but-not-quite effects, since it can decide at exactly what height to place the barrier which cuts us off."[63] In her revelation and concealment, Catherine metonymizes the cinematic apparatus itself: the stall door, under her manipulation, a kind of wipe transition. In her performance of ostension and obfuscation, Catherine invites and rejects, exposes and conceals.

Thus, while *Basic Instinct* invokes cultural phenomena related to patriarchal and neoliberal politics, these invocations are deployed perversely. The film's invocation of the imagery of bisexual marketability is twofold. The promise of feminine, girl-on-girl display is certainly a central aspect of the film's allure, but the duality of this image also comes to bear. The second time that Nick meets Roxy is at Catherine's beach house, where he becomes aware of the romantic relationship between the two of them. Catherine beckons Roxy over and the two share a passionate, perhaps uncomfortably long kiss. Rather than dwell on this erotic image—scan the women's bodies or cut to a close-up of entangled lips perhaps—the film cuts to Nick's reaction in reverse shot. The distance between Nick and the pair is not that comfortable lacuna secured by the voyeur's hiddenness. Nick is simply there—frustrated, awkward—and the women do not care. An image that, at first glance, might seem typical of nineties bisexual chic—the carefree feminine women embrace unencumbered by the company of men—jointly comes to signify, through its reaction shot, the threats of male exclusion. Nick is both an unnecessary participant and a confused interpreter. Whereas the marketing of female bisexuality works through these images being rendered palatable for patriarchal consumption, this moment promises the former but, instead, evokes patriarchal anxieties around the woman's unreadability and self-sufficiency.

Similarly, the film's engagement with the semiotics of the postfeminist sensibility undermines this sensibility's patriarchal functions through narrative. Catherine embodies the fantastical female figure of the postfeminist sensibility: rich, intelligent, glamorously well-kempt, comfortable with discussing and performing sexuality in public. Yet her power, presentability, and sexual frankness belie malevolent motives. Such a cinematic figuration is not simply a reification of the postfeminist sensibility but a projection of this sensibility's anxieties. Despite Catherine's figural allusions to the semiotics of the postfeminist sensibility, horror lurks in the suggestion that she might not be using these tools to acquiesce to the men around her but, instead, to harm them. *Basic Instinct*'s image of the woman-with-power is at once a sexy fantasy of postfeminist female success under capitalism and an erotic nightmare around the unpredictability of her deployment of this very power.

Queer Investments Under Financialization: Projecting Risk and Uncertainty

In *Black Widow*, Justice Department agent Alexandra (Debra Winger) investigates a series of suspicious deaths of men who share the same wife (Theresa Russell). This woman, who uses various aliases, is revealed to be Catharine, a shapeshifting serial seducer who marries men and murders them, accruing a hefty sum of inheritances along the way. Alexandra's investigation into Catharine involves befriending her at a beach resort, where sexual tension brews between the two women. At Catharine's wedding to her newest beau-cum-victim, Paul (Sami Frey), Alexandra pays a visit, gifting Catharine a brooch in the style of a black widow spider. Catharine instantly recognizes the symbolism, remarking, "Black widow. She mates, then she kills." Before Catharine leaves, she kisses Alexandra forcefully and abruptly on the mouth, extradiegetic high strings accenting the aggression of the kiss. In *Black Widow*'s Catharine, the nefarious accumulation of wealth is achieved through an ability to seduce others. In the allure of the seductive woman and the social power of the woman with wealth, patriarchal fears around desire's unmanageability and capitalist fears around a gendered recalibration of its channels of exploitation both come to bear.[64] Central to these fears, I contend, is a reckoning with risk and uncertainty, both as broad concepts and in their particularized economic iterations. The erotic thriller's bisexual femmes fatales, often enriched via devious machinations, embody specific anxieties around the unpredictability of capital's flow, its distribution within sexual economies, and the intensified paranoia around risk and uncertainty that characterizes finance capitalism.

Frank H. Knight, the preeminent economic thinker of risk and uncertainty, explicates these two concepts: "The practical difference between the two categories, risk and uncertainty, is that in the former the distribution of the outcome in a group of instances is known (either through calculation *a priori* or from statistics of past experience), while in the case of uncertainty this is not true, the reason being in general that it is impossible to form a group of instances, because the situation dealt with is in a high degree unique."[65] Knight's account stresses that although informed decisions tend to be made through knowledge of past experience, there will always be unique situations in which no prior knowledge exists. Here, a decision must be made in the face of uncertainty. John Maynard Keynes (the namesake of the Keynesian school of macroeconomics) stresses similarly the uncertainty that characterizes all predictions of economic probability, given the necessity in prediction of induction (inference of the general from the particular) and "the uncertainty to which all inductions are liable."[66] Both these central figures of modern economic thought contend that risks and uncertainties can never be eliminated entirely in predicting economic change. These issues became multiplied in the latter half of the twentieth century, in which a move toward financialization necessitated more prediction than ever.

The early 1970s saw the collapse of Bretton Woods, the transnational system that governed economic relations between states by tying currency exchange rates to gold.[67] This system was superseded by a period in which exchange rates could float, subject, instead, to the increasingly liberalized monetary policies of the world's hegemonic states.[68] In this economic paradigm, capital flows became progressively mobile, now principally subject to the workings of the purportedly self-regulating market.[69] This paradigm, consolidated across the 1970s and 1980s, was buttressed by neoliberal economic policies among the governments of the world's most powerful states, characterized by increased deregulation of the private sector, antiunion laws, greater privatization of formerly state-operated apparatuses, and the curtailment of state welfare provisions. The Reagan administration's (1981–1989) policies typified this move toward neoliberalism: an embrace of supply-side economics that envisaged the United States' economic growth through increased corporate freedoms. This landscape of mobile capital flow and neoliberal economic policy signaled a shift in modes of capital accumulation, implemented within the world's hegemonic states and disseminated to the benefit of capitalist interests worldwide. In this emergent economic order, finance was king.

The 1980s marked the genesis of the phenomenon political economists term "financialization" or "finance capitalism."[70] Whereas, previously, profit had been generated chiefly through the creation of surplus value in trade and commodity production, financialization saw capital accumulation emanate increasingly from financial channels in the form of what Karl Marx calls "interest-bearing capital."[71] Marx identifies this form of capital as "a commodity of a special kind," because its use value is "its capacity to function as capital and as such to produce the average profit under average conditions."[72] In other words, the value of interest-bearing capital consists of it being capital and its promise of profit. It is this form of capital, "a self-valorizing value capable of increasing itself," that gained prominence in the wake of financialization in the world's most powerful states, wherein investment and return would become a significant channel of profit creation.[73] Under finance capitalism, processes of risky investment became more widespread, effecting a system defined by a specific logic of risk outlined by Carolyn Hardin: "In this universe, riskless profit is an oxymoron. Profit or return is the correlate of risk. Without one, you cannot have the other."[74] Financial capital accumulation necessitates risk.

The risks of sexuality beyond a hetero/homo binary to capitalist systems have been theorized in compelling ways: first, in relation to late nineteenth- and early twentieth-century Victorian capitalism and, second, in relation to late twentieth- and early twenty-first-century finance capitalism. Eli Zaretsky outlines how Freud's theories of a universal bisexual disposition and infantile polymorphous perversity challenged not only nineteenth-century notions of sexual difference and sexual inversion but also the ways these cultural ideas were deployed by a Victorian capitalist economy.[75] In an economic system that relied upon the cultural reification of social divisions (like class, race, and gender), the universalizing potential of Freud's ideas contested the natural status of any social order. Bisexuality, in both Freud's physiological and psychological articulations, laid bare the plasticity of identity and the permeability of those divisions between social types through which Victorian capitalism functioned. Bisexuality can be seen to pose a similar threat later under finance capitalism, inflected here with a particular anxiety around unpredictability. Poet Maz Hedgehog explores the threat of bisexuality to capitalist models of asset management, which speaks to this context of financialization. They argue: "Anglo-American capitalism presumes that everything can be made predictable, coherent and reliable . . . that human beings, with their endless variation of bodies and desires and needs, can be turned into an asset, providing endless growth and limitless profits."[76] Later, they identify the forms of trouble that certain articulations of bisexual politics can pose for such an economic system, writing, "Bi politics asserts that, if ways of engaging in romantic/sexual intimacy can vary and change across a lifetime, then insisting on the purity/primacy of one attraction over another is doomed to fail. . . . In a society which uses the past behaviours to create present assets which are projected into future products, embracing change, fluidity and unpredictability can be a site of resistance."[77] Hedgehog's vision of a bisexual anticapitalist politics leverages bisexuality's unpredictable temporality as a tool against capitalism's abstraction of individuals as predictable assets. Bisexual unpredictability is anathema to financial forecasting.[78]

The arguments outlined here should not be taken to mean that bisexual individuals cannot be participants in or assets for capitalism or that bisexuality per se challenges capitalism. Instead, I am suggesting that bisexuality as a conceptual possibility threatens certain capitalist mechanisms insofar as, in Félix Guattari's words, "economic and sexual exploitation cannot be dissociated. Bureaucracies and the bourgeoisie maintain their power by basing themselves on sexual segregation."[79] We must, however, heed Mandy Merck's warning against the "functionalist assumptions of an intrinsically heterosexist capitalism," which attest to queers' incommensurability to capitalist systems.[80] The past three to four decades have, indeed, seen the incorporation of certain queers into dominant capitalist modes of economic subjectivity. It is in the particularity of which queers were targeted by and incorporated into these systems, however, and the forms through which this incorporation took place, that we find clues as to bisexuality's place in this changing landscape of sexual-economic organization.

The late 1980s and 1990s saw the accommodation of a certain gay subject within American capitalist systems, a figure Merck identifies as the "'global gay' . . . [a] middle-class professional and consumer."[81] The emergence of such a figure cannot be explained without attention to what became a widely cited piece of research: a 1988 survey by the Simmons Market Research Bureau for Rivendell Marketing, an advertising firm for gay publications. This survey reported that gay people had an average per capita income of $36,800 versus a $12,287 national average and that gay people had a larger proportion of college degree attainment and representation in managerial and professional positions.[82] Despite the fact that this study was fundamentally misleading—its survey base was a limited readership of certain lesbian and gay magazines— Dan Baker observes how the Simmons survey, and a subsequent survey by marketing firm Overlooked Opinions, "got an enormous amount of publicity," promoting the idea that "the gay and lesbian market was disproportionately wealthy."[83] The nineties saw these demographics targeted by large corporations like telecommunications company AT&T, the mortgage broker Chase Manhattan Mortgage, and the homeware company IKEA. This consumer targeting differed from the images of bisexual chic I considered earlier. Here, the allure is not one of sexual intrigue around sexual and gendered boundary crossing but that of what Lauren Berlant calls "the political and affective economies of normativity," which structure "the good life promised by capitalist culture."[84] In 1995, a partnership between Visa USA, Subaru of America, and Travelers Bank launched the Rainbow Card, a credit card that supported "gay and lesbian causes" and was famously backed by Martina Navratilova. This was a pivotal moment in which the American gay subject became a targetable and investable consumer.

Corporate interest in the gay consumer signaled a literal investment in what David L. Eng terms "queer liberalism" and Lisa Duggan calls the politics of "the new homonormativity."[85] The promise of this politics, Duggan writes, is "a privatized, depoliticized gay culture anchored in domesticity and consumption."[86] The subsequent leveraging of this politics by international financial institutions is traced by Rahul Rao toward the creation of a paradigm he terms "global homocapitalism," which "seeks to reconcile the twin imperatives of efficiency and empowerment, making capitalism friendly to queers but also rendering queers safe for capitalism."[87] That the gay subject could now be considered a potential purchaser of homeware and landline communications packages— or someone to whom credit was lent in the form of mortgages and credit cards—suggests how, during the nineties, emergent ideas around the domestic, consumptive gay citizen were becoming both culturally aspirational and economically investable. A significant factor in the reification of this figure is the Food and Drug Administration's approval of various HIV/AIDS treatments between 1990 and 1996, concluding with the combination of drugs in highly active antiretroviral therapy. The arrival of these effective treatments, Dagmawi Woubshet argues, "displaced AIDS . . . as a demarcated past against which a new normative gay identity could be forged."[88] The arrival of these medications thus carried with it a kind of social promise that gayness might be freed of its association with disease transmission, illness, and death and be granted access to liberal forms of normative citizenship. This normative gay identity carried not only presumptions of whiteness and affluence but also a definitional gayness that was distinct from other queer identities becoming increasingly politicized in the 1990s.

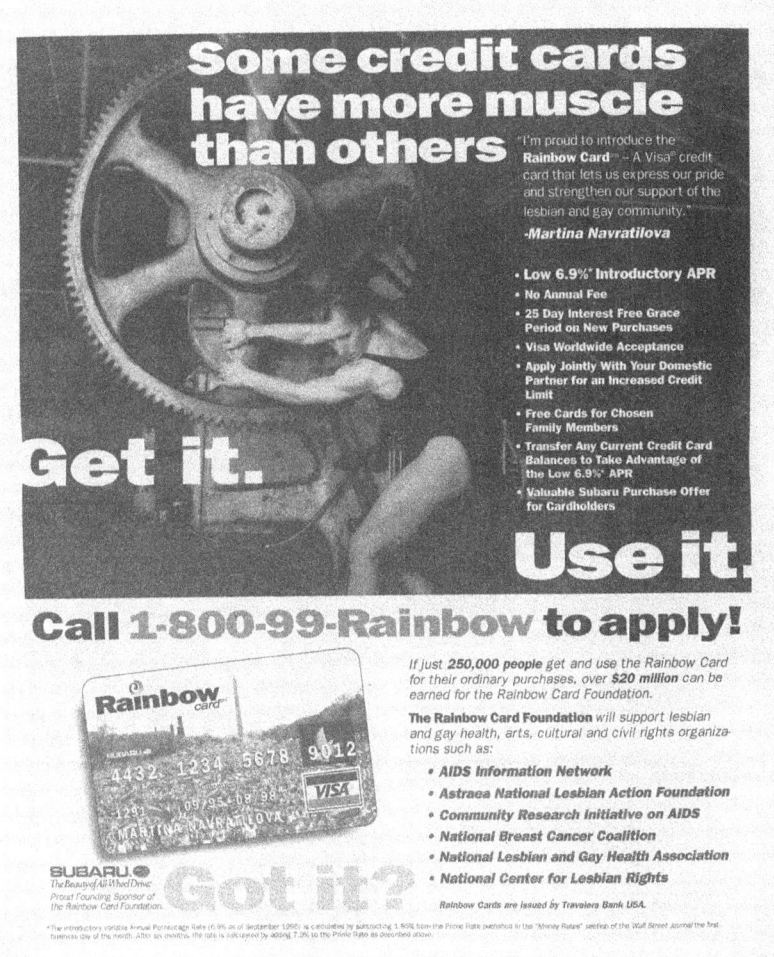

FIGURE 4.8 A 1995 advertisement for the Rainbow Card. Scanned document.

Christopher Chitty traces a trend in Western history whereby homosexuality's politicization is coterminous with shifts to financialized economies, resulting in newly calibrated sexual orders: "Historical periods of intensive politicization of homosexuality correspond to . . . periods in which a hegemonic power has entered a phase of financialization, deepening internal social divisions. . . . These periods of economic . . . destabilization and the subsequent periods of 'restoration' . . . were central to the disruption and establishment of the sexual orders in Western societies."[89] The politicization of gay and lesbian identities observable during the 1970s and 1980s can be understood in this framework as being followed by a restorative period in which the terms *gay* and *lesbian* were assigned meanings that explicitly excluded groups like bisexuals, transsexuals, transvestites, and intersex people.[90] Whereas, previously, these last groups had sometimes organized under the umbrellas of *gay* and *lesbian*, the nineties sexual order in the United States granted ascendance to a model of gayness that assumed monosexuality and cisness. The coevality of this sociopolitical shift with American financialization would not be incidental for Chitty, as financialization's deepening of social divisions necessarily involves a reification of social categories.[91] The work of bisexual theorists like Clare Hemmings and Jo Eadie demonstrates that with this exclusionary shoring up of gay identity came corollary anxieties around bisexual boundary crossing in both gay subculture and heterosexist society.[92] In this emergent paradigm of sexual-social organization, bisexuality threatened the security of a normative heterosexual/homosexual binary just as it threatened these groups' demarcation as discrete, normative, and investable populations.

This is a context in which the erotic thriller's wealthy bisexual figures take on particular resonances relating to capital, power, uncertainty, and risk. Finance capitalism's investment in a purportedly stable gay subject was driven by an expansionist promise to incorporate a new, productive, and consumptive population into extant economic systems. In the erotic thriller's wealthy bisexual, however, we witness a figure whose disruption of categories of social-sexual organization is enabled by their wealth. Rather than incorporate themselves into extant economic systems, these figures enter such systems dissimulatively, carrying with them the risk of a financially empowered form of dissidence. These bisexual figures embody a risk in capitalism's investment in queers: Rather than enriching a normative form of gay citizenship, this investment might effect the breakdown of forms of social-sexual categorization. That the erotic thriller regularly depicts bisexual figures made wealthy through nefarious means can thus be understood not as incidental but as an anxious projection around growing opportunities for queers to accumulate capital and the antinormative ends to which this wealth might be directed. Consider direct-to-video erotic thriller *Hourglass* (C. Thomas Howell, 1995), in which fashion executive Michael (Howell) enters into a dangerous affair with ambitious model Dara (Sofia Shinas). With the help of her girlfriend Kami (Colette O'Connell), Dara plots to take over Michael's business, killing anyone who gets in their way. Dara's bisexual duplicity is mobilized here toward her own enrichment. Her reactions to the murders of Michael's brother and Kami are nonplussed; the two are simply collateral damage in Dara's pursuit of wealth. Relevant here are the specificities around bisexuality that allow Dara's schemes to take place: She can pass as the heteronormative model but is hiding an intragender affair, and her playing off both sides against each other—with little care for either—allows her to accumulate wealth. The bisexual transgressor uses her interstitiality to effect social breakdown and gets rich in the process.

The distillation of fears around social breakdown in a wealthy bisexual figure is no more evident than in the financially powerful, alluringly destructive Catherine of *Basic Instinct*. She owns two California properties—one in San Francisco, the other in a gated community in Stinson Beach, Marin County. Catherine's expansive and expensive properties are a primary means of articulating her wealth, a classic example of John David Rhodes's observation that "the house is a medium for making publicly visible the wealth of its owners and inhabitants. When cinema looks at and/or takes place in the house, this spectacular function is multiplied."[93] Catherine's properties are examples of those cinematic houses Rhodes calls "a representation of wealth that is embodied in the private property of a house of enormous dimensions."[94] Catherine's homes are not the only pieces of property that convey her wealth: It is signified in her regularly-alluded-to penchant for Hermès scarves, the two Lotus Esprits in her San Francisco driveway, and her Latina maid who, in line with Rosa E. Soto's analysis of this figure in American film and television, "signifies the class status that [her employer] has achieved."[95] *Basic Instinct*'s mise-en-scène is populated by spaces and objects attesting to Catherine's wealth, which are, in turn, contrasted with the modest apartments of Nick and Beth. In the process of investigating Catherine, officers discover a hefty inheritance from her parents, who were killed in a mysterious boating accident, in addition to an inheritance from ex-fiancé boxer Manuel Vasquez, whose death, like those of *Black Widow*'s Catharine's lovers, enriched her. In their investigating, officers report Catherine's estimated net assets at $110 million, putting her in the top 0.01 percent of real wealth in the United States in 1992.[96] This is a year in which the median family net worth in the United States was $52,200, making Catherine over two thousand times wealthier than the average American household.[97] Though it might seem strange to ruminate here on the personal finances of a fictional character vis-à-vis historical economic data, I want to underscore the superlative level of wealth this character possesses in relation to the social context in which the film was produced and viewed. To call Catherine "successful" or "rich" would be far too general a characterization. In providing specific information around Catherine's economic assets, the film conveys something more specific: her wealth is inordinate.

Economic calculations of risks and returns are made in the hopes of maximizing the latter relative to the former; in the cinematic figure of the inordinately wealthy bisexual transgressor, however, risk has dwarfed return—the investment has nosedived. This potential misdirection of funds risks endowing a bisexual figure embodying the threats Hedgehog identifies: unpredictability, incoherence, unreliability, impurity, nonhierarchality.[98] This anxiety plays out in the erotic thriller's portrayals of wealthy bisexual transgressors, whose threats to the normative everyman and everywoman draw upon those bisexual qualities most troubling for finance capitalism. As inchoate financial investment in the gay consumer began in the late 1980s and 1990s, these cinematic images proliferated in the erotic thriller genre and functioned as reminders of the routine axiom that forewarns any financial investor: "Your capital is at risk."

Intrinsic to Catherine's display of inordinate wealth are connections between her economic freedom and her sexual freedom. David Andrews writes that she displays a "chilly consumerism. . . . Catherine's consumerist ethos dominates the film, becoming largely identical to it."[99] Catherine's approach to lovers, like her accumulation of luxury commodities, is excessive. This "consumerist ethos" is redolent of the characteristics of the cinematic figure Maria San Filippo terms the "bisexual rich bitch," in whom "bisexuality becomes inextricably joined with the capitalist appetite for accumulation, whereby the latter as a socially sanctioned form of rapacity becomes tainted with the 'pathology' associated with bisexuality, and vice versa."[100] Following San Filippo, we might understand Catherine's machinations as a kind of projection of finance capitalism's fears of its own pathology—the necessity of exploitation and wealth inequality for its functioning—onto a figure of sexual exploitation and unequal power dynamics. Here, the bisexual figure functions in a way Jo Eadie observes as commonplace in film: "The threats of unchecked appetite and joyful promiscuity do not originate with the bisexual: s/he is only the vehicle for this anxiety."[101] The figuration of finance capitalism's fears around its own greed through the bisexual is far from arbitrary: The bisexual's excessive desire is made meaningful by being cast, metonymically, in the moral drama of what Eadie calls "the pull between uncontainable appetite and dour asceticism."[102] The erotic thriller's wealthy bisexual transgressors thus not only signify the embezzlement of capital by queer thieves or the radical breakdown of seemingly discrete gay and straight spaces; their excessive desires, exploitation of others, and social impunity reflect finance capitalism's cataclysms—of excess and impoverishment, power and exploitation, recklessness and indemnification—back to itself.

In the Hollywood independent erotic thriller *Bound* (Lana Wachowski and Lilly Wachowski, 1996), lovers Corky (Gina Gershon) and Violet (Jennifer Tilly) hatch a plan to steal $2 million from Violet's mafioso boyfriend Caesar (Joe Pantoliano). In a visually arresting scene, Violet lingers in a room where hundred-dollar bills hang from washing lines, newly cleansed of the blood with which they were sullied in Caesar's violent heist. As Violet looks out at the bills, Caesar irons the crumpled notes, a tableau reversing domestic labor's conventional gendered division. Caesar irons while Violet plots to steal his plunder, Violet's bisexual deception a prerequisite to pulling off her and Corky's scheme. In an earlier scene, Corky claims to Violet that she served time for "the redistribution of wealth" before commenting, "That's what I tell someone when I'm trying to get them in my bed." Corky's use of "the redistribution of wealth" (commonly describing governmental taxation policies seeking to alleviate income inequality) perverts its meaning away from state-sanctioned liberal economic models toward those of a radical, criminal Robin Hood figure. Casting herself as this revolutionary, Corky's theft from the rich is fashioned as a kind of redistributive justice.[103] Moreover, Corky suggests the allure of a Robin Hood figure who beds the notably gender-neutral "someone," a comment that, despite Corky's prized place in the lesbian cinematic canon, teems with bisexual erotic appeal. That a figure of wealth redistribution might be seductive speaks to a key feature of the erotic thriller's wealthy bisexuals: Theirs is a maldistributed wealth that risks wreaking further distributive irregularities, yet this chaos is markedly alluring. Like *Black Widow*'s Catharine, *Hourglass*'s Dara, and *Basic Instinct*'s Catherine, Violet and Corky are not simply transgressors whose bisexual allure mirrors a moral duplicity; more specifically, they invoke an economic anxiety around queers obtaining wealth and using it toward antinormative ends. The bisexual seductress puts the straight everyman's capital at risk.

Erotic thrillers like *Basic Instinct* pulse with the anxieties that mark investments under financialization, wherein prediction based on incomplete knowledge is requisite. A symptomatic reading finds here the social fears around investment in the normative gay subject that risks misdirection to an unpredictable bisexual boundary-breaker. We can also read, in the exploitative and inordinately wealthy bisexual embezzler, finance capitalism's paranoia around its own exploitative systems. Central to those social-economic fears with which the erotic thriller plays is the idea of a disturbance or disruption that cannot be anticipated. These films are at once an anxious financial projection, a paranoid augury of a worst-case scenario in which queers redirect capital toward the destruction of socioeconomic systems, and a projection in the psychoanalytic sense, a defense mechanism deployed by a culture sublimating its own iniquities onto the body of the bisexual transgressor.[104] Both projections are literally projected cinematically as images of sexually unreadable suspects flaunting inordinate wealth. Ever present in the erotic thriller's figuration of wealthy bisexual transgressors is this dovetailing of sexual unpredictability with the unpredictability that, as Knight and Keynes forewarned, is inherent in all financial investment. Fredric Jameson observes how finance capital's abstraction from classical models of production and consumption, its "internal metabolisms," are redolent of "a stereotypical postmodern language."[105] This semiotic system disavows a relation to "the former real world," stressing, instead, how "the real world has already been suffused with culture and colonized by it."[106] The sociocultural ramifications of finance capitalism thus involve a loosening of the ontological certainty with which our language refers to things in the world. The cinematic figure of the wealthy bisexual transgressor is a symptom of this uncertainty; their sexuality, like the import of their wealth, cannot be predicted. Pat O'Malley warns of how economic mechanisms of anticipating risks "are useless against . . . the types of event in which the processes that produce the harms usually go unrecognized until it's too late."[107] Finance capitalism's anxious dramas of unpredictability and unrecognizability constitute familiar narrative ground for the erotic thriller. One cannot strategize against a risk that cannot be recognized. And by the time the threat is recognized, it might be too late.

Resisting Ratiocination: The Figure of the Murderer and Bi-Trans Critical Allegiances

> External differentiations between criminal and normal subjects . . . [are] fewer in the female than in the male.
> —Cesare Lombroso and William Ferrero, *The Female Offender*

Questions of risk and uncertainty are implicated by questions of epistemology; risk's correlative is a lack of knowledge.[108] The erotic thriller, in its narrativization of risk and epistemological uncertainty, illuminates this interrelation: Questions about what we can know, predict, or ascertain are posed in the face of mysteries in which knowledge is wanting. The morally compromised investigator, who must strategize against that which is unknown, is a persistent figure across the erotic thriller genre. Although not all of these figures are investigators by profession, they are investigative figures insofar as they are guided by detectivelike goals, which orient them in the erotic thriller narrative. These figures seek to uncover a truth through processes of ratiocination typical of criminal investigation: researching suspects' personal histories, scrutinizing crime scenes and other places of interest for clues, following a suspect's movements, and interrogating the accused and those who know them. The investigator hopes to uncover an expository concatenation of events. Each piece of potential evidence carries the possibility of epistemic utility, yet often this evidence is itself confounding, drawing the investigator deeper into a labyrinthine maze replete with aporic culs-de-sac. That the evidence produced or performed by the suspect causes confusion is paramount: The more the investigator is presented with unintelligible evidence, the deeper their investigation must go.

This investigative drive toward the suspect routinely dovetails with the investigator's desire toward them. This double-edged impulse is characteristic of what Katherine Farrimond observes in the femme fatale, who, she writes—improvising on Laura Mulvey's oft-cited turn-of-phrase—"is presented not merely as to-be-looked-at, but as to-be-solved."[109] The enigmatic image of the female suspect—stunning in its allure—is, at once, an epistemological enigma redolent of the patriarchal axiom Simone de Beauvoir observes at play in André Breton's poetry: "Woman is an enigma and she poses enigmas."[110] Compounding the investigator's obstacles to discover evasive truths are their own problems: sometimes a guilty conscience, sometimes substance addition, but, more often than not, their own desires. In *Basic Instinct*, Catherine teases Nick with allusions to his problematic cocaine and alcohol use; she offers him cigarettes despite his claim to have given up smoking. Like Nick's attraction toward her, Catherine makes strategic use of those dangerous attachments that mark Nick's fallibility. These games of temptation illuminate one of the erotic thriller's regular suggestions: that desire clouds epistemological clarity. This is a problem with which canny suspects are strategically familiar. The investigator's personal problems, and the intelligent suspect's manipulation of them, can even result in the implication of the investigator in the crime, muddying the boundaries between investigator and investigated, hunter and prey, normative and dissident.

While the erotic thriller's suspect poses epistemological problems for the investigator, they sometimes also display an epistemological authority that threatens to supersede that of the investigator. A battle for epistemological authority animates Catherine and Nick's repartee.[111] Her calling him "shooter" is an analeptic reference to him having accidentally shot two civilians while working; this nickname reminds Nick, as murder investigator, that he too might be considered a murderer were it not for state protections afforded to police. Catherine's status as author carries with it the potential to reinscribe those around her. Catherine's incorporation of a character clearly based on

Nick in her forthcoming book, entitled *Shooter*, crystallizes this dynamic through mise en abyme. The import of Catherine's status as author has pertinent repercussions in the film's sequel, *Basic Instinct 2*, in which Catherine (Stone) is under psychiatric examination by Dr. Michael Glass (David Morrissey). Catherine's manipulation of Michael is linked to a series of murders he suspects she has committed but in which he is strongly implicated; in this sense, the film's narrative plays on a confusion of identity around Catherine and Michael. In the final scene of *Basic Instinct 2*, Catherine details the plot of her new novel, which—like *Basic Instinct*—mirrors that of the film, again in mise en abyme. The twist of Catherine's novel is that "the real killer all along was the shrink." After this revelation, the film presents a series of flashbacks, narrated by Catherine, in which David is cast as the perpetrator of each murder. The murder of journalist Adam (Hugh Dancy) results in him naked on a bed having been strangled with a studded leather belt, typical of fetish wear; the murder of Michael's ex-wife (Indira Varma) is motivated, according to Catherine, by a sense of vengeance over her having sex with other men; the killing of drug dealer Dicky (Peter Rnic) is established similarly by Catherine as rooted in jealousy, but our prior knowledge that he was found dead with his buttocks exposed suggests sex being part of the killing. The film thus ends with Catherine's counternarrative, visualized through flashback. Importantly, this ending not only grants Catherine epistemological or narrative authority; she is also able, through this authority, to queer Michael, who is implicated not only as killer but in a bisexual array of liaisons. As the *Basic Instinct* films display the centrality of epistemological uncertainty for the erotic thriller, so too do they highlight how questions of sexuality are implicated by questions of epistemology. As the investigator's hermeneutics of criminality prove unreliable, so too do the dominant hermeneutics of (mono)sexual signification. Catherine's epistemological authority troubles the dichotomization not only of investigator and criminal but also that of normative and queer, revealing that which is criminal in the criminal-hunter and that which is queer in the figure once assumed heterosexual. The erotic thriller's evocations of bisexuality use its troubling of the binary of (mono)sexual signification to suggest various ways in which the unknown and the mutable can trouble epistemological certainty.

As Nick follows Catherine's trail, he becomes curious about her relationship with a middle-aged woman called Hazel, who had been imprisoned previously for murdering her husband and children with no purported motive. Catherine justifies this friendship to Nick in relation to her work: She met Hazel researching her book, and a friendship developed. Though Hazel's appearances are fleeting, the key pieces of information provided about her are this murderous past and a relation to Catherine. Chris Holmlund calls Hazel "an aging mirror and possible stand-in 'mother' lover of Catherine as mirror/'daughter' lover," a suggestion that the erotic relation between these women carries two transgressive qualities: a pathological kind of mimesis and the taboo of mother-daughter incest.[112] Yet, further, this inscrutable relationship also suggests a kind of intergenerational kinship between a convicted murderer and a murder suspect. Catherine's closeness with Hazel, whom she calls "Honey," is intriguing. It suggests both women's bisexualities, it evokes the incest taboo, and it also teeters ever so close to implicating Catherine. But, as always, she has a suitable alibi. In the film's depiction of an intragender bond between murderer and murder suspect, *Basic Instinct* also makes reference to an extant cultural association that was revivified between the 1960s and the 1990s: that between queerness and murderousness.

The figure of the murderer is far from transhistorical. Lisa Downing traces a Foucauldian genealogy of the murderer from the eighteenth and nineteenth centuries onward, emerging in Western Europe in literary discourses that ontologize killing as a "primitive," creative-aesthetic, or superhuman activity and medical discourses geared toward the idea of a patient whose type is determined by the nature of their pathology.[113] For Michel Foucault, as for Downing, the development of the latter birthed a medicolegal paradigm in which a "defendant's behavior prior to his or her crimes was retroactively examined and *made* to be commensurate with his or her identity as a criminal."[114] Concerning the figure of the murderer, this epistemology of criminality sought—through purportedly expert medical testimony—to show that a defendant guilty of murder displays, and has always displayed, certain personal qualities unique to murderers. Downing's discursive historiography stresses how "murderers are considered special individuals, an ascription that serves both to render them apart from the moral majority on the one hand and, on the other, to reify, lionize, and fetishize them as 'individual agents.'"[115] It is this quality of personal exceptionality that sets the figure of the murderer apart: They are exceptional transgressors of moral standards to the same extent that they are exceptionally singular, compelling, or even, dare we admit it, alluring.

Queer murderers have played a significant role in this discursive history. Insofar as the murderer is understood as possessing personal qualities—either physical or behavioral—that symptomatize their murderousness, the deviance of queerness has regularly taken on expository meaning. The paradigmatic example of this tendency can be found in the case of Nathan Leopold and Richard Loeb, two young men who, in 1924, were found guilty of murdering a fourteen-year-old boy in Chicago. In the public discourses around this case, rumors of the men's romantic relationship abounded. These homoerotic undercurrents animate Alfred Hitchcock's *Rope* (1948), a film inspired by the case, which renders a passionate yet fraught relation between the two accomplices (John Dall and Farley Granger) that hints toward their mutual ardor.[116] In the case's contemporary context, however, Leopold and Loeb's queerness (and their racialized Jewishness) was rendered symptomatic of their homicidality via expository hypotheses by phrenologist James M. Fitzgerald, whose diagrams marked facial and cranial features purportedly pertaining to both immorality and sexual deviance.[117] These signifiers of abnormality worked to posit Leopold and Loeb's very bodies as containing physiognomic clues suggesting capacities for queerness and murderousness alike.

Although the epistemic claims of phrenology were later widely rejected, reports of queers who kill obtained in a media sphere populated by tawdry tales of criminality and licentiousness. In the latter half of the twentieth century, reports of purportedly bisexual murder suspects proliferated. This is not to say that reports of other forms of nonnormative sexuality among suspected murderers necessarily waned during this period; instead, I want to highlight how bisexuality is cited increasingly at this time—both explicitly and implicitly—in media discussions of murder suspects. Between the 1960s and the 1990s, American newspaper reporting of a number of high-profile murder cases would identify specifically as bisexual a range of men who were either convicted murderers or alleged murder suspects, including John Wayne Gacy, John Barrett Hawkins, Jim Jones, William Robert Jones Jr., Patrick Kearney, Henry Lee Lucas, and David Scott Harrison.[118] I am not concerned here with the veracity of these claims but with how, on numerous occasions, media reports around murder cases incorporated information of the accused's purported bisexuality, sometimes as an aside, sometimes as a salacious revelation. The latter tendency is discernible in a 1992 episode of Fox reality legal series *America's Most Wanted* (1988–2011; 2021–) that features the case of John Kelly Gentry Jr.: a bisexual fugitive who was charged in 1983 with the murders of both his girlfriend and his boyfriend.[119] The series' format combines direct-to-camera segments typical of newscasting with dramatized segments, transposing the generic-aesthetic codes of melodrama and detective crime television onto news broadcasting.[120] In one such stylized reenactment, Gentry's soon-to-be girlfriend, Barbara, invites him to eat at her house; when she asks him, "What kind of food do you like? Spicy or mild?" he responds, "Me? I like it both ways." Delivering this pun on bisexual desire, Gentry raises his eyebrows; an ominous synth bass note rings as the scene fades to black. Curiously, *America's Most Wanted* is alluded to in *Basic Instinct* as Catherine ends a conversation with Nick, who had been following Hazel and her: "I promised I'd get [Hazel] home by six o' clock; she just loves *America's Most Wanted*."

As with the male murder suspects whose alleged bisexuality was deemed noteworthy in media reporting of these cases, queerness also played a role in media discourses around particular female murder suspects, infused here with notions of departure from feminine ideals of virginity or motherliness. As Downing observes, the female murderer appears to be "a woman so divorced from 'natural' (passive, maternal, caregiving) femininity that her agentic individuality represents a pure form of evil. . . . Female murderers are special . . . because they are seen to *lack* something that is perceived as being essential to femininity."[121] Lest we forget how, in late nineteenth-century discourses around female inversion, it was, in Lynda Hart's words, "the female invert's *aggressiveness* [that] marked her as deviant and therefore dangerous, *not* her object choice."[122] Hart's historiographic observation is key to understanding the development of the figure of the female murderer, suggesting the role aggressiveness has played in conceptions of female queerness and giving clues to the latter's expository function in relation to female murderers over a century after the conception of female inversion. Three years after the release of *Basic Instinct*, a front-page story in British tabloid the *Daily Mail* reported on an alleged tryst in prison between the high-profile murderers Myra Hindley and Rosemary West (a relationship that both later denied). The article reads: "The two most evil women in Britain—both openly bisexual—have been seen holding hands in Durham Prison."[123] This reporting draws upon those same cultural touchpoints as *Basic Instinct*'s portrayal of the relationship between Catherine and Hazel: an incestuous, intergenerational queer kinship between two women implicated in murder. In both of these instances, a nonnormative relationship serves a symptomatizing function: In the former, it evidences the depravity of Britain's "most evil" women; in the latter, it serves as grounds for suspicion that Catherine might be displaying the murderer's purportedly ontological qualities. Yet, it is Catherine's marrying of close relations with women to a feminine amenability to sex with men that marks her suspected duplicity most discernibly. Like the "both openly bisexual" between the em dashes of the *Daily Mail*'s salacious speculations, a doubling of desire in Catherine comes to mirror further incongruous facets that render the murderer exceptional.

It is in this sense that Catherine's duplicity cannot be separated from the discourses around the most high-profile contemporary case involving a female murderer. As Camilla Griggers writes, there is a "lesbian body which Sharon

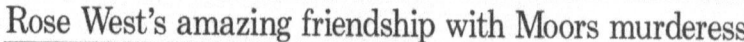

HAND IN HAND WITH HINDLEY

Rose West's amazing friendship with Moors murderess

By PAUL HENDERSON
and STEPHEN WRIGHT

ROSE WEST and Myra
Hindley have formed a macabre friendship in jail, it was
revealed last night.

The two most evil women in Britain —
both openly bisexual — have been seen
holding hands in Durham Prison.

They were drawn together by shared religion, and the 51-year-old Moors Murderess
became West's confidante and adviser. They
have made unsupervised visits to each
other's cell, and prayed together in the jail
chapel.

Hindley even sent a 'Good Luck' card before
the start of the 31-day trial at Winchester
Crown Court which has appalled the nation.

Prison sources described the relationship as
41-year-old West began ten life sentences for
the 'House of Horrors' killings.

Mr Justice Mantell told her: 'If attention is
paid to what I think you will never be
released.'

West's face stayed as expressionless as it
had been through all the evidence of the
unimaginable cruelty she inflicted on her
daughter Heather, stepdaughter Charmaine
and eight other girls and women.

But her lawyers, who said they would
appeal, admitted later that she had wept
uncontrollably after the first three guilty verdicts were brought in on Tuesday.

As the trial ended, a furious row broke over
how the Wests were able to go on sexually
abusing their own children and torturing and
killing other victims for 25 years.

An independent report by child care experts
highlighted blunders and communication
failures involving doctors, nurses, health visitors, teachers and social workers. But after it
became clear they would escape virtually
unscathed, Gloucester Tory MP Douglas
French demanded a public inquiry, branding
the report 'woefully inadequate'.

Police are sure West holds the key to the
fate of nine more missing girls, known to have

Turn to Page 2, Col. 1

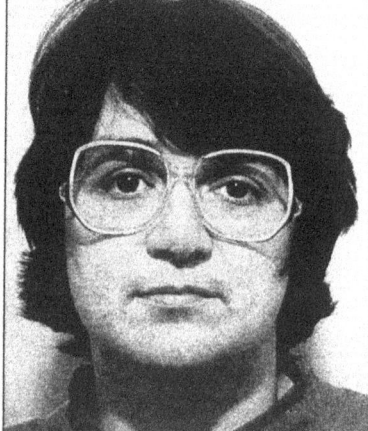

Prison bond: Myra Hindley

Ten guilty verdicts: Rose West in a new police picture

**The verdicts and
the victims:
PAGES 4 and 5**

**Scandal of the
missed signals:
PAGES 6 and 7**

**How could society
breed such evil?
PAGES 10 and 11**

**Girl who grew
into a monster:
PAGES 37 to 44**

INSIDE: Weather 2, Andrew Neil 13, Diary 35, Femail 46-59, Letters 60-61, TV & Radio 62-64, Coffee Break 65-66, City 71-73, Sport 74-80

FIGURE 4.9 The *Daily Mail* reports on rumors of a relationship between Myra Hindley and Rose West (1995). Scanned document.

Stone's projection in *Basic Instinct* screens as body double. That body . . . belongs to Aileen Wuornos."[124] Following her arrest in 1991, Wuornos confessed to killing seven men between 1989 and 1990, in what she claimed were acts of self-defense against rape by sex work clients. Wuornos's first trial began in January of 1992; by the end of her final trial in 1993, she had amassed six death sentences. Animating media discourses around Wuornos's case were details of her sex work and her alleged rapes, as well as interest in her relationship with girlfriend Tyria Moore. The discursive construction of Wuornos's exceptionality is not simply rooted in the amalgam of femaleness and murderousness. This combination is made more deviant by her embodiment of two seemingly contradictory figures: "the prostitute" and "the lesbian."[125]

These aspects of Wuornos's public image constitute nodal points through which her exceptionality was constructed: to be both *prostitute* and *lesbian* is to embody, at once, two different, perhaps seemingly paradoxical, poles of non-normative womanhood.[126] We can thus observe in Wuornos's public image a compelling compresence of, first, a dissident form of extragender sexuality and, second, a dissident form of intragender sexuality. In this sense, Wuornos's exceptionality is rooted in a bisexual kind of polysemy.[127] Wuornos's extensively televised case hinged upon a thwarted desire to look at and thus comprehend her; the curious gaze directed toward Wuornos was animated by the confound-ment produced by a figure whose amalgam of woman-murderer-prostitute-lesbian has no visual analogue. This phenomenon of visual noncomprehension vis-à-vis the female criminal has pertinent roots in criminal anthropology and its foremost theorist, Cesare Lombroso. This section's epigraph features Lom-broso and historian William Ferrero's contention, in 1893, that female crimi-nals were less physiognomically identifiable than their male counterparts.[128] The anxiety around the female murderer is thus occasioned not by what can be discerned in her physicality but that which cannot.

The critical praise of Charlize Theron's rendition of Wuornos in *Monster* (Patty Jenkins, 2003) centered around the glamorous actor's physical embodi-ment of monstrosity, the versatility associated with her star image displayed through a visual transformation. That a woman as glamorous as Theron might embody Wuornos—or women as wholesome as sitcom star Jean Smart or ex-Disney Channel tween star Peyton List in their respective portrayals of her—speaks to the extratextual visual appeal elicited by a specifically female form of transformability.[129] *Basic Instinct*'s narrative of investigation is driven precisely by the inability to identify women's potential murderousness, manifested by their potential for transformation. It is this phenomenon that undergirds the narrative twist of direct-to-video erotic thriller *Night Rhythms* (Gregory Dark, 1992), in which the queerness of the unassuming radio producer Bridget (Delia Sheppard) is revealed in concert with her being the killer. Another feminine, blond woman, the revelation that Bridget murdered the straight Honey (Tracy Tweed) out of an unrequited desire for her is a simultaneous disclosure of both queerness and murderousness in a body assumed to be normative. The unread-ability of the bisexual transgressor's queerness renders precarious the knowledge of her criminal culpability.

These kinds of epistemological uncertainty plague the narrative of *Basic Instinct* comparatively. Although both Hazel and Roxy are understood to be murderers who have previously served their time, their culpability in the current investigation is equivocal. Suspicion toward criminal psychologist Beth mounts as details of her past relationship with Catherine—and their having been students of a professor murdered with an ice pick—come to bear. Nick's investigation into Beth reveals that she previously assumed the name Lisa, colored her hair blond, and had relationships with women as well as men. As Nick looks through police records, he flicks between two photographs of Lisa/Beth—one blond and one brunette—her suspected bisexual duplicity playing out in a visual effect redolent of the thaumatrope. This early nineteenth-century optical toy consists of a double-sided disk that, when spun, gives the illusion of a single image. *Basic Instinct*'s quick back-and-forth between these two images is structurally isomorphic to the thaumatrope, but it is deployed to different effects. Whereas the classical thaumatrope combines two separate images into the illusion of one, *Basic Instinct*'s thaumatrope effect reveals a duplicity in one woman: It suggests that Lisa/Beth's metaphysical unity is itself illusive.

It is in the erotic thriller's pernicious play with the fallibility of perceptions vis-à-vis the queer female murder suspect that generative links can be forged with the genre's iterations of transfemininity. These iterations sometimes overlap with notions of bisexual transgression, the transfeminine figure's bisexual desires and desirability intersecting with the significations of their transness. But, more precisely here, it is this figure's confoundment of cis(gendered) expectations that functions homologously in the erotic thriller as both an investigative hurdle and as a site of intrigue. Consider *Dressed to Kill*, in which Dr. Elliott/Bobbi's identity as murderer remains as hidden from viewers as it is from investigators. This obfuscation is as formal as narrative, achieved through editing (earlier shots of Bobbi are cut quickly) and mise-en-scène (she wears a wig and sunglasses). A similar technique of both narrative and formal concealment can be found in Katt Shea's erotic thriller *Stripped to Kill* (1987), in which the murderer of local strippers is revealed to be one of the stripper's younger siblings, Eric (Pia Kamakahi), a transfeminine figure passing for their sister. Like *Dressed to Kill*, *Stripped to Kill* obscures the murderer's identity through form: extreme close-ups and decentered framing hide her identity for most of the film. The revelation of Roxanne-as-Eric occurs as they tear off their prosthetic breasts, a Cronenbergian moment of abject catharsis. Both films' engagement of transfemininity is rooted in the unexpectedness and unreadability of transness in a suspect and the spectacle of feminine adornment's destruction—Bobbi's detached wig, Eric's rent breasts—revealing a body that a cissexist logic can read as "man."

These figurations of transfeminine murderers can be understood as being made meaningful through what Cáel M. Keegan calls a "cissexist gaze."[130]

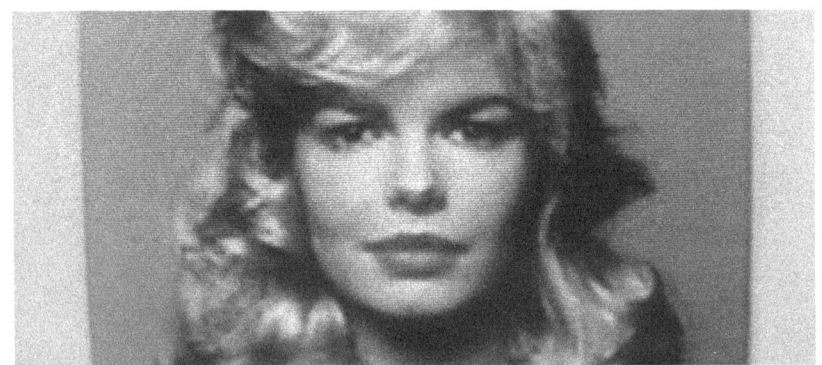

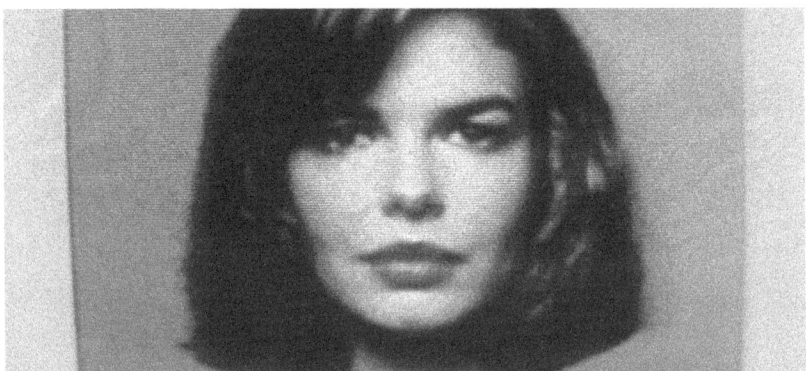

FIGURES 4.10–4.11 Lisa/Beth's (Jeanne Tripplehorn) traumatropic mug shots. *Basic Instinct* (Paul Verhoeven, 1992). Digital screen captures.

Keegan articulates this gaze as one invested in the "realness, perceptibility, and meaningfulness of assigned sex . . . a structure of cissexism itself, which demands that the sexed body is real and that [a trans person's] felt gender is imaginary."[131] Insofar as both *Dressed to Kill*'s and *Stripped to Kill*'s forms mirror the perceptions of their investigators, the confusion transness poses to a cissexist epistemology of gender is sated by a cissexist visual logic in which the revelation of a body's transness secures its interpellation as normatively sexed. As Danielle M. Seid writes, although the cinematic trans reveal "stages a denaturalization of widespread assumptions about gender and sex . . . it typically does so in a manner that regulates and corrects gender noncompliance, narratively reinscribing a binary gender system as 'natural' and desirable."[132] Such a revelation thus works to reify the investigators' epistemological authority as it secures the murderer's alterity in their sexual deviance.

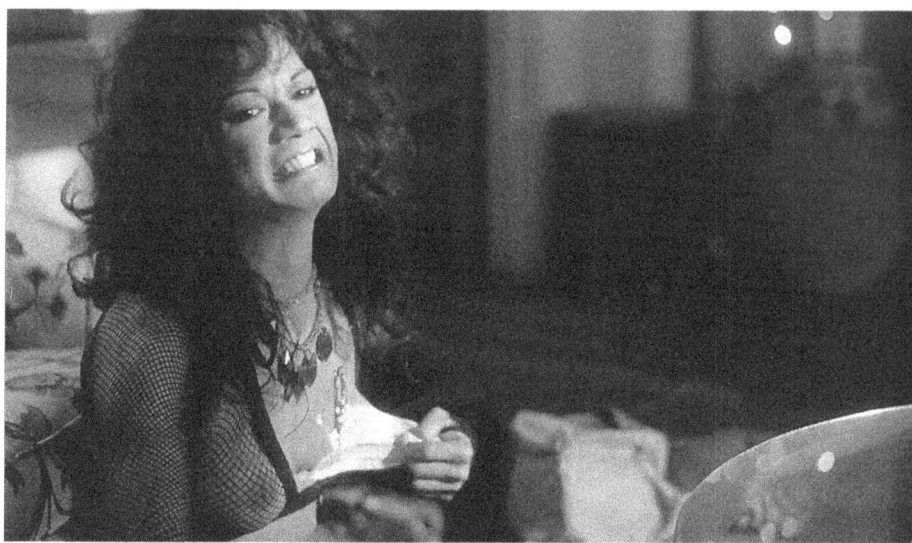

FIGURE 4.12 Eric (Pia Kamakahi) tears off their prosthetic breasts. *Stripped to Kill* (Katt Shea, 1987). Digital screen capture.

Yet despite the reification of cissexist logic observable in these moments of revelation, we should not forget these films' rupturing of expectations around a suspect's gender. What Seid identifies as their "denaturalization" effects importantly trouble cissexist assumptions. While the investigators may have found their culprits, the epistemological foundations through which gender is recognized, and through which gendered crime is identified (that which is considered symptomatic of a male murderer or a female murderer), have been destabilized. Thus, even while the murderer's identity is made manifest with reference to cissexist understandings of sexed bodies and transness-as-pathology, it is this same logic that the films reveal to have hamstrung investigators in their search for truth. In direct-to-video erotic thriller *Cover Me* (Michael Schroeder, 1995), the revelation of the murderer's identity and transness occurs early in the narrative when Demi's (Stephen Nicols) wig slips mid-murder. While this is itself a typical trans reveal, compounded by a pathologizing narrative that symptomizes Demi's transness as the product of maternal abuse, it is key that the film uses two different actors' voices—one higher pitched and one lower pitched—depending on whether or not the characters around Demi are aware of her transness. Rather than interpret this technique as simply augmenting the purported falsity of Demi's femininity, the film might be read as suggesting, instead, that the cissexist logic of perception through which gendered phenomena like voices and appearances are identified is itself false. By assuming the perceptions of ignorant cisgender characters, *Cover Me* illuminates Judith Butler's proposal that "'sex' denotes . . . a language that forms perception by forcibly shaping the interrelationships through which physical bodies are perceived."[133] By configuring the field of perception as itself contingent, subject to change, *Cover Me* gestures toward those forms of queerness for which cissexist visual logic cannot account. These are present in other erotic thrillers in which transfeminine figures, though not all suspects, are to be found in illicit milieux: the transfeminine performers in *Mascara*'s (Patrick Conrad, 1987) underground nightclub; Mike's (Peter Berg) big secret in *The Last Seduction* (John Dahl, 1994), his transgender ex-wife (Serena); and in *Heaven* (Scott Reynolds, 1998), whose eponymous character (Daniel Edwards) is a clairvoyant transgender dancer. These incorporations of transfeminine figures into the erotic thriller are not only typical of the genre's fascination with sexual nonnormativity; their figurations contribute toward an aura of epistemological uncertainty vis-à-vis gender that lingers long after the trans reveal. In these examples, we can thus observe both the reification of cissexist logic—that which has been promulgated by medicolegal discourses of sex and gender—and this logic's very deracination.

In the transfeminine and bisexual transgressors who stalk the erotic thriller, we find pertinent parallels that excavate generative critical ground for bi-trans alliances in our film theoretical interventions. First, in the face of a surfeit of transgressive cinematic figures aligned in various ways with notions of badness, we can take the nonaxiological approach that Keegan advocates, looking to their potential for disruption vis-à-vis sexual-social orders.[134] Second, we can attend to how these figures stage useful challenges to the attainment of knowledge around sexuality and gender through perception, metaphorized via the unreliability of ascertaining suspects' criminalities through the same means. Importantly, it is through these films' deployment of form—the plasticity of mise-en-scène, the opacity of off-screen space, the manipulability of image and sound—that these epistemic regimes become unsettled. As we see in Grace E. Lavery's reading of *The Silence of the Lambs* (Jonathan Demme, 1991), whose "intensifying mediation of the perceptual apparatus" she relates to the film's wrestling with notions of real and pseudo-transsexuality, attention to perception's requirement of a (fallible) apparatus of mediation is indispensable for bi and trans film theory alike.[135] As I discussed in this book's introduction, there are a number of sites upon which bisexual and transgender theorization have drawn and should continue to draw inspiration from one another, none more urgently than in the shared challenge these pose to dualistic, oppositional, and discrete taxonomies of sexual being. When Eliza Steinbock articulates their trans mode of media analysis as attending to "that which baffles the binary paradigm by seeming to confound its strictures, confuse its terms of engagement, or flummox the net that tries to capture meaning," they echo the mode of analysis I have demonstrated in relation to bisexuality in ways that speak to mutual investments and allegiances between our approaches.[136] It is here that we might join forces, as critical accomplices, to expose visual culture's promises of sexual-knowledge-through-perception as inherently unstable.

The erotic thriller stages conflicts between representational forms and epistemic concepts. Like one of its generic antecedents, detective fiction, it uses an aesthetic model that, in Franco Moretti's words, "implies the impossibility of verifying cultural forms."[137] The cultural forms that the erotic thriller exposes as unverifiable are those categories of sexuality and gender disturbed by queer transgressors, who, in their yoking of murderousness and polysemy, launch an attack on normative systems of both social organization and epistemological meaning-making. Catherine Tramell embodies the erotic thriller's potential to engage such an attack with an effectiveness dependent on the film's complicity with her. For the telos that secures the *who* and *why* of the erotic thriller murder mystery narrative is notably absent from *Basic Instinct*. The question of whether Catherine, Roxy, Beth, Hazel, or someone else is responsible for *Basic Instinct*'s series of murders goes unanswered. The epistemological trouble occasioned by the bisexual transgressor abides.

Catherine Didn't Do It

Ahead of *Basic Instinct*'s release in 1992, in one of the final actions against it, a group calling themselves Catherine Did It set out to ruin the film's ending for unsuspecting cinemagoers with chants, signs, and wheat-pasted posters revealing the purported spoiler.[138] These actions, which concluded a two-year-long campaign against the film, homed in on one of the central objects of the protestors' ire: that the duplicitous, manipulative, and murderous Catherine was also bisexual.

A number of *Basic Instinct*'s detractors were driven by a desire to see images of queers reflecting values of citizenship and normality, a desire *Basic Instinct* could never satisfy. John Weir accuses *Basic Instinct* of suggesting that lesbianism "implies villainy"; he longs, instead, for different images of queerness: "There are millions of homosexuals who are responsible citizens in real life; why not in the movies?"[139] Queer Nation activist Annette Gaudino strikes a similar tone,

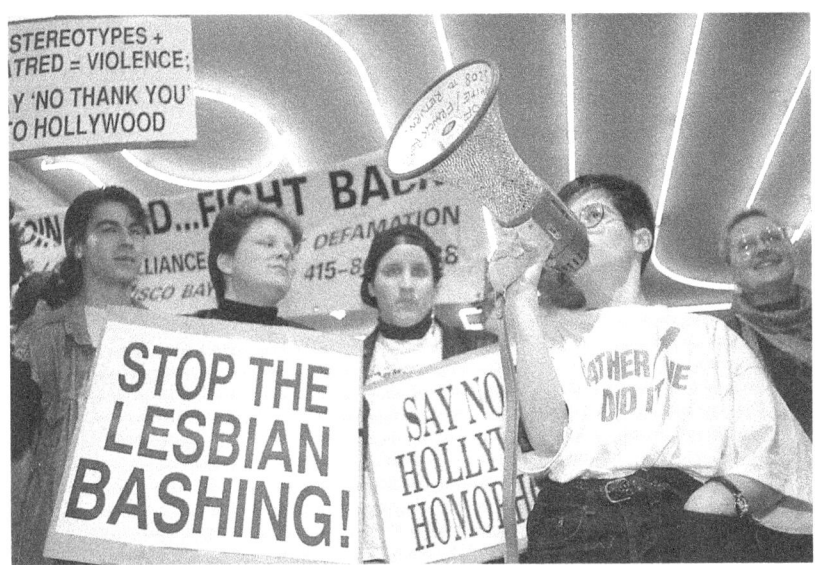

FIGURE 4.13 Protesting *Basic Instinct* at the Metro Theater, San Francisco. March 3, 1992. © Rick Gerharter.

reflecting on her involvement in the *Basic Instinct* protests: "When I look back ten years [since the protests] and I see *Ellen*, I see *Will and Grace*, I honestly don't believe that would have happened if not for the fact that there was . . . a vocal activist movement out in the streets demanding that Hollywood change its tune."[140] The liberal incorporation of gayness into established American media vehicles—here, the television sitcom—signals, for Weir's and Gaudino's politics, social progression. This is a process that broadly mirrors the nineties' homonormative turn I have traced involving the assimilation of particular depoliticized gay citizen-subjects into the liberal body politic. It is through this process of incorporation that purportedly bad stereotypes about queers are eschewed in favor of ideas of gay citizenship, rights-holding, and subjecthood. This aspiration is a bisexual formation of queer liberalism or homonormativity—what Jo Bower, Maria Gurevich, and Cynthia Mathieson term "binormativity"—wherein "'legitimate' bisexuality is . . . constructed through the delegitimation of other sexual categories."[141] This normative politics—which undergirds much of the movement against *Basic Instinct*—is guided by a desire for queerness to be incorporated on-screen into ideas of upstanding citizenship, virtue, and respectability. However, not all the queer responses to *Basic Instinct* followed this schema.

A pertinent opposition to the arguments proposed by other queer contemporaries highlights the heterodox allure in images of queers behaving badly and the alignment of these images with a queer political sensibility. Martha Ertman is most passionate in her article for the Chicago gay and lesbian magazine *Outlines*, which demands extended quotation:

> *Basic Instinct* presents and revels in lesbian and bisexual characters who are smarter, richer, stronger, and ultimately triumphant over the male buffoons on the film's landscape. . . . Best of all, the plot unfolds to reveal that all the women in the film are lesbians, which furthers the gay agenda by publicizing the reality that "we are everywhere." . . . It is arguably the mainstream version of Queer Nation's suggestion that queers bash back. . . . Rather than picket the film, I'd act on the information given in *Basic Instinct* by purchasing an ice pick at K-Mart for $3.69. I'd hang it on my belt-loop as a symbol of empowerment.[142]

Though Ertman's tone is irreverent, her observations are clear: There are many aspects of *Basic Instinct*'s portrayal of queerness that chime with contemporary queer politics' subversion of the normative, its militant passion, its reveling in the badness with which heterosexist society has cast it. These were, in fact, the sensibilities undergirding the contemporaneous New Queer Cinema movement, which had already seen vengeful queer killers in the likes of Todd Haynes's *Poison* (1991) and Tom Kalin's *Swoon* (1992). For B. Ruby Rich, *Basic Instinct*, alongside *Thelma and Louise* (Ridley Scott, 1991), "echoed the [New Queer Cinema's] contention that 'negative images' could be reclaimed. . . . I loved the movie and wondered why, with half a dozen films in the multiplex showing men murdering women, I was expected to boycott the only film in which a woman killed men instead."[143] Both Ertman's and Rich's approaches suggest the possibility of assuming a queer spectatorial sensibility, particularly when viewing Hollywood film. Disabused of the inclination to find truth in these images, we might discover, they suggest, a radical kind of fantasy.

In an interview with *Time Out* published a month after *Basic Instinct*'s release, Paul Verhoeven responds to debates around the film's portrayal of sexuality with this provocation: "Catherine is the devil, that's why she is bisexual."[144] This comment was unlikely to assuage the critiques of Verhoeven's detractors; in fact, it seemed to confirm their accusation that the film associated bisexuality with evil. Yet, in the comments that follow, Verhoeven offers a curious reasoning behind his words: "Genesis says that God created man in his image—male and female. . . . That's why I think the devil is male and female, and that's why I think bisexuality is appropriate to Catherine's character."[145] In this remark we can observe, as Jo Eadie does, the common slippage between bisexuality as a form of desiring and bisexuality as synonymous with intersexuality.[146] This claim—that the devil is intersex—has some cultural precedent. In John Milton's *Paradise Lost*, for example, Satan is among a class of spirits who "when they please / Can either sex assume or both."[147] In this sense, Verhoeven's alignment of Catherine with the devil speaks to her capacity for dissimulation, her combination of traits deemed traditionally masculine or feminine, and both her constitutional and desirous rejection of the paradigm of sexual difference. Yet, beyond Milton's and Verhoeven's unorthodox mythologies, the idea that the devil or Satan is alluring or attractive to all is widespread, both within Christianity, where Satan's capacity for temptation precipitated the Fall, and beyond. Indeed, it is the allure of Satan as a figure of "indulgence," "vital existence," "wisdom," "vengeance," and "gratification" that signals his iconicity for LaVeyan Satanism.[148] Verhoeven's alignment of Catherine with a bisexual devilishness thus can be read as a profession not of bisexuality's evil but of her similarities to this enduring figure of antinormative rebellion. She is, like Satan, a figure of power and knowledge and (bisexually) alluring to all. As Eadie contends, "To be the Devil Catherine must be . . . a woman whom anyone could desire."[149] To reject Verhoeven's alignment of Catherine's bisexuality with the devil as phobic is to be constrained hermeneutically by a Christian framework of morality. Catherine's bisexuality might thus render her devilish, even Satanic, not because bisexuality is immoral but because it involves transgressive forms of knowledge, it contests dominant systems of social organization, and it is characterized by a gratification-driven refusal to settle upon a single gendered object.

For the activists—bisexual, gay, and lesbian alike—who protested *Basic Instinct*, the film's entanglement of bisexuality with murderousness could only ever be read as conveying a negative, phobic truth-value. Although the rallying call of "Catherine did it" intended to function as a means of preventing an audience's enjoyment of the film, it is better understood as symptomatic of the flattening, parochial approach to cinema of those who chanted it. As other scholars, critics, and even Verhoeven himself note, *Basic Instinct* refuses to tell its audience who "did it." In the film's final shot, the camera pans from Catherine and Nick in bed to an ice pick beneath it. While this is, of course, a suggestive shot, it importantly does not confirm anything but there being an ice pick beneath Catherine's bed. In this sense, the ice pick exemplifies Roland Barthes's contention that "all images are polysemous; they imply, underlying their signifiers, a 'floating chain' of signifieds. . . . Polysemy poses a question of meaning and this question always comes through as a dysfunction . . . in the cinema itself,

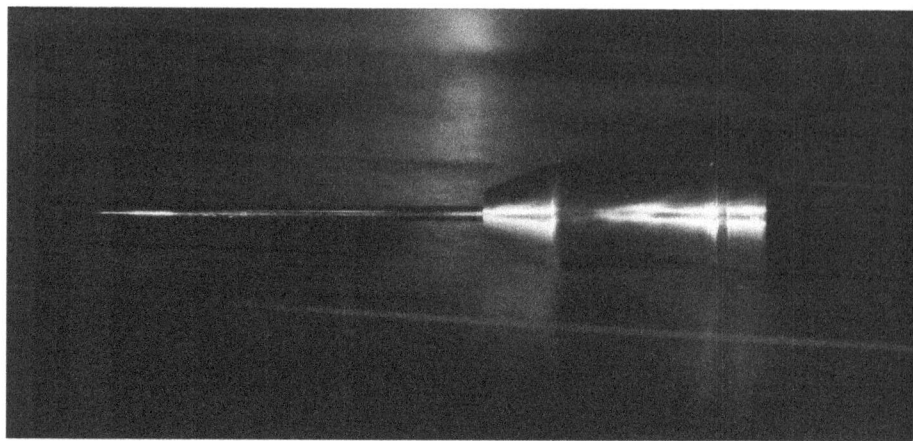

FIGURE 4.14 The overdetermined ice pick. *Basic Instinct* (Paul Verhoeven, 1992). Digital screen capture.

traumatic images are bound up with an uncertainty (an anxiety) concerning the meaning of objects . . . various techniques are developed intended *to fix* the floating chain of signifieds in such a way as to counter the terror of uncertain signs."[150] The terror of the ice pick as uncertain sign is assuaged by the interpretation that "Catherine did it," but this solution is similarly troubled by the question as to what "it" is. Did Catherine commit *all* the murders? Did Catherine commit only some of the murders? These particularities haunt the pretense of univocality purported by some of the film's interpreters. Unavoidably, however, the questions as to who has murdered Johnny (Bill Cable), Marty (Daniel von Bargen), and Gus (George Dzundza)—and as to whether Catherine's parents and Catherine's and Beth's ex-husbands were murdered—remain unanswered. Incertitude endures.

Given this lack of narrative conclusion, we would be justified in entertaining the possibility that Catherine did not do it. Any of it. Read thus, what comes into view are the frenzied neuroses of Nick and his colleagues' perceptual fallibilities in the face of a bisexual figure who elicits in them both intense arousal and epistemology-shattering confoundment. In Viviane Namaste's analysis of *Basic Instinct*, she observes how "every time a bisexual takes an everyday sign, she corrupts it, she destroys the 'natural order.'"[151] Later, she elaborates that because "bisexuals cannot access signs according to the dominant culture's mode, they are inscribed as a rupture in this circulation of signs."[152] Although Namaste seems to lament this exclusion of the bisexual from the natural order's circulation of signs, we might, instead, appreciate how bisexuality's exclusion from a normative semiotic system spells bisexuality's potential for contesting logocentrism itself. Eadie argues that one of the key threats bisexuality poses concerns dominant notions of sexual semiotics. Whereas certain styles, cultures, bodies, or sex acts carry symbolic associations with one or other monosexuality, bisexual figures' potential to possess such symbols breaks apart these semiotic links to the extent that these signs must be said to "not . . . tell us anything."[153] This realization leads to what is perhaps the more terrifying (non)reading of the ice pick beneath Catherine's bed. In a film animated by the drive to know through seeing—a film that suggests that efforts toward understanding the visual through dominant epistemologies are routinely ineffectual—the horror of Catherine's ice pick might actually lie in its semiotic overdetermination.

Afterword

Toward the beginning of Gaspar Noé's *Irreversible* (2002), we see Marcus (Vincent Cassel) and his friend Pierre (Albert Dupontel) navigating an underground male sex club in search of a man known only as the Tapeworm (Jo Prestia). When Marcus finds a man (Mick Gondouin) he believes to be the Tapeworm, the two begin to scrap; the man overpowers Marcus, breaks his arm, and attempts to rape him. Pierre then intervenes, proceeding to pummel the man's face with a fire extinguisher, killing him. *Irreversible's* narrative is structured in reverse chronology and, as the film proceeds, we learn that Marcus and Pierre's actions were precipitated by the Tapeworm's rape of Marcus's girlfriend, Alex (Monica Bellucci). The man we have seen Marcus and Pierre attack, however, is revealed not to be the Tapeworm, who, in fact, was looking on—slightly smirking—as the other man was killed in front of him. The Tapeworm escapes the men's retribution with impunity.

I conclude with a brief consideration of this figure as he is, at once, beyond reclamation for a politics that looks to film for "positive" images of bisexuality while being, undeniably, a figure of bisexual transgression. Our witnessing of the Tapeworm raping Alex in concert with his presence within a male sex club establishes his object choices as in excess of a single gender. While it might be unsettling to understand rape as involving object choice, given that some of the most impactful feminist theories of rape stress its political and violent motivations over the sexual, other accounts warn against dismissing the role of the assailant's sexuality.[1] Ann J. Cahill writes that "it *matters* that sexuality is the medium of the power and violence that are imposed on the victim. . . . The rapist's sexuality *is* engaged. . . . That these sexual experiences may be the result of the violence and the asymmetric power relations inherent in the assault makes them no less sexual in nature."[2] To understand the Tapeworm's

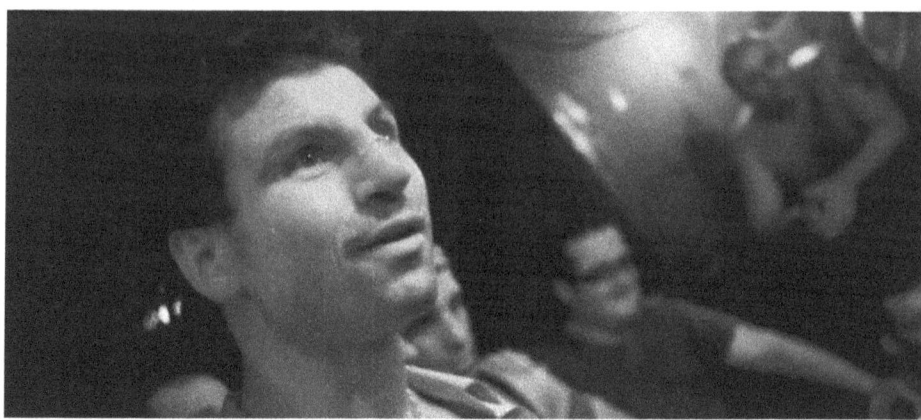

FIGURE A.1 The Tapeworm (Jo Prestia) watches on as he evades retribution for his violence. *Irreversible* [*Irréversible*] (Gaspar Noé, 2002). Digital screen capture.

sexual interest in both Alex and the men patronizing the sex club is not to deny the violence of the former but to acknowledge the imbrication of desire in sexual violence. Like the other cinematic bisexual transgressors I have traced, the Tapeworm inheres across disparate spaces of sexual demarcation and, importantly, it is his unidentifiability, his unreadability, that allows him to escape retribution.

The Tapeworm's rape of Alex is anal; the sex club to which Marcus and Pierre are led is called Rectum. Similarly to *Salò's* (Pier Paolo Pasolini, 1975) staging of a competition of genderless asses, we find, in *Irreversible*, bisexuality aligned with an anal focus: an alignment toward that organ irreducible to gender. The tapeworm—the Cestoda class of parasitic flatworms—also evades sexual classification within an oppositional and discrete binary. It is bisexual in the nineteenth-century sense of the term, hermaphroditic in the language of twenty-first-century zoology: It contains reproductive attributes assigned by bioscience the terms both *male* and *female*.[3] The tapeworm inheres unknowingly in the body of its host, as undetectable as the male bisexuals whose presence haunted media discourses around HIV/AIDS or as the erotic thriller's bisexual suspects. The tapeworm feeds off its host like the les(bi)an vampire feeds off her targets or like the bisexual women in lesbian feminist communities were accused of having "fed on lesbian energy."[4] The tapeworm finally makes itself known in its exit through the anus. We are returned to the rectum, the anus, the ass, where we began. Diarmuid Hester's formalist reading of *Irreversible* describes how "the Rectum persists as something like an inescapable primal scene, to which one is psychologically compelled to return again and again."[5] Here, I am compelled to enact a similar return to anality, back to the bodily cluster around which sexual significations accumulate but that are unattributable to a single binary gender. Like the primal scene in the film Jo makes in *She Must Be Seeing Things* (Sheila McLaughlin, 1987), as in Sigmund Freud's original conception of it, this is a scene where sexual positions find themselves unmoored. Desirously, the ass-as-object-choice evades monosexual classification, and it is here that both the tapeworm and the Tapeworm manifest.

Cinemas of Bisexual Transgression has sought to make the case for doing queer film studies differently, demonstrating the benefits of taking as our starting point cinema's figures of bisexual transgression. I have shown how, through these figures, we can model modes of queer film analysis that attend to sexuality's interstitiality, its mutability, and its irreducibility to signification—qualities whose conceptual alignments with bisexuality mark an underexploited affordance of *bisexuality* as a critical term. Attention to the contingencies of film form has been central to this undertaking, which stresses the unique connections between aesthetics and notions of sexual intelligibility, mapping both the ways film form has been deployed to consolidate the dominant monosexualities and also its potential to undo these forms of consolidation in ways that bespeak sexuality's extensive capacities beyond discrete oppositional binaries. This project has returned to bisexual theory as a critical practice that aids us in formulating complex approaches in sexuality studies, yet this is not a practice that requires isolated engagement. Positioned in conversation with a range of interlocutors—film theory, poststructuralist feminist theory, queer theory, lesbian feminist theory, trans theory, critical philosophies of race, political economy—bisexual theory is a lively, challenging, and rigorous critical practice whose contributions are richest in dialogue with other critical practices. Attention to the phenomenon of bisexual transgression on film responds critically to a recent return in popular media discourses to notions of so-called positive representation, an approach I have argued is anathema to critical engagement with the work of sexual-cinematic signification. To look, sometimes uncomfortably, at cinemas of bisexual transgression necessitates a critical textual practice unconcerned with flat or transparent reading. Instead, it demands analysis of how the illumination of structures of organization via transgression marks the most persistent and generative ways in which cinema has attested to bisexual capacities beyond a monosexual rule.

The cinematic figurations of bisexual transgression this book has traced speak to the troubling and persistent evocation of figures that are unthinkable within a sexuality binary, figures whose inherence across seemingly discrete spaces of sexual definition challenges the binary organization of sexuality it-self. The bisexual transgressor's alliance with the "and/or" enables a rethinking of structures of sexuality beyond extant conventions of signification. Among the reconsiderations these figures might inspire in queer studies is the incom-mensurability of oppositionality in accounting for them. In this sense, at-tention to the bisexual transgressor harmonizes with Robyn Wiegman and Elizabeth A. Wilson's call for a queer theory that interrogates the assumptions of antinormativity and disputes two regular claims about the norm: "that it is *restrictive* and that it *excludes*."[6] The bisexual transgressor, in fact, dem-onstrates that the norm is remarkably permeable, even infiltratable, that its boundaries are more precarious than we might assume. Wiegman and Wilson warn against turning normativity's "systemic play" into "unforgiving rules and regulations," concretized by a methodological approach of "moving against."[7] They stress, instead, "the relationality that is at the heart of normativity" is better approached through a methodology of "moving athwart."[8] The bisexual transgressor's athwart movements—within and beyond spaces of normativity and dissidence—model such an approach, whose lessons for queer epistemol-ogy are plentiful.

The bisexual transgressor's refutation of the laws of binary opposition ren-ders their figuration on film an indispensable locus for queer film inquiry. Nev-ertheless, bisexual theoretical approaches and bisexual textual foci remain few and far between in queer film studies. *The Oxford Handbook of Queer Cinema*, published in 2021, contains no chapters focused on bisexuality; the handful of times the term appears in the edited collection do not even warrant an entry in the volume's index.[9] The repetition of the term *LGBTQ* throughout the collection instantiates how a cursory acknowledgment of bisexuality's being-there (in a *B* whose utterance depends on its subsumption within the abbreviation) can, in fact, work to preclude critical engagement with bisexu-ality, its theories, its modes of reading, its social and discursive histories. My identification of this elision is less an indictment of this particular work and more a diagnosis of a consistent ignorance in queer film studies regarding the viability, usefulness, or relevance of bisexuality for queer film inquiry. I hope to have shown that bisexuality's eschewal in queer film studies comes at the ex-pense of the formulation of complex, rigorous investigation into the workings of sexuality and the cinema.

With the limited historical and geographical scope of this book, I have ob-viously not been able to account for the sheer extent of figurations of bisexual transgression across cinema history. I have found stirring images in 1920s stag films, including *The Modern Household of Madame Butterfly* (1920) and *Tea Time*

(1925), wherein performers' transgressions between intragender and extragender sex acts constitute a cinematic attraction.[10] Bisexual transgressors can be found disparately in cinema's silent period, from muse Eugène (Lars Hanson) of *The Wings* (Mauritz Stiller, 1916)—torn between his sculptor Claude (Egil Eide) and his crush Lucia (Lili Beck)—to the figure of the female cross-dresser, who appeared in many films across the period and in whose gender transgression bisexual possibilities become all the more likely.[11] *Impetuous Youth*'s (Paul Czinner, 1926) cross-dressed Renée (Elisabeth Bergner), for instance, is taken in by an artsy Florentine couple (Conrad Veidt and Nora Gregor), both of whom develop an attraction toward her as a boy yet, upon the revelation of her womanhood, both share an ardent kiss with her, the gender of their object choice having become inconsequential. Figures of bisexual transgression have also continued to surface in the decades following my corpus: from the deceptive Rose (Allison Williams) of *Get Out* (Jordan Peele, 2017), in which the revelation of her serial seduction of Black victims makes an additional revelation that these were not all men, to the narcissistic Tomas (Franz Rogowski) of *Passages* (Ira Sachs, 2023), whose embodiment of bisexual greed effects various forms of social breakdown. Beyond the loose 1970s to 1990s framework this book has deployed, cinema's bisexual transgressors linger.

While I have justified the geographical scope of my corpus through the shared epistemologies of sexuality in Western contexts, bisexual transgressors persist beyond this purview. Prem Kapoor's independent Hindi film *Infamous Neighborhood* (1971) centers around a bisexual bandit, Sarnam (Nitin Sethi), whose savvy navigation of the criminal underworld mirrors his manipulation of men and women alike. Bisexual transgression is equally discernible among the male sex worker figures of Filipino director Lino Brocka's *Manila in the Claws of Light* (1975) and *Macho Dancer* (1988). Bisexual sadomasochist figures populate the gay pink films of Japan's Hisayasu Sato, such as the brutal dom Ishikawa (Takeshi Ito) of *Hunters' Sense of Touch* (1995). The titular Karmen (Djeïnaba Diop Gaï) of *Karmen Geï* (Joseph Gaï Ramaka, 2001) leads a transgressive life of hedonism in Dakar, Senegal, where she enjoys male and female lovers. These are just some of the films from cinemas beyond the West in which figures of bisexual transgression are equally identifiable. I have shown, however, that analysis of these figures must attend to the respective cultural, political, historical, and epistemological contexts through which transgressive bisexuality is made meaningful. Herein lies rich potential for future scholarship on a wide cinematic array of bisexual transgressors.

While narrative cinema has been the predominant focus of this book, I am open to its theoretical transposability to other media forms. I would be remiss not to mention the significant corpus of television that exceeds this book's scope but that would warrant similar investigations into the operations of bisexual transgression. It was, indeed, a televised episode of *Midnight Caller* depicting a bisexual man purposefully transmitting HIV to others that prompted what is likely bisexual politics' first organized action in relation to a media object. Although considering this corpus has not been my task to take up, I am interested in the interrelation between television's seriality and bisexuality that, Maria San Filippo argues, "makes it the medium with the most *bi-potential* . . . (multi-)seasonal arcs allow[ing] time for bisexuality to develop."[12] Here, I would be curious to see investigations into how the potential of the serialized television format affects forms of bisexual transgression, the extent to which these developments might involve sexual, social, or even bodily transformations in ways unrealizable in shorter media formats. Another media form that I have explored only briefly (with my analysis of Midi Onodera's *The Basement Girl* [2000]) is that of avant-garde cinema. Although figuration is key to my theoretical grounding, and much avant-garde work deprivileges figurativity in favor of the materiality of image and sound, figures still populate avant-garde work. Here, bisexual approaches might consider invocations of orgiastic, multigendered groups in works like Enrico Cocozza's *Bongo Erotico* (1959), Jack Smith's *Flaming Creatures* (1963), or Carolee Schneemann's *Meat Joy* (1964). Maybe we could look to queer experimental filmmaker Edward Owens's aptly named *Once I Loved a Woman* (1966), which features the same male figure in two different pairings, one with a woman and one with a man, or perhaps we could consider the consecutive presentations of differently gendered sexual configurations in films like Andy Warhol's *Kiss* (1963–64) and *Couch* (1964).[13] To consider bisexual transgression in relation to avant-garde film would necessitate a consideration of how avant-garde formal techniques enable an opening up of desirous configurations in ways that are meaningful to bisexual interpretation. Beyond this book's predominant historical, geographic, and stylistic foci are promising sites of media analysis that would expand and complicate media theories of bisexual transgression further.

Over four decades ago, Félix Guattari established two levels upon which homosexuality had articulated itself. The first is "the global social field," in which homosexuality is defined by secretiveness and notions of perversion; the second is the oppositional "militant homosexuality," whereby "homosexuality confronts heterosexual power on its own terrain. Now heterosexuality must account for itself."[14] Guattari then gestures toward a third level, "a more molecular one in which categories, groupings and 'special instances' would not be differentiated in the same way, in which clear cut oppositions between types would be repudiated, in which, on the contrary, one would look for similarities . . . among all forms of sexual minorities once it is understood that in this realm there could only be minorities. . . . All forms of sexual activity are fundamentally on this side of the personological oppositions homo-hetero."[15] While Guattari is perhaps guilty of the tendency I have described earlier whereby something akin to bisexuality is cast as a possibility of a utopian future and unavailable in the present, he nevertheless underscores a vital direction for queer inquiry. This path leads to a consideration of the various ways our sexualities fall outside of the homo-hetero binary, effecting a splitting open of sexual categorization. The bisexual approaches I have outlined are crucial tools, I contend, in this movement toward Guattari's third level.

That bisexuality might trouble extant oppositional frameworks still enjoying purchase in queer film scholarship might be daunting, but this is a challenge that chimes with queer studies' initial aims to, in the words of Teresa de Lauretis, "transgress" the "given terms" of *lesbian* and *gay*, "not to assume their ideological liabilities."[16] Elizabeth Wilson laments that "the demand for the recognition of bisexuality challenges the foundations of the lesbian and gay movement which . . . is predicated on the assumption that the lesbian/gay identity is at least relatively fixed. . . . The bisexual movement . . . has been insensitive to these difficulties."[17] I contend, however, that a foundational challenge to sexual-subjective fixity should be one of queer inquiry's central guiding forces, and bisexuality's ability to produce such effects evidences its critical utility. Wilson's and others' dismissal of bisexuality symptomatizes a phenomenon Martin Duberman had already identified in the 1970s: that "to suggest, as practicing bisexuals do, that each of us may contain within ourselves all those supposed diametric opposites we've been taught to divide humanity into is to suggest that we might not know ourselves as well as we like to pretend. . . . Such suggestions are discomforting. Few people welcome discomfort."[18] I call upon queer film scholarship, written with the implicit assurance of a settled object choice, to let down its protective guard and welcome discomfort, to loosen its grip to oppositionality and allow itself to become unfixed in the analytically rich space of cinema's bisexual potentialities.

In 1997, the Bi Academic Intervention compelled us to go in search of the "different meanings that become invested" in bisexuality.[19] Central to their call was an insistence that bisexuality "necessarily partakes of the pleasures and problematics of partiality and of vacillation: it can never be *one* thing."[20] This book, with its focus on bisexual transgression and film, has attended to the heterogeneous, heterologous, and heterodox affordances to be found herein. Although the workings and effects of these cinematic figurations vary, the persistent phenomenon they attest to involves bisexual transgression's ability to illuminate the precarities inherent in structures of organization, be they so- cial, sexual, cinematic. Jo Eadie's analysis of the bisexual-as-cinematic-figure contends that they carry "the stigma of passions for which there is no place in anyone, and yet which find in everyone a place prepared for them."[21] The excesses, unintelligibilities, and metamorphoses of cinema's bisexual trans- gressors, in whom anxieties around structures of organization are made mean- ingful, may leave some appalled, some compelled, some confounded. These figures' value, however, is to be found in their elucidation of cinema's capac- ity to convey that which lies beyond homosexual-heterosexual opposition through violations of rules that render systems of categorization unstable. Queer film studies is impoverished without them.

Acknowledgments

A function of an acknowledgments section that I appreciate involves its mapping out of the vast intersubjective network that is the condition of the author's work. While these efforts can only ever be partial, unfinished, I appreciate the opportunity to attempt to lay out mine.

The research that composes this book first began with the support of the London Arts and Humanities Partnership, for which I am grateful. My greatest debt is owed to Rosalind Galt and Elena Gorfinkel, whose generous, incisive, and critical attention to my work has been the condition of this book's possibility. For their attentive and thoughtful feedback on this research, I am also thankful to Mandy Merck and Maria San Filippo; I hope the fruits of our generative exchanges are readable herein.

The first mentors to offer me encouragement in conducting research around bisexuality and cinema were Blanka Nyklová, Rachel O'Connell, and Samuel Solomon; I am eternally grateful for your encouragement of me pursuing these lines of thought. My development as a researcher is equally indebted to many others, but particularly, I would like to thank Olga Kourelou, Michael Lawrence, John David Rhodes, and Cynthia Weber, who inspired, challenged, and supported me in formative ways. I am thankful in particular for a small but significant email exchange with Clare Hemmings back in 2015, which pushed me to think more critically about sexual representability and to pursue cinema's bad bisexual figures; bisexual theory would not exist as it does today without your contributions, and neither would this book.

My research was aided by a number of organizations, whose generosity I appreciate: Arsenal—Institute for Film and Video Art e.V (Arsenal—Institut für Film und Videokunst e.V.); the Austrian Film Archive (Filmarchiv Austria);

the British Board of Film Classification; Cinenova; the Croatian Audiovisual Centre (Hrvatski audiovizualni centar); the Czech National Film Archive (Národní filmový archiv); the Hall-Carpenter Archives at the London School of Economics Library; the International Institute of Social History, Amsterdam; the National Film Institute Hungary (Nemzeti Filmintézet); the National Library of Scotland (Leabharlann Nàiseanta na h-Alba); the Norwegian Film Institute (Norsk filminstitutt); the University of Michigan Library Special Collections Research Center; and the University of Toronto Mark S. Bonham Centre for Sexual Diversity Studies.

I am thankful to the filmmakers who gave up their time to speak with me about their work and ideas: Lizzie Borden, Bruna Fionda, Polly Gladwin, Sheila McLaughlin, and Zachary Nataf. For support with tricky research questions, from rare translations to the laws of trigonometry, I am grateful for the friendly help of Sophie Abrahams, Marie-Aude Baronian, Evgenii Bershtein, Clara Bradbury-Rance, Cüneyt Çakırlar, Alasdair Cameron, Farrah Freibert, Laura Gill, Donna Haraway, Alice Haylett Bryan, Grace Lavery, Carolina McPhail, and Michael L. Thomas. I also owe much to friends who served as critical interlocutors as I thought through a range of ideas relating to this research; thank you to Khaled Alsaleh, Jules Douglas, Nea Ehrlich, Diarmuid Hester, Tom Houlton, Jules O'Dwyer, Tilly Scantlebury, Rhys Steven Jones, and Joseph Ronan.

I received feedback on various arguments presented in this book at a number of conferences: Queer Conversations: Looking to Art History and Visual Culture (the Courtauld Institute of Art), the European Geographies of Sexualities Conference, the Society for Cinema and Media Studies Conference, and the World Picture Conference. Thank you to the copanelists and attendees whose engagement with my work gave me eminently useful challenges and considerations.

This work has taken shape in academic community, and I would like to acknowledge the vibrant networks of colleagues and friends who have made up mine as I completed this research. At King's College London, I was grateful for Mark Betz, Sarah Cooper, Victor Fan, Michael Grace, Theresa Heath, Berenike Jung, Laurence Kent, Robert Mills, Lawrence Napper, Martha Shearer, Laura Staab, and Belén Vidal. At the University of Amsterdam and Amsterdam University College, I am grateful for Jacqueline Antonissen, Sruti Bala, Erica Biolchini, Bogna Bochińska, Balázs Boross, Eugenie Brinkema, Isadora Campregher Paiva, Pei-Sze Chow, Emily Clark, Sudeep Dasgupta, Linda Duits, Nermin Elsherif, Augustin Ferrari Braun, Roberto Filippello, Jamil Fiorino-Habib, Zachary Furste, İdil Galip, Abe Geil, Erella Grassiani, Slava Greenberg, Gert

Jan Harkema, Mona Hegazy, Hemen Heidari, Kirsten van der Holt, Yolande Jansen, Sara Janssen, Misha Kavka, Jaap Kooijman, Halbe Kuipers, Catherine Lord, Emiel Martens, Juliëtte Molenaars, Gavin Mueller, Alex Muller, Aslı Özgen-Havekotte, Floris Paalman, Toni Pape, Patricia Pisters, Thomas Poell, Kimberly Poole, Noa Roei, Erinç Salor, Derk van Santvoort, Sidra Shahid, Markus Stauff, Jan Teurlings, Rika Theo, Stephen Turner, Tjalling Valdés Olmos, Vesna Vravnik, Amir Vudka, Maryn Wilkinson, and Marissa Willcox. At both of these institutions, I would like to thank the administrative staff, catering staff, cleaning staff, facility services staff, librarians, and information technology and audiovisual services personnel, whose work undergirds the professional communities we share. I also have deep appreciation for my students, who continue to inspire and to challenge me.

For friendships that have buoyed me during this research, I would like to thank Alison Clare, Martyn Lewis, Sarah Liewehr, Lan McArdle, Catherine O'Sullivan, Jasmine Scott, and Kate Wood. For showing me the values of critical thinking, lively discussion, and love as I grew up, I am especially thankful to Paul Devlin and Barbara-Anne Walker. I am also indebted to Lesley Marks, whose nurturing of my intellectual curiosity and supportive encouragement have been invaluable. For support with my well-being, I am grateful to Judith Ellenbogen, Jo Lawton, David Norton, and many other fellows.

The team at Duke University Press has been wonderful to work with, and I am particularly indebted to Elizabeth Ault for seeing something worth pursuing in my work and guiding me so clearly through the process of publication. Also at Duke University Press, I would like to thank Benjamin Kossak, Cameron M. Ludwick, Chad Royal, Olivia Schmitz, Liz Smith, and Lee Willoughby Harris. I am grateful to the Camera Obscura collective, Patricia White in particular, for their generous support. My heartfelt thanks also go out to my diligent and judicious copyeditor, Ziggy Snow. To my not-so-anonymous reader, Maria Pramaggiore, and to each of my two subsequent anonymous readers: Your rigor, attention to detail, and faith in the project made for a gratifying review process; thank you for your work. It was an absolute pleasure to work with my indexer, Josh Rutner, whose careful and meticulous approach has resulted in a wonderfully dynamic index that serves as an meaningful paratext in and of itself.

To Jo Waghorn: Thank you for returning me to what matters, steering me away from the perils of a life taken too seriously, and reminding me of the necessities that are joy, humor, and happiness.

To my mother, Jackie Engelberg: The love, support, and dedication you have shown me are part and parcel of your indefatigable drive to make the world better for others. Thank you, *mamele*, for all you have taught me.

And to Gary Needham: It is so very special that one of my most valued interlocutors is also a loved and loving partner. Your tenderness, intellect, cooking, and care throughout the writing of this book are gifts that I will always treasure. It is a privilege that I get to share a life with you.

Inchoate formulations of my arguments around bisexual intelligibility and film aesthetics were published in "'How Could Any One Relationship Ever Possibly Be Fulfilling?' Bisexuality, Nonmonogamy, and the Visualization of Desire in the Cinema of Gregg Araki," *Journal of Bisexuality* 18, no. 1 (2018): 102–17. An earlier version of some arguments from chapter 3 was published online by Club des Femmes for their Culture Club series: "She Must Be Seeing Men," 2021, https://perma.cc/7VGW-TLW3. Early formulations of some of my arguments around bisexuality and film form were also published in "Call Me Bi Any Other Name: Anal Monstration, Formal Bisexualization, Gay Indigestion," in *Call Me by Your Name: Perspectives on the Film*, ed. Edward Lamberti and Michael Williams (Intellect Books, 2024).

Notes

PREFACE

1   Angelides, *A History of Bisexuality*, 173.
2   Ahmed, *What's the Use?*, 4.
3   Angelides, *A History of Bisexuality*, 15 (emphasis removed).
4   Janssen, "Monosexual/Plurisexual." I am indebted to this article for enlightening me on the work of Ulrichs, Gley, Tarnowsky, Moll, Eulenburg, Raffalovich, and Saint-Paul, which I detail in the following sentences.
5   In his formulation, this was *Uranodionäismus* and *Uranodioning* for men and *Uranodioningin* for women. Ulrichs, *Formatrix*, xxii–xxiii; Ulrichs, *Vindicta*, 37.
6   Gley, "Les Aberrations de l'instinct sexuel," 70 (my translation).
7   Tarnowsky, *Die krankhaften Erscheinungen des Geschlectssinnes*, 38–49, quoted in and translated by Janssen, "Monosexual/Plurisexual," 7.
8   Krafft-Ebing, *Psychopathia Sexualis*, 447–48 (my translation); Moll, *Die konträre Sexualempfindung*, 14; Eulenburg, "Neuropathia sexualis virorum," 68, quoted in and translated by Janssen, "Monosexual/Plurisexual," 6.
9   Raffalovich, "Inversion sexuelle congénitale," 122; Saint-Paul, *Tares et poisons*, 27 (my translation).
10 Freud, "Three Essays," 169 et seq., 122; Freud, "Letter 52," 265.
11 Kinsey et al., *Sexual Behavior in the Human Male*, 638; F. Klein, *The Bisexual Option*, 19.
12 See Payne, "Some Freudian Contributions," 93n5; Ferenczi, "Über die Rolle der Homosexualität," 144; Nass et al., *Sexual Choices*, 159.
13 Peraldi, "Polysexuality."
14 Lacquer, *Making Sex*; Repo, *The Biopolitics of Gender*. With my historical account of *gender*, I am discussing it linguistically; obviously, gender's operations preceded the popularization of it as a term.
15 These rearticulations are observable in one of the draft manifestos from the first Politics of Bisexuality Conference in London (1984) (*Bi-Monthly*, "Bisexual Manifesto," 6), the statement of purpose of the Bay Area Bisexual Network's magazine *Anything That Moves* (n.p.) from their third issue onward, and in Julia Serano's

history of alliances between bisexual and transgender activism during the 1990s (*Excluded*, 94).

16   Here I am in alignment with Judith Butler's account of the suggestion that *sex* is "always already gender . . . the distinction between sex and gender turns out to be no distinction at all" (*Gender Trouble*, 10–11).

17   Villarejo, *Lesbian Rule*, 11.

INTRODUCTION

1   Andreas-Salomé, "'Anal' and 'Sexual,'" 28. Here, I am drawing on S. Pearl Brilmyer and Filippo Trentin's reading of Andreas-Salomé, in which they propose that it is "a fundamental corporeal sameness that must be erased in order for the regime of sexual difference to be established" ("Introduction," 14).

2   From one angle, seventeen genderless asses are discernible, but from another, only fourteen can be discerned.

3   This arrangement also recalls Guy Hocquenghem's assertion that the anus "does not practice sexual discrimination" (*Homosexual Desire*, 101).

4   I borrow the term *primary identification* from Christian Metz, who, drawing on Jean-Louis Baudry's articulation of the first level of identification, posits it as identification with the camera as an "all-seeing and invisible subject." Metz, *The Imaginary Signifier*, 97; Baudry, "Ideological Effects," 45.

5   Although Italian fascism was expressly homophobic, Barbara Spackman's analysis of Italian fascist writing demonstrates how sexual contact between men in the context of "nationalistic ardor" could be rendered permissible. One of fascist propagandist Filippo Tommaso Marinetti's speeches, cited by Spackman, proffers the purported period of homosexuality of men in their twenties as a "highly respectable taste" developed "out of a sort of intensification of camaraderie and friendship in athletic sports." Marinetti differentiates this kind of queerness from the "born invert, the false man, [and] the half-woman." It would seem, therefore, that there is some national-historical precedent for the permissibility of certain forms of queer sexuality under the auspices of fascist power. Spackman, *Fascist Virilities*, 15; Marinetti, "Discorso futurista agli inglesi," 283, quoted in and translated by Spackman, *Fascist Virilities*, 16.

6   San Filippo, *The B Word*, 17–18, 22.

7   The particularities of these works' sexual politics obviously precede the late nineteenth-century consolidation of sexual categorization, including bisexuality, with the context of libertinage and the juridico-religious notions of sodomy being of particular relevance. Nevertheless, they endure as texts attesting to the equally troubling and alluring transgressions of sexual unboundedness, with their particular emphasis on boundary crossings between differently gendered objects.

8   Sade, *La Philosophie dans le boudoir*, 14 (my translation).

9   See de Beauvois, "First Memoir of Observations," 211.

10   See Carter, "On a Bisexual Nematoid Worm."

11   Darwin, *The Descent of Man*, 207–8.

12 Haeckel, *Anthropogenie* , 5, quoted in and translated by Gould, *Ontogeny and Phylogeny*, 78.

13 Although systems of sexual governmentality in the West have varied tremendously across space and time, Erwin J. Haeberle makes the precise distinction that, prior to the eighteenth century, humans' "ambierotic potential was not doubted." These doubts, he writes, emerged with the eighteenth and nineteenth centuries' "bourgeoisification and scientification of life." Haeberle, "Bisexualitäten," 1 (my translation).

14 For greater detail on the developments of Freud's thinking on bisexuality, see Rapoport, *From Psychoanalytic Bisexuality*.

15 Fliess, *Der Ablauf des Lebens*, 437 (my translation).

16 Freud, "Three Essays," 127.

17 Freud, "Three Essays," 127.

18 Freud, "Three Essays," 177, 205.

19 See Freud, "The Interpretation of Dreams"; Freud, "Special Type of Choice." I am grateful to Mandy Merck for the suggestion of these two Freud papers in accounting for the differences between cultural understandings of male and female bisexuality.

20 Freud, "Some Psychical Consequences," 250–56. In a corrective to his earlier assertions that boys' and girls' experiences of the Oedipus complex were analogous, Freud proposes that while boys' Oedipus complexes are "smashed to pieces by the shock of threatened castration," girls' Oedipus complexes involve the rejection of clitoral masturbation, the embrace of the father as "love-object," the replacement of the wish for a penis with the wish for a child, and a concomitant embrace of femininity. Whereas the girl's Oedipus complex necessitates a journey from female love object (the mother) to male love object (the father), the boy's is obliged to stay fixed. Freud also concedes that "a number of women remain arrested in their original attachment to their mother and never achieve a true changeover towards men" ("Female Sexuality," 216).

21 Freud, "Female Sexuality," 217. Freud also concedes that many boys experience a double orientation during the Oedipus complex, involving the desire to take their mothers' places as the love objects of the fathers ("Some Psychical Consequences," 251).

22 Ideas of a universal bisexual disposition were shared by other writers in the early twentieth century. Philosopher Otto Weininger proposes that "from the outset all are *bisexual*, that is, capable of sexual intercourse with both men and women" (*Sex and Character*, 43). Freud's student Wilhelm Stekel was even more emphatic, declaring that "there are no monosexual persons! . . . All persons are bisexual. But persons . . . are compelled by particular circumstances and consequently act as if they were monosexual" (*Bisexual Love*, 27 [emphasis removed]).

23 J. Butler, *Gender Trouble*, 69.

24 These ideas would be influential for later sexological and psychological thinkers, including Alfred C. Kinsey, Li Shiu Tong, and Fritz Klein, whose work attests to bisexuality's enduring prevalence (Kinsey et al., *Sexual Behavior in the Human Male*;

Kinsey et al., *Sexual Behavior in the Human Female*; F. Klein, *The Bisexual Option*). Laurie Marhoefer's reading of Li Shiu Tong's archive (ca. 1980s) finds "an important and clear argument for bisexuality, for sexual fluidity, and against innate sexual identity" (*Racism and the Making of Gay Rights*, 189–90).

25 Ellis, *Studies in the Psychology of Sex*, 88; D. E. Hall, "Graphic Sexuality," 103.

26 Donaldson, "The Bisexual Movement's Beginnings," 34; Raymond and Highleyman, "Appendix A," 333.

27 *Newsweek*, "Bisexual Chic," 90.

28 Money et al., "Playboy Panel," 88.

29 *Newsweek*, July 17, 1995.

30 Eisner, *Bi*, 209. See also Feldman, "Reclaiming Sexual Difference."

31 Irigaray, *This Sex Which Is Not One*, 28.

32 Eisner, *Bi*, 143.

33 See Johnson and Grove, "Why Us?"

34 The only exception to this rule would seem to be homosocial phenomena like horseplay or hazing, in which intragender eroticism is nullified as unserious play.

35 Bergler, *Homosexuality*, 89.

36 For Freud, *bisexuality proper* is defined as "when there is virtually no difference between erotic responses to the body shapes of females and males" ("Male Homosexuality," 26, 39). Tom Waidzunas and Steven Epstein identify the scientific epistemology Freud deploys as one of "bodily truthing," in which physiological responses in laboratory settings are deemed indicative of the supposed truth of sexuality ("'For Men Arousal Is Orientation'"). Clearly, these observations also instantiate Michel Foucault's arguments around *scientia sexualis* (*The History of Sexuality*, 51–74).

37 Bailey's most well-known study is Rieger et al., "Sexual Arousal Patterns of Bisexual Men."

38 Bailey, *Man Who Would Be Queen*, 95–96. Ironically, Bailey later joined forces with the American Institute of Bisexuality to declare the existence of male bisexual attraction via penile plethysmography. These studies include Rosenthal et al., "Sexual Arousal Patterns of Bisexual Men Revisited"; Jabbour et al., "Robust Evidence for Bisexual Orientation." For critical discussion of these supposedly affirmative studies, see Eisner, *Bi*, 214–19; Engelberg et al., "Futile Search for 'Physiological Evidence.'"

39 I am thinking in particular of Helen Joyce's antitransgender book *Trans: When Ideology Meets Reality*.

40 Hegel, *The Science of Logic*, 59–60, §21.68–70.

41 Hegel, *The Science of Logic*, 59–82, §21.68–96.

42 Among the most compelling reformulations to this effect comes from McKenzie Wark, who first proposes bisexuality as "something that stands at the limit of the binary logic of an identity that can only exist negatively." Second, she proposes something beyond a monosexual-bisexual spectrum that she terms "an open vector . . . any possible relation that does not depend for its existence on the terms it relates in mirror opposition to each other, but which could head for the unknown, the unnamed." Wark's former formulation speaks to the potential for something intelligibly bisexual to disrupt the heterosexual-homosexual binary's logic; her

second formulation looks toward spaces of unintelligibility as a vector toward which our thinking on sexuality might be drawn. Wark, "Bisexual Mediations," 69.

43   De Lauretis, "Queer Theory," v; Sedgwick, *Tendencies*, 7.

44   Halperin, "Thirteen Ways of Looking at a Bisexual," 454. These assumptions of a gay positioning in queer theory are also observed by bisexual theorist Jo Eadie, who, quoting Jonathan Dollimore's description of Western metaphysics, critiques the formulation of a "narrow queerness . . . precisely a 'regime of essential and absolute truth' with its own 'normative and prescriptive teleology' . . . that of exclusive and absolute homosexuality." Eadie, "Queer," 246, quoting Dollimore, *Sexual Dissidence*, 116.

45   Edelman, *Homographesis*, xvi, 250n8.

46   Eve Kosofsky Sedgwick, "Bi," *QSTUDY-L* mailing list, August 17, 1994, https://mailman.rice.edu/mailman/private/qstudy-l/1994-August/01424, archived August 19, 2022, at https://perma.cc/A6L7-VAPW.

47   Angelides, *A History of Bisexuality*, 194.

48   Angelides, *A History of Bisexuality*, 194–95.

49   Däumer, "Queer Ethics," 98.

50   Däumer, "Queer Ethics," 97–98.

51   Däumer, "Queer Ethics," 98.

52   Hemmings, *Bisexual Spaces*, 43; cf. James, "Denying Complexity."

53   Hemmings, "Bisexual Theoretical Perspectives," 27.

54   Pramaggiore, "BI-ntroduction I," 3.

55   For more on these processes of repudiation, see Hemmings, *Bisexual Spaces*, 25.

56   Hegel, *Encyclopedia of the Philosophical Sciences*, 133.

57   J. Butler, *Gender Trouble*, 73 et seq.; Sedgwick, *Epistemology of the Closet*, 10.

58   Hegel, *Encyclopedia of the Philosophical Sciences*, 132.

59   Eisner, "Monosexism," 792.

60   Hemmings, *Bisexual Spaces*, 29.

61   Hemmings, "From Landmarks to Spaces," 151.

62   Potentially useful here are various concepts in Black feminist theory that map the ways in which systems of oppression operate interdependently. See Combahee River Collective, "A Black Feminist Statement."

63   Hemmings, "From Landmarks to Spaces," 151.

64   Yoshino, "Epistemic Contract of Bisexual Erasure."

65   Hemmings, "From Landmarks to Spaces," 476n33.

66   Hemmings, *Bisexual Spaces*, 28.

67   Hemmings, *Bisexual Spaces*, 29. Another notable critique of the term comes from Merl Storr, who suggests that bisexual politics "reflect seriously on the implication of 'monosexual' and 'bisexual,' and that explicit attention must be paid to the racial heritage of both of those terms, before any such use is attempted" ("The Sexual Reproduction of 'Race,'" 85). I discuss the import of racist, colonialist epistemologies of race onto bisexuality in chapter 1. For now, suffice it to say that I am unconvinced that the racist contexts of these terms' developments preclude their use; indeed, one aspect of these terms' usefulness is precisely their illumination of the discursive alignment of monosexuality with civilization and bisexuality with "primitivity."

68 See Peyghambarzadeh, "Untellable Bisexual Asylum Stories." For a recent summary of social-scientific investigations into disparities between bisexuals and other sexuality groups, see Monro, *Bisexuality*, 52–54.

69 See also Angelos Bollas's assertion of monosexuality's theoretical utility, especially in relation to sociodicy ("Hegemonic Monosexuality").

70 Another figure central to the history of film studies who considers humans' bisexual potential is Jean Epstein, who wrote about sexuality (not in relation to film) under the pseudonym Alfred Kléber. Epstein posits that every organism "seems capable of continuing its development either in the heterosexual direction, or in the homosexual direction, and perhaps in both directions at the same time. . . . In certain cases, sexuality succeeds in pursuing an ambivalent evolution along the two paths on which it is engaged" ("Ganymède," 42 [my translation]).

71 Bershtein, "Eisenstein's Letter to Magnus Hirschfeld," 77.

72 Quoted and translated in Bershtein, "Eisenstein's Letter to Magnus Hirschfeld," 80.

73 Bershtein, "Eisenstein's Letter to Magnus Hirschfeld," 79.

74 Eisenstein, "'Shift' to the Biological Level," 21.

75 Firestone envisages "a reversion to an unobstructed *pansexuality*" and the supersession of "Freud's 'polymorphous perversity'"; Mieli envisages the unlearning of "educastration," the teaching that all are either heterosexual or homosexual (Firestone, *The Dialectic of Sex*, 11; Mieli, *Towards a Gay Communism*, 5). I am grateful to Mandy Merck for her suggestion of the parallels between Eisenstein's and Firestone's uses of bisexuality. I develop Mieli's ideas further in my critique of responses to *Call Me by Your Name* (2017), "Call Me Bi Any Other Name."

76 Quoted in Ivanov, *Ocherki po istorii semiotiki v SSSR*, 113–14, quoted and translated in Salazkina, *In Excess*, 126.

77 This aspect of sexuality served, for Eisenstein, a primary means of mobilizing dialectics: "Bisexual conflict, *le plus saillant* [the most prominent] in a subject becomes . . . the main mechanism for the realization of a [dialectical] phenomenon." *Metod*, 495, quoted and translated in Salazkina, *In Excess*, 129.

78 Eisenstein, "'Shift' to the Biological Level," 17. For N. M. Lary, Eisenstein's reading of *L'Âge de Juliette* underscores these characters' having "rediscovered the bisexuality of our ontogenetic being" ("Eisenstein and Shakespeare," 141). The term *ontogenesis* is key here, as it situates a conception of sexuality as a process of becoming, a horizon of possibility. That this changing of clothes might indicate or agitate such a process speaks to Eisenstein's contention that the artistic representation of sexual mutability reminds us of both gender's and desire's plasticity. This phenomenon is observable in disparate moments across film history. From early cinema's cross-dressing/gender-shifting drama *A Florida Enchantment* (Sidney Drew, 1914), to Marlene Dietrich's renowned stage act in *Morocco* (Josef von Sternberg, 1930), to François Ozon's subversive short *A Summer Dress* (1996), a transgression of gender occurs in tandem with a transgression of monosexuality. The mutability of gender and sexuality come into view at once.

79 Eisenstein, *Diary*, 139, quoted and translated in Bulgakowa, "Sergei Eisenstein's System Thinking," 93.

80   I am thinking in particular of, first, Cáel M. Keegan's discussion of the trans media object as that which "cultivate[s] trans consciousness by offering an aesthetic space in which the subject might feel a way forward through the closed phenomenological horizon of binary gender." In the space of bisexual film and media studies, I am thinking of Maria San Filippo's discussion of "missed moments" in which bisexual meaning accrues. Keegan, "Revisitation," 27; San Filippo, *The B Word*, 15.

81   Mulvey, "Afterthoughts on 'Visual Pleasure and Narrative Cinema,'" 13.

82   Steinbock, "Towards Trans Cinema." Cf. Teresa de Lauretis's positioning of the female spectator "between the look of the camera and the image on the screen" as "double identification" (*Alice Doesn't*, 69, 143–44).

83   Laplanche and Pontalis, "Fantasy and the Origins of Sexuality," 17.

84   Cowie, "Fantasia," 87.

85   Cowie, "Elizabeth Cowie," 129 et seq.; Bergstrom, "Enunciation and Sexual Difference," 58; Clover, *Men, Women, and Chainsaws*, 215–16; Hansen, "Pleasure, Ambivalence, Identification," 13; Modleski, *Women Who Knew Too Much*, 5; Morse, "Margaret Morse," 246; Studlar, *In the Realm of Pleasure*, 32–35; L. Williams, *Hard Core*, 206; L. Williams, "Film Bodies," 8.

86   Cowie, "Elizabeth Cowie," 131.

87   Bazin, "Marginal Notes on Eroticism," 174.

88   Stacey, "Desperately Seeking Difference," 61.

89   Pramaggiore, "Straddling the Screen," 282.

90   San Filippo, *The B Word*, 18.

91   For a fuller account of the deployments of bisexuality in theoretical writing on spectatorship, and suggestions as to its development specifically in relation to pornographic spectatorship, see my article "Bisexual and Transgender Potentialities."

92   Udis-Kessler, "Identity/Politics."

93   ACT UP New York, "NBC Protest." Jack Bradigan Spula, from the Rochester Bisexual Men's Network, penned a critique of the *Midnight Caller* episode in "'Midnight Caller' Episode."

94   *New Line Presentations*, n.p., 1975, box 1, Robert Shaye–New Line Cinema Papers 1958–2008 (inclusive), University of Michigan Special Collections Library.

95   As cited in Herbert, *Maverick Movies*, 40.

96   *New Line Presentations*, n.p.

97   Russo, *The Celluloid Closet*, 249.

98   Borah, "Media Effects Theory."

99   S. Hall, "The Work of Representation"; Dyer, *The Matter of Images*.

100 Bryant, *Bisexual Characters in Film*; Bryant, "Stereotyping Bisexual Men in Film"; Bryant, "Is That Me up There?"; Vicari, *Male Bisexuality in Current Cinema*; J. D. White, "Bisexuals Who Kill"; Martinez, "11 Bisexual Tropes"; Rude, "9 Bisexual TV and Film Characters"; TV Tropes, "Depraved Bisexual." See also Brown et al., "Crimes of Duplicity."

101 I should note, however, that not all bisexual writing that discusses tropes and stereotypes necessarily leads to media-effects-informed conclusions. These concepts

are discussed by B. C. Roberts and Maria San Filippo, for instance, in ways that attend to questions of plot, narrative, and genre. Roberts, "Neither Fish nor Fowl"; San Fillipo, *The B Word*.

102 B. C. Roberts critiques this tendency, whereby "bi critics inadvertently attribute to [film images] a truth-value that belongs as much to the properties of the medium as to the content of the film" ("Muddy Waters," 334).

103 Spivak, "Can the Subaltern Speak?," 278–79. Spivak is drawing on Karl Marx's use of these terms in *The Eighteenth Brumaire of Louis Bonaparte*.

104 Keeling, *The Witch's Flight*, 41; Chow, "A Phantom Discipline."

105 Eisner, *Bi*, 42.

106 *Respectability politics* is a term coined by Evelyn Brooks Higginbotham to describe strategies of assimilation and reform in Black American politics (*Righteous Discontent*, 187). It has since enjoyed use beyond this context.

107 Eadie, "'That's Why She Is Bisexual,'" 143.

108 Keegan, "On the Necessity of Bad Trans Objects," 36.

109 Keegan is drawing upon Eliza Steinbock's equally expository work that interrogates the problematic of visual representations of transness being most intelligible "when set against an ambient background consisting of gender normative conditions." Steinbock, "Wavering Line of Foreground and Background," 171.

110 Keegan, "On the Necessity of Bad Trans Objects," 29.

111 For the discussion of *Tootsie*, see Keegan, "On the Necessity of Bad Trans Objects," 29–31; for the discussion of *The Silence of the Lambs*, see Keegan, "In Praise of the Bad Transgender Object."

112 For more on sites of solidarity between bisexuality and transness, see Nagle, "Framing Radical Bisexuality"; du Plessis, "Blatantly Bisexual"; Prosser and Storr, "Part III"; Hemmings, *Bisexual Spaces*, 99–144; Meyer, "Looking Toward the InterSEXions"; Serano, *Excluded*, 81–98.

113 The following sentences paraphrase arguments from Eisner, *Bi*, 239–45.

114 D. E. Hall, "BI-ntroduction II," 9.

115 Ochs, "Why We Need to 'Get Bi,'" 172.

116 Pramaggiore, "Straddling the Screen," 276.

117 San Filippo, "The Politics of Fluidity," 71.

118 Here, I am thinking in particular of the work of Ferdinand de Saussure and his insistence that "the sign must be studied as a social phenomenon" (*Course in General Linguistics*, 16§34).

119 Needham, *Brokeback Mountain*, 47.

120 San Filippo, *The B Word*, 168, 176.

121 This practice is characteristic of what Martin Heidegger terms "hermeneutic violence," explicated by John D. Caputo as "pushing back against the pressure of received readings . . . desedimentation, stirring up the sedimented forms a tradition has taken." Heidegger, *Being and Time*, 298, §311; Caputo, *Hermeneutics*, 54.

122 Gadamer, *Truth and Method*, 280; Gadamer, *Warheit und Methode*, 252. Joel Weinsheimer and Donald G. Marshall's translation is "being pulled up short," but I am grateful to Sarah Liewehr and Alasdair Cameron for their suggestions, which I have also used.

123　Gadamer, *Truth and Method*, 280.

124　Jordan, "A New Politics of Sexuality," 13.

125　Barthes, *S/Z*, 77. Here, I am inspired by Cynthia Weber's use of Barthes's logoi to discuss sexual epistemology in *Queer International Relations*.

126　Barthes, *S/Z*, 77.

127　Barthes, *S/Z*, 77.

128　Barthes, *S/Z*, 77 (emphasis removed). See also Jo Eadie's bisexual reading of Barthes's articulation of connotation (also in *S/Z*) ("Indigestion," 78–80).

129　San Filippo, "The Politics of Fluidity," 78.

130　Alexander Doty stipulates a critical approach to film bisexuality as involving a resistance to "thinking monosexually"; Maria San Filippo, in a similar vein, encourages the film analyst to be attentive to the "missed moments" in which bisexual meaning accumulates. My articulation of a bisexual hermeneutic expands upon these approaches, but with a particular focus on the centrality of interpretation— and its being frustrated—for bisexual meaning-making. Doty, *Flaming Classics*, 136; San Filippo, *The B Word*, 15.

131　Lyotard, *Discourse, Figure*, 7. For Lyotard's discussion of film, see 268–76.

132　Vidal, *Figuring the Past*, 39, 41–42.

133　This approach to filmic figures echoes that of Jacques Aumont, for whom the figure traces the operations of tropes, metaphors, metonymies, and synecdoches on film. Aumont, *The Image*, 191–92.

134　"Conceptually," Michael du Plessis writes, "the bisexual can then only be an antisubject" ("Blatantly Bisexual," 35). Further, bisexuality's embrace of the mutability of desire challenges any notions of sexual identity as stable, even in bisexuality itself. As Judith Butler reminds us, "The very meaning and lived experience of bisexuality can also shift through time" (*Undoing Gender*, 80).

135　See Althusser, *Lenin and Philosophy*, 119.

136　Haraway, *When Species Meet*, 4.

137　Haraway, "Introduction," 1. Kathrin Thiele stresses how Haraway's figures "make us aware of a concrete problem; they are material-semiotic creatures that help us sense the world . . . differently" ("Figuration and/as Critique," 231).

138　These expansive dimensions of the cinematic figure speak to Luc Vancheri's assertion that "cinematic figuration is born truly when bodies set out in search of escaping their characters' fiction, when their figurative reality ceases to be their only filmic reality" (*Les Pensées figurales de l'image*, 16 [my translation]).

139　Haraway, personal communication, June 23, 2022.

140　Farajajé, "Fictions of Purity," 147.

141　Lacan, "The Paradox of *Jouissance*," 177.

142　Foucault, "A Preface to Transgression," 35.

143　Foucault, "A Preface to Transgression," 35.

144　Bataille, *The Accursed Share*, 124. Marjorie Garber echoes Bataille's words half a century later, in the context of bisexual cultural criticism, with her postulation that "eroticism and desire are always to some degree transgressive" (*Vice Versa*, 31).

145　Dean, "The Erotics of Transgression," 68.

146　Hemmings, *Bisexual Spaces*, 6.

147   Hemmings, *Bisexual Spaces*, 197.
148   See also Sharon Morris and Merl Storr's critique of bisexual transgression "Bisexual Theory," 2.
149   Foucault, "A Preface to Transgression," 35.
150   Dollimore, *Sexual Dissidence*, 121. Elsewhere, Dollimore warns against conceptualizing bisexual transgression as that which can change the social order. Dollimore, "Bisexuality, Heterosexuality, and Wishful Theory," 526–27.
151   Dollimore, *Sexual Dissidence*, 121.
152   Dean, "The Erotics of Transgression," 78.
153   F. Klein, *The Bisexual Option*, 7.
154   Hemmings, "Resituating the Bisexual Body," 130.
155   Mezey, "Response," 1102.
156   San Filippo, *The B Word*, 41.
157   San Filippo, *The B Word*, 53, 42, 96.
158   Eadie, "'That's Why She Is Bisexual,'" 142.
159   Däumer, "Queer Ethics," 103.

1. THE LES(BI)AN VAMPIRE'S CARNAL STAKES

1   San Filippo, *The B Word*, 118; Lacan, "The Mirror Stage," 3–9.
2   Hemmings, "Resituating the Bisexual Body," 129.
3   Weinstock, *The Vampire Film*, 21.
4   Krafft-Ebing, *Psychopathia Sexualis*, 162–63.
5   See Rigby, "'Prey to Some Cureless Disquiet.'"
6   Mariam Wassif calls *The Vampyre*'s Ruthven "a portrait of Byron's portraits," a reflection of fantastical cultural depictions of Byron ("Polidori's *The Vampyre*," 53). We might also consider the connection between Bram Stoker and Oscar Wilde insofar as it relates to the novel *Dracula*. See Schaffer, "'A Wilde Desire Took Me.'"
7   There are some examples of more minor male vampire characters presented through codes of queerness: for instance, the dandyish vampire Herbert (Iain Quarrier) of the British bawdy horror film *The Fearless Vampire Killers* (Roman Polanski, 1967) and Vampire Roman (Vladimír Marek) of the Czech fantasy-horror film *The Vampire Wedding* (Jaroslav Soukup, 1993), who is presented through codes of male drag.
8   Hanson, "Lesbians Who Bite," 184.
9   A. Weiss, "The Lesbian Vampire Film," 22.
10   In this sense, I agree with Nicole Richter that "in the case of vampire theory, a bisexual perspective is better suited to account for the fluid, polymorphous desire that is central to the genre" ("Bisexual Erasure," 279). On this point, we are in agreement, but I am less convinced of the utility of notions of bisexual erasure and appropriation without representation, of which this article makes use, to guide bisexual approaches to vampire film. Maria San Filippo also critiques how these vampires have been "staked off . . . as lesbian" in a way that forgets their "unmistakable sexual significations" ("(Re)Constructing Bisexual Space," 143).

11   While all these examples are from American and European contexts, female vam-
     pires that might be understood as queer are also discernible in non-Western cin-
     emas beyond the scope of this project.

12   James Craig Holte outlines some of the religious, mythical, and literary traditions
     out of which the female vampire emerges in "Not All Fangs Are Phallic" (163–65).
     Drawing on the research of Robert Eighteen-Bisang and Elizabeth Miller, Rosalind
     Galt suggests the high plausibility of Bram Stoker being influenced by colonial an-
     thropological accounts of the Malay pontianak. Galt, *Alluring Monsters*, 5–9; Stoker,
     Bram Stoker's Notes for Dracula.

13   These accusations were made in a letter from György Thurzó, the palatine of Hun-
     gary, to Matthias, the king of Hungary (Thorne, *Countess Dracula*, 167). The ques-
     tion as to Countess Báthory's guilt, however, is the subject of historical debate.

14   Turóczi, *Ungaria Suis cum Regibus*, quoted in and translated by Thorne, *Countess Drac-
     ula*, 204.

15   Le Fanu, *Carmilla*, 40.

16   In the European context, the liberalization of censorship codes can be observed
     across the 1960s, to differing degrees, in Belgium, Denmark, France, Greece, Italy,
     the Netherlands, Sweden, and West Germany.

17   These prohibitions obviously did not exist in the hardcore vampire films that
     emerged during this period, which include *The Mad Love Life of a Hot Vampire* (Ray
     Dennis Steckler, 1971), *Sexcula* (John Holbrook, 1974), and *Dracula Sucks* (Philip Mar-
     shak, 1978).

18   The corpus I have in mind comprises *Whirlpool* (1970), *Deviation* (1971), *The Uncertain
     Death* (1973), *The House That Vanished* (1973), *Emma, Dark Doors* (1974), and *Symptoms*
     (1974). Female bisexuality is portrayed in *Whirlpool, Deviation, Emma, Dark Doors*, and
     Symptoms.

19   Larraz's *Symptoms* in fact competed for the Grand Prix at the 1974 Cannes Film Festival.

20   Larraz in "Archival Interview with José Larraz." Owen's short stories have been un-
     derstood within the French tradition of *le fantastique*, coined by Tzvetan Todorov
     to describe works of literature in which the supernatural intrudes within a realist
     narrative. See Todorov, *Introduction à la littérature fantastique*.

21   Vaines, "On Doing the Unexpected," 87.

22   While the Motion Picture Association of America (MPAA)—the United States' film
     censorship and certification board—used the X rating, it was not trademarked by
     them like their other ratings. A distributor was therefore at liberty to self-impose
     an X rating without the MPAA's approval, as was the case with Cambist's distribu-
     tion of *Vampyres*. Dwyer, "Censorship," 32.

23   Fallows, "'More than Rutting Bodies,'" 87.

24   This organization's name was changed to the British Board of Film Classification in
     the mid-1980s.

25   Greaves, *Vampyres*, 44; British Board of Film Censors, *Exception Form No. 20942*.

26   British Board of Film Censors, *Vampyres* letter.

27   *Video Watchdog* 63 (2000): 70. Fox-Rank ultimately decided on a relatively limited
     distribution strategy, releasing the film as a somewhat ill-fitting double bill with

The *Devil's Rain* (Robert Fuest, 1975), an American B movie capitalizing on the inchoate Satanic panic.

28   Eadie, "Activating Bisexuality," 161.

29   A. Weiss, *Vampires and Violets*, 84.

30   Gorfinkel, *Lewd Looks*, 179.

31   A. Weiss, *Vampires and Violets*, 90; Holte, "Not All Fangs Are Phallic," 166.

32   For instance, this term is deployed in Guerrero-Pica et al., "Killing of Lexa."

33   Pramaggiore, "Straddling the Screen," 291.

34   McKenzie Wark describes being in this position as feeling "vaulted," a word that chimes with this moment in *Vampyres* in its metaphorization of the penis as a supportive or propelling apparatus in the service of its user's leap (*Reverse Cowgirl*, 169).

35   James Craig Holte identifies Lilith as a cultural influence on the female vampire ("The Vampire," 244).

36   "The Alphabet of Ben Sira," 183–84.

37   Zemon Davis, "Women on Top"; Koedt, "Myth of the Vaginal Orgasm."

38   Zimmerman, "Daughters of Darkness," 23.

39   A. Weiss, *Vampires and Violets*, 90.

40   Zimmerman, "Daughters of Darkness," 23.

41   Auerbach, *Our Vampires, Ourselves*, 149–50.

42   Comella, *Vibrator Nation*, 5.

43   Zimmerman, "Daughters of Darkness," 23; Heller-Nicholas, "Seductive Kindness," 215.

44   Larraz quoted in Greaves, *Vampyres*, 23.

45   Eadie, "'That's Why She Is Bisexual,'" 151.

46   For a fascinating exploration of *Dracula Sucks*, and other hardcore vampire films, see Marks, "I Want to Suck Your . . ."

47   Creed, *The Monstrous-Feminine*, 70.

48   L. Williams, "When the Woman Looks," 65.

49   Adamczak, "On Circlusion."

50   San Filippo, *The B Word*, 115.

51   Krzywinska, "La Belle Dame sans Merci?," 104.

52   Eisenstein, *Disney*, 15.

53   Craft, "'Kiss Me with Those Red Lips,'" 109.

54   J. Butler, *Undoing Gender*, 48. This point recalls Sandy Stone's reading of the vampire Lestat from Anne Rice's vampire novels, about whom, she writes: "He sees people trapped, stuck in their particular gender positions, in their particular subjectivities, not able to make the jump to seeing subject position as a boat that's momentarily at anchor, but that can actually move through a sea of possible subject positions." Sandy Stone, "What Vampires Know: Transsubjection and Transgender in Cyberspace," paper presented at In Control: Mensch-Interface-Maschine, Kunsthaus, Graz, Austria, May 1993, https://sandystone.com/pupik/eyes-of-the-vampire, archived August 19, 2022, at https://perma.cc/KB5R-N3PV.

55   This is a sexual-corporeal realignment that evokes Michel Foucault's description of "physical practices . . . that one might call devirilized, nay desexuated . . . extraordinary fabrications of pleasure" ("Le Gai Savoir," 34 [my translation]).

56 Connor, "Integuments," 52.

57 Foucault, "A Preface to Transgression," 34.

58 Brinkema, *Life-Destroying Diagrams*, 271.

59 Brinkema, *Life-Destroying Diagrams*, 272.

60 Although she is discussing necrophilia, Patricia MacCormack explores instances of sex with wounds and viscera on film through Gilles Deleuze and Félix Guattari's concept of the Body without Organs in her work "Necrosexuality."

61 Adams, "Cars and Scars," 62.

62 Adams, "Cars and Scars," 60.

63 Andreas-Salomé, "'Anal' and 'Sexual,'" 28.

64 I am thinking, first, of Jules Gill-Peterson's theorization of racialized and trans embodiment as technical capacities inherent to the body ("Technical Capacities of the Body"). Second, I am thinking of Marquis Bey's description of the *they* pronoun as "a refutation of immutable ontologization" (*Cistem Failure*, 58). Third, I am thinking of David A. Rubin's genealogy of intersex gender in *Intersex Matters* (21–48).

65 Hayward, "Lessons from a Starfish," 255.

66 See Riki Wilchins's response to Andrea Long Chu's assertion ("My New Vagina Won't Make Me Happy") of her body's regard of her vagina as a wound in "A New Vagina Didn't Make Her Sad."

67 Adams, "Cars and Scars," 70.

68 This abstraction speaks to Jean-Luc Nancy's observation that gender's stability is, in fact, disturbed by the sex act: "Gender is troubled not only because the stability of sex and gender assignments has been shaken but also because this shaking bears witness to a trouble inherent to sex—non-'gendered' sex, one might dare say" (*Sexistence*, 74).

69 Doane, *Femmes Fatales*, 1.

70 Doane, *Femmes Fatales*, 46.

71 Galt, *Pretty*, 249.

72 Galt, *Pretty*, 250–51.

73 Haraway, *Modest_Witness*, 179.

74 Bazin, "Ontology of the Photographic Image," 13.

75 J. Butler, *Gender Trouble*, 30.

76 Wittig, "The Straight Mind," 110.

77 J. Butler, *Gender Trouble*.

78 Larraz quoted in Greaves, *Vampyres*, 19. The voices of Morris and Dziubinska were, in fact, dubbed in postproduction, in part because of Larraz's dissatisfaction with the actors' delivery of dialogue.

79 Morris in "'By This Sign, I'll Recognise You. . . .'" Morris had previously appeared in *Corruption* (Robert Hartford-Davis, 1968), *Lovebox* (Tudor Gates and Wilbur Stark, 1972), *Just One More Time* (Maurice Hamblin, 1974), and *It's Not the Size That Counts* (Ralph Thomas, 1974).

80 Brode, *Deadlier than the Male*, 174; Fisons, "What's a Nice Girl like You Doing in a Firm like This?," 7; *Playboy*, August 1972; *Playboy*, May 1973. Prior to *Vampyres*, Dziubinska turned down the role of O in Just Jaeckin's *The Story of O* (1975); she later would appear in Ken Russell's *Lisztomania* (1975).

81　Midwinter dressed some of British 1970s exploitation cinema's most striking female screen villains, including Vanessa Howard in *Girly* (Freddie Francis, 1970) and
Adrienne Cori in *Madhouse* (Jim Clark, 1974).

82　Caws, "What to Wear in a Vampire Film," 47.

83　In "Unhappy Camper," Sally Faulkner, who portrays Harriet, remembers her character's "very unattractive beanie hat . . . very ordinary simple clothes; they probably got them from a charity shop."

84　Caws, "What to Wear in a Vampire Film," 47.

85　Wilson, "A Note on Glamour," 96, 99, 100, 105.

86　Wilson, "A Note on Glamour," 99.

87　Doane, *Femmes Fatales*, 3.

88　Larraz quoted in Greaves, *Vampyres*, 27.

89　A. Weiss, *Vampires and Violets*, 90–91.

90　A. Weiss, *Vampires and Violets*, 106.

91　Weiss takes this dichotomy a step further, arguing that these facets of the les(bi)an
vampire also render her sexually undesirable for lesbian spectators. The questionable assumption here is that images made by and intended to be viewed by heterosexual men are unable to be arousing for queer women.

92　J. Butler, afterword, 228.

93　Whatling, "Femme to Femme," 74–75.

94　A. Weiss, *Vampires and Violets*, 91.

95　Hemmings, "Waiting for No Man," 96.

96　While there are Black female vampires in 1970s Blaxploitation vampire films,
queerness tends not to be part of their figuration.

97　Dyer, *White*, 210. Dyer reads the vampire film as both a vivid conveyance of whiteness's
hunger for control and capacity for causing death and a disavowal of this very link.

98　Haraway, *Modest_Witness*, 214.

99　*Mayfair*, October 1976, 44; Morris in "By This Sign, I'll Recognise You . . ."

100　San Filippo, *The B Word*, 41.

101　Tohill and Tombs, *Immoral Tales*, 194.

102　Tohill and Tombs, *Immoral Tales*, 194; Shipka, *Perverse Titillation*, 253.

103　Malchow, *Gothic Images of Race*, 149–53.

104　Hudson, *Vampires, Race, and Transnational Hollywoods*, 104.

105　H. L. Malchow discusses "the Jew" as a male figure, and the Hollywood vampires
to which Hudson is referring are also male, his main example being Bela Lugosi in
Dracula (Tod Browning, 1931).

106　Krobb, "'La Belle Juive.'"

107　Boyarin et al., "Strange Bedfellows," 5.

108　Le Fanu, *Carmilla*, 26.

109　Le Fanu, *Carmilla*, 18.

110　Hoad, "Arrested Development," 135.

111　Hoad, "Arrested Development," 136–40.

112　Burton, "Terminal Essay," 207. Burton's euphemism "the vice" is first introduced
as "le vice contre nature" (the vice against nature). Although this phrase is directly

followed by the provocation "as if anything can be contrary to nature which includes all things," Burton positions himself as morally opposed to "the vice," calling it "a great and growing evil deadly to the birth-rate" (204).

113 Burton, "Terminal Essay," 207.

114 Burton, "Terminal Essay," 208.

115 Burton, "Terminal Essay," 238.

116 Similar articulations of so-called primitive bisexuality would go on to inform the fin-de-siècle sexology of Richard von Krafft-Ebing and Havelock Ellis, wherein, Merl Storr argues, bisexuality is conceptualized as "an original physical state . . . phylogenetically, as a primitive state of 'species'" ("Sexual Reproduction of 'Race,'" 84; Storr is discussing Krafft-Ebing, *Psyhopathia Sexualis*; Ellis, *Studies in the Psychology of Sex*). Later in the early twentieth century, English social reformer Edward Carpenter would argue that the sexual "customs" observable among "primitive folk" were not "homosexuality" per se but "variations in sex temperament from the normal" (*Intermediate Types*, 171).

117 Darwin's previous success, *On the Origin of Species*, concentrates predominantly on nonhuman animals and plants.

118 Darwin, *The Descent of Man*, 372.

119 Burton, "Terminal Essay," 181. These are Burton's unique spellings of *fricatrices* and *rubsters*, both of which denote tribadism, a sexual activity between women.

120 Horace, "Epistle XIX," 46; Reynolds, *The Sappho Companion*, 72–73; Burton, "Terminal Essay," 181n1.

121 *Oxford English Dictionary*, s.v. "fricatrice," revised June 2018, https://doi.org/10.1093/OED/7630671001.

122 In *Carmilla*, Laura describes the vampire as having an "amphibious existence," a term that might recall the "amphigenic invert" Sigmund Freud theorizes three decades later, in whom "sexual objects may equally well be of their own or of the opposite sex." Both terms use the Greek prefix *amphi-* (on both sides, of both types) to delineate the capacity to transcend a binary taxonomy. Le Fanu, *Carmilla*, 72; Freud, "Three Essays," 136.

123 Bradley, *Anteaesthetics*, 214. Bradley's analysis is part of a wider account of the simultaneous vestibularity and subjection of Black aesthesis to the aesthetics and metaphysics of the anti-Black world.

124 BBC News, "1973."

125 F. Klein, *The Bisexual Option*; Hemmings "Resituating the Bisexual Body." The case of Ethel "Bunty" Gee, a British woman who spied for the Soviet Union, would have been fresh in viewers' minds following her much-publicized release from prison in 1970.

126 Angelides, *A History of Bisexuality*, 72–73.

127 The house used for exterior footage was the Victorian Gothic country house Oakley Court in Berkshire; the interiors were shot in Harefield Grove, an early nineteenth-century country house in the London borough of Hillingdon (Pykett, *British Horror Film Locations*, 167; Greaves, *Vampyres*, 12; British Listed Buildings, "Harefield Grove"). Oakley Court was a prized location for British camp horror

films, including *The Old Dark House* (William Castle, 1963), *And Now the Screaming Starts!* (Roy Ward Baker, 1973), and *The Rocky Horror Picture Show* (Jim Sharman, 1975).

128 Southerton et al., "Social Worlds of Caravaning," para. 3.2.

129 This moment might be understood as an instance of mise en abyme, in which the caravan window's frame mirrors that of the cinematic screen and, accordingly, Harriet's dangerous fascination mirrors a spectator's own.

130 P. White, "Female Spectator, Lesbian Specter," 142; Castle, *The Apparitional Lesbian*, 2.

131 Merck, "Figuring Out Andy Warhol," 233; Castle, *The Apparitional Lesbian*, 60-62.

132 Hemmings, "Resituating the Bisexual Body," 129-30.

133 Hemmings, *Bisexual Spaces*, 1.

134 Merleau-Ponty, *Phenomenology of Perception*, 284.

135 Ahmed, *Queer Phenomenology*, 21.

136 Hemmings, "Locating Bisexual Identities," 52 (emphasis removed).

137 Balázs, "Visible Man," 72.

138 This point is echoed by Rosemary Jackson, for whom "the act of vampirism is the most violent and extreme attempt to negate, or reverse, the subject's insertion into the symbolic" (*Fantasy*, 120).

139 San Filippo, *The B Word*, 15.

140 Case, "Tracking the Vampire," 15.

141 Deleuze and Guattari, *A Thousand Plateaus*, 241-42. For a compelling reading of the bisexual vampire in relation to Deleuze and Guattari's Body without Organs, see Woo, "Queer Vampiric Desire."

2. TREACHERY IN LESBIAN CINEMA

1 The filmmakers were active in lesbian feminist politics and conceived of the film as an expression of this involvement, a subversion of the vampire genre, and a deconstruction of patriarchal film production. Zachary Nataf, email message to author, January 26, 2020; Bruna Fionda, email message to author, January 2, 2020.

2 Lillia's bisexual desires are conveyed in the film's opening sequence, when her companion Luke (Jeremy Peters) remarks: "I take men and women, as you do; the two equally satisfy my needs."

3 See Chu, "The Impossibility of Feminism."

4 Bruna Fionda, email message to author, January 2, 2020. Nataf reflects on this aspect of the film: "I was grappling with the reality of bisexual identity. . . . I think that representing a bisexual woman in the lesbian community was actually quite radical at the time!" Zachary Nataf, email message to author, January 26, 2020.

5 See Rich, *Chick Flicks*, 29-31.

6 Samer, "Lesbian Feminist Cinema's Archive," 98.

7 While lesbian cinema can often be seen as responding to feminist film theory at this time, lesbian approaches to film were not prioritized in feminist film theory in a comparative fashion. See de Lauretis, *Technologies of Gender*, 138-39; Mayne, *Framed*, xvi-xix.

8 S. Smith, "Image of Women in Film"; Mulvey, "Visual Pleasure and Narrative Cinema." Clare Johnston critiques this position, arguing that while realist

narrative cinema has tended to reproduce iconic images of women that lack differentiation, we cannot necessarily surmise that avant-garde or documentary film is more amenable to feminist intervention ("Women's Cinema as Counter-Cinema").

9   Kuhn, *Women's Pictures*, 136.
10 Dyer, "Gays in Film," 15.
11 Becker et al., "Lesbians and Film," 37.
12 McLaughlin in "Interview with Sheila McLaughlin."
13 Becker et al., "Lesbians and Film," 36.
14 Villarejo, *Lesbian Rule*, 191.
15 Villarejo, *Lesbian Rule*, 6–7.
16 Samer, *Lesbian Potentiality and Feminist Media*, 3.
17 For an extensive sociological account of this phenomenon in the United States, see Rust, *Bisexuality and the Challenge to Lesbian Politics*.
18 Morgan, "Lesbianism and Feminism," 34. From the publication of Morgan's speech in *The Lesbian Tide*.
19 Ault, "Hegemonic Discourse in an Oppositional Community"; Ault, "Ambiguous Identity"; S.-D. Stone, "Bisexual Women."
20 Hoagland, *Lesbian Ethics*, 198.
21 Däumer, "Queer Ethics," 103.
22 Faderman, "A Bisexual Moment," 43.
23 Armstrong, "Traitors to the Cause?," 201.
24 See Clausen, "My Interesting Condition."
25 Finkler, "Lesbians Who Sleep with Men," 4.
26 Jeffreys, "Bisexual Politics," 283.
27 Murphy, *Are You Girls Traveling Alone?*, 39. Amia Srinivasan outlines how this articulation of lesbian feminism considers sex with men "an eroticisation of gender inequality . . . from which there can be no true liberation without a revolution in relations between men and women" (*The Right to Sex*, 36).
28 The term *false consciousness* is often misattributed to Karl Marx. It was, in fact, coined by Friedrich Engels and theorized most extensively by György Lukács. Engels, "Letter to F. Mehring"; Lukács, *History and Class Consciousness*.
29 Weise, introduction, xii.
30 J. Johnston, *Lesbian Nation*, 179–80.
31 Ulmschneider, "Bisexuality," 2.
32 S.-D. Stone, "Bisexual Women," 107.
33 Gutter Dyke Collective, "Over the Walls," 27.
34 Murphy, "Thinking About Bisexuality," 88.
35 Murphy, "Thinking About Bisexuality," 87.
36 Murphy, "Thinking About Bisexuality," 88.
37 Hemmings, "Resituating the Bisexual Body," 130–31.
38 C.L.I.T. Collective, "C.L.I.T. Statement No. 2," 363.
39 In her reading of *The Potluck*, Valerie Smith finds that "the explicit coding of the racial and sexual identities of Dunye's characters is not contingent upon their ability to pass one kind of litmus test or another" (*Not Just Race, Not Just Gender*, 110).

In this sense, Dunye's film can be understood as opening up spaces that resist the reification of stable racial and sexual identities.

40 The period between the 1970s and the 1990s also saw transgressive figurations of female bisexuality outside of lesbian feminist cinema; first, in a number of European art films directed by women: Nouchka van Brakel's *A Woman like Eve* (1979) in the Netherlands, Nelly Kaplan's *A Young Emmanuelle* (1976) and Diane Kurys's *Entre Nous* (1983) in France, Lina Wertmüller's *Softly . . . Softly* (1984) in Italy, and Alexandra von Grote's *November Moon* (1985) in West Germany. In Hollywood at this time, there were also notable engagements with female bisexuality, including Robert Towne's *Personal Best* (1982), John Sayles's *Lianna* (1983), and Mike Nichols's *Silkwood* (1983). These films were box office successes and were received with varying levels of enthusiasm among lesbian audiences—*Personal Best* being the most lauded. See Ellsworth, "Illicit Pleasures."

41 Weise, introduction, xi.

42 Ardill and O'Sullivan, "Sex in the Summer of '88," 127.

43 *Pink Paper*, "Opening Up Pandora's Box"; Koller, *Lesbian Discourses*, 82.

44 Ardill and O'Sullivan, "Sex in the Summer of '88," 128.

45 Smyth, *Lesbians Talk Queer Notions*, 40.

46 Andermatt, "There Were Troubling Events . . ."

47 Wilton, "Introduction," xxix; Healey, *Lesbian Sex Wars*, 115–16.

48 Healey, *Lesbian Sex Wars*, 116.

49 Germane to this heated reception context is the status of bisexuality in contemporary British gay and lesbian politics. Martha Robinson Rhodes reflects on the "unfortunate irony that radical [1970s British gay] politics, which often expressed a desire for inclusive alliances . . . were more likely to exclude bisexuals" ("Bisexuality, Multiple-Gender-Attraction," 141). In 1985, three years before the Lesbian Summer School, the London Lesbian and Gay Centre banned bisexual groups. See D. Smith, "Banned."

50 *Artificial Memory* has since been revised into a short film called *Inside Out* (1978). During the 1980s, McLaughlin had a brief career as an actor, appearing in *Ordinary Sentence* (Heinz Emigholz, 1982), *Born in Flames* (Lizzie Borden, 1983), *Committed, Seduction: The Cruel Woman* (Monika Treut, 1985), *The Basis of Make-Up* (Heinz Emigholz, 1985), *The Big Blue* (Andrew Horn, 1988), and *The Meadow of Things* (Heinz Emigholz, 1988).

51 McLaughlin in "Interview with Sheila McLaughlin."

52 Both actors were associated with New York's experimental feminist theater scene. Weaver was active in WOW Café, and Dabney worked with La MaMa Experimental Theatre Club. Rich, *New Queer Cinema*, 8.

53 There is much scholarly debate as to the correct and most respectful way to refer to de Erauso, as they used different names and pronouns throughout their life. This sentence prioritizes the name Antonio, as this was how de Erauso identified toward the end of their life (Vicente, "Trans Visual Narratives"). In reference to Jo's film within *Seeing Things*, however, I will use "Catalina," to reflect the sole usage of this name in the film.

54   Ardill and O'Sullivan, "Sex in the Summer of '88," 128.
55   Raymond, "Putting the Politics Back into Lesbianism," 273; Jeffreys, *Anticlimax*, 5
     (for Jeffreys's comments on *Seeing Things*, see *The Lesbian Revolution*, 126; *Trigger
     Warning*, 141). Two years after *Seeing Things'* release, radical feminist legal scholar
     Catharine A. MacKinnon published an influential article where she offers the
     suggestion: "It may also be that sexuality is so gender marked that it carries domi-
     nance and submission with it, no matter the gender of its participants" ("Sexuality,
     Pornography, and Method," 331).
56   McLaughlin quoted in A. Butler, "'She Must Be Seeing Things,'" 21–22.
57   De Lauretis, "Film and the Visible," 240.
58   *Pink Paper*, "Opening Up," 13.
59   Gorham, "Our Standards Should Be Higher," 15.
60   McLaughlin quoted in A. Butler, "'She Must Be Seeing Things,'" 22.
61   Martin and Lyon, *Lesbian/Woman*, 189.
62   Casetti, "Objects on the Screen," 34. Casetti is drawing on Jean Epstein's suggestion
     that, on film, "objects take on airs. . . . Every prop becomes a character" ("Le Ciné-
     matographe vu de l'Etna," 289).
63   Casetti, "Objects on the Screen," 36.
64   Vidal, *Figuring the Past*, 163.
65   Nussbaum, "Toward Conceptualizing Diary," 135.
66   Hogan quoting Bunkers, "Reading and Interpreting Unpublished Diaries," 15, in
     Hogan, "Engendered Autobiographies," 97–98. Nussbaum suggests that the diarist
     "imitate[s] human chronology without overt rearrangement, evaluation, or clo-
     sure" ("Toward Conceptualizing Diary," 137).
67   Michel, "Do Bats Eat Cats?," 65.
68   Buse, "40,000 Roses," 44.
69   Buse, "40,000 Roses," 45.
70   Barthes, *Camera Lucida*, 79.
71   The excerpts of the diary's prose to which a viewer is made privy are opaque in
     meaning. There is a recollection of a time when Jo thought she was pregnant with
     a dead baby, a record of a dream that Jo had grown older and was making drawings,
     and laconic sentences expressing wanderlust, anger, and apathy toward men. While
     these entries might be interpreted in different ways (they certainly invite psycho-
     analytic interpretation), this is beyond the scope of my focus. Suffice to say that
     these entries' meanings or import are unclear; in Martha Gever's words, Jo's diary
     "never yield[s] the required clues" ("Girl Crazy," 17).
72   Ahmed quoting de Lauretis, *The Practice of Love*, 300, in Ahmed, *Queer Phenomenol-
     ogy*, 100.
73   Hemmings, *Bisexual Spaces*, 9.
74   Barthes, *Camera Lucida*, 14.
75   Çakırlar and Needham, "The Monogamous/Promiscuous Optics," 419, 406–16;
     Schoonover and Galt, *Queer Cinema in the World*, 267–71.
76   Cavell, *The World Viewed*, 24.
77   De Lauretis, "Film and the Visible," 225.

78 Gadamer, *Truth and Method*, 283.
79 Ault, "Hegemonic Discourse in an Oppositional Community," 212.
80 San Filippo, *The B Word*, 21.
81 Doane, *The Desire to Desire*, 124, 126.
82 There is a similarity here with Deborah Linderman's assertion that in *Vertigo*, "the spectator is deliberately set up as an agent of misrecognition." We might also recall Tania Modleski's identification of "Hitchcock's preoccupation with female bisexuality" and Robert Samuels's thesis that "Hitchcock's films . . . present multiple forms of sexual identification and desire," which suggest bisexuality itself as a mutual point of investment between these works. Linderman, "Mise-en-Abîme in Hitchcock's *Vertigo*," 55; Modleski, *Women Who Knew Too Much*, 8; Samuels, *Hitchcock's Bi-Textuality*, 1.
83 The effectiveness of this sequence's disruption is rooted in its manipulation of visual techniques to effect uncertainty around a spectator's relation to the characters, the characters' relation to one another, and McLaughlin's relation to both her spectators and her characters. The appositeness of a Hitchcockian style for the sequence is signaled by how, as Gilles Deleuze argues, Hitchcock "makes relation itself the object of the image" (*Cinema 1*, 203).
84 Cavell, *The World Viewed*, 85.
85 Rose, "Paranoia and the Film System," 89.
86 Doane, *The Desire to Desire*, 148.
87 This moment also corresponds to what Deleuze outlines as the "implied dream" in cinema, in which "it is no longer the character who reacts to the optical-sound situation, it is a movement of world which supplements the faltering movement of the character" (*Cinema 2*, 59). Deleuze is developing the concept of the implied dream from Michel Devillers, "Rêves informulés."
88 McLaughlin quoted in *Square Peg*, "She Must Be Seeing Things," 35.
89 Onodera, "Camera Obscura for Dreams," 151.
90 San Filippo, "The Politics of Fluidity," 78.
91 Freud, "Draft H. Paranoia," 238 (emphasis removed).
92 Quimby, "*She Must Be Seeing Things* Differently," 193.
93 Freud, "Draft H. Paranoia," 236.
94 De Lauretis, "Film and the Visible," 225.
95 Quimby, "*She Must Be Seeing Things* Differently," 194.
96 Teresa de Lauretis also reads this moment in relation to the primal scene, albeit differently from me, theorizing its relation to lesbian desire ("Film and the Visible," 230–36; *The Practice of Love*, 81–148).
97 Freud, "From the History of an Infantile Neurosis," 39.
98 Quoted in Treasure, "Attempting to Impose an All Flavour Ban," 43.
99 Quoted in Treasure, "Attempting to Impose an All Flavour Ban," 43.
100 Hemmings, "Out of Sight, Out of Mind?," 453.
101 Halberstam, *Female Masculinity*, 176.
102 I am borrowing the term *lesbian verisimilitude* from Elizabeth Ellsworth, who uses it to discuss lesbian spectators' identification of lesbian authenticity in a film. "Illicit Pleasures."

103 As Chris Holmlund articulates: "With the femme, far more than with the butch . . . it is obvious that images can be misleading, and clear that reception and context are key" ("When Is a Lesbian Not a Lesbian?," 148).

104 Bazin, "Ontology of the Photographic Image," 13.

105 Hemmings, "Waiting for No Man," 93.

106 Hemmings, "Waiting for No Man," 93. Chris Holmlund cites a filmic example of this credo in *Personal Best*, where "the moral of this story is: a lesbian, and especially a femme, is *not* a lesbian when there's a man around" ("When Is a Lesbian Not a Lesbian?," 154).

107 Jeffreys, "The Essential Lesbian," 99. For more on the butch-femme debates, see Roof, "1970s Lesbian Feminism."

108 For more on the politics of butch-femme and its relation to the figure of the bisexual woman, see Straayer, *Deviant Eyes, Deviant Bodies*, 271–79.

109 Mulvey, "Visual Pleasure and Narrative Cinema," 18. For a more detailed analysis of the striptease on film, see Doane, *Femmes Fatales*, 99–118.

110 McLaughlin discusses this shift in the scene: "When Jo does her dance in her little baby-doll outfit, the camera starts off with a very 'male' point of view, as she does this traditional sex-strip dance. But it's undermined by the music that she puts on. The image-sound tension makes it into a very weird thing that she's doing, and she makes it absolutely ridiculous" (quoted in A. Butler, "'She Must Be Seeing Things,'" 24).

111 Case, "Towards a Butch-Femme Aesthetic," 70.

112 Hemmings, "Out of Sight, Out of Mind?," 453.

113 De Lauretis, "Film and the Visible," 251.

114 I am grateful to Alasdair Cameron for his elucidation of this opera.

115 Quimby, "*She Must Be Seeing Things* Differently," 193.

116 Sedgwick, *Touching Feeling*, 131 (emphasis removed); M. Klein, "Notes on Some Schizoid Mechanisms."

117 McLaughlin quoted in A. Butler, "'She Must Be Seeing Things,'" 23; Quimby, "*She Must Be Seeing Things* Differently," 193.

118 Quimby, "*She Must Be Seeing Things* Differently," 193.

119 Munt, "The Butch Body," 95.

120 Stacey, "Butch Noir," 33–34. Stacey's discussion of "butch noir" includes examples from theater groups WOW Café and Split Britches, in which both Dabney and Weaver were active, suggesting a creative attention to butchness across the actors' work.

121 Graham et al., "Discussion," 268, 270; Muñoz, "Dead White," 129, 131.

122 Catholicism has played a significant and often contradictory role in Afro-Brazilian history. Most of the Christian Africans who were enslaved in Brazil were Catholic prior to their enslavement, but slavery in Brazil would later use Catholicism's hegemony to enact social domination in what is known as plantation Catholicism. Complicating the picture further is Catholicism's subsequent role in the abolition of slavery in the country. By the twentieth century, Catholicism was practiced by many Afro-Caribbeans, some of whom also incorporated traditions from the Afro-Brazilian religion candomblé syncretically. *Seeing Things'* allusion to a Catholic

Afro-Brazilian heritage thus evokes a dense cultural history in which notions of race, religion, and cultural identity are enmeshed. Selka, "Black Catholicism in Brazil," 288–91; Selka, *Religion and the Politics of Ethnic Identity*, 15–17.

123 Graham et al., "Discussion," 264.

124 McLaughlin quoted in *Square Peg*, "She Must Be Seeing Things," 34.

125 McLaughlin quoted in A. Butler, "'She Must Be Seeing Things,'" 25.

126 Chua, *Deviant Intersections*, 197–98. Chua is partially paraphrasing Tyler, "Desiring Machines?," 154–93.

127 Z. I. Jackson, *Becoming Human*, 10.

128 Z. I. Jackson, *Becoming Human*, 10.

129 Findlay, "Freud's 'Fetishism,'" 563–64.

130 Findlay, "Freud's 'Fetishism,'" 565.

131 Preciado, *Countersexual Manifesto*, 61.

132 Preciado, *Countersexual Manifesto*, 61.

133 In Lynn Comella's interview with Black sex shop founder Nenna Joiner from as late as 2015, Joiner discusses how it is difficult to find "chocolate and caramel colored" dildos and packers at other sex stores (*Vibrator Nation*, 168).

134 Findlay, "Freud's 'Fetishism,'" 574; Reich, "Genderfuck," 121.

135 *Clips, Hungry Hearts*, and *Shadows* were codirected with Nan Kinney.

136 Preciado, *Countersexual Manifesto*, 64. See also Chris Straayer's discussion of the penis and the dildo in *Deviant Eyes, Deviant Bodies*, 262–71, 280–87.

137 See Creed, "Lesbian Bodies," 99.

138 Ault, "Hegemonic Discourse in an Oppositional Community," 204, 212. A similar tendency is observable in some political lesbian arguments that female bisexuality's pervasiveness in the fantasies of heterosexual men is indicative of their lack of social penalization (an argument whose applicability to lesbians is conveniently elided). For an example of such an argument, see Murphy, "Thinking About Bisexuality," 88.

139 Preciado, *Countersexual Manifesto*, 71. Although I am purposely orienting my discussion away from psychoanalytic conceptions of the phallus, Judith Butler's consideration of the lesbian phallus is pertinent to these discussions. They outline how the incorporation of phallic symbols into lesbian eroticism undoes the phallus's conventional (heterosexual) mode of signification precisely *through* the phallus's resignification (*Bodies That Matter*, 55).

140 Preciado, *Countersexual Manifesto*, 9–10.

141 J. Butler, "Gender as Performance," 34.

142 De Lauretis, "Film and the Visible," 240.

143 Klotz, "Queer and Unqueer Spaces of Monika Treut's Films," 75.

144 Chris Straayer writes of *Virgin Machine*: "Many scenes . . . collapse male-female and hetero-homo dualities within the more accommodating category of inventive pleasure-seekers" (*Deviant Eyes, Deviant Bodies*, 38).

145 Uncited review of *My Father Is Coming* in the *Village Voice*, quoted in Schwartzberg, "Treut Films the Outer Edges of Sexuality," n.p.

146 Another filmmaker who can be considered within this framework is Lizzie Borden, a bisexual director whose *Working Girls* (1986) depicts a woman (Louise Smith) in a

relationship with another woman (Amanda Goodwin) while engaging in sex work with male johns.

147 Bradbury-Rance, *Lesbian Cinema After Queer Theory*, 141. Bradbury-Rance is drawing on P. Phelan, *Unmarked*. See also Villarejo, *Lesbian Rule*, 6–7; Jagose, *Inconsequence*, 143.

148 Foucault, *The History of Sexuality*, 101.

149 Callis, "Playing with Butler and Foucault," 225–26.

150 S. Phelan, *Getting Specific*, 96.

151 S. Phelan, *Getting Specific*, 96.

152 Lieb, *Mother of the Blues*, 17.

3. AMBIGUITY, MASCULINITY, AIDS

1 Depardieu plays an equally chaotic bisexual figure in Blier's *Going Places* (1974).

2 Bob's antics chime with Joseph Ronan's description of "bisexual camp," which "refashions the uncertainty, unresolvedness and hypersexualization of stereotypical constructions of bisexuality as weapons" ("Ostentatiously Discreet," 102). Whereas, in Ronan's formulation, these qualities are weaponized against "monosexist gay culture," their deployment here is firmly against a bourgeois sexual conservatism. Another example of such a figure of bisexual camp can be found in the enigmatic Journalist (Miran Javorović) of Croatian comedy *Calvary* (Zvonimir Maycug, 1996), who begins a tryst with his closeted male lover's daughter; chaos ensues.

3 Haraway, *Modest_Witness*, 11.

4 *Love Condemned* was never translated into English. It appears in this book's bibliography as Collard, *Condamné amour*.

5 While *art cinema* should not refer exclusively to European cinema, this chapter's geographical focus is rooted in the predominant Europeanness of the films the term *art cinema* encompassed up until the 1990s. Betz, *Beyond the Subtitle*, 14.

6 Bordwell, "The Art Cinema," 57–58.

7 Bordwell, "The Art Cinema," 60–61.

8 Heck, *After Authority*, 10.

9 Atherton, *The Stoics on Ambiguity*, 135.

10 Kierkegaard, *The Concept of Anxiety*, 41; Beauvoir, *The Ethics of Ambiguity*, 18. We might also remember the importance of *ambiguity* for Maurice Merleau-Ponty's phenomenology as the term he uses to describe the human's mode of existing in relation to their experience of the body. See G. Weiss, "Ambiguity"; Merleau-Ponty, *Phenomenology of Perception*.

11 For Aristotle's discussion of ambiguity, see Aristotle, *On Sophistical Refutations*.

12 San Filippo, *The B Word*, 48–49.

13 *Concise Oxford Dictionary of English Etymology*, s.v. "ambiguous," revised 2003, http://doi.org/10.1093/acref/9780192830982.001.0001. We might also recall the term *ambisexual*, proposed by some twentieth-century psychologists and sexologists as a preferable term to *bisexuality*. See Masters and Johnson, *Homosexuality in Perspective*.

14 Pramaggiore, "Straddling the Screen," 277.

15 T. Carroll, "Invisible Sissy," 195.

16 San Filippo, *The B Word*, 48.

17 Galt and Schoonover, "Introduction," 6.

18 For Bordwell, the concept of the auteur unifies the art film ("The Art Cinema," 59).

19 Gilles, "Les Enfants des 'Nuits fauves,'" n.p. (my translation).

20 Durham, "Portrait of a Generation," 512.

21 Riding, "Discovering a Film Idol's Feet"; Austin, *Contemporary French Cinema*, 79.

22 Durham, "Portrait of a Generation," 513.

23 Worth, *"Le Sacré et le SIDA,"* 105.

24 *F2 Le Journal 13H.*

25 This is not to say that these were the first queer directors in France. Around the mid-twentieth century, some established authors of French literature, who were known publicly as homosexual, turned their hand to filmmaking, including Jean Cocteau, Jean Genet, and Jean Marais. Post-1968, queer men were also some of the most prominent figures in French avant-garde filmmaking, including Georges Bensoussan, Jean-Michel Sénécal, and Lionel Soukaz.

26 Bourcier, *Q comme Queer*, 15, quoted in and translated by Rees-Roberts, *French Queer Cinema*, 6.

27 Deschamps, *Le Miroir bisexuel*, 51 (all my translations henceforth).

28 Grélois's comments typify a tendency, observed in lesbian and gay activism by Steven Angelides, in which bisexuality is determined to be "a viable practice only *after* sex roles and sexual categories had been abolished" (*A History of Bisexuality*, 127). These sentiments are echoed by Guy Hocquenghem in *Gay Liberation After May '68*, 92.

29 Hennig, *Bi*, 18, 31, 103 (all my translations henceforth).

30 For a discussion of this process in Anglophone gay activism, see Eadie, "Indigestion."

31 Collard, *L'Ange sauvage*, 90–92 (my translation).

32 Cheshire comments that "as a bisexual . . . [Jean] casts himself, bodily and emotionally, against the whole system of imposed choices and divisions, binary oppositions and long-enforced cultural schisms" ("Self Expressions," 75–76).

33 Eisenstein, "'Shift' to the Biological Level," 16, 17.

34 Kalmár, *Post-Crisis European Cinema*, 28.

35 The ascendency of misogynistic and patriarchal cultural norms in French cinema is stressed by Ginette Vincendeau and Geneviève Sellier. Vincendeau, "France"; Sellier, *Masculine Singular*.

36 hooks, *The Will to Change*.

37 Lipman, "Les Nuits fauves," 62.

38 Kinsey et al., *Sexual Behavior in the Human Male*, 656.

39 Kinsey et al., *Sexual Behavior in the Human Male*, 639.

40 Simon et al., *Rapport sur le comportement sexuel des Français*, 12 (my translation).

41 Spira et al., *Les comportements sexuels en France*, 140 (my translation).

42 Kinsey et al., *Sexual Behavior in the Human Male*, 639.

43 Kogout, *Le Monde animalier*, 18. This term was used previously to describe intersexuality, which hearkens the fin-de-siècle slippages in bisexuality's meanings between physical and psychical "hermaphroditism" (for the earlier sense, see Gazier, *Lettres à Grégoire*, 242). It was also a term used to refer to homosexuality insofar as the latter

was conceived of epistemologically, in Michel Foucault's words, as "a hermaphro-ditism of the soul" (*The History of Sexuality*, 43).

44 Sinfield, *On Sexuality and Power*, 28.

45 *AIDS: Love in Danger* is set in West Berlin.

46 Ivascu, "Les Maris secrètement bisexuels," 118 (my translation).

47 Nordheimer, "AIDS Specter for Women"; Randolph, "The Hidden Fear"; Japenga, "Hidden Dangers"; Warren, "How to Cope When Your Man Is Bisexual." For an insightful analysis of Randolph's article in *Ebony*, see C. Cohen, "Unsuspecting Women and the Dreaded Bisexual."

48 Grover, "AIDS," 21.

49 Grigorieff, *Non au sida*, 71 (my translation).

50 Dollimore, "Bisexuality," 250; Grover, "AIDS," 21; Weinberg et al., *Dual Attraction*, 206.

51 Martel, *The Pink and the Black*, 367.

52 Martel, *The Pink and the Black*, 422n38.

53 Steffen, "AIDS Policies in France"; Boulé, *HIV Stories*.

54 Caron, "*Liberté, Égalité, Séropositivité*," 284.

55 Boulé, *HIV Stories*, 12.

56 Boulé, *HIV Stories*, 12.

57 Deschamps, *Le Miroir bisexuel*, 39.

58 Hennig, *Bi*, 37.

59 We should note, however, that reports on male bisexuality during the 1980s were not altogether limited to discussions of HIV/AIDS. A feature in gay weekly maga-zine *Gai Pied Hebdo* announces a "bi boom" in France, without reference to HIV/AIDS. Fontenay and Darnett, "Le Boom des bi."

60 Gelman et al., "Perilous Double Love Life," 44.

61 Grosz, *Volatile Bodies*, 153. The question as to whether Grosz is herself reproduc-ing the stigmatization of the male bisexual in the family is equivocal. One could interpret her words as parodying heterosexual culture's fears but, equally, I under-stand McKenzie Wark's criticism of Grosz casting bisexuality as "a 'clandestine' practice of the dominant group. It doesn't qualify for the moral high ground of the 'marginalised'—and so Grosz marginalises it, ethically and actually." Wark, "Bisex-ual Mediations," 66.

62 Lamien, "Bisexualité," 10 (my translation).

63 Nash, "Chronicle(s) of a Death Foretold," 102. A notable exception to this trend in American cinema is Gavin Millar's *Tidy Endings* (1988), which centers on the re-lationship between a man and a woman whose shared bisexual male lover dies of AIDS-related illnesses.

64 The late 1980s also saw the release of narrative films about AIDS containing no ref-erence to queerness. These include *A Hoof Here, a Hoof There* (Věra Chytilová, 1989), *On the Make* (Sam Hurwitz, 1989), and *The Ryan White Story* (John Herzfeld, 1989).

65 Act Up–Paris, *Le Sida*, 176 (my translation).

66 Glucksmann, *La Fêlure du monde*, 18, translated in Worth, "*Le Sacré et le SIDA*," 105.

67 Simon Watney understands this aspect of the film as illustrative of "the psychologi-cal working of a culture which is so profoundly homophobic that the very idea of

a *collective* social or cultural response to Aids on the part of homosexuals is all but unthinkable" ("The French Connection," 24–25).

68 Cyril Collard quoted in Baube, "Décès du réalisateur et acteur français Cyril Collard," n.p. (my translation with the help of Jules O'Dwyer).

69 *Bouillon de culture* (all my translation henceforth).

70 *Bouillon de culture.*

71 Quoted in and translated by Nash, "Chronicle(s) of a Death Foretold," 98.

72 Agar, "Fragments of Wholeness," 125.

73 Mulligan, "Queer Cinema of Jacques Demy," 138–48. Demy had initially intended to cast David Bowie in the role of Orphée; Bowie was bisexual, and his star image is also associated with the bisexual aesthetics of glam rock.

74 Sébastien Ministru reads this song as Orphée's bisexual coming-out and draws parallels between these lyrics and the moment of bisexual candidness in Stanley Kubrick's *Spartacus* (1960), when Crassus (Laurence Olivier) tells Antonius (Tony Curtis), "My taste includes both snails and oysters" ("Orphée au parking," 354).

75 Mulligan, "Queer Cinema of Jacques Demy," 145–47.

76 This is a dynamic that Lee Edelman would later theorize, in which the figure of the (unborn) Child is positioned against an exterior queerness that threatens its future. Edelman, *No Future.*

77 Hewitt, "Homosexual Demography," 394–95.

78 Engelmann, *Mapping AIDS*, 121.

79 Westel, "The Best of Times," 95.

80 Grigorieff, *Non au sida*, 97.

81 Hemmings, "What's in a Name?," 25–26.

82 Mack, *Sexagon*, 50, 172.

83 *Les Nuits fauves* [compact disc insert], 8. The song is entitled "Aït Douz" (The people of Douz [a Tunisian town]) in Arabic. Thank you to Khaled Alsaleh for his help in identifying this piece of music.

84 For further consideration of what Maxime Cervulle and Nick Rees-Roberts call "gay orientalism" in French queer cinema, see Cervulle and Rees-Roberts, "Le Cineaste gay et le garçon arabe." Thank you Jules O'Dwyer for recommending this text.

85 MacCannell, *The Tourist*, 183.

86 Merck, *In Your Face*, 162, 164.

87 Urry and Larsen, *The Tourist Gaze*, 4.

88 Hennig, *Bi*, 69.

89 Bell, "Bi-Sexuality," 135.

90 This phrase also takes the forms *être* (to be), *marcher* (to walk), and *naviguer* (to sail) *à voile et à vapeur.* Jean-Marc Richard, *Dictionnaire des expressions paillardes et libertines de la littérature française* (Filipacchi, 1993), 263, s.v. "voile."

91 Giaccardi, "Fluidité et plasticité," 4 (all my translations henceforth).

92 Oakes and Schein, "Translocal China."

93 M. P. Smith, "Translocality," 181.

94 San Filippo, *The B Word*, 53.

95 Howes, "Introduction," 7.

96   Oakes and Schein, "Translocal China," 20.

97   Eadie, "Living in the Past," 23.

98   Eadie, "Bodyscapes, Resources and Social Change," 85.

99   Maliepaard, "Bisexuals in Space and Geography," 154.

100 Handyside, *Cinema at the Shore,* 187.

101 Delany, *Times Square Red,* 32. Such a process, in fact, took place in the San Francisco
     fisting venue the Catacombs, where Gayle S. Rubin describes its transformation from
     a gay male space to a space of mixed-gender sex parties that "provided opportunities
     for experimentation . . . [and] created a comfortable atmosphere in which diverse pop-
     ulations could . . . discover what they did have in common" ("The Catacombs," 131).

102 Foucault, "A Preface to Transgression," 34.

103 Hemmings, "Locating Bisexual Identities," 46–47.

104 Foucault, "Friendship as a Way of Life."

105 Wood, *Hollywood from Vietnam to Reagan,* 65.

106 Klesse, *The Spectre of Promiscuity,* 78.

107 Brilmyer et al., "The Ontology of the Couple," 223.

108 Brilmyer et al., "The Ontology of the Couple," 234.

109 Brilmyer et al., "The Ontology of the Couple," 238.

110 Engelberg, "'How Could Any One Relationship,'" 111.

111 Bryant, *Bisexual Characters in Film,* 73–81.

112 Deschamps, *Le Miroir bisexuel,* 170.

113 Bersani, "Against Monogamy," 3.

114 Bersani, "Against Monogamy," 11, 21.

115 Çakırlar and Needham, "The Monogamous/Promiscuous Optics," 411.

116 Roberts, "Neither Fish nor Fowl," vii.

117 Galt and Schoonover, "Introduction."

118 Salamon, "Unsafe Sex in Paris," 12.

119 Gabara, "Screening Autobiography," 68.

120 Dean, *Unlimited Intimacy,* 66.

121 Hunt, "Risk and Moralization in Everyday Life," 182–83.

122 Hunt, "Risk and Moralization in Everyday Life," 183.

123 Dean, *Unlimited Intimacy,* 77.

124 Muller, *Un amour sérodifférent,* 38 (my translation).

125 Condé, *Les Nuits fauves,* 56 (my translation).

126 Foucault, *The History of Sexuality,* 38.

127 Brilmyer et al., "The Ontology of the Couple," 247.

128 Deschamps, *Le Miroir bisexuel,* 170.

129 Hemmings, *Bisexual Spaces,* 134.

130 This was not the first campaign of its kind. The French Office for Fighting AIDS,
     an entity created by the French Minister of Health, ran campaigns between 1989
     and 1992 that were "philosophically, a way of reaching men with homosexual prac-
     tices, who were not integrated in the community, because they were married, lived
     in the provinces, were bisexual, or did not fit with the codes of the gay community."
     Gérard Pelé quoted in de Oliveira, "Communication publique," 111 (my translation).

131 To name just a handful of examples from art cinema depictions of male bisexuality between 1969 and 2000: *The Ages of Lulu* (Bigas Luna, 1990), *Life and Death* (Petter Vennerød and Svend Wam, 1980), *One Night at Dinner* (Giuseppe Patroni Griffi, 1969), *Serious as Pleasure* (Robert Benayoun, 1975), *To the Extreme* (Étienne Faure, 2000), and *Why Not!* (Coline Serreau, 1977).

132 Pramaggiore, "Straddling the Screen," 277.

133 Garber, *Vice Versa*, 433.

134 Lévi-Strauss, *Elementary Structures of Kinship*, 63.

135 G. Rubin, "The Traffic in Women," 174.

136 Girard, *Deceit, Desire, and the Novel*, 1–52.

137 Sedgwick, *Between Men*, 1–2.

138 Sedgwick, *Between Men*, 47.

139 Hao, "Chinese Visual Representation," 62n1.

140 Baudry, "Ideological Effects," 42.

141 Van Brummelen, *Mathematics of the Heavens and the Earth*, 9–10.

142 Van Brummelen, *The Doctrine of Triangles*, 3.

143 *Oxford English Dictionary*, s.v. "reflex (*adj.*)," last updated September 2023, http://doi .org/10.1093/OED/1101386157.

144 To read cinema's triangular bisexual embraces in relation to polygons, vertices, proportions, and lines is to remind us, as Eugenie Brinkema does, that "sex is a form of composition . . . [that] love and sex are designated *in form*" (*Life-Destroying Diagrams*, 323).

145 As outlined in Euclid, *Euclid's Elements*, 2.

146 Because, in Euclidean geometry, a reflex angle is always greater than 180°, and a triangle's interior angles always add up to 180°, the reflex angle's adjacent angle can never exceed 180°.

147 I am grateful to Sophie Abrahams and Farrah Freibert for their patience in helping me comprehend the rules of Euclidean geometry and allowing me to test out my theoretical proposals on them.

148 Bersani, "Sociality and Sexuality," 655–56 (emphases removed). Bersani is drawing on the words of Aristophanes in Plato's *Symposium*.

149 Bersani, "Is There a Gay Art?," 33. Here Bersani is referencing examples from Jean Genet's *Funeral Rites*.

150 Giaccardi, "Fluidité et plasticité," 2 (my translation).

151 Dusseau, "Les Bisexualités," 36 (my translation).

152 Giaccardi, "Fluidité et plasticité," 2 (my translation with the help of Carolina McPhail and Marie-Aude Baronian).

153 For psychoanalytic thinkers like Sheldon George and Todd McGowan, the appeal of the notion of racial difference lies in its being a fantasy that provides pleasure. George, *Trauma and Race*, 4; McGowan, *The Racist Fantasy*, 25.

154 Strauss, "Cyril Collard," 6 (my translation).

155 Quoted in Toubiana, "Carpe Diem and Night," 30 (my translation).

156 Nancy, *Being Singular Plural*, 30.

157 N. Carroll, introduction, 2.

158   This camera movement recalls Roger Caillois's term *ilinx*, describing the excitement to be found in vertiginous disorientation (*Man, Play, and Games*, 24).

159   Brinkema, *The Forms of the Affects*, 261. Brinkema is discussing Hollis Frampton's *Zorns Lemma* (1970) in a way that is equally expository here.

160   Roy, "La Vie à tout prix," 58 (my translation).

161   Quoted in and translated by Nash, "Chronicle(s) of a Death Foretold," 103.

162   Quoted in Loud, "Savage Love," 65.

163   Watney, "The French Connection," 25; Nash, "Chronicle(s) of a Death Foretold," 101; Nadeau, "Life with Pinky Dots," 143, 144n14. Nadeau's other examples of this supposed trend include *Ménage*, *Dry Cleaning* (Anne Fontaine, 1997), and *Man Is a Woman* (Jean-Jacques Zilbermann, 1998). I would argue that it is Nadeau's monosexist hermeneutic, more so than the films themselves, that produces this heterosexual reading.

164   Eadie, "Living in the Past," 17.

165   J. Butler, "Doubting Love," 66.

166   Brinkema, *Life-Destroying Diagrams*, 341.

167   Du Plessis, "Blatantly Bisexual," 19. See also Eisner, *Bi*, 134; MacDowall, "Present Tense Bisexuality," 220.

168   Muñoz, *Cruising Utopia*, 12.

169   See Tamagne, "Histoire des homosexualités"; Guérin, *Homosexualité et révolution*, particularly 22.

170   Guérin, "Géographie passionnelle," 6 (my translation).

171   Mandy Merck, in a discussion of the novel *Savage Nights*, relates the term *fauve* to both "the savagery of [Jean's] sexual encounters" and the Fauvists' "cultivated primitivism," which echoes the novel's (and perhaps the film's) orientalizing depictions of Maghrebi men (*In Your Face*, 162). My invocation of Fauvism, however, centers on its approach to the figural. While these approaches are not in conflict per se, they speak to different aspects of *Savage Nights*' (both the novel's and the film's) worldview.

172   Malabou, *Plasticity at the Dusk of Writing*, 61 (emphasis removed). Carolyn Durham also discusses *Savage Nights* in relation to Fauvism in "Portrait of a Generation," 516.

173   Schuller and Gill-Peterson, "Introduction," 4.

174   Giaccardi, "Fluidité et plasticité," 3.

175   As Carolyn Durham observes, the film is edited so that "Jean's most idyllic moments are ironically undermined even as they unfold" ("Portrait of a Generation," 518).

176   Cixous, "Sorties," 84–85.

4. THE EROTIC THRILLER'S ALLURING CONFOUNDMENTS

1   GLAAD, "Hollywood Images Fuel Gay/Lesbian Bashing," n.p. The films they cite as fueling antigay violence are *Basic Instinct*, *Bird on a Wire* (John Badham, 1990), *Darkman* (Sam Raimi, 1990), *House Party* (Reginald Hudlin, 1990), *Men at Work* (Emilio Estevez, 1990), *Miller's Crossing* (Joel Coen and Ethan Coen, 1990), *Ticking Man* (listed because of its screenplay; it was never produced), *Q & A* (Sidney

Lumet, 1990), and *Wild at Heart* (David Lynch, 1990). A similar link is made in a report by the National Gay and Lesbian Task Force Policy Institute. In a section that seeks to contextualize a 31 percent increase in antigay violence and victimization between 1990 and 1991, the report's authors state: "Destructive stereotyping of gay people in films such as *Silence of the Lambs* and the soon-to-be released *Basic Instinct* . . . contributed to the siege under which lesbian and gay Americans lived in 1991" ("Anti-Gay/Lesbian Violence," 3).

2 GLAAD, *The GLAAD Bulletin*, n.p.

3 Lyons, *The New Censors*, 126–31.

4 Following these meetings, Eszterhas submitted thirteen pages of changes to the screenplay, containing a reported thirty-seven revisions, reflecting: "I want to help better the lives of gay people. In my mind these changes are very important in terms of the perception of gay people and women in our society" (*Pink Paper*, "*Basic Instinct*"). These revisions were rejected by Carolco, who wrote in a press release that *Basic Instinct* "is a psychological thriller about a police detective investigating a series of brutal, baffling murders. It is not a negative depiction of lesbians and bisexuals," and that Eszterhas's proposed changes "undermine the strength of Eszterhas's original material, weaken the characters . . . and lessen the integrity of the picture itself" (quoted in Lew, "Gay Groups Protest a Film Script"). Eszterhas also requested that a disclaimer—similar to the one shown in screenings of *Cruising*—precede the film, stating: "The movie you are about to see is fictional. Its gay and bisexual characters are fictional and not based on reality" (D. Cohen, "Contested Terrain"). Carolco also rejected this suggestion.

5 *Cruising* was also produced by Lorimar, the production company behind *Midnight Caller*.

6 L. R. Williams, *The Erotic Thriller*, 3.

7 To varying extents, bisexuality is involved in stylizing these figures' transgressions. The acts of violence Andrea orchestrates for her gratification involve a man's intervention, a bisexualized mise-en-scène of desire. *Dressed to Kill*'s pathologizing explanation behind Bobbi's actions comes from its psychiatrist figure, Dr. Levy (David Margulies), who contends that it is Dr. Elliott's "male side" desiring women that causes their "female side," queer in its transness, to kill. The film's diagnosis, therefore, is rooted in the inability for Bobbi's bisexual desires to coexist. *Cruising* is the most relevant of the three films vis-à-vis bisexual inquiry, in its suggestion that one or more of its murders has been carried out by police officer Steve (Al Pacino), who is in a relationship with Nancy (Karen Allen); in Robin Wood's words, it becomes "clear that his confidence in his heterosexuality becomes progressively undermined" (*Hollywood from Vietnam to Reagan*, 60).

8 Spielrein, "Destruction as the Cause of Coming into Being"; Freud, "Beyond the Pleasure Principle."

9 Bauman, *Liquid Love*, 8, 58.

10 Bataille writes that Sade "states and restates, as an established truth, the paradox of crime's being a condition of sensual pleasure" (*The Accursed Share*, 176).

11 Garber, *Vice Versa*; Dean, "The Erotics of Transgression."

12 Sexploitation roughies with similar preoccupations to the erotic thriller include *Scum of the Earth* (Herschell Gordon Lewis, 1963), *Strange Compulsion* (Irvin Berwick, 1964), and *Aroused* (Anton Holden, 1966) (see Gorfinkel, *Lewd Looks*, 134–35). *Gialli* that may be considered precursors to the erotic thriller include *Libido* (Ernesto Gastaldi and Vittorio Salerno, 1965), *The Sweet Body of Deborah* (Romolo Guerrieri, 1968), *Orgasmo* (Umberto Lenzi, 1969), and *One on Top of the Other* (Lucio Fulci, 1969).

13 L. R. Williams, *The Erotic Thriller*, 3.

14 L. R. Williams, *The Erotic Thriller*, 1.

15 L. R. Williams, *The Erotic Thriller*, 25, 28.

16 Conrad, introduction, 1–2.

17 Conrad, introduction, 2.

18 L. R. Williams, *The Erotic Thriller*, 25.

19 Alilunas, *Smutty Little Movies*, 41–42.

20 By 1985, adult video's market share had declined, though it still made up a not-insignificant 15 percent of video sales in the United States. Davis, "X-Rated Video," 1.

21 L. R. Williams, *The Erotic Thriller*, 25.

22 L. R. Williams, *The Erotic Thriller*, 25.

23 San Filippo, *Provocauteurs and Provocations*, 111.

24 Krzywinska, *Sex and the Cinema*, 217.

25 L. R. Williams, *The Erotic Thriller*, 11. For a more focused consideration of direct-to-video erotic thrillers, see Andrews, "Sex Is Dangerous."

26 Alilunas, *Smutty Little Movies*, 219n105.

27 Moorman, "Bi for Pay?"

28 L. R. Williams, *The Erotic Thriller*, 44.

29 Holmlund, "Introduction," 2.

30 Gomery, "The Hollywood Blockbuster," 80–81.

31 *The Numbers*, "Basic Instinct."

32 *The Numbers*, "Jagged Edge." Rounded up to the nearest 100,000. Eszterhas also wrote erotic thriller screenplays subsequent to *Basic Instinct*, including *Sliver* (Phillip Noyce, 1993), *Showgirls* (Paul Verhoeven, 1995), and *Jade* (William Friedkin, 1995). For discussion of Eszterhas as the erotic thriller's paradigmatic screenwriter, see L. R. Williams, *The Erotic Thriller*, 149–62.

33 *The Numbers*, "Fatal Attraction"; "International Box Office Figures," Statista.

34 Simkin, *Basic Instinct*, 4.

35 Eller, "Eszterhas Script Picks Up Record $3-Mil."

36 Hillier, *The New Hollywood*, 19.

37 "A negative pickup deal is one in which a distributor acquires the right to distribute a completed motion picture that has been fully financed by someone other than the distributor itself." Sobel, "Financing the Production of Theatrical Motion Pictures," 4.

38 Hillier, *The New Hollywood*, 19–20.

39 Simkin, *Basic Instinct*, 4–5.

40 Simkin, *Basic Instinct*, 5, 7.
41 Eszterhas, *Hollywood Animal*, 293. Eszterhas had initially wanted Miloš Forman to direct the film. Simkin, *Basic Instinct*, 5.
42 Eszterhas, *Hollywood Animal*, 295–96; van Scheers, *Paul Verhoeven*, 245.
43 Verhoeven in the documentary *Blonde Poison*.
44 Galvin, "Paul Verhoeven," 50–51; van Scheers, *Paul Verhoeven*, 35.
45 Van Scheers, *Paul Verhoeven*, 257; Sharon Stone, *The Beauty of Living Twice*, 97.
46 Sharon Stone, *The Beauty of Living Twice*, 98.
47 Freud, "On the Sexual Theories of Children"; Freud, "Analysis of a Phobia in a Five-Year-Old Boy"; Freud, "Fetishism."
48 Such as a male protagonist's primary love interest (*King Solomon's Mines* [J. Lee Thompson, 1985], *Allan Quatermain and the Lost City of Gold* [Gary Nelson, 1986], *Above the Law* [Andrew Davis, 1988]); the "other woman" (*Irreconcilable Differences* [Charles Shyer, 1984], *He Said, She Said* [Ken Kwapis and Marisa Silver, 1991]); or the wife of a secondary character (*Action Jackson* [Craig R. Baxley, 1988], *Beyond the Stars* [David Saperstein, 1989]).
49 Feasey, "Neo-Noir's Fatal Woman," 187.
50 Gulam, "Film Stardom, Gender, and Philanthropy."
51 Sharon Stone, *The Beauty of Living Twice*, 101.
52 Gill, "Postfeminist Media Culture."
53 Gill, "Postfeminist Media Culture," 163.
54 Feasey, "'Sharon Stone, Screen Diva,'" 182.
55 Farrimond, *The Contemporary Femme Fatale*, 9, 108.
56 For contemporary discussions of 1970s bisexual chic, see J. Carroll, "Bisexual Chic"; *Time*, "The New Bisexuals"; *Newsweek*, "Bisexual Chic."
57 King, "'There Are No Lesbians Here,'" 42–43.
58 Clark, "Commodity Lesbianism," 494.
59 San Filippo, *The B Word*, 22.
60 San Filippo, *The B Word*, 22.
61 Farrimond, *The Contemporary Femme Fatale*, 110.
62 Freud, "Beyond the Pleasure Principle," 14–17.
63 Metz, *The Imaginary Signifier*, 95.
64 This film is among those Teresa de Lauretis identifies as "antagonistic, anti-feminist attempts to devalue the gains that . . . *very few* women may have made in social equality," a projection of a patriarchal ideology's fears around women obtaining wealth ("Guerrilla in the Midst," 18).
65 Knight, *Risk, Uncertainty and Profit*, 233.
66 Keynes, *A Treatise on Probability*, 95.
67 B. Cohen, "Bretton Woods."
68 Helleiner, *States and the Reemergence of Global Finance*, 146; Eichengreen, *Globalizing Capital*, 134.
69 LiPuma and Lee, *Financial Derivatives*, 70–71.
70 Orhangazi, *Financialization and the US Economy*, 3–6.
71 Marx, *Capital*, 459–79.

72 Marx, *Capital*, 459–60, 474.

73 Marx, *Capital*, 459.

74 Hardin, *Capturing Finance*, 3.

75 Zaretsky, "Bisexuality, Capitalism and the Ambivalent Legacy."

76 Hedgehog, "Where Fatness and Bisexuality Meet," 141.

77 Hedgehog, "Where Fatness and Bisexuality Meet," 144, 145.

78 Also of interest here is Catherine Deschamps's argument that bisexuality's so-cial treatment more as "behavior"—as something that is "done," as opposed to an identity—unshackles it, unwittingly, from neoliberal conceptions of identity ("Les Recherches sur la sexualité et le sida," 147 [my translation]).

79 Guattari, "I Have Even Met Happy Travelos," 81.

80 Merck, "Sexuality, Subjectivity and . . . Economics?," 57.

81 Merck, "Sexuality, Subjectivity, and . . . Economics?," 57. This is not to say that there were not preexisting alignments between gay and lesbian cultures and con-sumer cultures (see D'Emilio, "Capitalism and Gay Identity"), but, instead, that the late 1980s and 1990s saw an intensification of these alignments on a much larger scale, and with reference to a particular homosexual figure of investable normativity.

82 Figures cited in Baker, "A History in Ads," 12.

83 Baker, "A History in Ads," 13, 12.

84 Berlant, *Cruel Optimism*, 167.

85 Eng, *The Feeling of Kinship*; Duggan, *The Twilight of Equality?*, 50.

86 Duggan, *The Twilight of Equality?*, 50.

87 Rao, "Global Homocapitalism," 39.

88 Woubshet, *The Calendar of Loss*, 23.

89 Chitty, *Sexual Hegemony*, 35.

90 My use of the terms *transexuals* and *transvestites* here reflects their prevalence dur-ing the 1970s and 1980s.

91 Nor would this shift be incidental for John D'Emilio, for whom it is "the historical development of capitalism . . . that has allowed large numbers of men and women in the late twentieth century to call themselves gay, see themselves as part of a community of similar men and women, and to organize politically on the basis of that identity" ("Capitalism and Gay Identity," 468).

92 Hemmings, "Resituating the Bisexual Body"; Eadie, "Indigestion."

93 Rhodes, *Spectacle of Property*, ix.

94 Rhodes, *Spectacle of Property*, 14.

95 Soto, "'Made to Be the Maid'?," 254.

96 Saez and Zucman, "Wealth Inequality in the United States Since 1913," appendix, table B2.

97 Kennickell and Starr-McCluer, "Changes in Family Finances," 865.

98 Hedgehog, "Where Fatness and Bisexuality Meet."

99 Andrews, "Sex Is Dangerous," 66–67.

100 San Filippo, *The B Word*, 99–100.

101 Eadie, "'That's Why She Is Bisexual,'" 156.

102 Eadie, "'That's Why She Is Bisexual,'" 157.
103 Kolb, *Encyclopedia of Business Ethics*, s.v. "Redistribution of Wealth."
104 Jean Laplanche and Jean-Bertrand Pontalis note that projection has taken on various different meanings; their general definition of it describes "the operation whereby a neurological or psychological element is displaced and relocated in an external position, thus passing either from centre to periphery or from subject to object" (*The Language of Psycho-Analysis*, 349).
105 Jameson, "Culture and Finance Capital," 265.
106 Jameson, "Culture and Finance Capital," 265.
107 O'Malley, *Risk, Uncertainty and Government*, 2.
108 Hansson, "Panorama of the Philosophy of Risk."
109 Farrimond, *The Contemporary Femme Fatale*, 16; Mulvey, "Visual Pleasure and Narrative Cinema," 11. See also Deleyto, "The Margins of Pleasure."
110 Beauvoir, *The Second Sex*, 241.
111 See also Danziger, "*Basic Instinct.*"
112 Holmlund, "Cruisin' for a Bruisin'," 37. We might also recall San Filippo's examples of female bisexuality accruing meaning on screen through motifs of "mother-daughter surrogacy" (*The B Word*, 39).
113 Downing, *The Subject of Murder*, 3–24.
114 Downing, *The Subject of Murder*, 8. Downing is drawing on Foucault's ideas in "8 January 1975."
115 Downing, *The Subject of Murder*, 1.
116 A number of those involved with this film's production were queer, including screenwriter Arthur Laurents, Dall, and Granger, who is bisexual.
117 Fitzgerald's diagrams were reproduced in the *Chicago Daily Tribune*. Doherty, "Grand Jury to Indict Boy Slayers Today," 2.
118 Martin, "Man Sentenced in 'Trash Bag Murders'"; Lindsey, "Jim Jones"; Mober, "Murder Most Foul?"; Galloway, "Gacy Case Heading for Trial"; Taylor, "Two Drifters"; Gorman, "Judge, Calling Killing 'Sinister'"; Kazmin, "'Chameleon Fugitive'"; *Miami Herald*, "Condemned Killer."
119 *America's Most Wanted*.
120 A. Williams, "Domestic Violence and the Aetiology of Crime," 102.
121 Downing, *The Subject of Murder*, 123–24.
122 Hart, *Fatal Women*, 9.
123 Henderson and Wright, "Hand in Hand with Hindley," 1.
124 Griggers, "Phantom and Reel Projections," 167.
125 Whereas I use *sex work* to describe Wuornos's labor, my use of *prostitute* relates to it being the term through which this particular cultural figure has circulated discursively. This usage is reflected by writing in sex work theory and activism, see Grant, *Playing the Whore*; McClanahan and Settell, "Service Work, Sex Work, and the 'Prostitute Imaginary.'"
126 This particular figuration might be understood as drawing on similar associations as the "fricatrice," briefly discussed in chapter 1 in relation to its use by Richard Burton, insofar as it carries associations of both "the prostitute" and "the lesbian."

127 Wuornos herself affirmed feelings of romantic love toward both women and men from her past (*Dear Dawn*, 162).

128 Lombroso and Ferrero, *The Female Offender*, 74. See also Hart, *Fatal Women*, 11–12.

129 Smart played Wuornos in *Overkill: The Aileen Wuornos Story* (Peter Levin, 1992); List played Wuornos in *Aileen Wuornos: American Boogeywoman* (Daniel Farrands, 2021).

130 Keegan, *Lana and Lilly Wachowski*, 25.

131 Keegan, *Lana and Lilly Wachowski*, 25.

132 Seid, "Reveal," 177.

133 J. Butler, *Gender Trouble*, 146.

134 Keegan, "On the Necessity of Bad Trans Objects."

135 Lavery, *Pleasure and Efficacy*, 156.

136 Steinbock, *Shimmering Images*, 145.

137 Moretti, *Signs Taken for Wonders*, 134 (emphasis removed).

138 Lyons, *The New Censors*, 134–35; Kane, "RE: March 1992 Staff Report."

139 Weir, "Gay-Bashing, Villainy and the Oscars," 17.

140 In the documentary *Blonde Poison*.

141 Bower et al., "(Con)Tested Identities," 47.

142 Ertman, "Follow Your 'Basic Instinct,'" 45. Obviously, I would interpret these figures as bisexual and not lesbian, but I remain in agreement with Ertman's overriding points.

143 Rich, *New Queer Cinema*, 105.

144 McGregor, "Sex Crimes," 19.

145 McGregor, "Sex Crimes," 19.

146 Eadie, "'That's Why She Is Bisexual,'" 144.

147 Milton, *Paradise Lost*, 15.

148 LaVey, *The Satanic Bible*, 25.

149 Eadie, "'That's Why She Is Bisexual,'" 144.

150 Barthes, "Rhetoric of the Image," 38–39. We might also recall Claude Lévi-Strauss's "floating signifier," "a sign marking the necessity of a supplementary symbolic content over and above that which the signified already contains, which can be any value at all" (*Introduction to the Work of Marcel Mauss*, 63–64).

151 Namaste, "Le Déplacement et la crise du réel," 231 (my translation).

152 Namaste, "Le Déplacement et la crise du réel," 233 (my translation).

153 Eadie, "Indigestion," 83 (emphasis removed).

AFTERWORD

1 With the former, I am thinking in particular of Brownmiller, *Against Our Will*.

2 Cahill, *Rethinking Rape*, 27.

3 Rastogi, *Modern Text Book of Zoology*, 359–61.

4 S.-D. Stone, "Bisexual Women," 108.

5 Hester, "Diagramming *Irréversible*," 27. Cf. Eugenie Brinkema's articulation of how *Irreversible* returns us to the rectum as a site of Bersanian sexual shattering. Brinkema, "Rape and the Rectum"; Bersani, *Homos*.

6   Wiegman and Wilson, "Introduction," 12.

7   Wiegman and Wilson, "Introduction," 18.

8   Wiegman and Wilson, "Introduction," 18.

9   Gregg and Villarejo, *Oxford Handbook of Queer Cinema*.

10   The relations between bisexuality, transgression, and pornographic film have begun to be explored more broadly in, for example, Freibert, "Bad Bis Go to Hell," and Roberts, "The Imperfect Text."

11   See Chris Straayer's articulation of the encouragement of bisexual eroticism in the "temporary transvestite film" in *Deviant Eyes, Deviant Bodies*, 43.

12   San Filippo, *The B Word*, 34.

13   Both films present intragender and extragender configurations, and in roll twelve of *Couch*, there is a male-male-female threesome between Gerard Malanga, Rufus Collins, and Kate Heliczer (see also its unused take labeled by the Warhol Foundation "1964.18.23 *Couch*"). Jenkins, "*Couch*."

14   Guattari, "Becoming-Woman," 86.

15   Guattari, "Becoming-Woman," 86. Guattari's words are paralleled in Guy Hocquenghem's call, in the same issue of *Semiotext(e)*, "to be rid of sexual segregation . . . to be rid of the categories of man and woman, gay and straight, possessor and possessed, greater and lesser, master and slave" ("To Destroy Sexuality," 264).

16   De Lauretis, "Queer Theory," v.

17   Wilson, "Is Transgression Transgressive?," 112–13.

18   Duberman, "The Bisexual Debate," 207–8. This also recalls Jonathan Dollimore's argument that "we protect ourselves against those instabilities intrinsic to desire and which threaten to dislocate us psychically and socially, even, or especially, when our sexuality or object choices are relatively settled" ("Bisexuality, Heterosexuality, and Wishful Theory," 524).

19   Davidson et al., introduction, 2.

20   Davidson et al., introduction, 11.

21   Eadie, "'That's Why She Is Bisexual,'" 156.

Filmography

Note: Bisexuality-related titles are presented **in bold**.

Above the Law (a.k.a. *Nico*). Dir. Andrew Davis, 1988. USA.
Action Jackson. Dir. Craig R. Baxley, 1988. USA.
Adieu je t'aime. Dir. Claude Bernard-Aubert, 1988. France.
The Ages of Lulu [Las edades de Lulú]. Dir. Bigas Luna, 1990. Spain.
AIDS: Love in Danger [A.I.D.S.—Trop jeune pour mourir / Gefahr für die Liebe—Aids].
    Dir. Hans Noever, 1985. France and West Germany.
Aileen Wuornos: American Boogeywoman. Dir. Daniel Farrands, 2021. USA.
Alien. Dir. Ridley Scott, 1979. UK and USA.
Alien Resurrection. Dir. Jean-Pierre Jeunet, 1997. USA.
Aliens. Dir. James Cameron, 1986. USA and UK.
Alien 3. Dir. David Fincher, 1992. USA.
Allan Quatermain and the Lost City of Gold. Dir. Gary Nelson, 1986. USA and Israel.
Anatomy of Hell [Anatomie de l'enfer]. Dir. Catherine Breillat, 2004. France and Portugal.
And Now the Screaming Starts! (a.k.a. *Bride of Fengriffen*). Dir. Roy Ward Baker, 1973. UK.
Apartment Zero [Conviviendo con la muerte]. Dir. Martin Donovan, 1988. UK and
    Argentina.
"Archival Interview with José Larraz." Prod. Pete Tombs. Special feature in *Blood Hunger:
    The Films of José Larraz, Vampyres*. Arrow Video, 2019. Blu-ray disc.
Aroused. Dir. Anton Holden, 1966. USA.
Artificial Memory. Dir. Sheila McLaughlin, 1976. USA.
Atomic Blonde. Dir. David Leitch, 2017. USA.
At the Golden Crown, or The Good Inn [À l'écu d'or ou la Bonne auberge]. Dir. anony-
    mous, 1908. France.
The Basement Girl. Dir. Midi Onodera, 2000. Canada.
Basic Instinct. Dir. Paul Verhoeven, 1992. USA, UK, and France.
Basic Instinct 2: Risk Addiction. Dir. Michael Caton-Jones, 2006. UK, Germany, Spain,
    and USA.

The Basis of Make-Up [*Die Basis des Make-Up*]. Dir. Heinz Emigholz, 1985. West Germany.

Before the Bat's Flight Is Done [*Mielőtt befejezi röptét a denevér*]. Dir. Péter Tímár, 1989. Hungarian People's Republic.

Behind the Green Door. Dir. Artie Mitchell and Jim Mitchell, 1972. USA.

Benedetta. Dir. Paul Verhoeven, 2021. France, Belgium, and Netherlands.

The Berlin Affair [*Interno Berlinese / Leidenschaften*]. Dir. Liliana Cavani, 1985. Italy and West Germany.

The Best Way to Walk [*La Meilleure Façon de marcher*]. Dir. Claude Miller, 1976. France.

Beyond Good and Evil [*Al di là del bene e del male*]. Dir. Liliana Cavani, 1977. Italy and France.

Beyond the Stars. Dir. David Saperstein, 1989. USA and Canada.

The Big Blue. Dir. Andrew Horn, 1988. USA and West Germany.

Bird on a Wire. Dir. John Badham, 1990. USA.

Black Widow. Dir. Bob Rafelson, 1987. USA.

Bliss. Dir. Joe Begos, 2019. USA.

Blonde Poison: The Making of "Basic Instinct." Dir. Jeffrey Schwarz, 2001. USA.

Blood and Roses [. . . *Et mourir de plaisir / Il sangue e la rosa*]. Dir. Roger Vadim, 1960. France and Italy.

Blood and Sand [*Sangre y arena*]. Dir. Javier Elorrieta, 1989. Spain and USA.

The Blood Spattered Bride [*La novia ensangrentada*]. Dir. Vicente Aranda, 1972. Spain.

Blue Velvet. Dir. David Lynch, 1986. USA.

Body Heat. Dir. Lawrence Kasdan, 1981. USA.

Bongo Erotico. Dir. Enrico Cocozza, 1959. UK.

Born in Flames. Dir. Lizzie Borden, 1983. USA.

Bound. Dir. Lana Wachowski and Lilly Wachowski, 1996. USA.

Bram Stoker's Dracula. Dir. Francis Ford Coppola, 1992. USA.

Brokeback Mountain. Dir. Ang Lee, 2005. USA and Canada.

Buddies. Dir. Arthur J. Bressan Jr., 1985. USA.

But I'm a Cheerleader. Dir. Jamie Babbit, 1999. USA.

"By This Sign, I'll Recognise You . . ." Prod. Ewan Cant. Special feature in *Blood Hunger: The Films of José Larraz, Vampyres*. Arrow Video, 2019. Blu-ray disc.

Calendar Girl Murders. Dir. William A. Graham, 1984. USA.

Calvary [*Kalvarija*]. Dir. Zvonimir Maycug, 1996. Croatia.

Claire of the Moon. Dir. Nicole Conn, 1992. USA.

Clips. Dir. Debi Sundahl and Nan Kinney, 1988. USA.

Cold Steel. Dir. Dorothy Ann Puzo, 1987. USA.

A Comedy in Six Unnatural Acts. Dir. Jan Oxenberg, 1975. USA.

Coming Out. Dir. Heiner Carow, 1989. East Germany.

Committed. Dir. Sheila McLaughlin and Lynne Tillman, 1984. USA.

Confessions of a Congressman [*El diputado*]. Dir. Eloy de la Iglesia, 1978. Spain.

Confusion of Genders [*La Confusion des genres*]. Dir. Ilan Duran Cohen, 2000. France.

Corruption. Dir. Robert Hartford-Davis, 1968. UK.

Couch. Dir. Andy Warhol, 1964. USA.

Countess Dracula. Dir. Peter Sasdy, 1971. UK.

Cover Me. Dir. Michael Schroeder, 1995. USA.

Crash. Dir. David Cronenberg, 1996. Canada.

Cruising. Dir. William Friedkin, 1980. USA and West Germany.

Dark Harbor. Dir. Adam Coleman Howard, 1998. USA.

Darkman. Dir. Sam Raimi, 1990. USA.

Daughter of Dracula (a.k.a. Dracula's Daughter) [La Fille de Dracula]. Dir. Jesús Franco, 1972. France and Portugal.

Daughters of Darkness [Les Lèvres rouges / Le Rouge aux lèvres]. Dir. Harry Kümel, 1971. Belgium, France, and West Germany.

Dear Boys [Lieve jongens]. Dir. Paul de Lussanet, 1980. Netherlands.

Desert Hearts. Dir. Donna Deitch, 1985. USA.

Deviation. Dir. José Ramón Larraz, 1971. UK, Sweden, and Spain.

The Devil's Commandment (a.k.a. Lust of the Vampire) [I Vampiri]. Dir. Riccardo Freda and Mario Bava, 1957. Italy.

The Devil's Plaything (a.k.a. Vampire Ecstasy) [Der Fluch der schwarzen Schwestern]. Dir. Joseph W. Sarno, 1973. Sweden, Switzerland, and West Germany.

The Devil's Rain. Dir. Robert Fuest, 1975. Mexico and USA.

The Devil's Wedding Night [Il plenilunio delle vergini]. Dir. Luigi Batzella, 1973. Italy.

The Does [Les Biches]. Dir. Claude Chabrol, 1968. France and Italy.

The Doom Generation. Dir. Gregg Araki, 1995. USA and France.

Dracula. Dir: Tod Browning, 1931. USA.

Dracula in Brianza (a.k.a. Dracula in the Provinces) [Il cav. Costante Nicosia demoniaco ovvero: Dracula in Brianza]. Dir. Lucio Fulci, 1975. Italy.

Dracula's Daughter. Dir. Lambert Hillyer, 1936. USA.

Dracula Sucks. Dir. Phillip Marshak, 1978. USA.

Dressed to Kill. Dir. Brian De Palma, 1980. USA.

Dry Cleaning [Nettoyage à sec]. Dir. Anne Fontaine, 1997. France and Spain.

Duffer. Dir. Joseph Despins and William Dumaresq, 1971. UK.

An Early Frost. Dir. John Erman, 1985. USA.

Emma, Dark Doors [Emma, puertas oscuras]. Dir. José Ramón Larraz, 1974. Spain.

Entre Nous [Coup de foudre]. Dir. Diane Kurys, 1983. France.

Fascination. Dir. Jean Rollin, 1979. France.

Fatal Attraction. Dir. Adrian Lyne, 1987. USA.

The Fearless Vampire Killers (a.k.a. *Dance of the Vampires*). Dir. Roman Polanski, 1967. UK and USA.

Female Vampire (a.k.a. The Bare-Breasted Countess) [La Comtesse]. Dir. Jesús Franco, 1973. France and Belgium.

Flaming Creatures. Dir. Jack Smith, 1963. USA.

Flesh for Frankenstein (a.k.a. Andy Warhol's Frankenstein). Dir. Paul Morrissey, 1973. Italy and France.

Flesh on Glass. Dir. Ann Turner, 1981. Australia.

A Florida Enchantment. Dir. Sidney Drew, 1914. USA.

The 4th Man [De vierde man]. Dir. Paul Verhoeven, 1983. Netherlands.

Gayracula. Dir. Roger Earl, 1983. USA.

Get Out. Dir. Jordan Peele, 2017. USA and Japan.

Gilda. Dir. Charles Vidor, 1946. USA.

Girly (a.k.a. *Mumsy, Nanny, Sonny, and Girly*). Dir. Freddie Francis, 1970. UK.

Go Fish. Dir. Rose Troche, 1994. USA.

Going Places [Les Valseuses]. Dir. Bertrand Blier, 1974. France.

Goodbye Emma Jo. Dir. Cheryl Newbrough, 1998. USA.

Hamam (a.k.a. Steam: The Turkish Bath) [Il bagno turco]. Dir. Ferzan Özpetek, 1997. Italy, Turkey, and Spain.

Heaven. Dir. Scott Reynolds, 1998. New Zealand and USA.

Henry: Portrait of a Serial Killer. Dir. John McNaughton, 1986. USA.

He Said, She Said. Dir. Ken Kwapis and Marisa Silver, 1991. USA.

A Hoof Here, a Hoof There (a.k.a. *Snowball Reaction / Tainted Horseplay*) [*Kopytem sem, kopytem tam*]. Dir. Věra Chytilová, 1989. Czechoslovakia.

Hourglass. Dir. C. Thomas Howell, 1995. USA.

House Party. Dir. Reginald Hudlin, 1990. USA.

The House That Vanished (a.k.a. *Scream . . . and Die! / Please! Don't Go in the Bedroom*) Dir. José Ramón Larraz, 1973. UK and Spain.

The Hunger. Dir. Tony Scott, 1983. UK and USA.

Hungry Hearts. Dir. Debi Sundahl and Nan Kinney, 1989. USA.

Hunters' Sense of Touch [Karyudo-tachi no shokkaku]. Dir. Hisayasu Sato, 1995. Japan.

I Can't Sleep [J'ai pas sommeil]. Dir. Claire Denis, 1994. France.

I Don't Kiss [J'embrasse pas]. Dir. André Téchiné, 1991. France and Italy.

I Love You, I Don't [Je t'aime moi non plus]. Dir. Serge Gainsbourg, 1976. France.

Immoral Tales [Contes immoraux]. Dir. Walerian Borowczyk, 1973. France.

Impetuous Youth (a.k.a. The Fiddler of Florence) [Der Geiger von Florenz]. Dir. Paul Czinner, 1926. Weimar Republic.

The Incredibly True Adventure of Two Girls in Love. Dir. Maria Maggenti, 1995. USA.

Infamous Neighborhood [Badnam basti]. Dir. Prem Kapoor, 1971. India.

In My Skin [Dans ma peau]. Dir. Marina de Van, 2002. France.

Inside Out. Dir. Sheila McLaughlin, 1978. USA.

"Interview with Sheila McLaughlin." Special feature in *She Must Be Seeing Things*. First Run, 2015. DVD.

Interview with the Vampire. Dir. Neil Jordan, 1994. USA.

Irreconcilable Differences. Dir. Charles Shyer, 1984. USA).

Irreversible [Irréversible]. Dir. Gaspar Noé, 2002. France.

It's Not the Size That Counts (a.k.a. *Percy's Progress*). Dir. Ralph Thomas, 1974. UK.

Jade. Dir. William Friedkin, 1995. USA.

Jagged Edge. Dir. Richard Marquand, 1985. USA.

Just One More Time (a.k.a. *The Over-Amorous Artist*). Dir. Maurice Hamblin, 1974. UK.

Karmen Geï. Dir. Joseph Gaï Ramaka, 2001. Senegal, France, and Canada.

Katzelmacher. Dir. Rainer Werner Fassbinder, 1969. West Germany.

King Solomon's Mines. Dir. J. Lee Thompson, 1985. USA.

Kiss. Dir. Andy Warhol, 1963–1964. USA.

Last Action Hero. Dir. John McTiernan, 1993. USA.

The Last Emperor [*L'ultimo imperatore*]. Dir. Bernardo Bertolucci, 1987. UK, Italy, France, and China.

The Last Seduction. Dir. John Dahl, 1994. USA and UK.

L.A. Zombie. Dir. Bruce LaBruce, 2010. Germany and USA.

Le F.H.A.R. Dir. Carole Roussopoulos, 1971. France.

The Legend of Blood Castle (a.k.a. *Blood Ceremony*) [*Ceremonia sangrienta*]. Dir. Jorge Grau, 1973. Spain and Italy.

Lesbian Vampire Killers. Dir. Phil Claydon, 2009. UK.

Lianna. Dir. John Sayles, 1983. USA.

Libido. Dir. Ernesto Gastaldi and Vittorio Salerno, 1965. Italy.

The Lie [*Mensonge*]. Dir. François Margolin, 1993. France.

Life and Death [*Liv og død*]. Dir. Petter Vennerød and Svend Wam, 1980. Norway.

Lips of Blood [*Lèvres de sang*]. Dir. Jean Rollin, 1975. France.

Lisztomania. Dir. Ken Russell, 1975. UK.

Longtime Companion. Dir. Norman René, 1989. USA.

Looking for Mr. Goodbar. Dir. Richard Brooks, 1977. USA.

Loulou. Dir. Maurice Pialat, 1980. France.

Lovebox (a.k.a. *The Love Box*). Dir. Tudor Gates and Wilbur Stark, 1972. UK.

Macho Dancer. Dir. Lino Brocka, 1988. Philippines.

Madhouse (a.k.a. *The Revenge of Dr. Death*). Dir. Jim Clark, 1974. UK and USA.

The Mad Love Life of a Hot Vampire. Dir. Ray Dennis Steckler (as Sven Christian), 1971. USA.

Maîtresse. Dir. Barbet Schroeder, 1976. France.

Manila in the Claws of Light [*Maynila, sa mga kuko ng liwanag*]. Dir. Lino Brocka, 1975. Philippines.

Man Is a Woman [*L'homme est une femme comme les autres*]. Dir. Jean-Jacques Zilbermann, 1998. France.

The Mark of Lilith. Dir. Bruna Fionda, Polly Gladwin, and Zachary Nataf, 1986. UK.

Martyrs. Dir. Pascal Laugier, 2008. France and Canada.

Mascara [*Make-up voor een moord*]. Dir. Patrick Conrad, 1987. Belgium, Netherlands, and France.

The Meadow of Things [*Die Wiese der Sachen*]. Dir. Heinz Emigholz, 1988. West Germany.

Meat Joy. Dir. Carolee Schneemann, 1964. USA.

Ménage (a.k.a. *Evening Dress*) [*Tenue de soirée*]. Dir. Bertrand Blier, 1986. France.

Men at Work. Dir. Emilio Estevez, 1990. USA.

Miller's Crossing. Dir. Joel Coen and Ethan Coen, 1990. USA.

The Modern Household of Madame Butterfly [*Le Ménage moderne du* [*sic*] *Madame Butterfly*]. Dir. anonymous, 1920. France.

Monster. Dir. Patty Jenkins, 2003. USA and Germany.

Morocco. Dir. Josef von Sternberg, 1930. USA.

MURDER and murder. Dir. Yvonne Rainer, 1996. USA.

My Father Is Coming. Dir. Monika Treut, 1991. Germany.

My Mother [*Ma mère*]. Dir. Christophe Honoré, 2004. France, Portugal, Austria, and Spain.

Nadja. Dir. Michael Almereyda, 1994. USA.

Night Rhythms. Dir. Gregory Dark, 1992. USA.

9½ Weeks. Dir. Adrian Lyne, 1986. USA.

Nosferatu: A Symphony of Horror [*Nosferatu—Eine Symphonie des Grauens*]. Dir. F. W. Murnau, 1922. Weimar Republic.

November Moon [*Novembermond*]. Dir. Alexandra von Grote, 1985. West Germany and France.

The Nude Vampire [*La Vampire nue*]. Dir. Jean Rollin, 1970. France.

The Old Dark House. Dir. William Castle, 1963. UK and USA.

Once I Loved a Woman [*Autrefois j'ai aimé une femme*]. Dir. Edward Owens, 1966. USA.

Once More [*Encore*]. Dir. Paul Vecchiali, 1988. France.

One Night at Dinner (a.k.a. *Love Circle*) [*Metti, una sera a cena*]. Dir. Giuseppe Patroni Griffi, 1969. Italy.

One on Top of the Other (a.k.a. *Perversion Story*) [*Una sull'altra*]. Dir. Lucio Fulci, 1969. Italy, France, and Spain.

On the Make. Dir. Sam Hurwitz, 1989. USA.

Ordinary Sentence [*Normalsatz*]. Dir. Heinz Emigholz, 1982. West Germany.

Orgasmo (a.k.a. *Paranoia*). Dir. Umberto Lenzi, 1969. Italy and France.

Overkill: The Aileen Wuornos Story. Dir. Peter Levin, 1992. USA.

Parking. Dir. Jacques Demy, 1985. France and Japan.

Passages. Dir. Ira Sachs, 2023. France.

Personal Best. Dir. Robert Towne, 1982. USA.

Play Misty for Me. Dir. Clint Eastwood, 1971. USA.

Poison. Dir. Todd Haynes, 1991. USA.

The Potluck and the Passion. Dir. Cheryl Dunye, 1993. USA.

Q & A. Dir. Sidney Lumet, 1990. USA and UK.

The Rape of the Vampire (a.k.a. *The Queen of the Vampires*) [*Le Viol du vampire*]. Dir. Jean Rollin, 1968. France.

Rebecca. Dir. Alfred Hitchcock, 1940. USA.

Requiem for a Vampire (a.k.a. *Caged Virgins*) [*Requiem pour un vampire*]. Dir. Jean Rollin, 1971. France.

"Ring the Alarm." Beyoncé. Music video. Dir. Sophie Muller, 2006. USA.

The Rocky Horror Picture Show. Dir. Jim Sharman, 1975. UK and USA.

Rope. Dir. Alfred Hitchcock, 1948. USA.

The Ryan White Story. Dir. John Herzfeld, 1989. USA.

Safe Is Desire. Dir. Debi Sundahl, 1993. USA.

Salò, or The 120 Days of Sodom [*Salò o le 120 giornate di Sodoma*]. Dir. Pier Paolo Pasolini, 1975. Italy and France.

Savage Nights [*Les Nuits fauves*]. Dir. Cyril Collard, 1992. France and Italy.

Scum of the Earth! (a.k.a. *Sam Flynn*). Dir. Herschell Gordon Lewis, 1963. USA.

Secret Games. Dir. Gregory Dark, 1992. USA.

Seduction: The Cruel Woman [*Verführung: Die grausame Frau*]. Dir. Monika Treut, 1985. West Germany.

See the Sea [*Regarde la mer*]. Dir. François Ozon, 1997. France.

Serious as Pleasure [*Sérieux comme le plaisir*]. Dir. Robert Benayoun, 1975. France.

Sexcula. Dir. John Holbrook, 1974. Canada.

Shadows. Dir. Debi Sundahl and Nan Kinney, 1985. USA.

She Must Be Seeing Things. Dir. Sheila McLaughlin, 1987. USA.

The Shiver of the Vampires [*Le Frisson des vampires*]. Dir. Jean Rollin, 1971. France.

Showgirls. Dir. Paul Verhoeven, 1995. USA and France.

The Silence of the Lambs. Dir. Jonathan Demme, 1991. USA.

Silkwood. Dir. Mike Nichols, 1983. USA.

Sliver. Dir. Phillip Noyce, 1993. USA.

Softly . . . Softly . . . [*Sotto . . . sotto . . . strapazzato da anomala passione*]. Dir. Lina Wertmüller, 1984. Italy.

Something for Everyone. Dir. Harold Prince, 1970. USA.

Sons of Satan. Dir. Tom DeSimone, 1973. USA.

Spartacus. Dir. Stanley Kubrick, 1960. USA.

Speak like a Child. Dir. John Akomfrah, 1998. UK.

Spetters. Dir. Paul Verhoeven, 1980. Netherlands.

The Spiral Staircase. Dir. Robert Siodmak, 1946. USA.

The Story of O [*Histoire d'O*]. Dir. Just Jaeckin, 1975. France, West Germany, and Canada.

Strange Compulsion. Dir. Irvin Berwick, 1964. USA.

Stranger than Paradise. Dir. Jim Jarmusch, 1984. USA.

Stripped to Kill. Dir. Katt Shea, 1987. USA.

Suburban Dykes. Dir. Debi Sundahl, 1990. USA.

Such a Crime. Dir. Cheryl Newbrough, 1998. USA.

A Summer Dress [*Une robe d'été*]. Dir. François Ozon, 1996. France.

Sunday Bloody Sunday. Dir. John Schlesinger, 1971. UK.

The Sweet Body of Deborah [*Il dolce corpo di Deborah*]. Dir. Romolo Guerrieri, 1968. Italy and France.

Swoon. Dir. Tom Kalin, 1992. USA.

Symptoms. Dir. José Ramón Larraz, 1974. UK, Belgium, and Spain.

Taboo Parlor. Dir. Monika Treut, 1994. Germany. This short film appears in the anthology feature *Erotique* (dir. Lizzie Borden, Clara Law, Ana Maria Magalhães, and Monika Treut, 1994).

Tea Time [*L'Heure du thé*]. Dir. anonymous, 1925. France.

Thelma and Louise. Dir. Ridley Scott, 1991. USA, UK, and France.

Theorem [*Teorema*]. Dir. Pier Paolo Pasolini, 1968. Italy.

Tidy Endings. Dir. Gavin Millar, 1988. USA.

Tootsie. Dir. Sydney Pollack, 1982. USA.

To Our Loves [*À nos amours*]. Dir. Maurice Pialat, 1983. France.

Total Recall. Dir. Paul Verhoeven, 1990. USA.

To the Extreme [*In extremis*]. Dir. Étienne Faure, 2000. France.

The Uncertain Death [*La muerte incierta*]. Dir. José Ramón Larraz, 1973. Spain, Italy, and India.

"Unhappy Camper." Prod. Ewan Cant. Special feature in *Blood Hunger: The Films of José Larraz, Vampyres*. Arrow Video, 2019. Blu-ray Disc.

The Vampire Lovers. Dir. Roy Ward Baker, 1970. UK and USA.

The Vampire Wedding [*Svatba upírů*]. Dir. Jaroslav Soukup, 1993. Czechia.

Vampyres. Dir. José Ramón Larraz, 1974. UK and Spain.

Vampyros Lesbos [*Las vampiras*]. Dir. Jesús Franco, 1971. West Germany and Spain.

The Velvet Vampire (a.k.a. **Cemetery Girls**). Dir. Stephanie Rothman, 1971. USA and Philippines.

Vertigo. Dir. Alfred Hitchcock, 1958. USA.

Videodrome. Dir. David Cronenberg, 1983. Canada.

Virgin Machine [*Die Jungfrauenmaschine*]. Dir. Monika Treut, 1988. West Germany.

The Werewolf Versus the Vampire Woman (a.k.a. **Shadow of the Werewolf / Werewolf Shadow**) [*La noche de Walpurgis*]. Dir. León Klimovsky, 1971. Spain and West Germany.

Whirlpool (a.k.a. **She Died with Her Boots On / Whirlpool of Sex**). Dir. José Ramón Larraz, 1970. UK and Denmark.

Why Not! [*Pourquoi pas!*]. Dir. Coline Serreau, 1977. France.

Wild at Heart. Dir. David Lynch, 1990. USA.

Windows. Dir. Gordon Willis, 1980. USA.

The Wings [*Vingarne*]. Dir. Mauritz Stiller, 1916. Sweden.

A Woman like Eve [*Een vrouw als Eva*]. Dir. Nouchka van Brakel, 1979. Netherlands.

Working Girls. Dir. Lizzie Borden, 1986. USA.

Year of the Gun. Dir. John Frankenheimer, 1991. USA.

A Young Emmanuelle [*Néa*]. Dir. Nelly Kaplan, 1976. France and West Germany.

Zorns Lemma. Dir. Hollis Frampton, 1970. USA.

SERIALIZED TELEVISION

America's Most Wanted. "John Kelly Gentry." Aired May 29, 1992, on Fox. USA.

Bouillon de culture. Aired October 18, 1992, on France 2. France.

Divorce Court. Aired 1984–1993 on USA Network. USA.

Ellen. Aired 1994–1998 on ABC. USA.

F2 Le Journal 13H. Aired March 10, 1993, on France 2. France.

Magnum, P.I. Season 5, episodes 1 and 2, "Echoes of the Mind: Part 1" and "Echoes of the Mind: Part 2." Aired September 27, 1984, and October 4, 1984, on CBS. USA.

Midnight Caller. Season 1, episode 3, "After It Happened." Aired March 11, 1989, on NBC. USA.

The New Mike Hammer. Season 1, episode 5, "Shots in the Dark." Aired March 3, 1984, on CBS. USA.

Remington Steele. Season 1, episode 16, "Steele Crazy After All These Years." Aired February 18, 1983, on NBC. USA.

Saturday Night Live. Season 17, episode 17, "Sharon Stone/Pearl Jam." Aired April 11, 1992, on NBC. USA.

The Simpsons. Season 6, episode 25, "Who Shot Mr. Burns? Part Two." Aired September 17, 1995, on Fox. USA.

Will and Grace. Aired 1998–2006, 2017, on NBC. USA.

Bibliography

ACT UP New York. "NBC Protest," n.d. Series xi, Ephemera, Flyers, Handbills, Act Up box 194, folder 24. New York Public Library.

Act Up-Paris. *Le Sida: Combien de divisions?* [AIDS: How many divisions?]. Éditions Dagorno, 1994.

Adamczak, Bini. "On Circlusion." *mask magazine*, July 2016. http://www.maskmagazine .com/the-mommy-issue/sex/circlusion. Archived February 8, 2020, at https://perma .cc/QM25-Y5YS.

Adams, Parveen. "Cars and Scars." *New Formations* 35 (1998): 60–72.

Agar, James N. "Fragments of Wholeness and Filmic Healing: Collard's *Les Nuits Fauves.*" *Contemporary French Civilization* 34, no. 2 (2010): 115–40. https://doi.org/10.3828/cfc.2010.16.

Ahmed, Sara. *Queer Phenomenology: Orientations, Objects, Others.* Duke University Press, 2006.

Ahmed, Sara. *What's the Use? On the Uses of Use.* Duke University Press, 2019.

Alilunas, Peter. *Smutty Little Movies: The Creation and Regulation of Adult Video.* University of California Press, 2016.

"The Alphabet of Ben Sira." Translated by Norman Broznick, David Stern, and Mark Jay Mirsky. In *Rabbinic Fantasies: Imaginative Narratives from Classical Hebrew Literature,* edited by David Stern and Mark Jay Mirsky. Varda, 2001.

Althusser, Louis. *Lenin and Philosophy and Other Essays.* Translated by Ben Brewster. Monthly Review Press, 2001.

Andermatt, Sonia. "There Were Troubling Events . . ." *Pink Paper,* February 18, 1989.

Andreas-Salomé, Lou. "'Anal' and 'Sexual.'" Translated by Nina Hausmann, S. Pearl Brilmyer, Filippo Trentin, Matt ffytche, and Melanie Adley. *Psychoanalysis and History* 24, no. 1 (2022): 19–40. https://doi.org/10.3366/pah.2022.0409.

Andrews, David. "Sex Is Dangerous, So Satisfy Your Wife: The Softcore Thriller in Its Contexts." *Cinema Journal* 45, no. 3 (2006): 59–89. https://doi.org/10.1353/cj.2006.0024.

Angelides, Steven. *A History of Bisexuality.* University of Chicago Press, 2001.

Ardill, Susan, and Sue O'Sullivan. "Sex in the Summer of '88." *Feminist Review* 31 (1989): 126–34. https://doi.org/10.2307/1395096.

Aristotle. *On Sophistical Refutations on Coming-to-Be and Passing-Away.* Translated by E. S. Forster. Harvard University Press, 1955.

Armstrong, Elizabeth. "Traitors to the Cause? Understanding the Lesbian/Gay 'Bisexuality Debates.'" In *Bisexual Politics: Theories, Queries, and Visions,* edited by Naomi Tucker, Liz Highleyman, and Rebecca Kaplan. Harrington Park, 1995.

Atherton, Catherine. *The Stoics on Ambiguity.* Cambridge University Press, 1993.

Auerbach, Nina. *Our Vampires, Ourselves.* University of Chicago Press, 1995.

Ault, Amber. "Ambiguous Identity in an Unambiguous Sex/Gender Structure: The Case of Bisexual Women." In *Bisexuality: A Critical Reader,* edited by Merl Storr. Routledge, 1999.

Ault, Amber. "Hegemonic Discourse in an Oppositional Community: Lesbian Feminist Stigmatization of Bisexual Women." In *Queer Studies: A Lesbian, Gay, Bisexual, and Transgender Anthology,* edited by Brett Beemyn and Mickey Eliason. New York University Press, 1996.

Aumont, Jacques. *The Image.* Translated by Claire Pajackowska. British Film Institute, 1997.

Austin, Guy. *Contemporary French Cinema: An Introduction.* Manchester University Press, 1996.

Bailey, J. Michael. *The Man Who Would Be Queen: The Science of Gender-Bending and Transsexualism.* Joseph Henry Press, 2003.

Baker, Dan. "A History in Ads: The Growth of the Gay and Lesbian Market." In *Homo Economics: Capitalism, Community, and Lesbian and Gay Life,* edited by Amy Gluckman and Betsy Reed. Routledge, 1997.

Balázs, Béla. "Visible Man or the Culture of Film." Translated by Rodney Livingstone. In *Béla Balázs: Early Film Theory,* edited by Erica Carter. Berghahn, 2010.

Barthes, Roland. *Camera Lucida: Reflections on Photography.* Translated by Richard Howard. Hill and Wang, 1981.

Barthes, Roland. "Rhetoric of the Image." Translated by Stephen Heath. In *Image Music Text.* Fontana, 1977.

Barthes, Roland. *S/Z.* Translated by Richard Miller. Blackwell, 1990.

Bataille, Georges. *The Accursed Share: An Essay on General Economy.* Vol. 2. Translated by Robert Hurley. Zone, 1993.

Bataille, Georges. *Death and Sensuality: A Study of Eroticism and the Taboo.* Translated by Mary Dalwood. Walker and Company, 1962.

Baube, Olivier. "Decès du réalisateur et acteur français Cyril Collard" [Death of French director and actor Cyril Collard]. *Agence France Presse,* March 5, 1993.

Baudry, Jean-Louis. "Ideological Effects of the Basic Cinematographic Apparatus." Translated by Alan Williams. *Film Quarterly* 28, no. 2 (1974–75): 39–47. https://doi.org/10.2307/1211632.

Bauman, Zygmunt. *Liquid Love: On the Frailty of Human Bonds.* Polity, 2003.

Bay Area Bisexual Network. *Anything That Moves* 3 (1991).

Bazin, André. "Marginal Notes on Eroticism in the Cinema." Translated by Hugh Gray. In *What Is Cinema?* Vol. 2. University of California Press, 1971.

Bazin, André. "The Ontology of the Photographic Image." Translated by Hugh Gray. In *What Is Cinema?* Vol. 1. University of California Press, 1967.

BBC News. "1973: Britain Joins the EEC." n.d. http://news.bbc.co.uk/onthisday/hi/dates /stories/january/1/newsid_2459000/2459167.stm. Archived February 8, 2020, at https://perma.cc/QYR7-WQBT.

Beauvoir, Simone de. *The Ethics of Ambiguity.* Translated by Bernard Frechtman. Citadel, 1976.

Beauvoir, Simone de. *The Second Sex.* Translated by H. M. Parshley. Jonathan Cape, 1953.

Becker, Edith, Michelle Citron, Julia Lesage, and B. Ruby Rich. "Lesbians and Film." In *Out in Culture: Gay, Lesbian, and Queer Essays on Popular Culture,* edited by Corey K. Creekmur and Alexander Doty. Cassel, 1995.

Bell, David. "Bi-Sexuality—a Place on the Margins." In *The Margins of the City: Gay Men's Urban Lives,* edited by Stephen Whittle. Arena, 1994.

Bergler, Edmund. *Homosexuality: Disease or Way of Life?* Hill and Wang, 1957.

Bergstrom, Janet. "Enunciation and Sexual Difference (Part I)." *Camera Obscura* 7, no. 2–3 (1989): 33–69. https://doi.org/10.1215/02705346-1-2-3-1_3-4-32.

Berlant, Lauren. *Cruel Optimism.* Duke University Press, 2011.

Bersani, Leo. "Against Monogamy." *Oxford Literary Review* 20, no. 1–2 (1998): 3–21. https:// doi.org/10.3366/olr.1998.001.

Bersani, Leo. *Homos.* Harvard University Press, 1996.

Bersani, Leo. "Is There a Gay Art?" In *Is the Rectum a Grave? and Other Essays.* University of Chicago Press, 2010.

Bersani, Leo. "Sociality and Sexuality." *Critical Inquiry* 26, no. 4 (2000): 641–56. https:// doi.org/10.1086/448986.

Bershtein, Evgenii. "Eisenstein's Letter to Magnus Hirschfeld: Text and Context." In *The Flying Carpet: Studies on Eisenstein and Russian Cinema in Honor of Naum Kleiman,* edited by Joan Neuberger and Antonio Somaini. Éditions Mimésis, 2017.

Betz, Mark. *Beyond the Subtitle: Remapping European Art Cinema.* University of Minnesota Press, 2009.

Bey, Marquis. *Cistem Failure: Essays on Blackness and Cisgender.* Duke University Press, 2022.

Bi-Monthly. "Bisexual Manifesto—Draft III." *Bi-Monthly* 7 (1985): 6.

Bollas, Angelos. "Hegemonic Monosexuality." *Journal of Bisexuality* 23, no. 4 (2023): 441–55. https://doi.org/10.1080/15299716.2023.2248126.

Borah, Porismita. "Media Effects Theory." In *The International Encyclopedia of Political Communication,* edited by Gianpietro Mazzoleni. John Wiley and Sons, 2016. https:// doi.org/10.1002/9781118541555.wbiepc156.

Bordwell, David. "The Art Cinema as a Mode of Film Practice." *Film Criticism* 4, no. 1 (1979): 56–64.

Boulé, Jean-Pierre. *HIV Stories: The Archaeology of AIDS Writing in France, 1985–1988.* Liverpool University Press, 2002.

Bourcier, Sam M.-H. *Q comme Queer: Les Séminaires Q du zoo (1996–1997).* [Q as in queer: The Q seminars of zoo (1996–1997)]. Cahiers Gai Kitsch Camp, 1998.

Bower, Jo, Maria Gurevich, and Cynthia Mathieson. "(Con)Tested Identities: Bisexual Women Reorient Sexuality." In *Bisexual Women in the Twenty-First Century,* edited by Dawn Atkins. Harrington Park, 2002.

Boyarin, Daniel, Daniel Itzkovitz, and Ann Pellegrini, eds. "Strange Bedfellows: An Introduction." In *Queer Theory and the Jewish Question*. Columbia University Press, 2003.

Bradbury-Rance, Clara. *Lesbian Cinema After Queer Theory*. Edinburgh University Press, 2019.

Bradley, Rizvana. *Anteaesthetics: Black Aesthesis and the Critique of Form*. Stanford University Press, 2023.

Brilmyer, S. Pearl, and Filippo Trentin. "Introduction: The Genesis of '"Anal" and "Sexual."'" *Psychoanalysis and History* 32, no. 1 (2022): 5–17. https://doi.org/10.3366/pah.2022.0408.

Brilmyer, S. Pearl, Filippo Trentin, and Zairong Xiang. "The Ontology of the Couple: Or, What Queer Theory Knows About Numbers." *GLQ: A Journal of Lesbian and Gay Studies* 25, no. 2 (2019): 223–55. https://doi.org/10.1215/10642684-7367717.

Brinkema, Eugenie. *The Forms of the Affects*. Duke University Press, 2014.

Brinkema, Eugenie. *Life-Destroying Diagrams*. Duke University Press, 2021.

Brinkema, Eugenie. "Rape and the Rectum: Bersani, Deleuze, Noé." *Camera Obscura* 20, no. 1 (2005): 33–57. https://doi.org/10.1215/02705346-20-1_58-33.

British Board of Film Censors. "Exception Form No. 20942: *Vampyres*." July 8, 1974. Accessed in the BBFC's internal archives, London.

British Board of Film Censors. "*Vampyres* letter." July 9, 1974. Accessed in the BBFC's internal archives, London.

British Listed Buildings. "Harefield Grove." n.d. https://britishlistedbuildings.co.uk /101181148-harefield-grove-harefield-ward. Archived February 8, 2020, at https://perma .cc/Q79C-3W7W.

Brode, Douglas. *Deadlier than the Male: Femmes Fatales of 1960s and 1970s Cinema*. Bear-Manor Media, 2016.

Brown, Jason A., Brandon Golob, and Bruno Araujo. "Crimes of Duplicity: The Dangers of Demonizing Bisexuality." In *The (Mis)Representation of Queer Lives in True Crime*, edited by Abbie E. Goldberg, Danielle C. Slakoff, and Carrie L. Buist. Routledge, 2024.

Brownmiller, Susan. *Against Our Will: Men, Women, and Rape*. Penguin, 1975.

Bryant, Wayne M. *Bisexual Characters in Film: From Anaïs to Zee*. Haworth, 1997.

Bryant, Wayne M. "Is That Me up There?" *Journal of Bisexuality* 5, no. 2–3 (2005): 305–12. https://doi.org/10.1300/J159v05n02_35.

Bryant, Wayne M. "Stereotyping Bisexual Men in Film." *Journal of Bisexuality* 1, no. 2–3 (2000): 213–19. https://doi.org/10.1300/J159v01n02_09.

Bulgakowa, Oksana. "Sergei Eisenstein's System Thinking: Influences and Inspirations." *Cultural Science Journal* 13, no. 1 (2021): 85–100. https://doi.org/10.2478/csj-2021-0007.

Bunkers, Suzanne. "Reading and Interpreting Unpublished Diaries by Nineteenth-Century Women." *a/b: Auto/Biography* 2, no. 2 (1986): 15–17. https://doi.org/10.1080 /08989575.1986.10815405.

Burton, Richard Francis. "Terminal Essay." In *The Book of the Thousand Nights and a Night*. Vol. 10. London: Burton Club, 1886.

Buse, Peter. "40,000 Roses—or, The Perversity of Polaroid." In *The Polaroid Years*, edited by Mary-Kay Lombino. Prestel, 2013.

Butler, Alison. "'She Must Be Seeing Things': An Interview with Sheila McLaughlin by Alison Butler." *Screen* 28, no. 4 (1987): 20–29. https://doi.org/10.1093/screen/28.4.20.

Butler, Judith. Afterword to *Butch/Femme: Inside Lesbian Gender*, edited by Sally Munt. Cassel, 1998.

Butler, Judith. *Bodies That Matter: On the Discursive Limits of "Sex."* Routledge, 2011.

Butler, Judith. "Doubting Love." In *Take My Advice: Letters to the Next Generation from People Who Know a Thing or Two*, edited by James L. Harmon. Simon and Schuster, 2002.

Butler, Judith. "Gender as Performance: An Interview with Judith Butler." Interview by Peter Osborne and Lynne Segal. *Radical Philosophy* 67 (1994): 32–39.

Butler, Judith. *Gender Trouble: Feminism and the Subversion of Identity*. Routledge, 2007.

Butler, Judith. *Undoing Gender*. Routledge, 2004.

Byron, George Gordon. "A Fragment." In *Mazeppa: A Poem*. London: John Murray, 1819.

Cahill, Ann J. *Rethinking Rape*. Cornell University Press, 2001.

Caillois, Roger. *Man, Play, and Games*. Translated by Meyer Barash. University of Illinois Press, 2001.

Çakırlar, Cüneyt, and Gary Needham. "The Monogamous/Promiscuous Optics in Contemporary Gay Film: Registering the Amorous Couple in *Weekend* (2011) and *Paris 05:59: Théo & Hugo* (2016)." *New Review of Film and Television* 18, no. 4 (2020): 402–30. https://doi.org/10.1080/17400309.2020.1800329.

Callis, April S. "Playing with Butler and Foucault: Bisexuality and Queer Theory." *Journal of Bisexuality* 9, no. 3–4 (2009): 213–33. https://doi.org/10.1080/15299710903316513.

Caputo, John D. *Hermeneutics: Facts and Interpretation in the Age of Information*. Pelican, 2018.

Caron, David. "*Liberté, Égalité, Séropositivité*: AIDS, the French Republic, and the Question of Community." *French Cultural Studies* 9, no. 27 (1998): 281–93. https://doi.org/10.1177/095715589800902702.

Carpenter, Edward. *Intermediate Types Among Primitive Folk: A Study in Social Evolution*. George Allen, 1914.

Carroll, Jon. "Bisexual Chic." *Oui*, February 1974.

Carroll, Nathan. Introduction to *The Cinematic Sublime: Negative Pleasures, Structuring Absences*, edited by Nathan Carroll. Intellect, 2020.

Carroll, Traci. "Invisible Sissy: The Politics of Masculinity in African American Bisexual Narrative." In D. E. Hall and Pramaggiore, *RePresenting Bisexualities*.

Carter, Henry John. "On a Bisexual Nematoid Worm Which Infests the Common House-Fly (*Musca domestica*) in Bombay." *Annals and Magazine of Natural History* 3, no. 37 (1861): 29–32.

Case, Sue-Ellen. "Towards a Butch-Femme Aesthetic." *Discourse* 11, no. 1 (1988–89): 55–73.

Case, Sue-Ellen. "Tracking the Vampire." *differences: A Journal of Feminist Cultural Studies* 3, no. 2 (1991): 1–20. https://doi.org/10.1215/10407391-3-2-1.

Casetti, Francesco. "Objects on the Screen: Tools, Things, Events." In *Cinematographic Objects: Things and Operations*, edited by Volker Patenburg. August Verlag Berlin, 2015.

Castle, Terry. *The Apparitional Lesbian: Female Homosexuality and Modern Culture*. Columbia University Press, 1993.

Cavell, Stanley. *The World Viewed: Reflections on the Ontology of Film*. Harvard University Press, 1979.

Caws, Mary Ann. "What to Wear in a Vampire Film." In *Fashion in Film*, edited by Adrienne Munich. Indiana University Press, 2011.

Cervulle, Maxime, and Nick Rees-Roberts. "Le Cineaste gay et le garçon arabe" [The gay filmmaker and the Arab boy]. In *Homo exoticus: Race, classe et critique queer* [Homo exoticus: Race, class, and queer critique]. Armand Colin, 2010.

Cheshire, Godfrey. "Self Expressions: Cyril Collard's *Savage Nights*." *Film Comment* 30, no. 1 (1994): 74–77.

Chitty, Christopher. *Sexual Hegemony: Statecraft, Sodomy, and Capital in the Rise of the World System*, edited by Max Fox. Duke University Press, 2020.

Chow, Rey. "A Phantom Discipline." *PMLA* 116, no. 5 (2001): 1386–95. https://doi.org/10.1632/pmla.2001.116.5.1386.

Chu, Andrea Long. "The Impossibility of Feminism." *differences: A Journal of Feminist Cultural Studies* 30, no. 1 (2019): 63–81. https://doi.org/10.1215/10407391-7481232.

Chu, Andrea Long. "My New Vagina Won't Make Me Happy." *New York Times*, November 24, 2018. https://www.nytimes.com/2018/11/24/opinion/sunday/vaginoplasty-transgender-medicine.html. Archived April 12, 2025, at https://perma.cc/4EBB-MAG3.

Chua, Ling-Yen. "Deviant Intersections: Interrogating Discourses of 'Race,' Sexuality and Non-White Homosexuality in Contemporary Films." PhD diss., University of Warwick, 1998.

Cixous, Hélène. "Sorties: Out and Out: Attacks/Ways Out/Forays." Translated by Betsy Wing. In *The Newly Born Woman*, edited by Hélène Cixous and Catherine Clément. Manchester University Press, 1975.

Clark, Danae. "Commodity Lesbianism." In *Out in Culture: Gay, Lesbian, and Queer Essays on Popular Culture*, edited by Corey K. Creekmur and Alexander Doty. Duke University Press, 1995.

Clausen, Jan. "My Interesting Condition." *Journal of Sex Research* 27, no. 3 (1990): 445–59. https://doi.org/10.1080/00224499009551571.

C.L.I.T. Collective. "C.L.I.T. Statement No. 2." In *For Lesbians Only: A Separatist Anthology*, edited by Sarah Lucia-Hoagland and Julia Penelope. Onlywomen Press, 1988.

Clover, Carol. *Men, Women, and Chainsaws: Gender in the Modern Horror Film*. British Film Institute, 1992.

Cohen, Benjamin. "Bretton Woods." In *Routledge Encyclopedia of International Political Economy*, vol. 1, edited by R. J. Barry Jones. Routledge, 2001.

Cohen, Cathy J. "Unsuspecting Women and the Dreaded Bisexual." In *The Boundaries of Blackness: AIDS and the Breakdown of Black Politics*. University of Chicago Press, 1999.

Cohen, Dan. "Contested Terrain." *Guardian: Independent Radical Newsweekly* 44, no. 9 (1991): 20.

Collard, Cyril. *Condamné amour* [Love condemned]. Flammarion, 1987.

Collard, Cyril. *L'Ange sauvage* [The savage angel]. Flammarion, 1993.

Collard, Cyril. *Les Nuits fauves* [Savage nights]. Flammarion, 2015.

Combahee River Collective. "A Black Feminist Statement." In *All the Women Are White, All the Men Are Men, but Some of Us Are Brave: Black Women's Studies*, edited by Gloria T. Hull, Patricia Bell Scott, and Barbara Smith. Feminist Press, 1982.

Comella, Lynn. *Vibrator Nation: How Feminist Sex-Toy Stores Changed the Business of Pleasure*. Duke University Press, 2017.

Condé, Michel. *Les Nuits fauves: Un film de Cyril Collard* [Savage nights: A film by Cyril Collard]. Le Centre Culturel de Grignoux, 1993.

Connor, Steven. "Integuments: The Scar, the Sheen, the Screen." *New Formations* 39 (1999): 32–54.

Conrad, Mark. Introduction to *The Philosophy of Neo-Noir*, edited by Mark Conrad. University Press of Kentucky, 2007.

Cowie, Elizabeth. "Elizabeth Cowie" [individual response]. *Camera Obscura* 7, no. 2–3 (1989): 127–32. https://doi.org/10.1215/02705346-7-2-3_20-21-127.

Cowie, Elizabeth. "Fantasia." *m/f: a feminist journal* 9 (1984): 71–105.

Craft, Christopher. "'Kiss Me with Those Red Lips': Gender and Inversion in Bram Stoker's *Dracula*." *Representations* 8 (1984): 107–33. https://doi.org/10.2307/2928560.

Creed, Barbara. "Lesbian Bodies: Tribades, Tomboys and Tarts." In *Sexy Bodies: The Strange Carnalities of Feminism*, edited by Elizabeth Grosz and Elspeth Probyn. Routledge, 1995.

Creed, Barbara. *The Monstrous-Feminine: Film, Feminism, Psychoanalysis*. Routledge, 1993.

Danziger, Marie. "*Basic Instinct*: Grappling for Post-Modern Mind Control." *Literature/Film Quarterly* 22, no. 1 (1994): 7–10.

Darwin, Charles. *The Descent of Man, and Selection in Relation to Sex*. Vol. 1. London: J. Murray, 1871.

Darwin, Charles. *On the Origin of Species by Means of Natural Selection, or The Preservation of Favoured Races in the Struggle for Life*. London: John Murray, 1859.

Däumer, Elisabeth D. "Queer Ethics; or, The Challenge of Bisexuality to Lesbian Ethics." *Hypatia* 7, no. 4 (1992): 91–105. https://doi.org/10.1111/j.1527-2001.1992.tb00720.x.

Davidson, Phoebe, Jo Eadie, Clare Hemmings, Ann Kaloski, and Merl Storr. Introduction to *The Bisexual Imaginary: Representation, Identity and Desire*, edited by Bi Academic Intervention. Cassel, 1997.

Davis, Bob. "X-Rated Video Losing Share of Tape Sales." *Wall Street Journal*, January 19, 1984.

Dean, Tim. "The Erotics of Transgression." In *The Cambridge Companion to Gay and Lesbian Writing*, edited by Hugh Stevens. Cambridge University Press, 2011.

Dean, Tim. *Unlimited Intimacy: Reflections on the Subculture of Barebacking*. University of Chicago Press, 2009.

de Beauvois, Palisot. "First Memoir of Observations on the Plants Denominated Cryptogamick." *Transactions of the American Philosophical Society* 3 (1793): 202–13. https://doi.org/10.2307/1004869.

Delany, Samuel R. *Times Square Red, Times Square Blue*. 20th anniversary ed. New York University Press, 2019.

de Lauretis, Teresa. *Alice Doesn't: Feminism, Semiotics, Cinema*. Indiana University Press, 1984.

de Lauretis, Teresa. "Film and the Visible." In *How Do I Look? Queer Film and Video*, edited by Bad Object-Choices. Bay Press, 1991.

de Lauretis, Teresa. "Guerrilla in the Midst: Women's Cinema in the 80s." *Screen* 31, no. 1 (1990): 6–25. https://doi.org/10.1093/screen/31.1.6.

de Lauretis, Teresa. *The Practice of Love: Lesbian Sexuality and Perverse Desire*. Indiana University Press, 1994.

de Lauretis, Teresa. "Queer Theory: Lesbian and Gay Sexualities, an Introduction." *differences* 3, no. 2 (1991): iii–xviii. https://doi.org/10.1215/10407391-3-2-iii.

de Lauretis, Teresa. *Technologies of Gender: Essays on Theory, Film, and Fiction*. Indiana University Press, 1987.

Deleuze, Gilles. *Cinema 1: The Movement Image*. Translated by Hugh Tomlinson and Barbara Habberjam. University of Minnesota Press, 1986.

Deleuze, Gilles. *Cinema 2: The Time-Image*. Translated by Hugh Tomlinson and Robert Galeta. Athlone, 1989.

Deleuze, Gilles, and Félix Guattari. *A Thousand Plateaus: Capitalism and Schizophrenia*. Translated by Brian Massumi. University of Minnesota Press, 1987.

Deleyto, Celestino. "The Margins of Pleasure: Female Monstrosity and Male Paranoia in *Basic Instinct*." *Film Criticism* 21, no. 3 (1997): 20–42.

D'Emilio, John. "Capitalism and Gay Identity." In *The Lesbian and Gay Studies Reader*, edited by Henry Abelove, Michèle Aina Barale, and David M. Halperin. Routledge, 1993.

de Oliveira, Jean-Philippe. "Communication publique et formes de gouvernabilité contemporaines de l'état: Le Cas d'homosexualité dans les campagnes de prévention du sida en France (1987–2007)" [Public communication and contemporary forms of state governmentality: The case of homosexuality in AIDS prevention campaigns in France (1987–2007)]. PhD diss., Université de Grenoble, 2012.

Deschamps, Catherine. *Le Miroir bisexuel: Une socio-anthropologie de l'invisible* [The bisexual mirror: A socio-anthropology of the invisible]. Balland, 2002.

Deschamps, Catherine. "Les Recherches sur la sexualité et le sida sous les fourches caudines du néolibéralisme" [Research on sexuality and AIDS under the yoke of neoliberalism]. *L'Homme et la Société* 189–90 (2013): 145–62. https://doi.org/10.3917/lhs.189.0145.

Deval, Jacques. *L'Âge de Juliette: Pièce en trois actes* [The age of Juliette: A play in three acts]. L'Illustration, 1935.

Devillers, Michel. "Rêves informulés" [Unspoken dreams]. *Cinématographe* 35 (1978): 3.

Doane, Mary Ann. *The Desire to Desire: The Woman's Film of the 1940s*. Indiana University Press, 1987.

Doane, Mary Ann. *Femmes Fatales: Feminism, Film Theory, Psychoanalysis*. Routledge, 1991.

Doherty, James. "Grand Jury to Indict Boy Slayers Today." *Chicago Daily Tribune*, June 5, 1924.

Dollimore, Jonathan. "Bisexuality." In *Lesbian and Gay Studies: A Critical Introduction*, edited by Sally Munt and Andy Medhurst. Cassel, 1997.

Dollimore, Jonathan. "Bisexuality, Heterosexuality, and Wishful Theory." *Textual Practice* 10, no. 3 (1996): 523–39. https://doi.org/10.1080/09502369608582258.

Dollimore, Jonathan. *Sexual Dissidence*. Oxford University Press, 1991.

Donaldson, Stephen. "The Bisexual Movement's Beginnings in the 70s: A Personal Retrospective." In *Bisexual Politics: Theories, Queries, and Visions*, edited by Naomi Tucker, Liz Highleyman, and Rebecca Kaplan. Harrington Park, 1995.

Doty, Alexander. *Flaming Classics: Queering the Canon*. Routledge, 2000.

Downing, Lisa. *The Subject of Murder: Gender, Exceptionality, and the Modern Killer*. University of Chicago Press, 2013.

Duberman, Martin. "The Bisexual Debate." In *Human Sexuality in Today's World*, edited by John Gagnon. Little, Brown, 1977.

Duggan, Lisa. *The Twilight of Equality? Neoliberalism, Cultural Politics, and the Attack on Democracy*. Beacon, 2003.

du Plessis, Michael. "Blatantly Bisexual; or, Unthinking Queer Theory." In D. E. Hall and Pramaggiore, *RePresenting Bisexualities*.

Durham, Carolyn A. "Portrait of a Generation: Cyril Collard's *Les Nuits fauves*." *French Review* 75, no. 3 (2002): 512–25.

Dusseau, Félix. "Les Bisexualitiés: Un révélateur social de l'amour" [Bisexualities: Revealing social expectations of love]. *Revue des sciences sociales* 58 (2017): 30–17. https://doi.org/10.4000/revss.289.

Dwyer, Susan. "Censorship." In *The Routledge Companion to Philosophy and Film*, edited by Paisley Livingston and Carl Plantinga. Routledge, 2009.

Dyer, Richard. "Gays in Film." *Jump Cut* 18 (1978): 15–16.

Dyer, Richard. *The Matter of Images: Essays on Representation*. 2nd ed. Routledge, 2002.

Dyer, Richard. *White*. Routledge, 1997.

Eadie, Jo. "Activating Bisexuality: Towards a Bi/Sexual Politics." In *Activating Theory: Lesbian, Gay, Bisexual Politics*, edited by Joseph Bristow and Angelia R. Wilson. Lawrence and Wishart, 1993.

Eadie, Jo. "Bodyscapes, Resources and Social Change." *Body and Society* 9, no. 1 (2003): 73–87. https://doi.org/10.1177/1357034X030091005.

Eadie, Jo. "Indigestion: Diagnosing the Gay Malady." In *Anti-Gay*, edited by Mark Simpson. Cassel, 1996.

Eadie, Jo. "Living in the Past: *Savage Nights*, Bisexual Times." *Journal of Gay, Lesbian and Bisexual Identity* 2, no. 1 (1997): 7–26. https://doi.org/10.1023/A:1026385031442.

Eadie, Jo. "Queer." *Paragraph* 17, no. 3 (1993): 244–51. https://doi.org/10.3366/para.1994.17.3.244.

Eadie, Jo. "'That's Why She Is Bisexual': Contexts for Bisexual Visibility." In *The Bisexual Imaginary: Representation, Identity and Desire*, edited by Bi Academic Intervention. Cassel, 1997.

Edelman, Lee. *Homographesis: Essays in Gay Literary and Cultural Theory*. Routledge, 1994.

Edelman, Lee. *No Future: Queer Theory and the Death Drive*. Duke University Press, 2004.

Eichengreen, Barry. *Globalizing Capital: A History of the International Monetary System*. 2nd ed. Princeton University Press, 2008.

Eisenstein, Sergei. *Diary*. RG 1923, series 2, file no. 1123.1.1931. Russian State Archive for Literature and the Arts, Moscow.

Eisenstein, Sergei. *Disney*. Edited by Oksana Bulgakowa and Dietmar Hochmuth. Translated by Dustin Condren. Potemkin, 2011.

Eisenstein, Sergei. *Metod* [Method]. Vol. 2. Edited by Naum Kleiman. Muzei kino, 2002.

Eisenstein, Sergei. "A 'Shift' to the Biological Level." 1944. Translated by Evgenii Bershtein and Alex Fallow. Unpublished translation accessed courtesy of Evgenii Bershtein, 2019.

Eisner, Shiri. *Bi: Notes for a Bisexual Revolution*. Seal, 2013.

Eisner, Shiri. "Monosexism." In *The SAGE Encyclopedia of LGBTQ Studies*, edited by Abbie E. Goldberg. SAGE, 2016.

Eller, Claudia. "Eszterhas Script Picks Up Record $3-mil from Carolco." *Variety*, June 27, 1990.

Ellis, Henry Havelock. *Studies in the Psychology of Sex*. Vol. 1. William Heinemann, 1941.

Ellsworth, Elizabeth. "Illicit Pleasures: Feminist Spectators and *Personal Best*." *Wide Angle* 8, no. 2 (1986): 45–56.

Eng, David L. *The Feeling of Kinship: Queer Liberalism and the Racialization of Intimacy*. Duke University Press, 2010.

Engelberg, Jacob. "Bisexual and Transgender Potentialities in Pornographic Spectatorship." *Porn Studies* 11, no. 3 (2024): 271–89. https://doi.org/10.1080/23268743.2024.2310534.

Engelberg, Jacob. "Call Me Bi Any Other Name: Anal Monstration, Formal Bisexualization, Gay Indigestion." In *Call Me by Your Name: Perspectives on the Film*, edited by Edward Lamberti and Michael Williams. Intellect, 2024.

Engelberg, Jacob. "'How Could Any One Relationship Ever Possibly Be Fulfilling?': Bisexuality, Nonmonogamy, and the Visualization of Desire in the Cinema of Gregg Araki." *Journal of Bisexuality* 18, no. 1 (2018): 102–17. https://doi.org/10.1080/15299716.2017.1373263.

Engelberg, Jacob, Samuel Lawton, and Julia Shaw. "The Futile Search for 'Physiological Evidence' of Male Bisexuality: A Response to Jabbour et al. (2020)." *Psychology of Sexualities Review* 12, no. 2 (2021): 31–34. https://doi.org/10.53841/bpssex.2021.12.2.31.

Engelmann, Lukas. *Mapping AIDS: Visual Histories of an Enduring Epidemic*. Cambridge University Press, 2018.

Engels, Friedrich. "Letter to F. Mehring, July 14, 1893." In *Karl Marx and Friedrich Engels: Selected Works*. Vol. 3. Progress, 1970.

Epstein, Jean. "Ganymède, essai sur l'éthique homosexuelle masculine" [Ganymede, an essay on male homosexual ethics]. In *Écrits complets* [Complete writings], vol. 3. Independencia, 2014.

Epstein, Jean. "Le Cinématographe vu de l'Etna" [The cinema seen from Etna]. Translated by Stuart Liebman. In *Jean Epstein: Critical Essays and New Translations*. Amsterdam University Press, 2012.

Ertman, Martha. "Follow Your 'Basic Instinct.'" *Outlines: The Voice of the Gay and Lesbian Community* 5, no. 12 (1992): 45.

Eszterhas, Joe. *Hollywood Animal*. Vintage, 2005.

Euclid of Alexandria. *Euclid's Elements*. Edited by Dana Densmore. Translated by Thomas L. Heath. Green Lion, 2002.

Eulenburg, Albert. "Neuropathia sexualis virorum" [Sexual neuropathy in men]. In *Klinisches Handbuch der Harn- und Sexualorgane* [Clinical manual of the urinary and sexual organs], vol. 4, edited by Wolf Zuelzer. Leipzig: F. C. W. Vogel, 1894.

Faderman, Lillian. "A Bisexual Moment." *Advocate*, September 5, 1995.

Fallows, Tom. "'More than Rutting Bodies': Cambist Films, Quality Independents, and the 'Lost' Films of George A. Romero." *Journal of Popular Film and Television* 46, no. 2 (2018): 82–94. https://doi.org/10.1080/01956051.2017.1423018.

Farajajé, Ibrahim Abdurrahman. "Fictions of Purity." In *Recognize: The Voices of Bisexual Men—an Anthology*, edited by Robyn Ochs and H. Sharif Williams. Bisexual Resource Center, 2014.

Farrimond, Katherine. *The Contemporary Femme Fatale: Gender, Genre and American Cinema*. Routledge, 2018.

Feasey, Rebecca. "Neo-Noir's Fatal Women: Stardom, Survival and Sharon Stone." In *Neo-Noir*, edited by Mark Bould, Kathrina Glitre, and Greg Tuck. Wallflower, 2009.

Feasey, Rebecca. "'Sharon Stone, Screen Diva': Stardom, Femininity and Cult Fandom." In *Defining Cult Movies: The Cultural Politics of Oppositional Taste*, edited by March Jancovich, Antonio Lazario-Reboll, Julian Stringer, and Andy Willis. Manchester University Press, 2003.

Feldman, Susan. "Reclaiming Sexual Difference: What Queer Theory Can't Tell Us About Sexuality." *Journal of Bisexuality* 9, no. 3-4 (2009): 259-78. https://doi.org/10.1080/15299710903316562.

Ferenczi, Sándor. "Über die Rolle der Homosexualität in der Pathogenese der Paranoia" [On the role of homosexuality in the pathogenesis of paranoia]. In *Bausteine zur Psychoanalyse* [Building blocks for psychoanalysis], vol. 1, *Theorie* [Theory]. Internationaler Psychoanalytischer Verlag, 1927.

Findlay, Heather. "Freud's 'Fetishism' and the Lesbian Dildo Debates." *Feminist Studies* 18, no. 3 (1992): 563-79. https://doi.org/10.2307/3178083.

Finkler, Lilith. "Lesbians Who Sleep with Men." *Broadside: A Feminist Review* 5, no. 2 (1983): 4.

Firestone, Shulamith. *The Dialectic of Sex: The Case for Feminist Revolution*. Bantam, 1970.

Fisons. "What's a Nice Girl like You Doing in a Firm like This?" Advertisement. *The Times*, March 17, 1971.

Fliess, Wilhelm. *Der Ablauf des Lebens: Grundlegung zur exakten Biologie* [The course of life: Foundations for an exact biology]. Franz Deuticke, 1906.

Fontenay, Franck, and Patrick Genesis Darnett Jr. "Le Boom des bi" [The boom of bis]. *Gai Pied Hebdo*, July 12–August 1, 1986.

Foucault, Michel. "8 January 1975." In *Abnormal: Lectures at the Collège de France 1974-1975*. Translated by Graham Burchell. Verso, 2003.

Foucault, Michel. "Friendship as a Way of Life." Translated by John Johnston. In *Foucault Live: Collected Interviews, 1961-1984*, edited by Sylvère Lotringer. Semiotext(e), 1997.

Foucault, Michel. *The History of Sexuality*. Vol. 1, *The Will to Knowledge*. Translated by Robert Hurley. Penguin, 1998.

Foucault, Michel. "Le Gai Savoir" [Gay knowledge]. *Revista Mec* 5 (1988): 32-36.

Foucault, Michel. "A Preface to Transgression." Translated by Donald F. Bouchard and Sherry Simon. In *Language, Counter-Memory, Practice: Selected Essays and Interviews*. Cornell University Press, 1977.

Freibert, Farrah. "Bad Bis Go to Hell: Bisexuality as Transgressive and Lucrative in Doris Wishman's Roughies." In *ReFocus: The Films of Doris Wishman*, edited by Alicia Kozma and Farrah Freibert. University of Edinburgh Press, 2021.

Freud, Sigmund. "Analysis of a Phobia in a Five-Year-Old Boy." In Freud, *Revised Standard Edition*, vol. 10.

Freud, Sigmund. "Beyond the Pleasure Principle." In Freud, *Revised Standard Edition*, vol. 18.

Freud, Sigmund. "Draft H. Paranoia (January 24, 1895)." In Freud, *Revised Standard Edition*, vol. 1.

Freud, Sigmund. "Female Sexuality." In Freud, *Revised Standard Edition*, vol. 21.

Freud, Sigmund. "Fetishism." In Freud, *Revised Standard Edition*, vol. 21.

Freud, Sigmund. "From the History of an Infantile Neurosis." In Freud, *Revised Standard Edition*, vol. 17.

Freud, Sigmund. "The Interpretation of Dreams (Chapters I–VI (C))." In Freud, *Revised Standard Edition*, vol. 4.

Freud, Sigmund. "Letter 52. December 6, 1896." In Freud, *Revised Standard Edition*, vol. 1.

Freud, Sigmund. "On the Sexual Theories of Children." In Freud, *Revised Standard Edition*, vol. 9.

Freud, Sigmund. *The Revised Standard Edition of the Complete Psychological Works of Sigmund Freud.* 24 vols. Edited by Mark Solms and Ilse Gubrich-Simitis. Translated by James Strachey, Anna Freud, Alix Strachey, and Alan Tyson. Rowman and Littlefield and the Institute of Psychoanalysis, 2024.

Freud, Sigmund. "Some Psychical Consequences of the Anatomical Distinction Between the Sexes." In Freud, *Revised Standard Edition*, vol. 19.

Freud, Sigmund. "A Special Type of Choice of Object Made by Men (Contributions to the Psychology of Love I)." In Freud, *Revised Standard Edition*, vol. 11.

Freud, Sigmund. "Three Essays on the Theory of Sexuality." In Freud, *Revised Standard Edition*, vol. 7.

Freund, Kurt. "Male Homosexuality: An Analysis of the Pattern." In *Understanding Homosexuality: Its Biological and Psychological Bases*, edited by John A. Loraine. Medical and Technical Publishing, 1974.

Gabara, Rachel. "Screening Autobiography: Cyril Collard's *Nuits fauves.*" *French Cultural Studies* 16, no. 1 (2005): 55–72. https://doi.org/10.1177/0957155805049566.

Gadamer, Hans-Georg. *Truth and Method.* Translated by Joel Weinsheimer and Donald G. Marshall. Bloomsbury Academic, 2013.

Gadamer, Hans-Georg. *Warheit und Methode: Grundzüge einer philosophischen Hermeneutik* [Truth and method: Fundamentals of a philosophical hermeneutics]. J. C. B. Mohr, 1960.

Galloway, Paul. "Gacy Case Heading for Trial." *Chicago Sun-Times*, March 11, 1980.

Galt, Rosalind. *Alluring Monsters: The Pontianak and Cinemas of Decolonization.* Columbia University Press, 2021.

Galt, Rosalind. *Pretty: Film and the Decorative Image.* Columbia University Press, 2011.

Galt, Rosalind, and Karl Schoonover. "Introduction: The Impurity of Art Cinema." In *Global Art Cinema*, edited by Rosalind Galt and Karl Schoonover. Oxford University Press, 2010.

Galvin, Peter. "Paul Verhoeven." *Advocate*, September 19, 1995.

Garber, Marjorie. *Vice Versa: Bisexuality and the Eroticism of Everyday Life.* Penguin, 1997.

Gazier, Augustin. *Lettres à Grégoire sur les patois de France, 1790–1794: Documents inédits* [Letters to Grégoire on French dialects, 1790–1794: Unpublished documents]. Paris: G. Pedone-Lauriel, 1880.

Gelman, David, Lisa Drew, Mary Hager, Monroe Anderson, George Raine, and Sue Hutchison. "A Perilous Double Love Life." *Newsweek*, July 13, 1987.

Genet, Jean. *Funeral Rites*. Translated by Bernard Frechtman. Faber and Faber, 2009.

George, Sheldon. *Trauma and Race: A Lacanian Study of African American Racial Identity*. Baylor University Press, 2016.

Gever, Martha. "Girl Crazy: Lesbian Narratives in *She Must Be Seeing Things* and *Damned If You Don't*." *Independent*, July 1988.

Giaccardi, Thierry. "Fluidité et plasticité dans les *Nuits fauves* de Cyril Collard" [Fluidity and plasticity in Cyril Collard's *Savage Nights*]. *Entrelacs: Cinéma et audiovisuel* 9 (2012): 1–9. https://doi.org/10.4000/entrelacs.359.

Gill, Rosalind. "Postfeminist Media Culture: Elements of a Sensibility." *European Journal of Cultural Studies* 10, no. 2 (2007): 147–66. https://doi.org/10.1177/1367549407075898.

Gilles, Médioni. "Les Enfants des *Nuits fauves*" [The children of *Savage Nights*]. *L'Express*, February 18, 1993.

Gill-Peterson, Jules. "The Technical Capacities of the Body: Assembling Race, Technology, and Transgender." *Transgender Studies Quarterly* 1, no. 3 (2014): 402–18. https://doi.org/10.1215/23289252-2685660.

Girard, René. *Deceit, Desire, and the Novel: Self and Other in Literary Structure*. Translated by Yvonne Freccero. Johns Hopkins University Press, 1965.

GLAAD. *The GLAAD Bulletin*, May/June 1991.

GLAAD. "Hollywood Images Fuel Gay/Lesbian Bashing." *Daily Variety*, September 25, 1990.

Gley, Eugène. "Les Aberrations de l'instinct sexuel: D'après des travaux récents" [Aberrations of the sexual instinct: According to some recent work]. *Revue Philosophique de la France et de l'Étranger* 17 (1884): 66–92.

Glucksmann, André. *La Fêlure du monde: Éthique et sida* [The rift of the world: Ethics and AIDS]. Flammarion, 1994.

Gomery, Douglas. "The Hollywood Blockbuster: Industrial Analysis and Practice." In *Movie Blockbusters*, edited by Julian Stringer. Routledge, 2003.

Gorfinkel, Elena. *Lewd Looks: American Sexploitation Cinema in the 1960s*. University of Minnesota Press, 2017.

Gorham, Caz. "Our Standards Should Be Higher." *Pink Paper*, September 15, 1988.

Gorman, Tom. "Judge, Calling Killing 'Sinister,' Imposes 20 Years." *Los Angeles Times*, May 3, 1990.

Gould, Stephen Jay. *Ontogeny and Phylogeny*. Belknap Press of Harvard University Press, 1977.

Graham, Nancy, Teresa de Lauretis, Mandy Merck, et al. "Discussion." In *How Do I Look? Queer Film and Video*, edited by Bad Object-Choices. Bay Press, 1991.

Grant, Melissa Gira. *Playing the Whore: The Work of Sex Work*. Verso, 2014.

Greaves, Tim. *Vampyres: A Tribute to the Ultimate in Erotic Horror Cinema*. Shot 1, 1994.

Gregg, Ronald, and Amy Villarejo, eds. *The Oxford Handbook of Queer Cinema*. Oxford University Press, 2021.

Griggers, Camilla. "Phantom and Reel Projections: Lesbians and the (Serial) Killing-Machine." In *Posthuman Bodies*, edited by Jack Halberstam and Ira Livingston. Indiana University Press, 1995.

Grigorieff, Ghéorghiü. *Non au sida* [No to AIDS]. Marabot, 1986.

Grosz, Elizabeth. *Volatile Bodies: Toward a Corporeal Feminism.* Indiana University Press, 1994.

Grover, Jan Zita. "AIDS: Keywords." *October* 43 (1987): 17–30. https://doi.org/10.2307/3397563.

Guattari, Félix. "Becoming-Woman." Translated by Rachel McComas and Stamos Metzidakis. *Semiotext(e)* 10 (1981): 86–88.

Guattari, Félix. "I Have Even Met Happy Travelos." Translated by Rachel McComas. *Semiotext(e)* 10 (1981): 80–81.

Guérin, Daniel. "Géographie passionnelle d'une époque. Entretien avec Daniel Guérin" [Emotional topography of an era. Interview with Daniel Guérin]. Translated by Olga Luisa Balaguer. Interview by J. A. Gonzalez and Ignacio de Llorens. *Débattre* 10 (2000): 5–10.

Guérin, Daniel. *Homosexualité et révolution* [Homosexuality and revolution]. Spartacus, 2013.

Guerrero-Pica, Mar, María-José Establés, and Rafael Ventura. "Killing of Lexa: 'Dead Lesbian Syndrome' and Intra-Fandom Management of Toxic Fan Practices in an Online Queer Community." *Participations: Journal of Audience and Reception Studies* 15, no. 1 (2018): 311–33.

Gulam, Joshua. "Film Stardom, Gender, and Philanthropy: Sharon Stone at the World Summit of Nobel Peace Laureates." *Celebrity Studies* 5, no. 3 (2014): 360–63. https://doi.org/10.1080/19392397.2014.935634.

Gutter Dyke Collective. "Over the Walls, Separatism." In *For Lesbians Only: A Separatist Anthology,* edited by Sarah Lucia-Hoagland and Julia Penelope. Onlywomen, 1988.

Haeberle, Erwin J. "Bisexualitäten—Geschichte und Dimensionen eines modernen wissenschaftlichen Problems" [Bisexualities—History and dimensions of a modern scientific problem]. In *Bisexualitäten—Ideologie und Praxis des Sexualkontaktes mit beiden Geschlechtern* [Bisexualities—Ideology and practice of sexual contact with both sexes], edited by Erwin J. Haeberle and Rolf Gindorf. Gustav Fischer, 1994.

Haeckel, Ernst. *Anthropogenie: Oder, Entwickelungsgeschichte des Menschen* [Anthropogeny: Or, the history of human development]. Leipzig: Wilhelm Engelmann, 1877.

Halberstam, Jack. *Female Masculinity.* Duke University Press, 1998.

Hall, Donald E. "BI-ntroduction II: Epistemologies of the Fence." In D. E. Hall and Pramaggiore, *RePresenting Bisexualities.*

Hall, Donald E. "Graphic Sexuality and the Erasure of a Polymorphous Perversity." In D. E. Hall and Pramaggiore, *RePresenting Bisexualities.*

Hall, Donald E., and Maria Pramaggiore, eds. *RePresenting Bisexualities: Subjects and Cultures of Fluid Desire.* New York University Press, 1996.

Hall, Stuart. "The Work of Representation." In *Representation: Cultural Representations and Signifying Practices,* edited by Stuart Hall. Open University, 1997.

Halperin, David M. "Thirteen Ways of Looking at a Bisexual." *Journal of Bisexuality* 9, no. 3–4 (2009): 451–55. https://doi.org/10.1080/15299710903316679.

Handyside, Fiona. *Cinema at the Shore: The Beach in French Film.* Peter Lang, 2014.

Hansen, Miriam. "Pleasure, Ambivalence, Identification: Valentino and Female Spectatorship." *Cinema Journal* 25, no. 4 (1986): 6–32. https://doi.org/10.2307/1225080.

Hanson, Ellis. "Lesbians Who Bite." In *Out Takes: Essays on Queer Theory and Film*, edited by Ellis Hanson. Duke University Press, 1999.

Hansson, Sven Ove. "A Panorama of the Philosophy of Risk." In *Handbook of Risk Theory: Epistemology, Decision Theory, Ethics, and Social Implications of Risk*, edited by Sabine Roeser, Rafaela Hillerbrand, Per Sandin, and Martin Peterson. Springer, 2012.

Hao Dazheng. "Chinese Visual Representation: Painting and Cinema." Translated by Douglas Wilkerson. In *Cinematic Landscapes: Observations on the Visual Arts and Cinema of China and Japan*, edited by Linda C. Ehrlich and David Dessler. University of Texas Press, 2008.

Haraway, Donna. "Introduction: A Kinship of Feminist Figurations." In *The Haraway Reader*. Routledge, 2004.

Haraway, Donna. *Modest_Witness@Second_Millennium.FemaleMan©_Meets_ OncoMouse™: Feminism and Technoscience*. Routledge, 1997.

Haraway, Donna. *When Species Meet*. University of Minnesota Press, 2008.

Hardin, Carolyn. *Capturing Finance: Arbitrage and Social Domination*. Duke University Press, 2021.

Hart, Lynda. *Fatal Women: Lesbian Sexuality and the Mark of Aggression*. Routledge, 1994.

Hayward, Eva. "Lessons from a Starfish." In *Queering the Non/Human*, edited by Noreen Giffney and Myra J. Hird. Ashgate, 2008.

Healey, Emma. *Lesbian Sex Wars*. Virago, 1996.

Heck, Kalling. *After Authority: Global Art Cinema and Political Transition*. Rutgers University Press, 2020.

Hedgehog, Maz. "Where Fatness and Bisexuality Meet: Discipline and Anglo-American Capitalism." In *It Ain't Over til the Bisexual Speaks: An Anthology of Bisexual Voices*, edited by Vaneet Mehta and Lois Shearing. Jessica Kingsley, 2024.

Hegel, Georg Wilhelm Friedrich. *Encyclopedia of the Philosophical Sciences in Basic Outline, Part I: Science of Logic*. Edited and translated by Klaus Brinkmann and Daniel O. Dahlstrom. Cambridge University Press, 2010.

Hegel, Georg Wilhelm Friedrich. *The Science of Logic*. Translated by George Di Giovanni. Cambridge University Press, 2010.

Heidegger, Martin. *Being and Time*. Translated by Joan Stambaugh. State University of New York Press, 2010.

Helleiner, Eric. *States and the Reemergence of Global Finance: From Bretton Woods to the 1990s*. Cornell University Press, 1996.

Heller-Nicholas, Alexandra. "Seductive Kindness: Power, Space and 'Lesbian' Vampires." In *Hospitality, Rape and Consent in Vampire Popular Culture: Letting the Wrong One In*, edited by David Baker, Stephanie Green, and Agnieszka Stasiewicz-Bieńkowska. Palgrave Macmillan, 2017.

Hemmings, Clare. *Bisexual Spaces: A Geography of Sexuality and Gender*. Routledge, 2002.

Hemmings, Clare. "Bisexual Theoretical Perspectives: Emergent and Contingent Relationships." In *The Bisexual Imaginary: Representation, Identity and Desire*, edited by Bi Academic Intervention. Cassel, 1997.

Hemmings, Clare. "From Landmarks to Spaces: Mapping the Territory of a Bisexual Genealogy." In *Queers in Space: Communities, Public Places, Sites of Resistance*, edited by Gordon Brent Ingram, Anne-Marie Bouthillette, and Yolanda Retter. Bay, 1997.

Hemmings, Clare. "Locating Bisexual Identities: Discourses of Bisexuality and Contemporary Feminist Theory." In *Mapping Desire: Geographies of Sexualities*, edited by David Bell and Gill Valentine. Routledge, 1995.

Hemmings, Clare. "Out of Sight, Out of Mind? Theorizing Femme Narrative." *Sexualities* 2, no. 4 (1999): 451-64. https://doi.org/10.1177/136346099002004005.

Hemmings, Clare. "Resituating the Bisexual Body: From Identity to Difference." In *Activating Theory: Lesbian, Gay, Bisexual Politics*, edited by Joseph Bristow and Angelia R. Wilson. Lawrence and Wishart, 1993.

Hemmings, Clare. "Waiting for No Man: Bisexual Femme Subjectivity and Cultural Repudiation." In *Butch/Femme: Inside Lesbian Gender*, edited by Sally Munt. Cassel, 1998.

Hemmings, Clare. "What's in a Name? Bisexuality, Transnational Sexuality Studies and Western Colonial Legacies." *International Journal of Human Rights* 11, no. 1-2 (2007): 13-32. https://doi.org/10.1080/13642980601176258.

Henderson, Paul, and Stephen Wright. "Hand in Hand with Hindley." *Daily Mail*, November 23, 1995.

Hennig, Jean-Luc. *Bi: De la bisexualité masculine* [Bi: On male bisexuality]. Gallimard, 1996.

Herbert, Daniel. *Maverick Movies: New Line Cinema and the Transformation of American Film.* University of California Press, 2024.

Hester, Diarmuid. "Diagramming *Irréversible.*" *One+One Filmmakers Journal* 4 (2010): 22-27.

Hewitt, Christopher. "Homosexual Demography: Implications for the Spread of AIDS." *Journal of Sex Research* 35, no. 4 (1998): 390-96. https://doi.org/10.1080/00224499809551957.

Higginbotham, Evelyn Brooks. *Righteous Discontent: The Women's Movement in the Black Baptist Church, 1880-1920.* Harvard University Press, 1993.

Hillier, Jim. *The New Hollywood.* Continuum, 1992.

Hoad, Neville. "Arrested Development or the Queerness of Savages: Resisting Evolutionary Narratives of Difference." *Postcolonial Studies: Culture, Politics, Economy* 3, no. 2 (2000): 133-58. https://doi.org/10.1080/13688790050115277.

Hoagland, Sarah Lucia. *Lesbian Ethics: Toward New Value.* Institute of Lesbian Studies, 1988.

Hocquenghem, Guy. *Gay Liberation After May '68.* Translated by Scott Branson. Duke University Press, 2022.

Hocquenghem, Guy. *Homosexual Desire.* Translated by Daniella Dangoor. Duke University Press, 1993.

Hocquenghem, Guy. "To Destroy Sexuality." Translated by Tom Gora. *Semiotext(e)* 10 (1981): 260-64.

Hogan, Rebecca. "Engendered Autobiographies: The Diary as Feminine Form." *Prose Studies: History, Theory, Criticism* 14, no. 2 (1991): 95-107. https://doi.org/10.1080/01440359108586434.

Holmlund, Chris. "Cruisin' for a Bruisin': Hollywood's Deadly (Lesbian) Dolls." *Cinema Journal* 34, no. 1 (1994): 31-51. https://doi.org/10.2307/1225654.

Holmlund, Chris. "Introduction: Movies and the 1990s." In *American Cinema of the 1990s: Themes and Variations*, edited by Chris Holmlund. Rutgers University Press, 2008.

Holmlund, Chris. "When Is a Lesbian Not a Lesbian? The Lesbian Continuum and the Mainstream Femme Film." *Camera Obscura* 9, no. 1–2 (1991): 144–80. https://doi.org/10.1215/02705346-9-1-2_25-26-144.

Holte, James Craig. "Not All Fangs Are Phallic: Female Vampire Films." *Journal of the Fantastic in the Arts* 10, no. 2 (1999): 163–73.

Holte, James Craig. "The Vampire." In *Mythical and Fabulous Creatures: A Source Book and Research Guide*, edited by Malcolm South. Greenwood, 1987.

hooks, bell. *The Will to Change: Men, Masculinity, and Love*. Atria, 2004.

Horace [Quintus Horatius Flaccus]. "Epistle XIX." In *Horace: The Epistles*, edited by F. G. Plaitsower and F. P. Shipham. London: University Correspondence College Press, 1893.

Howes, David. "Introduction: Empires of the Senses." In *Empire of the Senses: The Sensual Culture Reader*, edited by David Howes. Berg, 2005.

Hudson, Dale. *Vampires, Race, and Transnational Hollywoods*. Edinburgh University Press, 2017.

Hunt, Alan. "Risk and Moralization in Everyday Life." In *Risk and Morality*, edited by Richard V. Ericson and Aaron Doyle. University of Toronto Press, 2003.

Irigaray, Luce. *This Sex Which Is Not One*. Translated by Catherine Porter and Carolyn Burke. Cornell University Press, 1985.

Ivanov, Viacheslav Vsevolodovich. *Ocherki po istorii semiotiki v SSSR* [Essays on the history of semiotics in the USSR]. Nauka, 1976.

Ivascu, Tessa. "Les Maris secrètement bisexuels: Danger, sida?" [Secretly bisexual husbands: AIDS danger?]. *Marie Claire* [France], June 1993.

Jabbour, Jeremy, Luke Holmes, David Sylva, et al. "Robust Evidence for Bisexual Orientation Among Men." *Proceedings of the National Academy of Science* 117, no. 31 (2020): 18369–77. https://doi.org/10.1073/pnas.2003631117.

Jackson, Rosemary. *Fantasy: The Literature of Subversion*. Routledge, 1981.

Jackson, Zakiyyah Iman. *Becoming Human: Matter and Meaning in an Antiblack World*. New York University Press, 2020.

Jagose, Annamarie. *Inconsequence: Lesbian Representation and the Logic of Sexual Sequence*. Cornell University Press, 2002.

James, Christopher. "Denying Complexity: The Dismissal and Appropriation of Bisexuality in Queer, Lesbian, and Gay Theory." In *Queer Studies: A Lesbian, Gay, Bisexual, and Transgender Anthology*, edited by Brett Beemyn and Mickey Eliason. New York University Press, 1996.

Jameson, Fredric. "Culture and Finance Capital." *Critical Inquiry* 24 (1997): 246–65. https://doi.org/10.1086/448873.

Janssen, Diederik. "Monosexual/Plurisexual: A Concise History." *Journal of Homosexuality* (2023): 1839–62. https://doi.org/10.1080/00918369.2023.2218957.

Japenga, Ann. "Hidden Dangers: Worried by AIDS Threat, Experts Focus on Bisexual Men Who Put Themselves, Families at Risk." *Los Angeles Times*, May 12, 1992.

Jeffreys, Sheila. *Anticlimax: A Feminist Perspective on the Sexual Revolution*. New York University Press, 1990.

Jeffreys, Sheila. "Bisexual Politics: A Superior Form of Feminism?" *Women's Studies International Forum* 22, no. 3 (1999): 273–85. https://doi.org/10.1016/S0277-5395(99)00020-5.

Jeffreys, Sheila. "The Essential Lesbian." In *All the Rage: Reasserting Radical Lesbian Feminism*, edited by Lynne Harne and Elaine Miller. Women's Press, 1999.

Jeffreys, Sheila. *The Lesbian Revolution: Lesbian Feminism in the UK 1970–1990.* Routledge, 2018.

Jeffreys, Sheila. *Trigger Warning: My Lesbian Feminist Life.* Spinifex, 2020.

Jenkins, Bruce. "*Couch*." In *The Films of Andy Warhol Catalogue Raisonné 1963–1965*, vol. 2, edited by John G. Hanhardt. Yale University Press, 2021.

Johnson, Nicole L., and MaryBeth Grove. "Why Us? Toward an Understanding of Bisexual Women's Vulnerability for and Negative Consequences of Sexual Violence." *Journal of Bisexuality* 17, no. 4 (2017): 435–50. https://doi.org/10.1080/15299716.2017.1364201.

Johnston, Claire. "Women's Cinema as Counter-Cinema." In *Notes on Women's Cinema*, edited by Claire Johnston. Society for Education in Film and Television, 1973.

Johnston, Jill. *Lesbian Nation: The Feminist Solution.* Simon and Schuster, 1973.

Jordan, June. "A New Politics of Sexuality." *Progressive* 55, no. 7 (July 1991): 12–13.

Joyce, Helen. *Trans: When Ideology Meets Reality.* Oneworld, 2021.

Kalmár, György. *Post-Crisis European Cinema: White Men in Off-Modern Landscapes.* Palgrave Macmillan, 2020.

Kane, Robin. "RE: March 1992 Staff Report." Box 3, folder 39, National Gay and Lesbian Task Force Records, 1973–2000. Cornell University Libraries, Ithaca, New York.

Kazmin, Amy Louise. "'Chameleon Fugitive' to Stand Trial for Murder." *Los Angeles Times*, July 28, 1992.

Keegan, Cáel M. "In Praise of the Bad Transgender Object: *The Silence of the Lambs*." *Flow Journal* (June 1, 2020). https://www.flowjournal.org/2020/06/in-praise-of-the-bad-silence/. Archived November 24, 2024, at https://perma.cc/XL59-7FTK.

Keegan, Cáel M. *Lana and Lilly Wachowski.* University of Illinois Press, 2018.

Keegan, Cáel M. "On the Necessity of Bad Trans Objects." *Film Quarterly* 75, no. 3 (2022): 26–37. https://doi.org/10.1525/fq.2022.75.3.26.

Keegan, Cáel M. "Revisitation: A Trans Phenomenology of the Media Image." *MedieKultur* 61 (2016): 26–41. https://doi.org/10.7146/mediekultur.v32i61.22414.

Keeling, Kara. *The Witch's Flight: The Cinematic, the Black Femme, and the Image of Common Sense.* Duke University Press, 2007.

Kennickell, Arthur B., and Martha Starr-McCluer. "Changes in Family Finances from 1989–1992: Evidence from the Survey of Consumer Finances." *Federal Reserve Bulletin* (October 1994): 861–82.

Keynes, John Maynard. *A Treatise on Probability.* Macmillan, 1921.

Kierkegaard, Søren. *The Concept of Anxiety: A Simple Psychologically Orienting Deliberation on the Dogmatic Issue of Hereditary Sin.* Translated by Reidar Thomte. Princeton University Press, 1980.

King, Katie. "'There Are No Lesbians Here': Lesbianisms, Feminisms, and Global Gay Formations." In *Queer Globalizations: Citizenship and the Afterlife of Colonialism*, edited by Arnaldo Cruz-Malavé and Martin F. Manalansan IV. New York University Press, 2002.

Kinsey, Alfred, Wardell Pomeroy, and Clyde Martin. *Sexual Behavior in the Human Male*. W. B. Saunders, 1948.

Kinsey, Alfred, Wardell Pomeroy, Clyde Martin, and Paul Gebhard. *Sexual Behavior in the Human Female*. W. B. Saunders, 1953.

Klein, Fritz. *The Bisexual Option*. 2nd ed. Haworth, 1993.

Klein, Melanie. "Notes on Some Schizoid Mechanisms." In *Developments in Psychoanalysis*, edited by Joan Riviere. Karnac, 1989.

Klesse, Christian. *The Spectre of Promiscuity: Gay Male and Bisexual Non-Monogamies and Polyamories*. Ashgate, 2007.

Klotz, Marcia. "The Queer and Unqueer Spaces of Monika Treut's Films." In *Triangulated Visions: Women in Recent German Cinema*, edited by Ingeborg Majer O'Sickey and Ingeborg von Zadow. State University of New York Press, 1998.

Knight, Frank H. *Risk, Uncertainty and Profit*. Houghton Mifflin, 1921.

Koedt, Anne. "The Myth of the Vaginal Orgasm." In *Notes from the First Year*. New York Radical Feminists, 1968.

Kogout, Vladimir. *Le Monde animalier dans les expressions et proverbes français* [The animal world in French expressions and proverbs]. Anthology, 2017.

Kolb, Robert W. "Redistribution of Wealth." In *Encyclopedia of Business Ethics and Society*, vol. 4, edited by Robert W. Kolb. SAGE, 2008.

Koller, Veronika. *Lesbian Discourses: Images of a Community*. Routledge, 2008.

Krafft-Ebing, Richard von. *Psychopathia Sexualis: The Classic Study of Deviant Sex*. Translated by Franklin S. Klaf. Arcade, 2011.

Krobb, Florian. "'La Belle Juive': 'Cunning in the Men and Beauty in the Women.'" *Jewish Quarterly* 39, no. 3 (1992): 5–11. https://doi.org/10.1080/0449010X.1992.10705865.

Krzywinska, Tanya. "La Belle Dame sans Merci?" In *A Queer Romance: Lesbians, Gay Men and Popular Culture*, edited by Paul Burston and Colin Richardson. Routledge, 1995.

Krzywinska, Tanya. *Sex and the Cinema*. Wallflower, 2006.

Kuhn, Annette. *Women's Pictures: Feminism and Cinema*. Verso, 1994.

Lacan, Jacques. "The Mirror Stage as Formative of the *I* Function as Revealed in Psychoanalytic Experience." Translated by Bruce Fink, Héloïse Fink, and Russell Grigg. In *Écrits*. W. W. Norton, 2002.

Lacan, Jacques. "The Paradox of *Jouissance*." Translated by Dennis Porter. In *The Ethics of Psychoanalysis 1959-1960: The Seminar of Jacques Lacan Book VII*, edited by Jacques-Alain Miller. W. W. Norton, 1986.

Lacquer, Thomas. *Making Sex: Body and Gender from the Greeks to Freud*. Harvard University Press, 1990.

Lamien, Eric. "Bisexualité: La Valse des identités" [Bisexuality: The shuffle of identities]. *3 Keller: Le Mensuel du Centre gai et lesbien* (1996): 10–11.

Laplanche, Jean, and Jean-Bertrand Pontalis. "Fantasy and the Origins of Sexuality." *International Journal of Psychoanalysis* 49, no. 1 (1968): 1–18.

Laplanche, Jean, and Jean-Bertrand Pontalis. *The Language of Psycho-Analysis*. Translated by Donald Nicholson-Smith. Karnac, 1973.

Lary, N. M. "Eisenstein and Shakespeare." In *Eisenstein Rediscovered*, edited by Ian Christie and Richard Taylor. Routledge, 1993.

Lavery, Grace E. *Pleasure and Efficacy: Of Pen Names, Cover Versions, and Other Trans Techniques.* Princeton University Press, 2023.

LaVey, Anton Szandor. *The Satanic Bible.* Avon, 1969.

Le Fanu, Joseph Sheridan. *Carmilla.* Enhanced Media, 2017.

Les Nuits fauves: Extraits de la bande originale du film de Cyril Collard [Savage nights: Extracts from the original soundtrack to the Cyril Collard film]. Compact disc insert. PolyGram, 1992.

Lévi-Strauss, Claude. *The Elementary Structures of Kinship.* Edited by Rodney Needham. Translated by James Harle Bell and John Richard von Sturmer. Beacon, 1969.

Lévi-Strauss, Claude. *Introduction to the Work of Marcel Mauss.* Translated by Felicity Baker. Routledge and Kegan Paul, 1987.

Lew, Julie. "Gay Groups Protest a Film Script." *New York Times,* May 4, 1991.

Lieb, Sandra R. *Mother of the Blues: A Study of Ma Rainey.* University of Massachusetts Press, 1981.

Linderman, Deborah. "The Mise-en-Abîme in Hitchcock's *Vertigo." Cinema Journal* 30, no. 4 (1991): 51–74. https://doi.org/10.2307/1224886.

Lindsey, Robert. "Jim Jones—From Poverty to Power of Life and Death." *New York Times,* November 26, 1978.

Lipman, Amanda. "Les Nuits fauves (Savage Nights)." *Sight and Sound,* June 1, 1993.

LiPuma, Edward, and Benjamin Lee. *Financial Derivatives and the Globalization of Risk.* Duke University Press, 2004.

Lombroso, Cæsar [Cesare], and William Ferrero. *The Female Offender.* New York: D. Appleton, 1898.

Loud, Lance. "Savage Love." *Advocate,* April 5, 1994.

Lukács, György. *History and Class Consciousness: Studies in Marxist Dialectics.* Translated by Rodney Livingstone. MIT Press, 1999.

Lyons, Charles. *The New Censors: Movies and the Culture Wars.* Temple University Press, 1997.

Lyotard, Jean-François. *Discourse, Figure.* Translated by Antony Hudek and Mary Lydon. University of Minnesota Press, 2020.

MacCannell, Dean. *The Tourist: A New Theory of the Leisure Class.* University of California Press, 1999.

MacCormack, Patricia. "Necrosexuality." *Rhizomes: Cultural Studies in Emerging Knowledge* 11/12 (2005/2006). http://www.rhizomes.net/issue11/maccormack/index.html. Archived May 1, 2025, at https://perma.cc/8NK3-TKSQ.

MacDowall, Lachlan. "Present Tense Bisexuality." Review of *A History of Bisexuality,* by Steven Angelides. *Cultural Studies Review* 9, no. 1 (2003): 220–23. https://doi.org/10.5130/csr.v9i1.3596.

Mack, Mehammed Amadeus. *Sexagon: Muslims, France, and the Sexualization of National Culture.* Fordham University Press, 2017.

MacKinnon, Catharine A. "Sexuality, Pornography, and Method: 'Pleasure Under Patriarchy.'" *Ethics* 99, no. 2 (1989): 314–46. https://doi.org/10.1086/293068.

Malabou, Catherine. *Plasticity at the Dusk of Writing: Dialectic, Destruction, Deconstruction.* Translated by Carolyn Shread. Columbia University Press, 2010.

Malchow, Howard L. *Gothic Images of Race in Nineteenth-Century Britain.* Stanford University Press, 1996.

Maliepaard, Emiel. "Bisexuals in Space and Geography: More-than-Queer?" *Fennia* 193, no. 1 (2015): 148–59. https://doi.org/10.11143/46303.

Marhoefer, Laurie. *Racism and the Making of Gay Rights: A Sexologist, His Student, and the Empire of Queer Love*. University of Toronto Press, 2022.

Marinetti, Filippo Tommaso. "Discorso futurista agli Inglesi" [Futurist speech to the English]. In *Teoria e invenzione futurista* [Futurist theory and invention], edited by Arnoldo Mondadori. Mondadori, 1983.

Marks, Laura Helen. "I Want to Suck Your . . . : Fluids and Fluidity in Dracula Porn." In *Alice in Pornoland: Hardcore Encounters with the Victorian Gothic*. University of Illinois Press, 2018.

Martel, Frédéric. *The Pink and the Black: Homosexuals in France Since 1968*. Translated by Jane Marie Todd. Stanford University Press, 2000.

Martin, Dave. "Man Sentenced in 'Trash Bag Murders' Tells Details." *Los Angeles Times*, December 23, 1977.

Martin, Del, and Phyllis Lyon. *Lesbian/Woman*. Volcano, 1991.

Martinez, Kelly. "11 Bisexual Tropes I'm Honestly Tired of Seeing in TV and Movies." *Buzzfeed*, December 11, 2021. https://www.buzzfeed.com/kellymartinez/bisexual-tropes -that-need-to-be-retired. Archived August 19, 2022, at https://perma.cc/2NQT-X26G.

Marx, Karl. *Capital: A Critique of Political Economy*. Vol. 3. Translated by David Fernbach. Penguin, 1981.

Marx, Karl. *The Eighteenth Brumaire of Louis Bonaparte*. Translated by Daniel De Leon. Mondial, 2005.

Masters, William H., and Virginia E. Johnson. *Homosexuality in Perspective*. Little, Brown, 1979.

Mayne, Judith. *Framed: Lesbians, Feminists, and Media Culture*. University of Minnesota Press, 2000.

McClanahan, Annie, and Jon-David Settell. "Service Work, Sex Work, and the 'Prostitute Imaginary.'" *South Atlantic Quarterly* 120, no. 3 (2021): 493–514. https://doi.org/10 .1215/00382876-9154870.

McGowan, Todd. *The Racist Fantasy: Unconscious Roots of Hatred*. Bloomsbury, 2022.

McGregor, Alex. "Sex Crimes." *Time Out*, April 22, 1992.

Merck, Mandy. "Figuring Out Andy Warhol." In *Pop Out: Queer Warhol*, edited by Jennifer Doyle, Jonathan Flatley, and José Esteban Muñoz. Duke University Press, 1996.

Merck, Mandy. *In Your Face: 9 Sexual Studies*. New York University Press, 2000.

Merck, Mandy. "Sexuality, Subjectivity and . . . Economics?" In *(Mis)recognition, Social Inequality and Social Justice*, by Nancy Fraser and Pierre Bourdieu, edited by Terry Lovell. Routledge, 2007.

Merleau-Ponty, Maurice. *Phenomenology of Perception*. Translated by Colin Smith. Routledge, 2005.

Metz, Christian. *The Imaginary Signifier: Psychoanalysis and the Cinema*. Translated by Celia Britton and Annwyl Williams. Indiana University Press, 1982.

Meyer, Michaela D. E. "Looking Toward the InterSEXions: Examining Bisexual and Transgender Identity Formation from a Dialectical Theoretical Perspective." *Journal of Bisexuality* 2, no. 3–4 (2003): 151–70. https://doi.org/10.1300/J159v03n03_11.

Mezey, Naomi. "Response: The Death of the Bisexual Saboteur." Public Law and Legal Theory Research Paper, no. 12-141. *Georgetown Law Journal* 100 (2012): 1093-104.

Miami Herald. "Condemned Killer Flees During Trip to Hospital." September 10, 1993.

Michel, Frann. "Do Bats Eat Cats? Reading What Bisexuality Does." In D. E. Hall and Pramaggiore, *RePresenting Bisexualities.*

Mieli, Mario. *Towards a Gay Communism: Elements of a Homosexual Critique.* Translated by David Fernbach and Evan Calder Williams. Pluto, 2018.

Milton, John. *Paradise Lost.* Edited by Gordon Teskey. W. W. Norton, 2005.

Ministru, Sébastien. "Orphée au parking" [Orpheus at the parking lot]. *Le Courage* 5 (2019): 347-70.

Mober, David. "Murder Most Foul? Youths' Mass Grave Stirs Primal Fears." *In These Times,* January 17, 1979.

Modleski, Tania. *The Women Who Knew Too Much: Hitchcock and Feminist Theory.* Routledge, 2005.

Moll, Albert. *Die konträre Sexualempfindung: Mit Benutzung amtlichen Materials* [The contrary sexual sensation: With the use of official documents]. 2nd expanded ed. Berlin: Fischer and H. Kornfeld, 1893.

Money, John, Madeline Davis, Betty Dodson, Al Goldstein, Phyllis Kronhausen, Eberhard Kronhausen, et al. "Playboy Panel: New Sexual Life Styles." *Playboy,* September 1973.

Monro, Surya. *Bisexuality: Identities, Politics, and Theories.* Palgrave Macmillan, 2015.

Moorman, Jennifer. "Bi for Pay? On Notions of Authenticity and Women's 'Compulsory Bisexuality' in US Adult Video." *Porn Studies* 11, no. 3 (2024): 208-26. https://doi.org/10.1080/23268743.2023.2297677.

Moretti, Franco. *Signs Taken for Wonders: Essays in the Sociology of Literary Form.* Translated by Susan Fischer, David Forgacs, and David Miller. Verso, 1997.

Morgan, Robin. "Lesbianism and Feminism: Synonyms or Contradictions?" *Lesbian Tide* 2, no. 10-11 (1973): 30-34.

Morris, Sharon, and Merl Storr. "Bisexual Theory: A Bi Academic Intervention." *Journal of Gay, Lesbian, and Bisexual Identity* 2, no. 1 (1997): 1-5. https://doi.org/10.1023/A:1026333014603.

Morse, Margaret. "Margaret Morse" [individual response]. *Camera Obscura* 7, no. 2-3 (1989): 246-48. https://doi.org/10.1215/02705346-7-2-3_20-21-246.

Muller, Isabelle. *Un amour sérodifférent* [A serodifferent love]. Seuil, 1995.

Mulligan, Georgia. "The Queer Cinema of Jacques Demy." PhD diss., University of Warwick, 2017.

Mulvey, Laura. "Afterthoughts on 'Visual Pleasure and Narrative Cinema' Inspired by King Vidor's *Duel in the Sun* (King Vidor, 1946)." *Framework* 15 (1981): 12-15. https://doi.org/10.1007/978-1-349-19798-9_4.

Mulvey, Laura. "Visual Pleasure and Narrative Cinema." *Screen* 16, no. 3 (1973): 6-18. https://doi.org/10.1093/screen/16.3.6.

Muñoz, José Esteban. *Cruising Utopia: The Then and There of Queer Futurity.* New York University Press, 2009.

Muñoz, José Esteban. "Dead White: Notes on the Whiteness of the New Queer Cinema." *GLQ: A Journal of Lesbian and Gay Studies* 4, no. 1 (1998): 127–38. https://doi.org/10.1215/10642684-4-1-127.

Munt, Sally R. "The Butch Body." In *Contested Bodies*, edited by Ruth Holliday and John Hassard. Routledge, 2001.

Murphy, Marilyn. *Are You Girls Traveling Alone? Adventures in Lesbian Logic.* Clothespin Fever, 1991.

Murphy, Marilyn. "Thinking About Bisexuality." *Resources for Feminist Research* 19, no. 3–4 (1990): 87–88.

Nadeau, Chantal. "Life with Pinky Dots." *GLQ: A Journal of Lesbian and Gay Studies* 6, no. 1 (2000): 137–44. https://doi.org/10.1215/10642684-6-1-137.

Nagle, Jill. "Framing Radical Bisexuality: Toward a Gender Agenda." In *Bisexual Politics: Theories, Queries, and Visions*, edited by Naomi Tucker. Harrington Park, 1995.

Namaste, Viviane. "Le Déplacement et la crise du réel: La Socio-sémiotique et la biphobie de *Basic Instinct*" [Movement and the crisis of the real: The socio-semiotic and the biphobia of *Basic Instinct*]. *Cinémas: Revue d'études cinématographiques* 3, no. 2 (1993): 223–38. https://doi.org/10.7202/1001200ar.

Nancy, Jean-Luc. *Being Singular Plural.* Translated by Robert D. Richardson and Anne E. O'Byrne. Stanford University Press, 2000.

Nancy, Jean-Luc. *Sexistence.* Translated by Steven Miller. Fordham University Press, 2021.

Nash, Mark. "Chronicle(s) of a Death Foretold, Notes Apropos of *Les Nuits Fauves.*" *Critical Quarterly* 36, no. 1 (1994): 97–104. https://doi.org/10.1111/j.1467-8705.1994.tb01018.x.

Nass, Gilbert D., Roger W. Libby, and Mary Pat Fisher. *Sexual Choices: An Introduction to Human Sexuality.* 2nd ed. Wadsworth Health Sciences Division, 1984.

National Gay and Lesbian Task Force Policy Institute. "Anti-Gay/Lesbian Violence, Victimization and Defamation in 1991" (1992). Box 61, folder 17, National Gay and Lesbian Task Force Records, 1973–2000. Cornell University Libraries, Ithaca, New York.

Needham, Gary. *Brokeback Mountain.* Edinburgh University Press, 2010.

Newsweek. "Bisexual Chic: Anyone Goes." May 27, 1974.

Nordheimer, Jon. "AIDS Specter for Women: The Bisexual Man." *New York Times*, April 3, 1987.

The Numbers. "Basic Instinct (1992)." https://www.the-numbers.com/movie/Basic-Instinct#tab=summary. Archived August 19, 2022, at https://perma.cc/86CU-YHMV.

The Numbers. "Fatal Attraction (1987)." https://www.the-numbers.com/movie/Fatal-Attraction#tab=summary. Archived August 19, 2022, at https://perma.cc/Q672-2JQ2.

The Numbers. "Jagged Edge (1985)." https://www.the-numbers.com/movie/Jagged-Edge#tab=summary. Archived August 19, 2022, at https://perma.cc/7X38-M97T.

Nussbaum, Felicity A. "Toward Conceptualizing Diary." In *Studies in Autobiography*, edited by James Olney. Oxford University Press, 1988.

Oakes, Tim, and Louisa Schein. "Translocal China: An Introduction." In *Translocal China: Linkages, Identities and the Reimagining of Space*, edited by Tim Oakes and Louisa Schein. Routledge, 2006.

Ochs, Robyn. "Why We Need to 'Get Bi.'" *Journal of Bisexuality* 11 (2011): 171–75. https://doi
.org/10.1080/15299716.2011.571983.

O'Malley, Pat. *Risk, Uncertainty and Government*. Glasshouse, 2004.

Onodera, Midi. "Camera Obscura for Dreams." In *Practical Dreamers: Conversations with
Movie Artists*, edited and interviewed by Mike Hoolboom. Coach House, 2008.

Orhangazi, Özgür. *Financialization and the US Economy*. Edward Elgar, 2008.

Payne, Charles R. "Some Freudian Contributions to the Paranoia Problem." *Psychoanalytic Review* 1 (1913–14): 76–93.

Peraldi, François, ed. "Polysexuality." Special issue, *Semiotext(e)* 10 (1995).

Peyghambarzadeh, Zeynab. "The Untellable Bisexual Asylum Stories." In *Bisexuality in
Europe*, edited by Emiel Maliepaard and Renate Baumgartner. Routledge, 2020.

Phelan, Peggy. *Unmarked: The Politics of Performance*. Routledge, 1993.

Phelan, Shane. *Getting Specific: Postmodern Lesbian Politics*. University of Minnesota Press,
1994.

The Pink Paper. "*Basic Instinct*: The Plot Thickens." June 22, 1991.

The Pink Paper. "Opening Up Pandora's Box." September 1, 1988.

Plato. *The Symposium*. Translated by Christopher Gill. Penguin, 2003.

Polidori, John. *The Vampyre: A Tale*. London: Sherwood, Neely, and Jones, 1819.

Pramaggiore, Maria. "BI-ntroduction I: Epistemologies of the Fence." In D. E. Hall and
Pramaggiore, *RePresenting Bisexualities*.

Pramaggiore, Maria. "Straddling the Screen: Bisexual Spectatorship and Contemporary
Narrative Film." In D. E. Hall and Pramaggiore, *RePresenting Bisexualities*.

Preciado, Paul B. *Countersexual Manifesto*. Translated by Kevin Gerry Dunn. Columbia
University Press, 2018.

Prosser, Jay, and Merl Storr. "Part III: Transsexuality and Bisexuality, Introduction." In
Sexology Uncensored: The Documents of Sexual Science, edited by Lucy Bland and Laura
Doan. University of Chicago Press, 1998.

Pykett, Derek. *British Horror Film Locations*. McFarland, 2008.

Quimby, Karin. "*She Must Be Seeing Things* Differently: The Limits of Butch/Femme." In
Lesbian Erotics, edited by Karla Jay. New York University Press, 1995.

Raffalovich, Marc-André. "Inversion sexuelle congénitale: Observations et conseils"
[Congenital sexual inversion: Observations and advice]. *Archives d'anthropologie crimi-
nelle de criminologie et de psychologie normale et pathologique* 10 (1895): 99–127.

Randolph, Laura B. "The Hidden Fear: Black Women, Bisexuals, and the AIDS Risk."
Ebony (1988): 120–26.

Rao, Rahul. "Global Homocapitalism." *Radical Philosophy* 194 (2015): 38–49.

Rapoport, Esther. *From Psychoanalytic Bisexuality to Bisexual Psychoanalysis: Desiring in the
Real*. Routledge, 2019.

Rastogi, Rakesh Kumar. *Modern Text Book of Zoology: Invertebrates*. 10th rev. ed. Capital
Offset, 2009.

Raymond, Danielle, and Liz A. Highleyman. "Appendix A: Brief Timeline of Bisexual Activism in the United States." In *Bisexual Politics: Theories, Queries, and Visions*,
edited by Naomi Tucker, Liz Highleyman, and Rebecca Kaplan. Harrington Park,
1995.

Raymond, Janice G. "Putting the Politics Back into Lesbianism." *Journal of Lesbian Studies* 1, no. 2 (1997): 273–86. https://doi.org/10.1300/J155v01n02_09.

Rees-Roberts, Nick. *French Queer Cinema*. Edinburgh University Press, 2008.

Reich, June L. "Genderfuck: The Law of the Dildo." *Discourse* 15, no. 1 (1992): 112–27.

Repo, Jemima. *The Biopolitics of Gender*. Oxford University Press, 2016.

Reynolds, Margaret. *The Sappho Companion*. Palgrave, 2001.

Rhodes, John David. *Spectacle of Property: The House in American Film*. University of Minnesota Press, 2017.

Rich, B. Ruby. *Chick Flicks: Theories and Memories of the Feminist Film Movement*. Duke University Press, 1998.

Rich, B. Ruby. *New Queer Cinema: The Director's Cut*. Duke University Press, 2013.

Richter, Nicole. "Bisexual Erasure in 'Lesbian Vampire' Film Theory." *Journal of Bisexuality* 13, no. 2 (2013): 273–80. https://doi.org/10.1080/15299716.2013.780198.

Riding, Alan. "Discovering a Film Idol's Feet of Clay." *New York Times*, April 28, 1994.

Rieger, Gerulf, Meredith L. Chivers, and J. Michael Bailey. "Sexual Arousal Patterns of Bisexual Men." *Psychological Science* 16, no. 8 (2005): 579–84. https://doi.org/10.1111/j.1467-9280.2005.01578.x.

Rigby, Mair. "'Prey to Some Cureless Disquiet': Polidori's Queer Vampyre at the Margins of Romanticism." *Érudit* 36–37 (2005): https://doi.org/10.7202/011135ar.

Roberts, B. C. "The Imperfect Text: Bisexual Transgression in *Score* (1974) and *Both Ways* (1975)." *Porn Studies* (2024): 241–51. https://doi.org/10.1080/23268743.2023.2220716.

Roberts, B. C. "Muddy Waters: Bisexuality in the Cinema." *Journal of Bisexuality* 11, no. 2–3 (2011): 329–45. https://doi.org/10.1080/15299716.2011.572018.

Roberts, B. C. "Neither Fish nor Fowl: Imagining Bisexuality in the Cinema." PhD diss., New York University, 2013.

Robert Shaye–New Line Cinema Papers 1958–2008 (inclusive). University of Michigan Special Collections.

Robinson Rhodes, Martha. "Bisexuality, Multiple-Gender-Attraction, and Gay Liberation Politics in the 1970s." *Twentieth Century British History* 32, no. 1 (2021): 119–42. https://doi.org/10.1093/tcbh/hwaa018.

Ronan, Joseph. "Ostentatiously Discreet: Bisexual Camp in *The Stranger's Child*." In *Alan Hollinghurst: Writing Under the Influence*, edited by Michèle Mendelssohn and Denis Flannery. Manchester University Press, 2016.

Roof, Judith. "1970s Lesbian Feminism Meets 1990s Butch-Femme." In *Butch/Femme: Inside Lesbian Gender*, edited by Sally R. Munt. Cassel, 1998.

Rose, Jacqueline. "Paranoia and the Film System." *Screen* 17, no. 4 (1976): 85–104. https://doi.org/10.1093/screen/17.4.85.

Rosenthal, Allen, David Sylva, Adam Safron, and J. Michael Bailey. "Sexual Arousal Patterns of Bisexual Men Revisited." *Biological Psychology* 88, no. 1 (2011): 112–15. https://doi.org/10.1016/j.biopsycho.2011.06.015.

Roy, André. "La Vie à tout prix: *Les Nuits fauves* de Cyril Collard" [Life at any price: Cyril Collard's *Savage Nights*]. *24 Images* 65 (1993): 58–59.

Rubin, David A. *Intersex Matters: Biomedical Embodiment, Gender Regulation, and Transnational Activism*. State University of New York Press, 2017.

Rubin, Gayle. "The Catacombs: The Temple of the Butthole." In *Leatherfolk: Radical Sex, People, Politics, and Practice*, edited by Mark Thompson. Daedalus, 1991.

Rubin, Gayle. "The Traffic in Women: Notes on the 'Political Economy' of Sex." In *Toward an Anthropology of Women*, edited by Rayna R. Reiter. Monthly Review, 1975.

Rude, Mey. "9 Bisexual TV and Film Characters Who Deserved Better than Tired Tropes." *Them*, September 18, 2018. https://www.them.us/story/bisexual-characters -who-deserved-better. Archived August 19, 2022, at https://perma.cc/3TGG-85VB.

Russo, Vito. *The Celluloid Closet: Homosexuality in the Movies*. Rev. ed. Harper and Row, 1987.

Rust, Paula C. *Bisexuality and the Challenge to Lesbian Politics: Sex, Loyalty, and Revolution*. New York University Press, 1995.

Sade, Donatien-Alphonse-François de. *La Philosophie dans le boudoir: Les quatre premiers dialogues* [Philosophy in the bedroom: The four first dialogues]. Gallimard, 2005.

Sade, Donatien-Alphonse-François de. *The 120 Days of Sodom*. Translated by Austryn Wainhouse and Richard Seaver. Arrow Books, 1990.

Saez, Emmanuel, and Gabriel Zucman. "Wealth Inequality in the United States Since 1913: Evidence from Capitalized Income Tax Data." *Quarterly Journal of Economics* 131, no. 2 (2016): 519–78. https://doi.org/10.1093/qje/qjw004.

Saint-Paul, Georges [pseud. Dr. Laupts]. *Tares et poisons: Perversion et perversité sexuelles* [Defects and poisons: Sexual perversion and perversity]. Paris: Georges Carré, 1896.

Salamon, Julie. "Unsafe Sex in Paris; Merchant, No Ivory." *Wall Street Journal*, April 14, 1994.

Salazkina, Masha. *In Excess: Sergei Eisenstein's Mexico*. University of Chicago Press, 2009.

Samer, Jed. "Lesbian Feminist Cinema's Archive and Moonforce Media's National Women's Film Circuit." *Feminist Media Histories* 1, no. 2 (2015): 90–124. https://doi.org /10.1525/fmh.2015.1.2.090.

Samer, Jed. *Lesbian Potentiality and Feminist Media in the 1970s*. Duke University Press, 2022.

Samuels, Robert. *Hitchcock's Bi-Textuality: Lacan, Feminisms, and Queer Theory*. State University of New York Press, 1998.

San Filippo, Maria. *The B Word: Bisexuality in Contemporary Film and Television*. Indiana University Press, 2013.

San Filippo, Maria. "The Politics of Fluidity: Representing Bisexualities in Twenty-First-Century Screen Media." In *The Routledge Companion to Media, Sex and Sexuality*, edited by Clarissa Smith, Feona Attwood, and Brian McNair. Routledge, 2018.

San Filippo, Maria. *Provocauteurs and Provocations: Screening Sex in 21st Century Media*. Indiana University Press, 2020.

San Filippo, Maria. "(Re)Constructing Bisexual Space in Contemporary Visual Culture." *English Language Notes* 45, no. 2 (2007): 141–47. https://doi.org/10.1215/00138282-45.2.141.

Saussure, Ferdinand de. *Course in General Linguistics*. Translated by Roy Harris. Open Court, 1986.

Schaffer, Talia. "'A Wilde Desire Took Me': The Homoerotic History of *Dracula*." *ELH* 61, no. 2 (1994): 381–425. https://doi.org/10.1353/elh.1994.0019.

Schoonover, Karl, and Rosalind Galt. *Queer Cinema in the World*. Duke University Press, 2016.

Schuller, Kyla, and Jules Gill-Peterson. "Introduction: Race, State, and the Malleable Body." *Social Text* 38, no. 2 (2020): 1–17. https://doi.org/10.1215/01642472-8164716.

Schwartzberg, Shlomo. "Treut Films the Outer Edges of Sexuality." *Eye Weekly*, February 20, 1992.

Sedgwick, Eve Kosofsky. *Between Men: English Literature and Male Homosocial Desire.* Columbia University Press, 1985.

Sedgwick, Eve Kosofsky. *Epistemology of the Closet.* University of California Press, 2008.

Sedgwick, Eve Kosofsky. *Tendencies.* Routledge, 1994.

Sedgwick, Eve Kosofsky. *Touching Feeling: Affect, Pedagogy, Performativity.* Duke University Press, 2003.

Seid, Danielle M. "Reveal." *TSQ: Transgender Studies Quarterly* 1, no. 1-2 (2014): 176-77. https://doi.org/10.1215/23289252-2399947.

Selka, Stephen. "Black Catholicism in Brazil." *Journal of Africana Religions* 2, no. 2 (2014): 287-95.

Selka, Stephen. *Religion and the Politics of Ethnic Identity in Bahia, Brazil.* University Press of Florida, 2007.

Sellier, Geneviève. *Masculine Singular: French New Wave Cinema.* Translated by Kristin Ross. Duke University Press, 2008.

Serano, Julia. *Excluded: Making Feminism and Queer Movements More Inclusive.* Seal, 2013.

Shipka, Danny. *Perverse Titillation: The Exploitation Cinema of Italy, Spain and France, 1960-1980.* McFarland, 2011.

Simkin, Stevie. *Basic Instinct.* Palgrave Macmillan, 2013.

Simon, Pierre, Jean Gondonneau, Lucien Mironer, and Anne Marie Dourlen-Rollier. *Rapport sur le comportement sexuel des Français* [Report on the sexual behavior of the French]. Julliard Charron, 1972.

Sinfield, Alan. *On Sexuality and Power.* Columbia University Press, 2004.

Smith, David. "Banned: Bisexual Groups Banned from the Lesbian and Gay Centre." *Bi-Monthly* 8 (April 1985): 2-3.

Smith, Michael Peter. "Translocality: A Critical Reflection." In *Translocal Geographies: Spaces, Place, Connections*, edited by Katherine Brickell and Ayona Datta. Routledge, 2016.

Smith, Sharon. "The Image of Women in Film: Some Suggestions for Future Research." *Women and Film* 1 (1972): 13-20.

Smith, Valerie. *Not Just Race, Not Just Gender: Black Feminist Readings.* Routledge, 1998.

Smyth, Cherry. *Lesbians Talk Queer Notions.* Scarlet, 1992.

Sobel, Lionel S. "Financing the Production of Theatrical Motion Pictures." *Entertainment Law Reporter* 5, no. 12 (1984): 3-6.

Soto, Rosa E. "'Made to Be the Maid'? An Examination of the Latina as Maid in Mainstream Film and Television." In *Contested Images: Women of Color in Popular Culture*, edited by Alma M. García. Altamira, 2012.

Southerton, Dale, Elizabeth Shove, Alan Warde, and Rosemary Deem. "The Social Worlds of Caravaning: Objects, Scripts and Practices." *Sociological Research Online* 6, no. 2 (2001): 71-78. https://doi.org/10.5153/sro.585.

Spackman, Barbara. *Fascist Virilities: Rhetoric, Ideology, and Social Fantasy in Italy.* University of Minnesota Press, 1996.

Spielrein, Sabina. "Destruction as the Cause of Coming into Being." *Journal of Analytical Psychology* 29, no. 2 (1994): 155-86.

Spira, Alfred, Nathalie Bajos, and ACSF. *Les Comportements sexuels en France* [Sexual behavior in France]. La Documentation française, 1993.

Spivak, Gayatri Chakravorty. "Can the Subaltern Speak?" In *Marxism and the Interpretation of Culture*, edited by Cary Nelson and Lawrence Greenberg. Macmillan Education, 1988.

Spula, Jack Bradigan. "'Midnight Caller' Episode Puts Our Lives on the Line." *Empty Closet*, February 2, 1989.

Square Peg. "She Must Be Seeing Things: Sheila McLaughlin." 21 (1988): 34–35.

Srinivasan, Amia. *The Right to Sex*. Bloomsbury, 2021.

Stacey, Jackie. "Butch Noir." *differences: A Journal of Feminist Cultural Studies* 30, no. 2 (2019): 30–71. https://doi.org/10.1215/10407391-7736035.

Stacey, Jackie. "Desperately Seeking Difference." *Screen* 28, no. 1 (1987): 48–61. https://doi.org/10.1093/screen/28.1.48.

Statista. "International Box Office Figures for the Highest Grossing Movies Each Year, from 1915 to 2021 (in Million US Dollars)." https://www.statista.com/statistics/1072778 /highest-grossing-movie-annually-historical/. Archived August 19, 2022, at https:// perma.cc/M44W-PQKG.

Steffen, Monika. "AIDS Policies in France." In *AIDS and Contemporary History*, edited by Virginia Berridge and Philip Strong. Cambridge University Press, 2000.

Steinbock, Eliza. *Shimmering Images: Trans Cinema, Embodiment, and the Aesthetics of Change*. Duke University Press, 2019.

Steinbock, Eliza. "Towards Trans Cinema." In *The Routledge Companion to Cinema and Gender*, edited by Kristin Lené Hole, Dijana Jelača, E. Ann Kaplan, and Patrice Petro. Routledge, 2017.

Steinbock, Eliza. "The Wavering Line of Foreground and Background: A Proposal for the Schematic Analysis of Trans Visual Culture." *Journal of Visual Culture* 19, no. 2 (2020): 171–83. https://doi.org/10.1177/1470412920944480.

Stekel, Wilhelm. *Bisexual Love*. Translated by James S. van Teslaar. Fredonia, 2003.

Stoker, Bram. *Bram Stoker's Notes for Dracula: A Facsimile Edition*, annotated and transcribed by Robert Eighteen-Bisang and Elizabeth Miller. McFarland, 2008.

Stone, Sharon. *The Beauty of Living Twice*. Alfred A. Knopf, 2021.

Stone, Sharon Dale. "Bisexual Women and the 'Threat' to Lesbian Space: Or What If All the Lesbians Leave?" *Frontiers: A Journal of Women Studies* 16, no. 1 (1996): 101–16. https://doi.org/10.2307/3346927.

Storr, Merl. "The Sexual Reproduction of 'Race': Bisexuality, History and Racialization." In *The Bisexual Imaginary: Representation, Identity and Desire*, edited by Bi Academic Intervention. Cassel, 1997.

Straayer, Chris. *Deviant Eyes, Deviant Bodies: Sexual Re-Orientation in Film and Video*. Columbia University Press, 1996.

Strauss, Frédéric. "Cyril Collard: Un art neuf" [Cyril Collard: A new art]. *Cahiers du cinéma* 466 (1993): 5–6.

Studlar, Gaylyn. *In the Realm of Pleasure: Von Strenberg, Dietrich, and the Masochistic Aesthetic*. University of Illinois Press, 1988.

Tamagne, Florence. "Histoire des homosexualités en Europe: Un état des lieux" [History of homosexualities in Europe: An overview]. *Revue d'histoire moderne et contemporaine* 53, no. 4 (2006): 7–31. https://doi.org/10.3917/rhmc.534.0007.

Tarnowsky, Benjamin. *Die krankhaften Erscheinungen des Geschlectssinnes: Eine forensisch-psychiatrische Studie* [The pathological manifestations of the sense of sex: A forensic-psychiatric study]. Berlin: August Hirschwald, 1886.

Taylor, Paul. "Two Drifters May Be Worst Mass Murderers of Modern Times." *Washington Post*, October 27, 1983.

Thiele, Kathrin. "Figuration and/as Critique in Relational Matters." In *How to Relate: Wissen, Künste, Pratiken / Knowledge, Arts, Practices*, edited by Annika Haas, Maximilian Haas, Hanna Magauer, and Dennis Pohl. Verlag, 2021.

Thorne, Tony. *Countess Dracula: The Life and Times of the Blood Countess, Elisabeth Báthory*. Bloomsbury, 1997.

Time. "The New Bisexuals." May 13, 1974.

Todorov, Tzvetan. *Introduction à la littérature fantastique* [Introduction to fantastique literature]. Éditions du Seuil, 1970.

Tohill, Cathal, and Pete Tombs. *Immoral Tales: European Sex and Horror Movies 1956–1984*. St. Martin's Griffin, 1994.

Toubiana, Serge. "Carpe Diem and Night." *Cahiers du cinéma* 460 (1992): 22–32.

Treasure, Catherine. "Attempting to Impose an All Flavour Ban." *Pink Paper*, October 6, 1988.

Turóczi, László. *Ungaria Suis cum Regibus Compendio Data* [Hungary with its kings, compendium data]. Trnava, Kingdom of Hungary: Typis Collegii Academici Societatis Jesu, 1744.

TV Tropes. "Depraved Bisexual." October 6, 2018. https://tvtropes.org/pmwiki/pmwiki.php/Main/DepravedBisexual. Archived August 19, 2022, at https://perma.cc/UB67-7VK3.

Tyler, Carole-Anne. "Desiring Machines? Queer Re-Visions of Feminist Film Theory." In *Coming Out of Feminism?*, edited by Mandy Merck, Naomi Segal, and Elizabeth Wright. Blackwell, 1998.

Udis-Kessler, Amanda. "Identity/Politics: A History of the Bisexual Movement." In *Bisexual Politics: Theories, Queries and Visions*, edited by Naomi Tucker, Liz Highleyman, and Rebecca Kaplan. Harrington Park, 1995.

Ulmschneider, Loretta. "Bisexuality." *Furies* (March–April 1973): 2.

Ulrichs, Karl Heinrich. *Formatrix: Anthropologische Studien über urnische Liebe* [Formatrix: Anthropological studies on urning love]. Leipzig: Heinrich Matthes, 1865.

Ulrichs, Karl Heinrich. *Vindicta: Kampf für freiheit von Verfolgung* [Vindicta: Struggle for freedom from persecution]. Leipzig: Heinrich Matthes, 1865.

Urry, John, and Jonas Larsen. *The Tourist Gaze 3.0*. SAGE, 2011.

Vaines, Colin. "On Doing the Unexpected." *Screen International*, May 14, 1977.

Van Brummelen, Glen. *The Doctrine of Triangles: A History of Modern Trigonometry*. Princeton University Press, 2021.

Van Brummelen, Glen. *The Mathematics of the Heavens and the Earth: The Early History of Trigonometry*. Princeton University Press, 2009.

Vancheri, Luc. *Les Pensées figurales de l'image* [The figural thoughts of the image]. Armand Colin, 2007.

van Scheers, Rob. *Paul Verhoeven*. Translated by Aletta Stevens. Faber and Faber, 1997.

Vicari, Justin. *Male Bisexuality in Current Cinema: Images of Growth, Rebellion and Survival*. McFarland, 2011.

Vicente, Marta V. "Trans Visual Narratives: Representing Gender and Nature in Early Modern Europe." *Journal of Women's History* 35, no. 4 (2023): 57–75. https://doi.org/10 .1353/jowh.2023.a913382.

Vidal, Belén. *Figuring the Past: Period Film and the Mannerist Aesthetic.* Amsterdam University Press, 2012.

Villarejo, Amy. *Lesbian Rule: Cultural Criticism and the Value of Desire.* Duke University Press, 2003.

Vincendeau, Ginette. "France." In *The Women's Companion to International Film*, edited by Annette Kuhn and Susannah Radstone. University of California Press, 1990.

Waidzunas, Tom, and Steven Epstein. "'For Men Arousal Is Orientation': Bodily Truthing, Technosexual Scripts, and the Materialization of Sexualities Through the Phallometric Test." *Social Studies of Science* 45, no. 2 (2015): 187–213. https://doi.org/10.1177 /0306312714562103.

Wark, McKenzie. "Bisexual Mediations: Beyond the Third Term." In *Sex in Public: Australian Sexual Cultures*, edited by Jill Julius Matthews. Allen and Unwin, 1997.

Wark, McKenzie. *Reverse Cowgirl.* Semiotext(e), 2020.

Warren, Jane. "How to Cope When Your Man Is Bisexual: Secret Passions Can Prove Deadly." *Daily Express*, June 2, 1994.

Wassif, Mariam. "Polidori's *The Vampyre* and Byron's Portraits." *Wordsworth Circle* 49, no. 1 (2018): 53–61. https://doi.org/10.1086/TWC49010053.

Watney, Simon. "The French Connection." *Sight and Sound* 3, no. 6 (1993): 24–25.

Weber, Cynthia. *Queer International Relations: Sovereignty, Sexuality and the Will to Knowledge.* Oxford University Press, 2016.

Weinberg, Martin, Colin Williams, and Douglas Pryor. *Dual Attraction: Understanding Bisexuality.* Oxford University Press, 1994.

Weininger, Otto. *Sex and Character: An Investigation of Fundamental Principles.* Translated by Ladislaus Löb. Indiana University Press, 2005.

Weinstock, Jeffrey. *The Vampire Film: Undead Cinema.* Wallflower, 2012.

Weir, John. "Gay-Bashing, Villainy and the Oscars." *New York Times*, March 29, 1992.

Weise, Elizabeth Reba. Introduction to *Closer to Home: Bisexuality and Feminism*, edited by Elizabeth Reba Weise. Seal, 1993.

Weiss, Andrea. "The Lesbian Vampire Film: A Subgenre of Horror." In *Dracula's Daughters: The Female Vampire on Film*, edited by Douglas Brode and Leah Deyneka. Scarecrow, 2014.

Weiss, Andrea. *Vampires and Violets: Lesbians in Film.* Penguin, 1992.

Weiss, Gail. "Ambiguity." In *Merleau-Ponty: Key Concepts*, edited by Rosalyn Diprose and Jack Reynolds. Routledge, 2008.

Westel, David. "The Best of Times, the Worst of Times: The Emerging Literature of AIDS in France." In *AIDS: The Literary Response*, edited by Emmanuel S. Nelson. Twayne, 1992.

Whatling, Clare. "Femme to Femme: A Love Story." In *Butch/Femme: Inside Lesbian Gender*, edited by Sally Munt. Cassel, 1998.

White, Jonathan David. "Bisexuals Who Kill: Hollywood's Bisexual Crimewave, 1985–1998." *Journal of Bisexuality* 2, no. 1 (2001): 39–54. https://doi.org/10.1300/J159v02n01_04.

White, Patricia. "Female Spectator, Lesbian Specter: *The Haunting*." In *Inside/Out: Lesbian Theories, Gay Theories*, edited by Diana Fuss. Routledge, 1991.

Wiegman, Robyn, and Elizabeth A. Wilson. "Introduction: Antinormativity's Queer Conventions." *differences: A Journal of Feminist Cultural Studies* 26, no. 1 (2015): 1–25. https://doi.org/10.1215/10407391-2880582.

Wilchins, Riki. "A New Vagina Didn't Make Her Sad (It Didn't Have To)." *TSQ: Transgender Studies Quarterly* 7, no. 3 (2020): 345–48. https://doi.org/10.1215/23289252-8552964.

Williams, Anna. "Domestic Violence and the Aetiology of Crime in America's Most Wanted." *Camera Obscura* 11, no. 1 (1993): 96–119. https://doi.org/10.1215/02705346-11-1_31-96.

Williams, Linda. "Film Bodies: Gender, Genre, and Excess." *Film Quarterly* 44, no. 4 (1991): 2–13. https://doi.org/10.2307/1212758.

Williams, Linda. *Hard Core: Power, Pleasure, and the "Frenzy of the Visible."* Pandora, 1990.

Williams, Linda. "When the Woman Looks." In *Re-Vision: Essays in Feminist Film Criticism*, edited by Mary Ann Doane, Patricia Mellencamp, and Linda Williams. University Publications of America, 1984.

Williams, Linda Ruth. *The Erotic Thriller in Contemporary Cinema*. Edinburgh University Press, 2005.

Wilson, Elizabeth. "Is Transgression Transgressive?" In *Activating Theory: Lesbian, Gay, Bisexual Politics*, edited by Joseph Bristow and Angelia R. Wilson. Lawrence and Wishart, 1993.

Wilson, Elizabeth. "A Note on Glamour." *Fashion Theory: The Journal of Dress, Body and Culture* 11, no. 1 (2007): 95–108. https://doi.org/10.2752/136270407779934605.

Wilton, Tamsin. "Introduction: On Invisibility and Mortality." In *Immortal, Invisible: Lesbians and the Moving Image*, edited by Tamsin Wilton. Routledge, 1995.

Wittig, Monique. "The Straight Mind." *Feminist Issues* 1, no. 1 (1980): 103–11. https://doi.org/10.1007/BF02685561.

Woo, Chris W. H. "Queer Vampiric Desire: Bisexuality on Body Without Organs." *IM: Interactive Media* 1 (2005): n.p. https://imjournal.murdoch.edu.au/index7425.html?media_dl=450. Archived May 1, 2025, at https://perma.cc/6TG9-MXLL.

Wood, Robin. *Hollywood from Vietnam to Reagan . . . and Beyond*. Columbia University Press, 2003.

Worth, Fabienne André. "*Le Sacré et le SIDA* (AIDS): Sexuality and Its Contradictions in France, 1971–1996." *Discourse* 19, no. 3 (1997): 92–121.

Woubshet, Dagmawi. *The Calendar of Loss: Race, Sexuality, and Mourning in the Early Era of AIDS*. Johns Hopkins University Press, 2015.

Wuornos, Aileen. *Dear Dawn: Aileen Wuornos in Her Own Words, 1991–2002*. Edited by Lisa Kester and Daphne Gottlieb. Soft Skull, 2011.

Yoshino, Kenji. "The Epistemic Contract of Bisexual Erasure." *Stanford Law Review* 52, no. 2 (2000): 353–461. https://doi.org/10.2307/1229482.

Zaretsky, Eli. "Bisexuality, Capitalism and the Ambivalent Legacy of Psychoanalysis." *New Left Review* 223 (1997): 69–89.

Zemon Davis, Natalie. "Women on Top." In *Society and Culture in Early Modern France*. Stanford University Press, 1975.

Zimmerman, Bonnie. "Daughters of Darkness: Lesbian Vampires." *Jump Cut* 24–25 (1981): 23–24.

Index

authenticity: vs. bisexuality, 88; lesbian, 111–15, 260n102; and screen sex, 184–85; and tourism, 147

autonomy: female creative, 84

Bailey, J. Michael: on male bisexuality, 10, 244n38

Baker, Dan: on the Simmons survey, 203–4

Balázs, Béla: on cinematic vampires and suspense film, 78–79

Barthes, Roland, 249n125, 249n128; and/or, 30; on the image, 225–26; on photography, 98–99

Basement Girl, The (Onodera), 106–7, 234

Basic Instinct (Verhoeven), 39, 179–227, 269n1, 270n4, 272n41; citations of, 189–90, 193–94; protests against, 179–80, 222–23, 225. See also Verhoeven, Paul

Basic Instinct 2: Risk Addiction (Caton-Jones), 194, 212

Bataille, Georges: on eroticism and transgression, 33, 182, 249n144, 270n10. See also transgression

bathing, in blood, 46, 50. See also Báthory, Countess Erzsébet

Báthory, Countess Erzsébet, 46–47, 73, 251n13

Baudry, Jean-Louis, 242n4; on Western classical cinema and monocular vision, 166

Bauman, Zygmunt: on Eros, 181

Bay Area Bisexual Network, 24n15

Bazin, André, 132; on cinema and desire, 20; on style vs. likeness, 63, 111

beauty: vs. acting ability, 64, 253n78; and bloodbaths, 46, 78

Beauvoir, Simone de: and the ethics of ambiguity, 130; on women in Breton's poetry, 211

Becker, Edith: on lesbian films/filmmakers, 84–85

Before the Bat's Flight Is Done (Tímár), 131

Behind the Green Door (Mitchell/Mitchell), 185

Bell, David: on accusations of bisexual tourism, 147

belle juive, 69–70. See also seduction

Bergler, Edmund: on male bisexuality, 10

Bergstrom, Janet, 19

Berlant, Lauren: on economies of normativity, 204

Berlin Affair, The (Cavani), 23, 25. See also Cavani, Liliana

Bersani, Leo, 268nn148–49, 275n5; on love and desire, 171–72; on monogamy, 156

Best Way to Walk, The (Miller), 134–35

Bey, Marquis: on the they pronoun, 253n64

Beyoncé, "Ring the Alarm," 190, 193. See also Basic Instinct (Verhoeven)

Beyond Good and Evil (Cavani), 156–57. See also Cavani, Liliana

Bi Academic Intervention, 235

bi-exclusionary lesbian ethics, 38, 85–91, 108, 121, 125, 258n49. See also ostracism

bi-exclusionary paranoia, 100–16. See also ostracism

bisexual camp, 263n2

bisexual chic, 9, 196–97, 199, 204

bisexuality: and abstraction, 77; and AIDS/HIV, 9, 21–22, 39, 128–78, 265n59, 265n63; and alienation, 77–78, 133; and Cold War anxieties, 74; and doubt, 6; as ever-present in humanity, 8; vs. femininity, 88; and gender, 7–12, 27; and glam rock, 196, 266n73; and goats, 137; vs. homosexuality, 133; "hunger" of, 56; and hybridity, 48–49; vs. lesbianism, 82, 112, 121, 124, 230; and marketability, 39, 196–200; and media, 21–28; vs. monogamy, 154–61, 176; and multiplicity, 10, 33, 135, 137; and murderousness, 210–22; and mutability, 26–27, 40, 129, 131; and narrative cinema, 84–85; and the natural sciences, 6; "nonexistence" of, 5, 9–12, 31, 88, 136, 138, 164, 185; and paranoia, 38, 95, 101–16, 119–22; partiality of, 13–14; and primitivity, 8, 44–45, 70–71, 136, 245n67, 254n112, 255n116; and privilege, 102–4; as problem, 85–87, 155; and queer theory, 12–15, 232; and race/racism, 145–49, 245n67; and reading, 98; as socially meaningful, 25; and song, 125; and stereotypes, 21–25, 146, 247n101, 263n2; suspicion of, 86, 111–12, 125, 133; of tapeworms, 230–31; and temporality, 13, 28, 36, 53, 131, 145–46, 157, 177–78, 203, 235; as term, xi–xv, 5–9; as threat, 35, 39, 45, 86, 88, 93, 114, 137, 181, 185–86, 189, 202–3, 206, 208, 227; as (not a) threat, 9–10, 198–200; as "tourism," 147; and translocality, 148–53; and transmissibility, 80, 128–78; and transness, xiii, 11, 24–26, 39, 221–22, 247n91; and triangularity, 161–71, 198, 268n144; and utopia, xi, 176–78, 235; and vacillation, 235; and vampirism, 41–80

gender: and bisexuality, 7–12, 27; and criminality, 210, 217; and desire, 63; (in)stability
of, 253n68; mutability of, 246n78; nonbinary, 11;and the Oedipus complex theory,
243nn20–21; and pornography, 184; vs. sex,
xiv, 6–7; and sexuality, 259n55; and subjectiv-
ity, 59; and truth, 62
Genet, Jean, 264n25; *Funeral Rites*, 268n149
Gentry Jr., John Kelly, 214
George, Sheldon: on racial difference, 268n153
Get Out (Peele), 233
Gever, Martha: on *She Must Be Seeing Things*,
259n71. See also *She Must Be Seeing Things*
(McLaughlin)
Giaccardi, Thierry: on *Savage Nights*, 148, 172,
177. See also *Savage Nights* (Collard)
Gilda (Vidor), 113
Gill, Rosalind: on the postfeminist sensibility,
194–95
Gilles, Guy, 133
Gill-Peterson, Jules, 253n64; on plasticity, 177.
See also plasticity
Girard, René: on the triangular nature of desire,
165–66
GLAAD. *See* Gay and Lesbian Alliance Against
Defamation
Gladwin, Polly: *The Mark of Lilith*, 81–83, 117,
256nn1–2, 256n4
Gley, Eugène: on bisexuality, xii
Glucksmann, André: on Collard, 142. *See also*
Collard, Cyril
Go Fish (Troche), 85, 89–91, 121
Gorfinkel, Elena: on bisexuality and lesbianism
in American sexploitation film, 49
Gorham, Caz: on reactions to *She Must Be Seeing
Things*, 94. See also *She Must Be Seeing Things*
(McLaughlin)
Granger, Farley: and *Rope* (Hitchcock), 214,
274n116
Grélois, Anne-Marie: on bisexuality vs. homo-
sexuality, 133, 264n28
Griggers, Camilla: on *Basic Instinct*, 215. See also
Basic Instinct (Verhoeven)
Grigorieff, Ghéorghiü: on bisexuality and the
AIDS crisis, 138, 145. *See also* AIDS/HIV
Grosz, Elizabeth: on bisexuality, 265n61; on
heterosexual anxiety during the AIDS crisis,
140. *See also* AIDS/HIV

Grover, Jan Zita: on the male bisexual during
the AIDS crisis, 138. *See also* AIDS/HIV
Guattari, Félix, 253n60, 276n15; on economic
and sexual exploitation, 203; on homo-
sexuality, 234–35; on the vampire, 80
Guérin, Daniel: on bisexuality, 176–77
Guibert, Hervé: on Collard, 142. *See also* Col-
lard, Cyril
Gurevich, Maria: on binormativity, 223
Gutter Dyke Collective, 88

Haeberle, Erwin J.: on humans' ambierotic
potential, 243n13
Haeckel, Ernst: on phylogenesis and ontogen-
esis, 6
Halberstam, Jack: on lesbian intelligibility, 111
Hall, Donald E.: on bisexuality, 6, 8, 27–28.
See also representation, media
Hall, Stuart, 23
Halperin, David M.: on queerness, 12
Hamam (Özpetek), 155
Handyside, Fiona: on films of Ozon, 150–51.
See also Ozon, François
Hansen, Miriam, 19
Hanson, Ellis: on bisexual/cinematic vampires,
44
Hao Dazheng: on perspective in East Asian
cinema, 166
Haraway, Donna: on figures, 31–32, 62, 128,
249n137; on vampires, 68. *See also* figure, the
Hardin, Carolyn: on profit and risk, 202. *See also*
financialization; risk
Harrison, David Scott, 214
Hart, Lynda: on the female invert's aggressive-
ness, 215
Haskell, Molly, 21
Hawkins, John Barrett, 214
Hayward, Eva: on the trans vagina, 60–61
Hayworth, Rita: and *Gilda* (Vidor), 113
Heath, Prime Minister Edward, 74
Heaven (Reynolds), 221
Heck, Kalling: on ambiguity and art cinema,
130. *See also* art cinema: and ambiguity
Hedgehog, Maz: on the threat of bisexuality,
202–3, 208
Hegel, Georg Wilhelm Friedrich, 11–12,14–15
Heidegger, Martin: on hermeneutic violence,
248n121

Mathieson, Cynthia: on binormativity, 223

Matisse, Henri: *Le Bonheur de vivre*, 177–78

McGowan, Todd: on racial difference, 268n153. *See also* race

McGuire, Dorothy: and *The Spiral Staircase* (Siodmak), 106

McLaughlin, Sheila: as actor, 101, 104–7, 123, 258n50; *Artificial Memory*, 92, 258n50; *Committed*, 92; on filmmaking, 84; on homosexuality, 94; *She Must Be Seeing Things*, 38, 83–125, 231, 258n53, 259n71, 260n96, 261n122; on *She Must Be Seeing Things*, 93–94, 106, 115, 117, 261n110. *See also She Must Be Seeing Things* (McLaughlin)

Meat Joy (Schneemann), 234

media effects theory, 22–23

Ménage (Blier), 127–28

Merck, Mandy, 111, 243n19, 246n75; on the homosexual phantom, 76; on queerness and capitalism, 203; on *Savage Nights*, 147, 269n171. *See also Savage Nights* (Collard)

Merleau-Ponty, Maurice: on space and the position of things, 77

Metz, Christian: on the cinema, 199; on primary identification, 242n4

Mezey, Naomi: on the "bisexual saboteur," 35

Michel, Frann: on reading bisexually, 98

Midnight Caller, 21–22, 234, 270nn4–5

Midwinter, Dulcie, 254n81; and *Vampyres*, 64. *See also Vampyres* (Larraz)

Mieli, Mario, 18, 246n75

Ministru, Sébastien: on *Parking*, 266n74. *See also Parking* (Demy)

mise en abyme, 110, 212, 256n129

mise-en-scène: as form, 28, 36, 38, 76, 148, 190, 207, 218, 221; as fantasy's setting, 19, 270n7

misogyny, 62–63, 68, 82, 114–15, 121, 135, 160, 192, 264n35

misrecognition, 101–5, 260n82

Modern Household of Madame Butterfly, The (stag film), 232–33

Modleski, Tania, 19; on Hitchcock's preoccupation with female bisexuality, 260n82. *See also* Hitchcock, Alfred

Moll, Albert: on bisexuality, xii

Money, John: on bisexuality and the '70s, 9

monogamy: vs. bisexuality, 154–61, 176; and heterosexuality, 76, 156, 160–61, 175

monosexuality, xii, 4–5, 246n69; and civilization, 8, 245; the problem of, 15–17

Monster (Jenkins), 217. *See also* Wuornos, Aileen

monstration, 3. See also *Salò, or The 120 Days of Sodom* (Pasolini)

Moorman, Jennifer: on pornographic film and queer sex, 185

Moretti, Franco: on detective fiction, 222

Morgan, Robin: and bisexuality, 85–86

Morocco (von Sternberg), 246n78

Morris, Marianne: and *Vampyres*, 44, 51–52, 64, 68, 253nn78–79. See also *Vampyres* (Larraz)

Morse, Margaret, 19

Muller, Isabelle: on unprotected sex and AIDS, 160. *See also* AIDS/HIV

Mulligan, Georgia: on *Parking*, 143. See also *Parking* (Demy)

multiplicity: and bisexuality, 10, 33, 135, 137; within Cyril Collard, 173; and erotic triangles, 162; of interpretations, 29; of sexual positions, 172; of spatial attachments, 148–50

Mulvey, Laura, 81–82, 84, 211; on cinematic spectatorship, 19; on the "invisible guest," 113

Muñoz, José Esteban: on hope and bisexual utopia, 176; on *She Must Be Seeing Things*, 116. See also *She Must Be Seeing Things* (McLaughlin)

Munt, Sally R.: on butch lesbians, 115. *See also* butch/femme

MURDER and murder (Rainer), 90–91

Murphy, Marilyn: on bisexual women in lesbian communities, 88–89. *See also* bi-exclusionary lesbian ethics

Murray, James, 21

mutability: and bisexuality, 26–27, 40, 129, 131; and the body, 59–61, 117; of desire, 14, 107, 249n134; and the figure, 31; and masculinity, 134–45; of perception, 122; of sexuality, 88, 231, 246n78; and spatiality, 151–53; and transness, 68; and vampires, 68, 69, 82; and women, 217. *See also* plasticity

My Father Is Coming (Treut), 123. *See also* Treut, Monika

My Mother (Honoré), 60

Nadeau, Chantal, 269n163; on *Savage Nights*, 175–76. See also *Savage Nights* (Collard)

Nadja (Almereyda), 45

Namaste, Viviane: on *Basic Instinct* and bisexuality, 226. See also *Basic Instinct* (Verhoeven)

Nancy, Jean-Luc: on gender's (in)stability, 253n68. *See also* gender

narrative cinema, 130, 150, 256n8; and bisexuality, 84–85

Nash, Mark: on French AIDS narratives, 142; on *Savage Nights*, 175–76. *See also* AIDS/HIV; *Savage Nights* (Collard)

Nataf, Zachary: *The Mark of Lilith*, 81–83, 117, 256nn1–2; on *The Mark of Lilith*, 256n4

National Bisexual Liberation Group, 9, 21

National Gay and Lesbian Task Force Policy Institute, 269n1

Navratilova, Martina: and the Visa Rainbow Card, 204–5. *See also* financialization

necrophilia, 42–43, 253n60. *See also* death

Needham, Gary: on *Brokeback Mountain*, 29; on gay cinema, 100, 156. *See also Brokeback Mountain* (Lee)

neoliberalism, 194–95, 199, 201–2, 273n78

neonoir, 183–84, 194. *See also* film noir

Newbrough, Cheryl, 85; *Goodbye Emma Jo*, 120; *Such a Crime*, 118, 120

New Line Cinema, "Presentations," 21–22

New Queer Cinema, 224

Night Rhythms (Dark), 217. *See also* Dark, Gregory

9½ Weeks (Lyne), 187

Nosferatu: A Symphony of Horror (Murnau), 43

November Moon (von Grote), 258n40

nudity, 95; and *Basic Instinct* (Verhoeven), 188, 190–93; frontal, 3, 49, 188, 190–93; *The Nude Vampire* (Rollin), 46; as promise of exploitation cinema, 64; and race, 72; and shame, 72

Nussbaum, Felicity A.: on diaries and temporality, 259n66. *See also* diaries

Ochs, Robyn: on bisexual intelligibility, 27

Oedipus complex theory, 7–8, 243nn20–21. *See also* Freud, Sigmund

O'Malley, Pat: on economic risk, 210. *See also* financialization; risk

omnisexuality, xii–xiii

Once I Loved a Woman (Owens), 234

Once More (Vecchiali), 142, 151, 157. *See also* Vecchiali, Paul

Onodera, Midi, 85; *The Basement Girl*, 106–7, 234

ontogenesis, 6–7, 246n78

ostracism, of bisexuals, 87, 133–34. *See also* bi-exclusionary lesbian ethics; bi-exclusionary paranoia

O'Sullivan, Sue: and the reaction to *She Must Be Seeing Things*, 91–93. *See also She Must Be Seeing Things* (McLaughlin)

Ottinger, Ulrike, 85

Ovid, *Metamorphoses*, 59

Owen, Thomas, 47, 251n20

Oxford Handbook of Queer Cinema, The: elision of bisexuality in, 232

Ozon, François, 133, 150–52; *See the Sea*, 151; *A Summer Dress*, 151–52, 246n78

painting, 65–66, 166; Fauvism, 177–78, 269nn171–72

pansexuality, xii–xiii, 246n75

Paradise Lost (Milton), 225

paranoia: and bisexuality, 38, 95, 101–16, 119–22; and lesbianism, 128. *See also She Must Be Seeing Things* (McLaughlin)

Parking (Demy), 143–44, 266nn73–74

Parmar, Pratibha, 85

Pasolini, Pier Paolo: *Salò, or The 120 Days of Sodom*, 1–4, 230, 242n2; *Theorem*, 131

Passages (Sachs), 233

passing: and Jewishness, 69; sexual, 26, 66, 69, 207; vampiric, 78

patriarchy: and female bisexuality, 10; and masculinity, 128, 135; and narrative form, 84

pegging, 123. *See also* dildos; penetration

Pellegrini, Ann: on the *belle juive*, 69. *See also belle juive*

penetration, 184–85; reciprocal, 136, 172; refigured, 56–58

penis: bestifed, 96–97; bitten, 57; celebrated (John Holmes's), 57; double, 118; erect (as filmic goal, for Verhoeven), 188; and hegemony, 121; identification with one's (in the Oedipus complex theory), 7; and lesbians, 118–22; as not required (for erotic fulfillment), 55; as propelling apparatus, 252n34. *See also* dildos

perception, 100–116; and contingency, 221; and the hermeneutic, 101–2; and mutability, 122; and sexuality, 109

Perche, Samuel: and *Confusion of Genders*, 158. See also *Confusion of Genders* (Cohen)

Personal Best (Towne), 258n40, 261n106

phallocentrism, 121–22

Phelan, Shane: on the presencing of lesbianism, 124

photography, 95–100

Pialat, Maurice: Loulou, 128; To Our Loves, 128

Pitt, Ingrid: and Countess Dracula, 78; and The Vampire Lovers, 63, 74. See also Countess Dracula (Sasdy); Vampire Lovers, The (Baker)

plasmaticity, 58, 60

plasticity, 177–78, 202, 221, 246n78. See also mutability

Play Misty for Me (Eastwood), 183

pleasure: and the body's organs, 60; female, 50–55, 185, 190; of lesbianism, 86; and monogamy, 161; and prohibition, 4 and semioticity, 122; and spectatorship, 84, 198–99; and tourism, 147

plurisexuality, xii–xiii

Poison (Haynes), 224

Polidori, John: The Vampyre, 43, 250n6

Politics of Bisexuality Conference (London), 241n15

Pontalis, Jean-Bertrand, 19; on projection, 274n104

Pool, Léa, 85

pornography: vs. erotic thrillers, 184–85; and gender, 184; lesbian-made, 120; and Polaroids, 98; and sex between women, 49; and simulated nonconsent, 35; stag films, 185, 232–33; and vampire narratives, 43

Potluck and the Passion, The (Dunye), 89–91, 257n39. See also Dunye, Cheryl

Pramaggiore, Maria: on bisexual epistemology, 14, 30; on bisexual reading strategies (and European art films), 131; on bisexual representation, 27–28; on bisexual triangulation, 162; on film spectatorship and desire, 20; on The Hunger, 50–53

Preciado, Paul B., 120–22; on countersexuality, 122; on dildos and sex toys in She Must Be Seeing Things, 120–21. See also dildos; She Must Be Seeing Things (McLaughlin)

primal scene, 109–10, 230–31. See also Freud, Sigmund

primitivity, and bisexuality, 8, 44–45, 70–71, 136, 245n67, 254n112, 255n116

privilege: bisexual, 102–4; and the bisexual-bohemian, 148; male, 114

protest: against Basic Instinct (Verhoeven), 179–80, 222–23, 225; against Midnight Caller, 21–22, 234, 247n93; against portrayals of bisexuality in media, 21–22; against She Must Be Seeing Things (McLaughlin), 92

Prou, Erica: and Collard, 159. See also Collard, Cyril

Pryor, Douglas W.: on bisexual men and AIDS, 138. See also AIDS/HIV

queerness, xi, xiii, 77; and aggression, 215; and credit, 182, 200–210; embodied (performative butchness), 115; vs. femininity, 63; vs. masculinity, 172–73; and murderousness, 210–22; New Queer Cinema, 224; and temporality, 266n76; and truth, 245n44, 260n102; and violence, 22, 179–81, 269n1

queer theory, 12–15, 232

Quimby, Karin: on She Must Be Seeing Things, 107–9, 114–15. See also She Must Be Seeing Things (McLaughlin)

race: and AIDS/HIV, 138, 145; and bisexuality, 145–49, 245n67; and epistemology, 245n67; and femininity, 117; and nudity, 72; and primitivity, 71; and racial difference, 268n153; and sex toys, 118, 120, 262n133; and sexuality, 70; and She Must Be Seeing Things (McLaughlin), 116–18; and vampirism, 68, 254n97. See also whiteness

Rafelson, Bob: Black Widow, 187, 200, 207, 209, 272n64

Raffalovich, Marc-André: on bisexuality, xii

Rainbow Card, 204–5. See also financialization

Rainer, Yvonne, 85, 92; MURDER and murder, 90–91

Rainey, Ma, 125. See also blues, the

Rao, Rahul: on "global homocapitalism," 204

Rape of the Vampire, The (Rollin), 46, 72–73. See also Rollin, Jean

ratiocination, 39. See also erotic thriller

Raymond, Janice G.: on male power modes, 93

reading: bisexual, 29, 98, 131; cinematic, 97–99; symptomatic, 209

record: skipping, 109; stuck, 113

Rees-Roberts, Nick: on French queer cinema, 266n84

Villarejo, Amy: on gender binarism and the visual terrain, xiv; on the term *lesbian*, 85

Vincendeau, Ginette: on French cinema, 264n35

violence: anti-gay, 22, 179–81, 269n1; and arousal, 172–73, 186–87; and desire, 230; and female bisexuality, 10; hermeneutic, 248n121

Virgin Machine (Treut), 123, 262n144. *See also* Treut, Monika

visual, the: and the erotic thriller, 182; and gender binarism, xiv; and knowledge, 36, 62; and the lesbian femme, 111; and pleasure, 147; and sexuality, 155–56

vulva: comparison of the wound with, 56–58, 60–61, 253n66; exposure of, 190, 192

Waidzunas, Tom: on bodily truthing, 244n36

Warhol, Andy: *Couch*, 234, 276n13; *Kiss*, 234, 276n13

Wark, McKenzie: on bisexuality, 244n42, 265n61; on feeling "vaulted," 252n34

Wassif, Mariam: on *The Vampyre*, 250n6. See also *Vampyre, The* (Polidori)

Watney, Simon: on *Savage Nights*, 175–76, 265n67. See also *Savage Nights* (Collard)

Weaver, Lois, 258n52, 261n120; and *She Must Be Seeing Things*, 92, 96, 111, 117. See also *She Must Be Seeing Things* (McLaughlin)

Weber, Cynthia, 249n125

Weinberg, Martin S.: on bisexual men and AIDS, 138. *See also* AIDS/HIV

Weininger, Otto: on bisexuality, 18, 243n22

Weinstock, Jeffrey: on cinematic vampires and sexual excess, 42

Weir, John: on *Basic Instinct*, 222–23. See also *Basic Instinct* (Verhoeven)

Weise, Elizabeth Reba: on bisexual women, 87–88, 91

Weiss, Andrea: on cinematic lesbian vampires, 44, 49–50, 66–67, 254n91; on second-wave feminism, 54

West, Rosemary: and Myra Hindley, 215–16

West Coast Lesbian Conference, 86

Whatling, Clare: on feminine lesbian representation on screen, 66–77

White, Jonathan David, 23

White, Patricia: on the lesbian specter, 76

whiteness: and heterosexuality, 111; and homosexuality, 204; and lesbian vampires, 63, 66, 68–69, 82, 254n97; and sex toys, 118, 120, 262n133. *See also* race

Wiegman, Robyn: on queer theory and normativity, 232

Wilde, Oscar, 250n6

Williams, Colin J.: on bisexual men and AIDS, 138. *See also* AIDS/HIV

Williams, Linda, 19; on vampirism and the threat of castration, 57–58

Williams, Linda Ruth: on the erotic thriller, 180, 183–85. *See also* erotic thriller

Wilson, Elizabeth: on bisexuality (as dismissed), 235; on glamour and vampire cinema, 64–65. *See also* femininity

Wilson, Elizabeth A.: on queer theory and normativity, 232

Windows (Willis), 180

Wings, The (Stiller), 233

Wittig, Monique: on lesbians (as "not women"), 63

Woman like Eve, A (Brakel), 102, 258n40

Wood, Robin: on bisexuality, 154; on *Cruising*, 270n7. See also *Cruising* (Friedkin); relationality, bisexual

Working Girls (Borden), 262n146. *See also* Borden, Lizzie

Worth, Fabienne André: on Collard's death, 132. *See also* Collard, Cyril

Woubshet, Dagmawi: on AIDS meds and the new normative gay identity, 204. *See also* AIDS/HIV

wound: continuous raw, 59; as object choice, 38, 56–61, 253n60; as unwriting of the body, 59–60; vagina as, 253n66

WOW Café, 258n52, 261n120

Wuornos, Aileen, 215–17, 274n125, 275n127

Xiang, Zairong: on the couple (and the shadowy third), 155, 161

Yoshino, Kenji: on bisexual erasure, 16

Young Emmanuelle, A (Kaplan), 258n40

Zaretsky, Eli: on bisexuality, capitalism, and psychoanalysis, 202

Zimmerman, Bonnie: on the cinematic lesbian vampire, 54–55

www.ingramcontent.com/pod-product-compliance
Lightning Source LLC
Chambersburg PA
CBHW041109280526
45792CB00011B/2353